W9-ASH-060

The Women Who
Wrote the War

The Women Who Wrote the War

The Compelling Story of
the Path-breaking Women
War Correspondents of
World War II

Nancy Caldwell Sorel

Arcade Publishing • New York

Copyright © 1999, 2011 by Nancy Caldwell Sorel

All Rights Reserved. No part of this book may be reproduced in any manner without the express written consent of the publisher, except in the case of brief excerpts in critical reviews or articles. All inquiries should be addressed to Arcade Publishing, 307 West 36th Street, 11th Floor, New York, NY 10018.

Arcade Publishing books may be purchased in bulk at special discounts for sales promotion, corporate gifts, fund-raising, or educational purposes. Special editions can also be created to specifications. For details, contact the Special Sales Department, Arcade Publishing, 307 West 36th Street, 11th Floor, New York, NY 10018 or info@skyhorsepublishing.com.

Arcade Publishing® is a registered trademark of Skyhorse Publishing, Inc.®, a Delaware corporation.

Visit our website at www.arcadepub.com.

10 9 8 7 6 5 4 3 2 1

Library of Congress Cataloging-in-Publication Data

Sorel, Nancy Caldwell.
 The women who wrote the war : the compelling story of the path-breaking women war correspondents of World War II / Nancy Caldwell Sorel.
    p. cm.
 Includes bibliographical references and index.
 ISBN 978-1-61145-049-1 (alk. paper)
 1. World War, 1939-1945--Journalists--Biography. 2. World War, 1939-1945--Photography. 3. War photographers--United States--Biography. 4. Women journalists--United States--Biography. 5. Women photographers--United States--Biography. I. Title.
 D799.U6S563 2011
 940.53082--dc22

                                     2011002501

Printed in the United States of America

For my sisters, Suzanne and Virginia,
my daughters, Jenny and Katherine,
Madeline, Suzanne, and Maria.
Also for Leo, and always for Ed.

Contents

Acknowledgments   ix

Prologue   xiii

A Note on the Foremothers   xvii

1. The Groundbreakers   1

2. Cassandras of the Coming Storm   12

3. Apprentices in Spain   25

4. The Lessons of Czechoslovakia   43

5. One Thought, One Holy Mission: Poland   58

6. Waiting for Hitler: The Phony War   71

7. Fleeing France   81

8. Braving the Blitz   92

9. Working Under the Swastika   106

10. Margaret Bourke-White Shoots the Russian War   117

11. Treading Water, Marking Time   125

12. China Hands   131

13. Facing the War That Is Our War Now   148

14. Women Behind Walls: Manila, Siena, Shanghai   159

15. Learning the Rules, Dressing the Part   170

16. Women on Trial: North Africa   180

17. Touching Base on Five Continents   193

18. Slogging Through Italy   200

19. New Women Come Over for Overlord   211

20. D Day   224

21. Trekking North from Rome   235

22. That Summer in France   242

23. Liberating Paris   256

24. Crossing the Siegfried Line   272

25. The Battle of the Bulge   283

26. Penetrating the Pacific Barriers   293

27. Iwo Jima   301

28. Of Rain, Ruin, Relationships, and the Bridge at Remagen   314

29. The Month of April: The Advance   330

30. The Month of April: The Camps   347

31. The Longed-for Day   362

32. "It Is Not Over, Over Here"   377

33. Women Winding Up a War   382

Epilogue   390

Notes   399

Selected Bibliography   439

Index   443

Acknowledgments

It is my deep regret that of the many correspondents I interviewed for this book, so few are here to read it now. Helen Kirkpatrick Milbank and Tania Long Daniell in particular became friends and offered me their experiences and insights over an interval of some years. Catherine Coyne Hudson, Eve Curie Labouisse, Shelley Mydans, Lael Wertenbaker, Iris Carpenter Akers, Lyn Crost Stern, Virginia Lee Warren Bracker, Mary Marvin Breckinridge, and Faye Gillis Wells were generous with their recollections. Annalee Jacoby Fadiman, Betty Wason, and Bonnie Wiley wrote from distant locations, and Patricia Lochridge recorded her story for her sons, who forwarded it to me. I also talked with male reporters, including Philip Hamburger, Carl Mydans, Harrison Salisbury, and William Walton, and corresponded with Allan Jackson, Lawrence LeSueur, Colonel Barney Oldfield, and David E. Scherman. Edith Iglauer Daly and Ruth Gruber did not report the war but knew many who had. I am immensely grateful to them all.

I wish to thank Frederick Voss, Historian/Curator, at the National Portrait Gallery; Margaret E. Wagner, Special Projects Coordinator, and Irene Ursula Burnham, Director of Interpretive Programs, Library of Congress; also Fern Ingersoll and Barbara Vandergriff at the Washington Press Club Foundation and National Press Club. Eva Mosely, Kathy Kraft, and Wendy Thomas at the Schlesinger Library, Radcliffe College, were consistently helpful. I am indebted to Emmett Chisum, Research Historian, and Jennifer King at the American

Heritage Center, University of Wyoming; Jim Gallagher, Library Coordinator, George H. Beebe Communications Library, and Margaret Goostray, Director, Special Collections, Mugar Memorial Library, at Boston University; Harold L. Miller, Reference Archivist, at the State Historical Society of Wisconsin; Amy Hague, Assistant Curator, Sophia Smith Collection, Smith College; Carolyn Davis, Special Collections, George Arents Research Library, Syracuse University; Diane E. Kaplan, Archivist, Yale University Library; Nicole L. Bouché, Manuscripts Division, Bancroft Library, University of California, Berkeley; Elaine Felcher, Archivist, *Time-Life*; and Bob Medina at the *New York Times*.

Gathering photographs for this book was not an easy task. I express my appreciation to Antony Penrose, Lee Miller's son and biographer, and Carole Callow, Archivist, at the Lee Miller Archives, Chiddingly, East Sussex, England; also to Barbara W. Brannon, Curator, Prints & Photographs Division, Library of Congress; Marie Helene Gold, Photograph Coordinator, Schlesinger Library, Radcliffe College; Beth Zarcone, Laura Giammarco, and George Hogan at *Time-Life*; Alan Goodrich, Audio-Visual Department, John F. Kennedy Library; Dan Fuller, Visual Materials Archivist, State Historical Society of Wisconsin; Camille Ruggiero at AP/Wide World Photos; and the staff of the Corbis-Bettman Archives.

The New York Public Library deserves a special vote of thanks; I all but lived there for several years, and could never have written this book without its voluminous resources and attentive staff.

I greatly benefited from the editorial observations of Ann Close, Byron Dobell, and Sara Blackburn. I owe much to Kirsten Bakis and Carole Spector for long hours spent transcribing tapes, and for research aid provided by my daughter Katherine and my loyal and tireless friend Helen Levacca. I also wish to recognize the effort on my behalf of Sonia Tomara's family, especially Tatiana de Fidler but also Blair Clark and C. Bassine; of Patricia Lochridge's son Steve Bull; of Catherine Coyne's sister-in-law Beatrice Coyne; and Marjorie Avery's good friend Kathleen Scott. Margaret Wolf's contribution to the Margaret Bourke-White story is much appreciated.

I am grateful to my agent, Irene Skolnick, for her blessed persistence and her devotion. My editors, Richard and Jeannette Seaver, are wise and wonderful; Jeannette's critical acumen and ready enthusiasm have been especially welcome. Tim Bent, Cal Barksdale, and Phillipa Tawn brought their individual expertise and good fellowship to this endeavor.

Finally, I would not have made it through the nine years spent on this book without the unwavering encouragement of my friends. Robert Kotlowitz, Dorothy Gallagher, and Richard Snow read the manuscript and offered their insight. Daniel Okrent at *Time-Life*, Peter Nichols at the *New York Times*, Neil Hickey at the *Columbia Journalism Review*, and Ben Sonnenberg proved valuable intermediaries. I am especially grateful to my husband Ed, who supplied the saving grace of daily laughter. Other friends, and family, were simply there, with abiding support and affection, and I thank them all.

Prologue

World War II was a great, tragic, drawn-out epic with a huge cast of characters. War correspondents were a tiny part of the whole, and women war correspondents — fewer than a hundred in all — comprised a fraction of that part. Most serious American journalists, male and female, wanted a piece of this story that was soon to cover much of the globe; the women were as determined as the men, although at the time few newspaperwomen had made it from the society desk into the newsroom. But the robustness of the American press was in their favor, with many more daily newspapers, news periodicals, and wire services than there are today, and with news bureaus in every capital of importance. Women benefited from this comprehensiveness if only because it left room for them. More than twenty-five newspapers, about the same number of magazines, eight wire services, and five radio networks employed women directly as war correspondents.

Although there was much that was common to the experience of all women correspondents, I was always struck by the variety of their perspectives. The longtimers often felt themselves participants in the action — understandable for someone dodging shells while taking notes, or typing a story during a bombing raid. Personal danger tends to blur one's vision. It also tests one's courage. Several women were close to fearless, others perpetually scared, most somewhere in between. They may not always have coped cheerfully with the lack of amenities, the endless rain, the cold, colds, foot blisters, aching limbs, and worse, but they all coped. It was essential to their pride that they not admit to small defeats.

Every woman felt vulnerable in regard to her professional status. Every woman, at one time or another, had first to buck the system before she could do the job her editor had sent her to do. Discriminatory treatment by generals or denigrating remarks from hostile male reporters were tougher to handle than adverse physical conditions. Fortunately, as time passed, military attitudes softened, and the majority of male colleagues were always open-minded and supportive. Often the danger lay in their being too sympathetic. Most male reporters were married, and rough moments shared with a feminine colleague could trigger a new but fragile alliance.

In spite of varying perspectives, there was much that united the women in these pages. All exhibited a kind of basic curiosity, an enjoyment of adventure, and a gutsiness without which they would not have lasted beyond the first week. I found no one inured to the horror of what she had witnessed. Barred from press briefings until late in the war, women reporters began by writing of the less combative side of the conflict — of the daily heroism of the medics, the miracles the doctors performed, how caring (even when bone-tired) the nurses were. They wrote of the young wounded far from home and of civilian victims close to home — families torn apart, old people cold and tired and homeless, mothers desperate for food for their children, children hungry and hurting and afraid. In some ways frontline reporting, which opened up for many women in the final months of the war, was easier. But both could be heartbreaking.

This book is not only about what the women saw and reported in their dispatches; it is also about that side of their lives they did not write about — their relationships with colleagues, buddies, lovers; what kept them sane in bad moments (or, alternatively, drove them crazy). And finally it is about how the war changed them, because, of course, it did. It gave them their breakthrough as journalists, their chance to prove themselves, and it allowed them to live more intensely than most of them ever would again. Experiencing the war through their eyes, hearing the urgency in their voices fifty-odd years later, I became their advocate, their champion. Theirs was a special opportunity which they themselves viewed as an honor, and their country was honored by the way they fulfilled that task.

When, after a modicum of preliminary investigation, I determined to write this book, my first thought was, how was I to locate women from a half century before, most of whom had never been famous, no longer bore the last name under which they had written, and, if still alive, might live just about anywhere? And if I did find them — women ranging from their late seventies to mid-nineties — was it not unconscionably intrusive to barge into their ordered lives with demands on their time and memory?

I had gathered a list of names (which in time would multiply several times over) and, just on the off chance, I looked them up in my Manhattan telephone book. I found two! That the first was within walking distance seemed a good omen; I called and, yes, this was the Irene Corbally Kuhn who had reported from the Pacific in the 1930s and, yes, she would love to talk with me. The next morning suited us both. She awaited me in the doorway of her small apartment in Greenwich Village, and the first thing she did was to give me a hug. The second was to talk, at length, with obvious joy.

This was the beginning. What evolved was a relationship with a rare group of women that I will always count one of the high points of my life. I carried my tape recorder into a Sutton Place apartment overlooking New York's East River, a sprawling Westchester house on a lake, a sunny tidewater home on Cape Cod, a retirement cottage in Williamsburg, Virginia, two large old homes in Washington, D.C., a simple country house in New Hampshire, and an even more modest one in a small Maryland town. One correspondent, down from Ottawa, met with me in the unexpectedly homey Park Avenue apartment of Clifton and Margaret Truman Daniel. Everywhere I was welcomed. Often my questions elicited a response on a subject that had been half buried for many years, and that in turn jogged another recollection, and another.

After our initial taping, I occasionally met with one or another of "my correspondents," as I had begun to think of them, for lunch, or over a drink at a hotel bar. At the same time I was acquiring their stories, available in college archives around the country, at the Library of

Congress, or on microfilm at the New York Public Library. I read them avidly, sprinkling paragraphs here and there throughout my rapidly growing manuscript. The stories offered access to women no longer alive — missed opportunities I have never ceased to regret. In time the manuscript grew to unwieldy size, requiring that half the original roster of reporters, and some whole areas of the war, be cut. The reader is perhaps relieved, but I mourn those women whose experiences I can no longer share with you.

The first women to cover war at the front on a par with men, the correspondents on these pages opened the way to new professional possibilities for women in journalism. They fought for and won the right to do their job on their own terms. Other battles for equality of gender they left for the women who would follow. It was a step-by-step process, and enough for them that they had established a single and irrevocable point of no return.

A Note on the Foremothers

The women in these pages were not first-generation American war correspondents. They had honorable predecessors, few in number but deserving recognition. Margaret Fuller, named European correspondent for the *New York Tribune* by editor Horace Greeley, covered the Italian uprisings of 1848 and the long bombardment of Rome by the French army. Cora Taylor Crane, Stephen Crane's wife, sent accounts of the Greco-Turkish war of 1897 to the *New York Journal*. Young and lovely Anna Benjamin, her bulky box camera slung over one shoulder, became the first female photojournalist when she covered first the Spanish-American war for *Leslie's Illustrated Newspaper* and then the Philippine insurrection for the *New York Tribune* and the *San Francisco Chronicle*. In August 1914, when the Germans invaded Louvain, Belgium, Mary Boyle O'Reilly, who happened to be there, dispatched stories of fire and devastation for three weeks to the *Boston Pilot*. Early the next year, armed with credentials from the *Saturday Evening Post*, best-selling author Mary Roberts Rinehart talked her way across the Channel from England to Dunkirk and sent back dramatic accounts of the German bombardment.

The career of Henrietta Eleanor "Peggy" Hull would span both world wars and reflect difficulties women encountered in the field. Reporting from Valdahon, France, in 1917 for the *El Paso Morning Times*, Hull described American doughboys learning to use trench mortars, a dispatch that prompted American generals to deny her further access to forward press camps. When she resorted to stories of the little things in the lives of the common soldier, popular with the Stateside papers, it was her fellow reporters who demanded her removal. Peggy returned home without having witnessed a battle, but her claim as a reporter of the Great War (and subsequent coverage of American troops in Vladivostok) led to her accreditation as the first American woman war correspondent.

The Women Who
Wrote the War

1

The Groundbreakers

In the early 1920s three American women, young then and unknown to each other, seized a chance at a reporter's life and never turned back. Each appreciated the rarity of her opportunity, her great luck, and gave back in kind. Their successes, both before and during the coming war, would prove pivotal in beckoning other women into the field.

Dorothy Thompson, Curtis syndicate

The oldest child of an English-born Methodist clergyman, Dorothy Thompson grew up in small towns in western New York. Her mother died when she was eight, and she rebelled against her stepmother's conventionality. As a scholarship student at Syracuse University, she was remembered as unusually articulate in class discussions, but also for monopolizing conversation and for the intense attachments she formed with other women students. She was tall and slender, with clear blue eyes and early indications of what would become a commanding presence. After three years of work with the women's suffrage movement, Dorothy went to Paris as a publicity writer for the American Red Cross, and from there to Vienna, where she supplemented her Red Cross duties by becoming a stringer for the *Philadelphia Public Ledger*. Freelance submissions were for women a time-honored means of entry into the newspaper world. Hearing that her firsthand account of an attempted coup by Emperor Franz Josef's grandnephew had impressed her editors, she applied for a salaried

Dorothy Thompson in her Berlin apartment, 1926.
GEORGE ARENTS RESEARCH LIBRARY FOR SPECIAL COLLECTIONS,
SYRACUSE UNIVERSITY.

position, and rushed off to the paper's Paris office to present her case. In person Dorothy could be magnificent. She got the job.

In the spring of 1921, now a bona fide foreign correspondent, Dorothy Thompson tentatively entered into the Viennese world of love, sex, and gossip. Gossip linked her with a handsome Hungarian writer, Josef Bard. Love was instantaneous; sex, her first, welcomed. Commitment was another story. "I am so scared of marriage," she confided to a friend, but marry him she did. Not long afterward the Curtis syndicate promoted her to the position of Central European bureau chief for the *Ledger* and the *New York Evening Post* — in Berlin. Berlin was many hours by train from Vienna. If Thompson weighed the pros and cons of a long-distance marriage, if for a moment she considered not accepting the job, she left no evidence.

Sigrid Schultz, Berlin, circa 1930.
STATE HISTORICAL SOCIETY OF WISCONSIN.

Sigrid Schultz, *Chicago Tribune*

Born in Chicago to parents of Norwegian descent, Sigrid Schultz grew up with the outward demeanor of a china doll complemented by a razor-sharp mind. Her father was a portrait painter, and when she was eight, the family moved to Paris. Sigrid graduated from the Sorbonne in 1914, then joined her parents, who had settled in Berlin. When World War I broke out a few months later, they remained, secure in their American citizenship. Even after the United States entered the war and they had to report daily to the authorities, their lives were little disrupted.

Supporting herself by teaching English and French, Schultz turned to international law, where her fluency in those languages in addition to Dutch, German, and Polish stood her in good stead. In 1919

3

the *Chicago Tribune* Berlin office took her on as an interpreter. She watched for her chance, and before long she was reporting, seizing initiatives available to one with her command of German politics. She was not averse to a little flirtation either: there were few attractive young single women in Berlin's professional circles, and if getting the story required charming the German establishment, why not? Schultz would have years of success in that arena before the political situation hardened. Sure that a reporter's best approach was to inspire confidence and be a good listener, she maintained a low profile. By the mid-1920s prominent men in government including the chancellor and foreign minister were seen at the *Tribune* office in the Hotel Adlon, talking with the knowledgeable young woman on staff there.

In late 1925 the *Tribune*'s Berlin bureau chief was reassigned to Rome, and Sigrid Schultz inherited his job.

That was the year that Dorothy Thompson was assigned to Berlin. Nothing at all like sleepy, romantic Vienna, the German capital was a bizarre metropolis, with its mix of stolid Weimar Republic officials and extravagantly garbed cabaret patrons of undetermined sex, its high culture of music and theater alongside pornography and drugs. The German nightmare of postwar inflation had waned; the mark stabilized, and with it the lives of the average Herrenvolk. An Austrian war veteran had recently been released from prison, where he had been detained for his part in an attempted coup d'état against the Munich city government; Adolf Hitler was still largely unknown.

On arrival in Berlin Thompson was warmly welcomed by the "news gang," Schultz said, even while she deplored Dorothy's "sketchy" grasp of languages and European history. They were friendly but never close, partly because Thompson shared a house facing the Tiergarten with Edgar Ansel Mowrer of the *Chicago Daily News*, the *Tribune*'s competition. Her share was sufficiently spacious to accommodate her husband, but Josef Bard stayed in Vienna. As was customary for an unmarried European woman, Schultz lived with her widowed mother, in a large atelier apartment.

In their early thirties, Thompson and Schultz were natural reporters, willing to go to great lengths for a story. Berlin offered plenty of material. By day there were chancelleries to visit, press conferences to cover, dignitaries to interview, and by night, the lights and bustle of the concert hall, opera, and theater. The evening often ended in the bar at the Hotel Adlon, second home to the American correspondents. When Josef Bard did visit Berlin, he found his wife distracted and the apartment without the requisite quiet for a contemplative writer like himself. He preferred Vienna; before long he preferred another woman as well. Although she had thought herself a sophisticated, modern wife (and logic hinted that it was she who had left first), Dorothy found the rejection devastating. The first solution to her distress was work. "Good old work!" she noted gratefully, "it stood by me and doesn't let me down. Good old routine, good old head that functions automatically at the sight of a newspaper." The second solution was another man.

In the summer of 1927 Sinclair Lewis, author of *Main Street* and *Babbitt*, arrived in Berlin. Thompson, who had read and admired both books, met him almost immediately, and although his (second) divorce was as yet incomplete, he proposed the next day. Lewis pursued his courtship over succeeding months. When in October Dorothy went to Moscow to cover the tenth anniversary of the Bolshevik Revolution, he followed her there, and proposed again. On their return, and despite warnings about his alcoholism, she accepted; the following spring she quit the bureau post and left Berlin to marry him.

That same spring the Nazi Party won 12 out of 491 seats in the Reichstag, less than half those held by women, but a beginning. Two years later that number multiplied by nine, and Sigrid Schultz, watching Hitler's lieutenants goose-step into Parliament in their brown uniforms, decided she could no longer afford to ignore them. She selected World War I ace pilot Captain Hermann Goering as the most likely candidate for reliable information, and "auditioned" him at lunch in a small elegant restaurant. Between the hors d'oeuvres of French snails and the coffee, he talked.

In return, when she later encountered him in the Kaiserhof, Goering introduced her to Hitler. At this time Hitler greeted all women with a kiss on the hand, Austrian style, while staring into their eyes. Schultz masked her animosity enough to remain part of a small group of correspondents who interviewed him several times in the early

1930s. Interviews were arranged and overseen by the half-American Harvard graduate head of the foreign press, Ernst Sedgwick Hanfstaengl, known as Putzi. Schultz later recalled that Hitler liked to take the first question asked him and extemporize an answer at length, after which he would declare the conference over. At one session, in order to deflect him from this practice, she zoomed in immediately with a question on a rather abstruse subject, commercial negotiations between Germany and India, and though momentarily brought up short, he gave a very intelligent answer. Schultz knew that although Hitler spoke no English, he kept tabs through his informants on the nature of the stories written about him in Berlin. She always knew just how far she could go.

Not so Dorothy Thompson Lewis when she interviewed Hitler in the fall of 1931:

> I was a little nervous. I considered taking smelling salts. And Hitler was late. An hour late. Waiting upstairs in the foyer of the Kaiserhof Hotel I saw him shoot by, on the way to his rooms, accompanied by a bodyguard who looked like Al Capone. Minutes pass. Half an hour. . . . When finally I walked in . . . I was convinced that I was meeting the future dictator of Germany. In something less than fifty seconds I was quite sure that I was not. It took just that time to measure the startling insignificance of this man who has set the whole world agog. . . . He is inconsequent and voluble, ill-poised, insecure. He is the very prototype of the "Little Man."

It was the kind of misjudgment that can haunt a journalist for years, but Thompson passed it off with her usual sangfroid. Her readers loved her, she knew, for her daring, her willingness to go out on a limb, and cared not at all when she took a tumble.

A year earlier — the same year her husband won the Nobel Prize for literature — Thompson had managed an accomplishment of her own: she had had a baby. During the first two years of her son's life, she traveled extensively in America and spent seven months abroad. She salved her conscience by hiring an excellent domestic staff and supplying them with detailed instructions. Having lost her own mother so early, Dorothy had no role model, and she felt little inclination for mothering. She had even fewer qualms about leaving her husband: it was already clear that their most congenial communication was by letter.

In 1933 Hitler was named chancellor of Germany, and the following year he assumed the post of president. Once again Thompson left her husband and son for Europe. As she reasoned, a serious journalist with expertise on Germany could do nothing else. Crossing from Austria into Germany that summer, she was greeted by an explosion of swastika flags and a Hitler youth camp — "six thousand boys between the ages of ten and sixteen," she wrote in a story for *Harper's*, "beautiful children. . . . They sang together, and no people sing in unison as the Germans do, thousands of them, in the open air, young voices, still soprano, and the hills echoing! It made one feel sentimental." But those romantic notions were undercut by the sight of an enormous banner stretched across the hillside. "It was so prominent that every child could see it many times a day. It was white, and there was a swastika painted on it, and besides that only seven words, seven immense black words: YOU WERE BORN TO DIE FOR GERMANY." With relief she thought of her own son back in the unadorned hills of Vermont.

In Berlin Thompson went to the Hotel Adlon, warmly familiar, with the same bartender, the same dry martinis, "the manager who always remembers how many people there are in your family and what room you had last time. . . . It was all the courtesy, all the cleanliness, all the exquisite order which is Germany." But she soon discovered it was all facade. Friends warned her not to use the hotel phones. A bank stenographer told her that wages were way down, and a car mechanic said that a man could eat but do little more on what he earned. She spent one afternoon in seclusion with a previous acquaintance, a tall young German now a storm trooper but not in uniform. He divulged details of Hitler's recent bloody purge of "mutinous" leaders and opponents of his dictatorship. A few days later the Adlon porter rang her from the desk: a member of the secret state police wished to see her. A young man wearing a trench coat served her with an order to leave the country within forty-eight hours.

Sigrid Schultz promptly wired the *Chicago Tribune*. "Dorothy Thompson, American writer and wife of Sinclair Lewis, noted novelist, has been banished from Germany," she wrote, and added that

Thompson had been requested to leave "because of her numerous anti-German articles in the American press." Not entirely displeased with the turn of events, Dorothy offered her own explanation of the expulsion: "My offense was to think that Hitler is just an ordinary man. That is a crime against the reigning cult in Germany, which says that Mr. Hitler is a Messiah sent of God to save the German people. . . . To question this mystic mission is so heinous that if you are German you can be sent to jail. I, fortunately, am an American, so I merely was sent to Paris. Worse things can happen to one."

On her return to Vermont she had the expulsion order framed, and hung it prominently on her wall.

Janet Flanner, *New Yorker*

In 1925, the same year Sigrid Schultz and Dorothy Thompson were appointed bureau chiefs in Berlin, Janet Flanner began writing her semimonthly "Letter from Paris" for the *New Yorker*. She wrote under the pseudonym Genêt, a name chosen for her by the fledgling magazine's editor. The *New Yorker* preferred its regulars to write under aliases, preferred objectivity to the point of detachment; the pronouns "I" and "me" hardly existed. Anything might be reported as long as it was neither boring nor tasteless, but pieces tended to be descriptive rather than analytical. The scope of Flanner's reporting would grow. In the beginning it was sophisticated but shallow.

That streak of rebellion shared by women who came to Europe as prospective journalists in the 1920s and 1930s surfaced early in Janet Flanner. As a chestnut-haired and already hawk-nosed teenager, she found it difficult to adapt to the social code of midwestern America. Her father was a funeral director, a not quite "acceptable" occupation, and when she was in her late teens, he killed himself. The nonconformist in her began to hold sway. She later gave a variety of explanations for leaving the University of Chicago after less than two years, but not attending classes and barely passing her courses would seem reason enough. She returned home and abruptly married — to get out of Indianapolis, she said later, but perhaps also because, at that time and in that place, marriage fell on the "acceptable" side of life's choices. It

Janet Flanner before portrait of Solita Solano, 1924.
LIBRARY OF CONGRESS.

was while living as a newlywed in Greenwich Village that Flanner came to realize how much less responsive she was to her young husband than to the beautiful women she met there, Solita Solano in particular. In 1921 Flanner abandoned her husband, with a finality Dorothy Thompson would not show on leaving hers, and she and Solano sailed together for Europe.

Four years later, in Paris and with a novel about to be published, Flanner was approached by the *New Yorker* to write a regular column from the French capital. The offer provided a legitimate reason for her to remain in Paris, as well as funds (thirty-five dollars per submission) to help with the rising expenses of her increasingly social life. She accepted. Although she could not be said to belong to the cultural elite, she wrote her "Letter from Paris" about the arts, fashion, cinema, and café life of the capital, as if she did.

Over the next decade both the *New Yorker* and Genêt flourished. The magazine gave Flanner room to experiment and improve her style. Happily ensconced at the small Hôtel Saint-Germain-des-Prés for less than a dollar a day, she felt she had made a real life for herself in Paris. Paris suited Janet, who considered it the capital not merely of France but of civilized Europe. The disapproval of midwestern America was far away. She lived as she chose. She continued to live with Solano even after she transferred her emotions to Noel Haskins Murphy, a nearly six-foot-tall high-cheekboned blonde training to become a singer. Noel Murphy (whose husband, brother of Gerald Murphy, had been killed in the war) owned a small farm outside the village of Orgeval; it was there that Flanner spent her weekends.

In addition to her regular "Letter from Paris," Flanner occasionally profiled a well-known European figure for the *New Yorker,* and she spent much of 1935 working on a long portrait of Adolf Hitler, titled "Fuehrer." She employed her usual detached, semisatiric approach, concentrating on the myriad details of his life and personality, but in the end she could not avoid taking into account what he was doing in, and to, Germany. She began her third and final section with an acute dissection of the man:

> As a ruler of a great European power, Herr Hitler is the oddest figure on the Continent today, but even as a humble individual,

he would still be a curious character. With a limited mind, slight formal education, a remarkable memory for print, uncanny powers as an orator, and a face inappropriate to fame, in fifteen years he planned, maneuvered, and achieved an incredible career. He is a natural and masterly advertiser, a phenomenal propagandist within his limits, the greatest mob orator in German annals, and one of the most inventive organizers in European history. He believes in intolerance as a pragmatic principle. He accepts violence as a detail of state . . .

Much of the information for "Fuehrer" Janet obtained from Ernst "Putzi" Hanfstaengl, that same chief of the foreign press in Berlin with whom Sigrid Schultz dealt regularly. Probably by this time Putzi could not have arranged an interview with Hitler even had Flanner wanted one. She did not. She felt insecure in her political acumen and not a little jittery about being in Germany as a reporter. Her role as correspondent for a primarily cultural magazine in a friendly country had required no particular courage, although that, she realized, might soon change.

Flanner was an accidental correspondent. She had been drafted into her job; the lure of reporting had not grabbed her the way it had other women. It was not the reason she had left her marriage, nor the real reason for her remaining in France — which may explain why, when later the going got tough, she would lack the will to stay.

2

Cassandras of the Coming Storm

Journalistic positions of some permanence and normality, such as those Dorothy Thompson and Sigrid Schultz and Janet Flanner had settled into in Berlin and Paris in the mid-1920s, were glittering prizes no longer available to women a decade later. Circumstances had changed. The establishment of the Italian Fascist state under Mussolini in the late 1920s and Hitler's rise to power in Germany in the early 1930s altered the psychic map of Europe long before the borders themselves were redrawn. American women who crossed the Atlantic with careers in mind came to observe as much as to write — came to assess, to prove or disprove, to try to make sense of the political scene if that was indeed possible.

For a young person with a bent for international politics, the League of Nations in Geneva was the place to go. That the United States was not a member of the League was a matter of dismay to many Americans, particularly idealistic college graduates who ardently hoped for its success and followed the course of its failures with increasing concern. With proper backing a young woman could join one of a number of peripheral programs that had sprung up in Geneva, explore matters currently before the League, attend sessions, and then look about to see where she could take her new expertise.

Helen Kirkpatrick, *Chicago Daily News*

This was Helen Kirkpatrick's plan. Tall, sandy-haired and blue-eyed, with a roguish smile and an inquiring mind, Helen grew up in Rochester, New York, and while at Smith spent a summer in Geneva with the Students' International Union. After graduation she returned there to help run the program, and then stayed on to study economics under Gunnar Myrdal and international relations with Count Sforza, the pre-Mussolini foreign minister of Italy. Simultaneously she was sending home articles for the Rochester papers.

Kirkpatrick's eventual return to the United States was a sobering experience. She could find no entry-level salaried positions in her field. In New York she tried Macy's management training, and then marriage — a double stab at becoming part of the American culture. Both proved a mistake. The Depression was in full swing, and a background in international affairs was neither pertinent to most job descriptions

Helen Kirkpatrick, 1942.
HELEN KIRKPATRICK PERSONAL COLLECTION.

nor helpful in a marriage she had had doubts about from the beginning. Desperate to recover a purposeful life, she took a summer job escorting thirty teenage girls about Europe, and at the furthermost point, Vienna, cabled her husband, "NOT RETURNING" — a cowardly solution, she admitted later. Once freed of her charges, Kirkpatrick returned to Geneva, where she was promptly hired to run the office of the Foreign Policy Association. This was an affirmation of her potential, and she was delighted. The FPA was in the League of Nations building, just below the press room, and before long Helen was covering for friends upstairs when they were ill or out of town. She wrote for the *Manchester Guardian* and the London *Daily Telegraph, Herald,* and *Express.* When the European office of the *New York Herald Tribune* offered her job as a stringer at a hundred dollars a month, she left the FPA. Reporting, she decided, was her calling. What she earned only barely sufficed, but that was to be expected. The point was, she was *in.*

It was as a *Herald Tribune* stringer that Kirkpatrick reported how the Nazis blew their own cover on rearmament. Against all intent and stipulation of the Versailles Treaty, the Reich army, navy, and air force were ballooning in size. Krupp, the armaments manufacturer, had been redesigning tanks for a decade. Submarines were being covertly assembled in Finland and Spain. I. G. Farben, the chemical trust, had discovered how to make gasoline and synthetic rubber from coal. Hitler reestablished universal military service and, in March 1936, sent his army into the demilitarized Rhineland.

In Basel, Kirkpatrick heard rumors of unusual activity along the riverfront. She and a friend left Switzerland at dawn and drove north along the east bank of the Rhine to investigate. Brand-new Nazi flags flew from every conceivable railing or pole. Soldiers crowded the streets of towns and villages, though Helen felt their presence was somehow tentative: they were positioned where they could withdraw quickly if a confrontation occurred. At Strasbourg she and her friend crossed over the Rhine and doubled back southward. On the French side the atmosphere was more apprehensive. Along the west bank the French had constructed an elaborate string of defenses known as the Maginot Line. Kirkpatrick was struck by the extent of the fortifications, the large numbers of antiaircraft and long-range guns, the thousands of newly summoned French troops. They seemed prepared, but she felt

that it was all a gamble on Hitler's part, that the Germans were bluff-
ing and the French were not calling the bluff. "The French and British
consulted, and decided that nothing had happened, so they wouldn't do
anything," she later recalled. "They were obligated to enforce the
treaty. But they didn't." Her story in the *Herald Tribune* European edition earned her considerable attention.

The same summer that Helen Kirkpatrick wired an airy farewell
to her husband from Vienna was the summer that Josephine Herbst,
enduring a wrenching separation from hers, took on a highly dangerous assignment in Berlin.

Josephine Herbst, *Nation, New Masses, New York Post*

Growing up poor in Sioux City, Iowa, Josephine Herbst was always
restless and filled with longing — for someplace that was not Iowa. At
the University of California at Berkeley she discovered radicals and
socialists, artists, poets, and writers, and especially the newspapermen
of the Bay Area. "I always knew that somewhere in the world were
people who could talk about the things I wanted to talk about and do
the things I wanted to do," she wrote home. Her new friends believed,
as she so passionately did, that it was possible to affect how things happened in the larger world.

Herbst graduated in 1918 and moved to New York — one of a
number of young women who migrated from the Midwest to live dangerously and try their talent. For Josephine, danger took the form of
an affair with the young socialist journalist and poet Maxwell Anderson,
who was trying to maintain his creative capacities while supporting a
wife and children. At the time she believed herself capable of free love,
no entanglements. She nabbed a job on an H. L. Mencken–George
Jean Nathan magazine, and in time two of her short stories were published in Mencken's *Smart Set*. Deciding to go where she could live
cheaply and write, she chose Berlin. In New York she met an aspiring
novelist, John Herrmann, friend of Ernest Hemingway, as Josie soon
was, too. Herrmann and Herbst returned home and married. There the
misfortune of needing jobs to pay the rent was offset by camaraderie
with fellow writers such as Katherine Anne Porter and John Dos
Passos, and for Herrmann by other women, something Herbst chose

to ignore. They were committed to each other as writers; free love still prevailed. But John's eventual departure left her devastated.

Herbst turned to reporting. She covered the Scottsboro case and Cuban politics for the radical *New Masses* and Iowa farm strikes for the *Nation*. In 1936 the *New York Post* asked her to go to Germany to gather information on underground resistance to Hitler, which correspondents in the Berlin bureaus knew about but were too visible to investigate. Government censors favored stories that stressed national unity and stability, but people who fled the country testified to unrest, and insisted there was still time to turn the situation around.

This kind of investigation was difficult, dangerous. Worn down by her personal troubles, Herbst was unsure she could take on so demanding an assignment. Still, it was a big story. She who felt so strongly that Americans must face the truth about Nazi Germany could hardly turn down a chance to help expose that truth. Besides, the trip would offer the best kind of distraction — wholly absorbing work in a changed environment.

Herbst arrived in Berlin with a scattering of names and addresses provided by exiles she had met in New York and elsewhere, and settled down in a comfortable hotel on Unter den Linden to get her bearings. The capital was both the same and very different. On her 1922 visit, rampant inflation had resulted in an often desperate populace, but people talked freely and the press published what it chose. Now everything seemed muzzled. To find the covert opposition, she had to pretend she was part of it, take every precaution they themselves were taking. No names or addresses could be written down, meetings must seem to happen by chance, the telephone was to be avoided. Other people's lives depended on her vigilance.

In the first of six installments (which could not be written until she left the country) she described the atmosphere in the capital:

> The newspaper, the radio and the newsreel repeat that all is quiet in Germany, everything is in order. To the eye, streets are clean, window boxes are choked with flowers, children hike to the country in droves, singing songs. The slogans of the opposition groups have been whitewashed from the walls. Only by word of mouth, in whispers, the real news circulates stealthily through

the German world. From hand to hand tiny leaflets inform the uninformed.

A worker tells me about the Bismarck strike in the secrecy of his home. It is in an apartment house where the doors are plastered with the different stickers of Nazi activities to show that the occupants have made their contributions. Within, we speak in lowered voices. The radio is turned on loudly and we sit near it with our heads close together. The walls have ears. . . .

Herbst found the tension hard to live with on a daily basis. People told her of strikes, and of retribution on the strikers. There was whisper of Gestapo jails and concentration camps. She noticed how, in bookstores, works once considered important were no longer on display. The Berlin of her youth seemed to have vanished:

For anyone who knew Germany in former years, it is a changed and sick country. Perhaps it is cleaner than before. The countryside is peculiarly orderly and beautiful. One may forget much in the country. Babies lie beside the wheat fields while mothers cut away with old-fashioned sickles. . . . Boys bicycle on country roads. Who sees a concentration camp? Yet silence is over the very countryside, in little inns where one is sharply scrutinized, in trains, along streets. Talk does not bubble up anymore.

To Josie, for whom talk was the supreme nourishment, the first necessity, it was as if civilization had vacated the country.

It was during the summer of 1936 that the virulence of German anti-Semitism hit American correspondents head on. They had grown up with the American variety, but in America one could combat anti-Semitism or try to avoid those who practiced it; even if Jewish, one had choices. By the mid-1930s choices for Jews in Germany were almost nonexistent. Herbst wrote despairingly of walking through Berlin and other cities and seeing sidewalks in front of small shops painted with red signs indicating Jewish ownership. Outside the capital, persecution was even more rampant. Many small-town Jews moved to Berlin to be

17

less conspicuous. But any sense of greater security there was nullified the night that storm troopers charged into cafés on the Kurfürstendamm demanding of patrons "Are you a Jew?" and, if there was no denial or the customer "looked Jewish," flinging his cup of coffee in his face. Men were hustled off and severely beaten. Herbst believed that the fiscal hardships of the working-class German increased his susceptibility to anti-Semitism, that racial consciousness was often the only thing he could take pride in. "The small disappointed shopkeeper gains some kind of distinction by being at least an 'Aryan,' " she wrote.

The Josephine Herbst who slipped out of Germany with her store of secrets was a different woman from the one who had entered a mere five weeks before. She went directly to Paris; saturated with her experience, she found it difficult to relate to her friends, and scorned their interests and concerns, although they were the same or similar to her own a short time before. Their failure to treat the situation in Germany seriously appalled her, even while she conceded that someone who had not seen what she had seen could not be expected to agonize as she did — or for that matter to plumb the depths of her despair at having heard nothing at all from her husband.

"Behind the Swastika," the six-part front-page series that appeared in the *New York Post*, documented the underside of Nazi Germany as no other journalist of either sex had yet done. But America slumbered on.

Like Herbst, Sigrid Schultz regretted the passing of the old Berlin. In the decade that she had served as bureau chief for the *Chicago Tribune*, the city had lost its cosmopolitan aura, its air of carefree emancipation. It was hard to take a morning stroll down Unter den Linden with uniformed men clicking their heels and heiling Hitler in stiff-armed salutes. Once-friendly neighbors were afraid to be seen talking with foreign reporters, particularly one with a reputation for anti-Nazi bias like Schultz.

Most foreign correspondents in Berlin tried to cover events objectively, irrespective of what light they cast on the Nazi regime. Hermann Goering, who saw reporters regularly, did his best to discourage a negative slant, and tried various tacks to that end — like favoring compliant correspondents with special interviews while boycotting others. Such stratagems seldom worked with American reporters who, over drinks at the Taverna, shared information any one of them had obtained.

So a backup ploy — planting incriminating documents in a reporter's residence and then staging a raid — was inaugurated, and Schultz was one of the first targets. An agent arrived at her apartment with a large sealed envelope which he handed to her mother with the directive that Fräulein Schultz should open it when she returned that evening. Forewarned, Frau Schultz phoned her daughter, and Sigrid rushed home, took one look at the design for an airplane engine inside the envelope, and burned it to ashes in the fireplace. On her way back to the office she passed a man she recognized, heading toward her home with two shady figures in tow. She planted herself squarely in their path and informed them it would be a waste of time to go any further as the contents of the envelope left at her house had already been destroyed. Then she flagged a taxi and loudly ordered the driver to take her to the American embassy.

Schultz decided the time had come to lodge a direct protest with Goering, and chose the occasion of a postwedding luncheon given by the Foreign Press Association to honor him and his new bride. Sigrid later described how Goering, scowling down the long banquet table, announced it was time these reporters began respecting the new Germany instead of constantly harping on concentration camps, which were needed to teach discipline to people who had forgotten about it during the days of the weak Weimar Republic. Schultz ignored that diatribe and began quietly to speak of her recent encounters with his agents provocateurs. "You are imagining things," he sputtered in response. Not at all, she said, and added that the American embassy was fully informed, which caused him to lose his temper and snarl about her never having learned proper respect for the authority of the state, probably a characteristic of people from "that crime-ridden city of Chicago." After that, Goering always referred to Sigrid as "the dragon lady from Chicago."

Schultz was not at all fazed by the intended slur, but now that the number two Nazi had declared openly against her, she had to be more on her guard than ever. The days when her working life and her private life meshed were over, and the latter was of necessity a lot more private and less fun than it had been. She enjoyed the respect of her colleagues, who admired her network of contacts, and relished the good fellowship at the Taverna, but she must have felt isolated. She was older than most of them by now and not privy to the banter she would have understood automatically had she grown up in the States.

Another matter separating Schultz from her colleagues at that time was a secret she was not sharing. The *Chicago Tribune* had begun a series of articles under the byline "John Dickson," which it prefaced with remarks to the effect that tight censorship and a controlled press having prevented a complete telling of the story of Nazi dictatorship, the *Tribune* had "sent one of its trained correspondents into Germany to obtain facts, which its accredited correspondents in the *Tribune*'s Berlin bureau have been unable to cable to America." In fact, Dickson and Schultz were the same.

The first series of stories, printed between May 15 and 19, 1937, and datelined Paris, explored problems currently facing Hitler, such as the resentment of farmers at the lack of available labor and the disgruntlement of the populace at the visibly increasing wealth of the Nazi leaders. There was friction in the ranks. Nazi leaders were unhappy that there was no immediate plan for the army to strike, while the army complained that the Hitler Youth, having been taught to think they were leaders, had to be retrained to obey before they were useful as soldiers. "Dickson" found the spring syllabus for Hitler Youth leaders of particular interest: eighteen-year-olds were advised what biological qualities to look for in a wife, to marry in a civil ceremony, and not to have their children christened since Christianity "undermines true heroic values."

For Schultz, to whom individuality and privacy were sacrosanct, her final "Dickson" piece was particularly damning. It described how in German society every citizen was "card-indexed" — not once but many times as he was registered with the local police, the central police, the secret police, the army, the "cell" in which his home fell and the "block" in which his "cell" fell, the guild of his profession, as either a donor or a recipient of winter relief, on the income tax lists, the city tax lists, the church unemployed insurance lists or the old-age insurance lists, as the owner of a house, a boat, a car, or a dog, and — if he were lucky — as a member of the Nazi Party.

Most *Chicago Tribune* readers accepted the stated identification of "John Dickson." If the Berlin correspondents were more skeptical, if they discerned in his writing the directness and style characteristic of their colleague Sigrid Schultz, they said nothing. The secret was hers alone — a cause of both satisfaction and unremitting anxiety.

Another American to confront the Germany of the mid-1930s was a young woman whose forebears were themselves German; her father, in fact, was a native of Breslau who had received his M.D. from the University of Würzburg and had come to America because of his anti-militarist beliefs. His children must often have heard from him, and discussed with him, events occurring in the country he still revered for its music and culture.

Martha Gellhorn, *Collier's* magazine

Martha Gellhorn grew up in Saint Louis, an only daughter in a family of four children. This was no ordinary family: her father and maternal grandfather were both practicing physicians and professors of medicine, her mother and grandmother deeply involved in education and civic affairs. Martha's mother in particular, the beautiful, loving Edna, immersed in all the best causes, of which women's suffrage was only the most prominent — even had Martha wanted to rebel against her, how could she? She adored her mother. She rebelled instead against Saint Louis, against its provinciality, against the upper-class society that her family moved among and yet (because her mother was half Jewish? because dinner conversation tended to be intellectual? because the Gellhorns thought a debut for their daughter too frivolous?) was never quite part of.

Martha was in the first class at the experimental (coed) John Burroughs School, founded under Edna's guidance, and when it came time for college, the daughter went off to the mother's alma mater, Bryn Mawr. Edna thought the college perfect, and perfect for her daughter,

Martha Gellhorn, 1940.
AP/WIDE WORLD PHOTOS.

but in Martha's view her fellow students were no more sophisticated than her friends in Saint Louis. She already knew more than they did, read more, smoked a lot more. And having led an unregulated youth among adults too busy to watch over her much, she resented the rules, or rather the fact that there were rules. She would always rebel against rules.

At twenty, to Edna's great disappointment, Martha left Bryn Mawr to live the life of a single and self-supporting woman in New York. She joined the staff of the *New Republic;* when that proved too academic, she took a job on the *Albany Times Union*, where as a cub reporter she covered the morgue. Two years later, in February 1930, she traded a favorable article on the Holland America Line for a one-way, third-class ticket to Europe. Paris did not disappoint her. She settled on the Left Bank, reported for *Vogue* and UP, and freelanced for the *Saint Louis Post-Dispatch*. On assignment for them she traveled to Geneva and interviewed women important in the structure of the League of Nations.

French had been a staple at both the John Burroughs School and

Bryn Mawr, and in Paris all Gellhorn's friends were French. With a delegation of male students from the Sorbonne, she went to Germany at the invitation of the young National Socialists, but found she could not take them seriously. Intellectually they were ridiculous, and she could imagine her father's scorn. When she returned the following year with a new friend, the titled (and married) French journalist Bertrand de Jouvenel, she revised this assessment. Stepson (and once lover) of the novelist Colette, Jouvenel left his wife to travel about with Gellhorn, two idealists united in struggle for the pacifist cause. But it was no longer possible not to take the young Nazis seriously. The situation in Germany had become alarming.

Jouvenel was strongly attracted to Gellhorn. Unlike the carefully sheltered young Frenchwomen of his station, she was as independent and opinionated as his stepmother, and at the same time young and beautiful. Both were cosmopolitan in outlook, had Jewish grandfathers on the mother's side, and shared an active devotion to peace and international community. But before long their politics were diverging. Martha had a gift for outrage; in their travels about Germany, she found herself much more incensed over the anti-Semitism they witnessed than Jouvenel was. He worried about young Germans feeling rejected by their contemporaries, a concern she thought naive. It was not long before her lack of commitment to his version of the world extended to himself. Her plan that they move to Paris and bring up his little son together was put on hold, and when she returned home in the fall of 1934, she went alone. She was twenty-six, she had completed her first novel, and now with the backing of Eleanor Roosevelt, a longtime friend of her mother's, she took a job as a field investigator with the Federal Emergency Relief Administration. The country was mired in the Depression; everywhere she found conditions appalling. The following year, at the invitation of both Roosevelts, she moved into the White House (austerely furnished then and lacking any security) and wrote a series of stories based on her field experience. *The Trouble I've Seen* was published in 1936 to rave reviews. By then Gellhorn was back in Germany, acquiring background material for a new novel and observing the strutting storm troopers and frightened people with despair.

After Christmas in Saint Louis that year, Martha, her mother, and a brother took a trip to Key West. They were sitting in a bar one afternoon when the town's most notable resident, Ernest Hemingway, walked in. In her simple black dress, with her tawny blond hair and long legs, her easy, knowledgeable conversation sprinkled with expletives and punctuated by puffs on a cigarette, Martha was more interesting than anyone Hemingway had seen for a long while. During the ensuing days Ernest devoted much of his time to her, and she spent hours at the Hemingway home. The subject of Spain came up often. The war there was six months old and attracting writers supportive of the Loyalist cause. Gellhorn was determined to go, and in opposition to the wishes of his wife, Pauline, Hemingway decided to go as well. He signed a contract with the North American Newspaper Alliance (NANA) and sailed in February. For Martha, obtaining proper credentials was less easily managed, but a sympathetic editor at *Collier's* dashed off a letter indicating her as a special correspondent for the magazine. Early in March 1937 she too set off for Spain.

3

Apprentices in Spain

Spain was where they gave a war and everybody came. The Spanish Civil War served as an apprenticeship for several young American female journalists who thought that world war looked likely. It offered them opportunity to hone their skills, earn their credentials, test their nerve. Older women went too, for ideological reasons. For both the press and the military, the conflict served as a preliminary to the main event to come. Spain was where Italy tested her troops, Germany her arms, and Russia her technicians; where Britain and France experimented with indecision, and America with isolation.

The war was especially irresistible to writers. W. H. Auden, Stephen Spender, George Orwell, and Rebecca West trooped down from England, André Malraux, Antoine de Saint-Exupéry, and Simone Weil crossed the border from France, and from America came Ernest Hemingway and John Dos Passos. They believed that the fate of the Spanish Republic was fused with the fate not only of democracy but of art, literature, all that mattered most in life. To awake the world to that danger they were doubling as correspondents. But there were other reporters too, unknown to the world at large, sent by their home offices to cover the war. Reynolds and Eleanor Packard were among the latter.

Eleanor Packard, United Press

In fact, Eleanor Packard was catapulted into the thick of the war from its start. In the summer of 1936 General Franco, hiding out in the

Eleanor Packard boarding an Italian observation plane in Ethiopia, 1936.
UPI/CORBIS-BETTMANN.

Canary Islands, was whisked back to Spain to lead his Nationalist army in a series of carefully coordinated uprisings. His success cut reporters in the capital off from the action. New reporters had to be sent at once to the areas of conflict, and UP turned to its trusty team, known to their friends as Pack and Peebee.

Although in most husband-wife teams the man was dominant, no one ever thought of Eleanor as playing a subordinate role. She had grown up on a ranch in Yakima, Washington, and there was always a rough frontierswoman quality about her. After attending the Columbia School of Journalism, she embarked for Paris and began reporting for UP. At home UP banned women from its staff, but Stateside rules did not always prevail abroad. Eleanor met her husband in a bar when, it was said, he got into a fight and she floored his adversary. They were a big, lusty couple.

After their marriage the Packards were posted to China, where the area to be covered was so vast that they worked independently, separated for weeks at a time. China was the testing ground of their marriage; it was in Peking that Reynolds became enamored of a Mongolian woman and, in a moment of passion, bit off her left nipple. The diplomatic consequences could be serious. Since the couple used the UP wires for private as well as business purposes, the scenario went public in daily communiqués between Peking and Shanghai, with relays to New York and other locations that expressed interest. Eleanor charged up to Peking to save her husband and both their careers. Reparations of some sort were made, and the matter settled. The experience was a defining one, but far from damaging their marriage, it seemed to cement it. If a bargain was struck, they kept that, at least, to themselves.

The Packards had been drawn together by lack of inhibition on both sides and a shared passion for the reporter's life. Transferred to Egypt, they worked out of a station wagon in the desert. In the fall of 1935 they were on their way to Ethiopia when the Italian army invaded. By spring, with Emperor Haile Selassie's army annihilated, the corps of reporters began an arduous five-day journey to General Pietro Badoglio's new headquarters along a road literally being carved out of the mountainside. In time, the hardships would fade from her mind, but Eleanor always remembered the gallantries of the simple Italian soldiers. She was the only woman present and the only white woman they had seen in months, and never mind that she was bigger than any of them. They crowded around the car at any opportunity, ignoring Reynolds and offering her everything from wine to Ethiopian castrating knives. At night, when they camped, the soldiers would request permission to serenade *la donna bianca*, and then would come choruses of popular Italian songs and, when they ran out of those, regimental songs. One evening, their tent pitched beside a shallow river, the couple headed for what they thought was a secluded spot to cool off with a swim. "Coming out of a thicket," Eleanor wrote later, "we suddenly found ourselves on the riverbank in front of some two hundred naked soldiers, standing knee-deep in the river, soaping themselves under the command of an Italian captain in uniform who stood on the opposite bank. More cries of *donna bianca* broke out. The captain quickly took charge of the situation and bellowed out a series of orders. 'About face. March to shore. Don drawers. Return to your bathing.' He then called to us, 'I hope la signora now finds everything satisfactory and will enjoy the water.' " After that Eleanor found the drive to Addis Ababa with General Badoglio in his Studebaker, meant to be a privilege, a real letdown.

Now, only two months later, the hot copy had moved to Spain. Deplaning in Paris from a vacation in New York, the Packards found a cable instructing them to go directly to the French border town of Hendaye, on the far side of which was Nationalist-held Spain. Within three days they had crossed over, into the middle of a war.

Frances Davis, London *Daily Mail, Chicago Daily News*

Frances Davis also made the trip from Paris down to Hendaye. Davis was Packard's physical opposite — small, slight of build, fine-featured — with few credentials but enormous verve. Reared in a utopian community outside Boston, she was intent on taking on the "real" world. Catherine Coyne, who later reported the larger war, remembered her at Boston University in 1926–27 as "a pretty little journalism student bursting with enthusiasm." Upon graduation she located an ex–foreign correspondent (unnamed), persuaded him to teach her all he knew, then applied to various papers and wire services for a European post. That effort failed. By chance one day in New York in the early 1930s, Davis met Dorothy Thompson, and over tea Thompson suggested she make up her own syndicate. Go out into the country and sell yourself to the little papers, Thompson told her. Although that was not easy in mid-Depression America, Davis managed to round up a dozen clients. With the last of her savings she bought a ticket for Paris where she could write her little columns and be available should any of the established papers need assistance.

Davis's entrance to the world of journalism, as a mail columnist for papers that could not afford to pay for cables, was a classic way for a clever woman to slip into a man's world. Edgar Ansel Mowrer, now at the Paris office of the *Chicago Daily News*, introduced her around, and after the Spanish story broke, he advised her to pack her clothes, take the next train to Hendaye, and stay at the Imatz Hotel with the rest of the press. The Imatz was glutted with reporters, most of whom seemed to know each other. But Edmond Taylor of the *Chicago Tribune*, whom she had met in Paris, introduced her to John Elliott of the *New York Herald Tribune*, and when the two men shared information, they included her. Davis had no information to trade, but she proved her worth a few days later when, having crossed into Spain together, they were attempting to get passes to Madrid, and the local *commandante* would deal only with her. The safe-conduct was made out in her name with the others listed as appendages. Davis was on her way.

After that, Elliott, Taylor, Major Cardozo of the London *Daily Mail*, and Bertrand de Jouvenel of *Paris-Soir* made room for her in their hired car. Every morning they drove out seeking the war. On their first day of real action, they drove south through sad, deserted towns where Franco's army had recently passed. After the city of Zaragoza nobody sat at the café tables in the sun or waved from doorways. At Medinaceli, a mountaintop Nationalist stronghold, they sighted Republican planes. Reporters, villagers, and a milk cow were shooed down a narrow stair-well into a deep wine cellar where Davis and her colleagues leaned against the walls and listened to the bombs. Afterward, back in the sun-shine and happy at having found a piece of the war, they could set up their typewriters on the green baize surface of a pool table and write their stories.

But the articles could not be sent from Spain. Someone would have to take them back to France. Promising to return the following day, Davis collected the stories with a thousand-franc note each for trans-mittal costs and got back into the car with the driver. Night was approaching, a dense fog had descended. She suggested they take a dif-ferent route, which appeared shorter on the map. Hearing artillery fire in the mountains, and feeling uneasy as they neared the frontier, she unzipped the side of her dress and secreted the stories inside her girdle. The extra money, four thousand more francs than the six hun-dred recorded on her border pass, posed another problem, so she unzipped her dress again and stuffed the money alongside the stories. As they reached the border town, Frances noticed that the flag on the guardhouse was not the red and gold Nationalist flag but the red, yellow, and purple of the Republic. Without knowing it, she had crossed the lines. Here the signatures on her pass were enemy signatures; the information burning against her skin was military information. But her youth and her American passport were in her favor. Through the car window an official questioned her courteously, cautioning her against returning to Spain. Davis nodded agreement. Her experience had been a frightening one, she said, and she had no intention of repeating it. The car was waved on to France.

Exhausted as she was, she had still to send out the stories. In Biarritz she rang the night bell of a darkened hotel, and within minutes was resting against down pillows under a warm comforter, the phone at her side. Carefully sorting the stories into four piles on the bedcovers, she picked up the receiver. "Elysées 1287. Oui. C'est ça. Herald Trib? I have a story from John Elliott. Are you ready? Dateline Medinaceli . . ."

Within hours the border closed. Davis could not return to Spain, and it was three days before it reopened and her colleagues made it back to Hendaye. But the *Daily Mail* was impressed by her resourcefulness. A call came through from London. Perhaps a permanent arrangement? Would she be free to assist Cardozo? Would ten pounds a week plus expenses do?

It would do very well. A woman with credentials need not fear being excess baggage in a car. A reporter for the *Mail* could hold her own at the Imatz. Frances had been made legitimate; she felt transformed.

In an early dispatch Davis described the tension in Hendaye:

> Reinforcements have been sent from the north. The atmosphere in the town is changing. Antagonism is growing between those who are for one side and those who are for the other. Violence flares up at a taunt, at the mimicking of a salute, at the whistling of a song.
>
> A half-dozen wild young workingmen take infinite pleasure in eluding the police and appearing upon the river road opposite the White army emplacements, to stand in the sunlight waving their clenched fists and singing the "Internationale."
>
> There are spies everywhere. They lie in the long grasses by the river bank. . . . At night they swim the river to report. Some

have been shot. The farming fields on the French side of the river are pitted with shell holes. . . .

Now the sound of the big guns ceases only at nightfall and, lying on the beach at St.-Jean-de-Luz, you can feel the impact as the shells hit the earth in Spain.

The press moved to Burgos, and Davis continued her role as courier. Shuttling over mountain roads, she ate, slept, and typed her own stories in the car. The tension of the steep mountain ascent and descent, of the guards monitoring her movements, was increasingly wearing. The official stories she carried openly, but sometimes she also carried an uncensored version tucked inside her girdle. Who knew when the guards might decide to search her.

By late September, when Toledo fell to the Nationalists, Davis's pleasure at her connection with the *Daily Mail* had begun to pale. She had come to resent the *Mail*'s slanted terminology and cozy relations with Franco; she had seen too much of the war by now to refer to his soldiers as "patriots." Frances weighed her options. She had worked for two months behind Franco's lines; to switch to the other side might brand her a double agent. Better try to move to a publication that would allow her a more skeptical approach. She caught the train to Paris, where she persuaded Edgar Mowrer to take her on for the *Chicago Daily News*.

The action moved to Madrid. From the town of Avila, Eleanor Packard covered Franco's attacks on the capital. She later recalled it as "a grim journalistic picnic." With other reporters she drove daily the ninety miles to the front lines, seeking eyewitness copy from the "top of windmills or behind chimneys, in deserted suburban villas surrounded by once-beautiful gardens now filled with the rubble of war, dead bodies, shrapnel-broken furniture and torn clothing. Every time we poked our heads out too far, the Madrid sharpshooters' bullets buzzed over us like wasps."

That fall the American contingent swelled as more young reporters arrived. Frances Davis ran into John Whitaker of the International News Service, black curls spilling out from under his beret, cape swinging back from his shoulders. He and a friend urged her to abandon the "older men" she had been associating with and join them. Ready for the companionship of her own kind, Frances concurred. Together they conspired to have a Thanksgiving and broached the subject to Eleanor Packard: a woman who grew up on a ranch was sure to know how to cook a turkey, even the tough, skinny Spanish variety. As it happened, Eleanor also made pumpkin pies. They borrowed the hotel kitchen and invited the press. There was a lull in the war, and the day was a huge success.

The weather turned cold, and fighting resumed. During most of her journalistic adventure with her new friends, Davis could barely talk: a bitter wind from the mountains had brought on a throat infection that steadily worsened. A shell sliver wound under her knee would not heal. In mid-December she and Whitaker set out for France. Their car ran the gauntlet between the armies, the two young reporters on the floor and the chauffeur slumped down as far as he could get and still see the road. In Paris, partially recovered, she was sent by the *Chicago Daily News* to bask in the warm sun of Majorca and learn what was going on there. Alone and often frightened, Frances discovered that the island was no longer a tourist paradise but a training ground for Italian conscripts bound for Spain, a storehouse of slave labor, a secret bomber base with underground hangars, and a concentration camp complete with torture chamber. She was thoroughly searched on leaving, and it was only by luck that her little black notebook, secreted in a lining pocket of the man's coat she wore, was not discovered. She had proved her status as a reporter and her value to the *News*, but back in Paris, her wound suppurated; she was hospitalized with septicemia and nearly died. Her recovery would be longer and more arduous than she could then imagine, but there were two bright spots. The senior intern confided to her that Edgar Mowrer, her boss and mentor, had paced the hospital corridors the night of her gravest danger. And on another day long-stemmed roses arrived with the cabled message FROM ONE NEWSPAPER WOMAN TO ANOTHER WHO ENORMOUSLY ADMIRES YOUR COURAGE AND GALLANTRY. DOROTHY THOMPSON.

During the spring of 1937 three American women writers arrived in Madrid. Martha Gellhorn and Josephine Herbst, both deeply political, went as much out of sympathy for the Republican cause as for journalistic reasons. For them it was a gesture of solidarity. If not technically a member of the Communist Party, Herbst was close enough to be called "comrade" by those who were, and in Russia and abroad the Communists were powerful supporters of the Republican "popular front" in Spain. Josie identified with them; she was active in strikers' marches, in the struggle against exploitation. Virginia Cowles had no such identification, coming as she did from the "exploiter class," but if she had been unsure of her career before, Spain settled her mind once and for all.

Virginia Cowles, Hearst Publications, London *Sunday Times*

It was the professional aspect of the reporter's life that attracted Virginia Cowles. A young, privately educated Boston socialite, she had moved beyond the conventions of her class to take a job on the staff of a New York fashion magazine, then rebelled against what she viewed as trivial assignments. Resigning her post, she set off on a twelve-month trip from London to Tokyo, regularly forwarding articles to the "March of Events" section of the Hearst papers (another entry into international journalism available only to a woman with a private income). Virginia spoke excellent French and Italian, and her social connections provided her with entrée far beyond that of the average correspondent. When at a party in Rome she dropped a hint to the Italian minister of propaganda that she would like to interview his boss, she was catapulted over a dozen others for a session at the great marble palazzo the next day. She expected a solemn black-uniformed dictator, and was at first nonplussed by the short, stocky, dapper man who shot questions at her like grapeshot, banged on the table in his anger at the League of Nations for opposing his takeover of Ethiopia, then abruptly concluded the interview by suggesting she go home and tell the American people that Italy was a great power and feared no one.

After war broke out in Spain, Cowles saw a chance for what she referred to as "more vigorous" reporting. She persuaded a Hearst editor that covering both sides and writing a series of articles contrasting the two would make a good story. Having no experience of war, she had

Virginia Cowles broadcasting on the BBC, London, 1943.
AP/WIDE WORLD PHOTOS.

no real idea what her suggestion would entail. Her plan was indicative of how, over the next few years, she would cover the larger war — by leaping blindly into one trouble spot after another.

The Loyalists, with whom Cowles sympathized even while insisting on her professional impartiality, were losing battle after battle. They held central Madrid, but only ten blocks away, in the University City area, the Nationalists were already entrenched. Virginia stayed with the other correspondents at the Hotel Florida, and it was there that Josephine Herbst, dragging a knapsack and coated with white dust residue from exploded shells, was greeted with a bear hug by her old friend Ernest Hemingway, dividing his time between NANA and work with John Dos Passos on a documentary film of the war.

Martha Gellhorn's arrival was less auspicious. She had traveled from the border on a train full of young, enthusiastic, and admiring Republican soldiers. From that heady experience, she entered the basement restaurant of the Gran Vía Hotel in Madrid, where the correspondents ate together at a long communal table, to find a far different Hemingway from the attentive semisuitor she had known in Key West.

34

Under the daily flattery of his companions in Madrid, he had reverted to his condescending Papa role. He knew she would get there, he said, because he had arranged it so. That, of course, was nonsense. In addition, Martha felt she had proved herself as a novelist and reporter, and believed herself more committed to anti-Fascism than he was. When she arrived, cold, dusty, and tired, to find herself patronized instead of appreciated, she was furious. Right then she was ready to declare that it was only by chance that she and this insufferable man had both landed in Madrid in the middle of a war.

Gellhorn, Herbst, and Cowles all had rooms at the Florida. In Madrid the normal city and the city at war existed side by side. "The shellholes, the camouflaged trucks and the stone barricades seemed as unreal as stage props," Virginia reported. Martha wrote that "the sun was too warm, the people too nonchalant for war." After a shelling "you could see people around Madrid examining the new shell holes with curiosity and wonder. Otherwise they went on with the routine of their lives, as if they had been interrupted by a heavy rainstorm but nothing more."

Josephine Herbst noted that it was like living in a tropical climate where it rained every day at about the same time:

> The heavy shelling usually came in the afternoon and if you got caught in it the only thing to do was to duck into some cafe. No one anywhere was well dressed, not even the tarts. There were no mantillas or black lace or shrinking girls with duennas. In the evening on the way to the restaurant the pavement was likely to be all hummocks and busted-up rubble. You picked your way with a flashlight. In the morning all this stuff would be swept up and new patches of cement would cover the holes. This went on, day by day, with the regularity of washing up the supper dishes.

Herbst and Cowles waited out a shelling together with Hemingway at the Gran Vía one afternoon. Josie liked Virginia, whom she described as "young and pretty, dressed in black with heavy gold bracelets on her slender wrists, and tiny black shoes with incredibly high heels." Herbst herself was no longer young, had never been pretty, and could not afford gold bracelets. Still, Cowles was a serious reporter, and Herbst respected that, even when wondering how Virginia managed to walk through the rubble-filled streets in such shoes. Both women remembered the afternoon at the Gran Vía vividly because of the man who joined them, whom Hemingway referred to as "the chief executioner of Madrid." Pepe Quintanilla knew all about how people in Madrid had died, including the "mistakes," as he called them — innocent townspeople who had been in the wrong place at the wrong time — as well as men who responded crazily to the war and charged the enemy with a butcher knife. Throughout the conversation he counted each shell as it landed and then resumed talking. Listening to his stories, tensed for the next shell, no one else said anything. Hemingway kept standing up to leave, but Quintanilla always pushed him back in his seat. "No one goes," he said, ordering more cognac, and then another shell would fall nearby, proving him right. When at last he allowed them to return to the Florida, they found it had received a direct hit.

Later Gellhorn, who had been caught in the Florida during the raid, described the shelling in an article in *Collier's*:

> Looking out the door, I saw people standing in doorways all around the square, just standing there patiently, and then suddenly a shell landed, and there was a fountain of granite cobblestones flying up into the air, and the silver lyddite smoke floated off softly. . . . Another shell hit, halfway across the street, and a window broke gently and airily, making a lovely tinkling musical sound.
>
> I went back to my room, and again suddenly there came that whistle-whine-scream-roar and the noise was in your throat and you couldn't feel or hear or think and the building shook and seemed to settle. Outside in the hall, the maids were calling to one another like birds, in high excited voices. The concierge ran upstairs looking concerned and shaking his head. On the floor above, we went into a room in which the lyddite smoke still hung mistily. There was nothing left in that room, the furniture was kindling wood, the walls were stripped and in places torn open, a great hole led into the next room and the bed was twisted iron and stood upright and silly against the wall.

For reasons of her own, Gellhorn did not immediately settle down to reporting. She later described how she had tagged along behind the other correspondents for weeks until "a journalist friend" remarked that it was time she began to write. Considering her experience, her ambition, and her natural work ethic, this would have been most uncharacteristic, unless her creativity was somehow blocked by living in close proximity to that same "journalist friend." Ernest and Martha had apparently reconciled. Their cohabitation became clear very early one morning when a rebel shell exploded in the hot water tank of the Florida. The corridors filled with steam, and all the guests rushed from their rooms in various stages of panic. Sefton Delmer of the London *Daily Express*, noting who burst out of which door, observed it was then that Hemingway's affair with Gellhorn became public knowledge. Josephine Herbst remembered how the correspondents flocked together into a front room, one with a coffeepot in his hand, another with a toaster and a little stale bread. She was most impressed by a French reporter in a blue satin robe (Saint-Exupéry?) "carrying an armful of grapefruit, which he passed out to each of us, bowing to us in turn."

Herbst was not happy about Hemingway's liaison with Gellhorn. Perhaps she saw something of herself in this young unattached woman having an affair with a famous writer, not himself unattached. Maxwell Anderson, whom she had loved as a young woman in New York, had been a husband and father; Hemingway was the same twice over. Josie had known his first wife, Hadley, in Paris, and his second, Pauline, in Key West. Now here was Martha, blue-eyed like herself but with silky blond hair where her own was nondescript and frizzled — not that she was *competing*. If anyone, it was Hemingway she measured herself against. As young writers in Paris they had been equals, but now he was more famous, much richer, with better press credentials, two cars at his disposal, and a mistress. Herbst chose to think of it that way, although Gellhorn, of course, did not. Josie, while condoning Cowles's high heels, thought Martha's "beautiful Saks Fifth Avenue pants with a green chiffon scarf wound around her head" inappropriate to a battle zone. Envy can work havoc with consistency.

For a journalist, the raison d'être in Madrid was to go to the front. Most convenient was the Casa de Campo and University City front, a bare two miles from the main shopping area. A car was unnecessary — the tram went halfway, and you walked the rest. You knew you were there when a stone barricade blocked your way and a Republican guard, attired in corduroys and a sweater, asked to see your pass. He carefully studied whatever you produced, raised a clenched fist in salute, and let you pass.

This front provided the baptism of trench warfare for many, including Virginia Cowles, invited to accompany the English scientist and Loyalist sympathizer J. B. S. Haldane there one afternoon. They dodged shells and crawled along the narrow communication trench with mud slopping into their shoes and bullets ringing over their heads. When Virginia questioned their position, the professor pompously noted that in the last war women were prohibited from the front lines and she should be grateful for this privilege. Further along he abandoned her entirely to have a look on the other side of the hill, just as the enemy started throwing trench mortars. Fortunately, a young officer came along to guide her through dark tunnels to a shack full of soldiers, where he explained that she was an American writer who had lost her way, and said they were to take care of her until he could locate her missing professor. Welcomed with exuberance, Virginia was installed by the tiny fire, her shoes (those little high heels?) cleaned, and stale bread offered as refreshment. It was a typical introduction to the troops of the Popular Front; in contrast to the cerebral scientist, they were all heart, and for that Virginia was grateful.

Such camaraderie with the fighting men, preferably the soldiers of the International Brigades, was what Josephine Herbst had come for. Her chance came one morning when she encountered a friend of Hemingway's about to take off for the village of Murata, near the front lines. He offered to take her along, and she leaped at the opportunity. The first rule a woman learned reporting a war was to seize any chance for a ride to the front.

Murata had been the scene of fierce fighting. During the winter Nationalist troops had made a concerted push against the Loyalists, including four hundred Americans of the Abraham Lincoln Brigade — many of them raw volunteers who had never held a rifle. A few battles later, only a hundred Americans remained. A Loyalist general arranged safe-conduct for Herbst to the front lines. She could stay a few days if she chose, he said; there was a café in the village where she could sleep. This was her break, and she was euphoric.

The route to the front began up an old donkey road by car, proceeded by foot across a stretch of open ground, then dipped down into an open dugout. Young American soldiers sitting around a table, bare except for a telephone, were astonished by her sudden appearance. They had been in the line for sixty days, and were expecting an attack. "The nucleus of Americans left from the big offensive was holding tight together," Herbst wrote, "but they must have felt during the prolonged stalemate, where men died one by one, that the real war was going on elsewhere. Or that only the enemy would remember them and on some dark night swoop down and take them by surprise."

When she returned to Madrid from her days at the front, Herbst found life tiresomely superficial. It was a readjustment problem women correspondents would have throughout the war — the same in 1940 when they returned to the United States from bombed-out London, or in 1945 to Paris from the ruins of Aachen or Cologne. In Madrid in 1937, Josie tried to hold on to the core of her experience. At night she would lie in bed and recall her room in Murata with its stone floor so cold that "the chill shot up your leg like a toothache if you put your bare foot down." Mornings she sat in the lobby of the Florida so that soldiers on leave could drop in to talk. With tea and a little dry bread saved from dinner the night before, they would sit munching and talking. Dos Passos was often there, too. Before long, odors of ham and coffee would drift downward from the fourth floor, and Hemingway would lean over the rail and invite them to breakfast. There was no such thing as ham anywhere except in his own private store, and Josie, always hungry, would be terribly tempted, but as she said, "You couldn't run off from your visitors. Tomorrow they might be dead."

Martha Gellhorn visited the Abraham Lincoln Brigade with Hemingway, and he took her on a ten-day inspection tour, on horseback, of the Guadarrama front, a series of Republican strongholds scattered over a wooded mountain range. Virginia Cowles went along for part of the trip. Back in Madrid, the two women visited hospitals and prisons together, interviewing personnel and recording their impressions. In one article for *Collier's*, Gellhorn described a visit to the Palace Hotel, now a military hospital, where the reading room had become an operating room. Hypodermic needles, surgical instruments, and bandages filled the old Empire bookcases, and surgeons performed their delicate work by the light of cut-glass chandeliers. Sun poured in the windows. The world seemed properly ordered until one visited the patients. The spectacle of a young blond aviator who had been shot down in his plane, his eyes saved by his goggles but his face a thick brown scab, would not leave her.

That women reporters might be doubling as spies was a concept as rife among the Republicans that spring as Frances Davis had found it with the Nationalist forces. Josephine Herbst noted that whenever she left Madrid and the car was stopped, the only papers the guards were interested in were hers.

Virginia Cowles became embroiled in a situation so serious that she had to leave the country. One afternoon in May she and Jerome Willis of the Agence d'Espagne, driving on the Murata road in search of the International Brigade headquarters, stumbled by accident on the Soviet divisional headquarters. Although some two thousand Soviet officers and technicians were in Spain to help train the Republican army, reporters were not allowed contact with them. The general who confronted them was curt and hostile — but afterward he had a change of heart. He sent Cowles an invitation to lunch, and as it seemed her only chance to see the Brigade lines, she accepted. A car was dispatched for her, and after a sumptuous meal the general personally escorted her through trenches ankle deep in mud. Most of the troops were idealists of various nationalities; Cowles thought them ill suited for soldiering. When she and the general reached the American sector, he encouraged her to converse at length with the soldiers there. Their faces were tired and worn, and she wondered how many of them would ever see America again.

Virginia might perhaps have wondered the same of herself when, on her return to headquarters, she discovered that she was not exactly free to leave. The general said he wished to convert her to Communism, and detained her for three days; each evening, over champagne, he instructed her in Marxism. He had sworn "eternal enmity to the privileged classes of the world," he told her, and convinced that the Revolution would reach America soon, he was preparing her to be on the right side. At the end of her stay he said, somewhat wistfully, that she would be welcome to return whenever she wished, but then concluded: "You won't return, but you will boast to your friends that a Red Army general took a fancy to you."

Back in Madrid Cowles learned that any such boast would be unwise. The Soviet ban on journalists was well known; already her visit to their headquarters had placed her in a dubious position. Friends warned her not to ride in a car by herself, as road accidents were a favorite way of dealing with suspected spies. It was time, Virginia concluded, to leave Spain. She drove to Valencia, where a German Communist who worked for the secret police insisted on taking her out for a drink. Why was she leaving Spain so soon after her trips to various army headquarters? he asked. Perhaps she could just as well write her stories from the "nice new jail at Albacete." But he did not arrest her, and the next morning she flew to France.

Josephine Herbst, too, thought it was time to move on. The war was at a stalemate, and there was dissension among the various Republican ideological factions. Dos Passos, deeply disillusioned, had quarreled with Hemingway. Food was scarcer than ever, and Josie told herself that she — a noncombatant, a foreigner — was consuming too much of it, although in fact she had lost twenty pounds. She made her way to Barcelona and flew to Toulouse, looking forward to ordering a real lunch in a normal restaurant, only to find herself sobbing over her omelette "and looking at people calmly passing by as if I had entered into a nightmare where the 'real' world had suddenly been wiped off with a sponge and vanished forever."

Martha Gellhorn and Hemingway also left during that summer of 1937, but in September they returned. Although Franco now held about two-thirds of Spain, the Republican forces had recently had some success in Aragon, and together with Herbert Matthews of the *New York Times* the couple surveyed the area for stories. Traveling the mountain paths on foot and horseback, they lived out of an open truck and cooked over campfires. Snow fell early in the mountains, and the wind was cold, but Martha bore it all with great equanimity, endearing herself even more to Hemingway.

The war — or perhaps Spain — continued to hold a magnetic attraction for reporters. True to her original plan to cover both sides,

Virginia Cowles managed to cross the border once more to compare the situation in Nationalist Spain, bedecked from one end to the other with German and Italian flags and swastikas, with what she had seen in and around Madrid. She visited Guernica. Accompanied by a Spanish officer, she followed Franco's army through the rugged province of Asturias, the soldiers on muleback forming "a long, silent procession winding through the mountains."

Having gone to war of her own volition, Cowles felt free to draw her own conclusion: for the common people, war was hard whether you were on the winning or losing side. Most civilians cared little about either military strategy or the isms thrown at them — Bolshevism, Fascism, Nationalism. War meant domestic upheaval, soaring prices, inadequate food, and houses with shell holes in them, if not worse. She found the soldiers on Franco's side less idealistic, although better disciplined and far better equipped. But she learned to keep her conclusions to herself. Comparisons could be dangerous; objectivity was not tolerated. Unthinking, she contradicted the views of a Nationalist officer. Finding herself once again in grave personal danger, she counted herself lucky to slip out of the country.

Madrid fell on March 28, 1939. The International Brigade, what was left of it, had long since been pulled from the lines. The Soviet general who had taken a fancy to Virginia Cowles had departed for Moscow and a very uncertain future. Most of the Italian troops had returned home as well, and at the end it was as it had begun — Spaniard against Spaniard.

Eleanor and Reynolds Packard reported the Nationalist victory parade in Madrid on May 11. They viewed the proceedings from the press gallery beside Franco's reviewing stand. For five hours the troops marched past in the rain. Tanks from Italy, German planes overhead, all were part of a show of strength that conveyed its own message: the civil war in Spain may have ended, but the Fascist onslaught had begun.

4

The Lessons of Czechoslovakia

The international scene attracted early women photographers as well as men, although seldom professionally and seldom in the middle of an armed conflict. Forty years had passed since Anna Benjamin, her box-shaped camera slung over her slender shoulder, covered wars in Cuba, Manila, and the Far East. In fact, few American women had broken into news photography as a career, until during the 1930s one emerged who coupled genius behind the lens with extraordinary determination and would become one of the great photojournalists of World War II.

Margaret Bourke-White, *Life*

Margaret (sometimes "Maggie" or "Peg") Bourke-White grew up in a small New Jersey town, in a family where standards of conduct — always doing one's best, and then a little better — substituted for pretty clothes and position in local society. In high school, where appearance mattered, she felt herself on the sidelines, but she was happier at Columbia, the first of her several colleges. She enrolled in a photography course with Clarence H. White (no relation), mainstay of the Photo-Secession group. Already a perfectionist herself, she adopted his passion for absolute control of each picture.

Margaret's father, who had introduced her to photography and to whom she was very close, died that year, and she migrated to the

Margaret Bourke-White at an American air base in England, 1942.
PHOTO BY LEE MILLER. © LEE MILLER ARCHIVES.

University of Michigan, where she spent as much time with her camera as her books. She discovered the link between photography and
adventure, clambering up and sliding down pitched roofs or lowering
herself into a manhole to get the desired shot. It was at Michigan that
she defined her goal to be "a news photographer-reporter," and where
she blossomed socially — joined a sorority, dated, fell in love with a fellow photographer. At twenty, and not without doubts, she married him.
She tried to be a good wife (had she not been trained to do her best in
every situation?), but her young husband's family, bitterly opposed and
supremely possessive, won out. When at last she left, having survived

two years of stressful courtship and two more of connubial blisslessness, Margaret was ready for life as an individual again.

At Cornell, her sixth college, she peddled her photos to help see her through to graduation. Wielding her old Ica Reflex with a crack through its lens, she shot fuzzy, soft-focus impressions of Cornell's fine old buildings. "Campus pattern pictures" she called them, or more romantically, "pseudo-Corots." Cornell alumni who saw them featured in the *Alumni News* were impressed, and when during Easter vacation Margaret took her portfolio to the associates of a large New York architectural firm, she received a resounding vote of affirmation.

Newly confident, Bourke-White made serious preparations for her career of star photographer. She had cut her hair to a smart bob and hyphenated her name when she left her husband; now she dropped both him from her record and two years from her life. Her new youth served to elevate her prodigy status. In Cleveland, selected as a stepping-stone for consolidating her reputation before she hit New York, she began shooting industrial locations — the Lake Erie waterfront, railways, steel mills. Some shots were possible only from the roofs of other buildings, or from precarious beams or ledges, and she became adept at conquering dizzy heights. Such antics were noticed, and contributed to a growing celebrity. Along with her newly vibrant, almost electric personality, she suddenly found she had sex appeal.

Perhaps employing that elusive quality, Bourke-White persuaded a reluctant president of the Otis Steel Mills to allow her to photograph there at will. Henry Luce happened upon a sampling in the rotogravure section of a midwestern paper and sent Margaret an invitation to come to New York and join the staff of his new business periodical, *Fortune*. The first issue concentrated on the meatpacking industry, and her photo-essay of "pattern pictures of giant hog shapes" established her as a pioneer in the new photojournalism. From that time on, the magazine made extravagant use of her photographs, sending her to Germany, and then on to the Soviet Union to cover the new Russia. She returned there twice over the next two years. Stalin was consolidating his power, but she saw none of the terrible cost of that endeavor, and the country was otherwise open to her. She responded in kind: all her pictures were flattering.

Her career moved at an ever accelerated pace. In New York in 1930 she photographed the Chrysler Building at every stage of its construction, even straddling the gargoyles for striking perspectives. In South Bend, Indiana, Luce himself accompanied her through the steel foundries, carrying her cameras from one site to the next. Many men in high positions would carry Bourke-White's equipment over the next quarter of a century. Almost all her friends were men, and some were more than friends. A few would have preferred to be more than lovers, but Margaret refused to consider a serious relationship. She had no time for love, she liked to say.

This mind-set dissolved in the summer of 1936 when she approached Erskine Caldwell about collaborating on a social documentary on America's poor. Almost exactly her age, he already had five novels to his credit — vivid naturalistic tales of the sharecroppers, tenant farmers, and mill hands of his native Georgia. He was a committed activist and had reported extensively for the *New York Post* on the poverty of the South and its crudeness and degenerate sexuality, while Bourke-White had only recently come to a social consciousness. The tour by car that covered six states and resulted in the widely acclaimed book *You Have Seen Their Faces* proved a pivotal experience for her. "I was learning that to understand another human being you must gain some insight into the conditions which made him what he is," she wrote in her autobiography. She was also becoming aware that a good photograph shows at a glance how events affect people.

Their collaboration was not without difficulties. The terrain was familiar to Caldwell; he mapped out the trip, and left Margaret no choice but to relinquish control. Perhaps for balance, she introduced sex into the picture. Within the first week they were lovers. During the second, Erskine's secretary, relegated to the backseat with cameras and tripods, left for home. Caldwell's wife and three children blurred into the background. Bourke-White was, and always would be, attracted by fame, but even more by the creative process behind the fame, and in Caldwell's case by the man behind the process. The ensuing relationship terminated whatever was left of his marriage, and by the spring of 1938 when they sailed together for Europe, he was pressing her for a commitment.

In the interim, Bourke-White had shifted from *Fortune* to Henry

Luce's newest creation, *Life. Life* was a weekly designed to present the news in photos that would tell a story as succinctly as words did in *Time*. Margaret's photo of the great earth-filled concrete dam at Fort Peck, Montana, graced the cover of the first issue on November 23, 1936. Now *Life* was sending her to Czechoslovakia. Caldwell would accompany her and gather material for a book on that country's predicament.

Czechoslovakia was rife with tension that spring of 1938. Pieced together after the First World War when the Austro-Hungarian monarchy fell, it was surrounded by hostile, or at least unsympathetic, countries — Poland, Hungary, Austria, Germany. The outer edges bordering Austria and Germany were known as the Sudetenland, and when his just-concluded annexation of Austria drew little opposition, Hitler determined to move in. He ordered Germans living in the Sudetenland to agitate for secession, forcing non-Germans, many of them Jews, to flee. Bourke-White and Caldwell found the population unfriendly, suspicious of each other and of foreigners.

Crossing the Tatras Mountains on the Kosice-Zilina Express, they watched in strained silence as a German Nazi in their car brought out a map of Czechoslovakia on which all the place-names were in German. He circled half of Bohemia and most of Moravia, and made smaller rings elsewhere. "These are German islands," he said. "Wherever German is spoken, that is German territory." Perhaps sensing opposition, he began to expostulate. "It belongs to the Fatherland. Soon the German people will claim it. The Czechs have no right to it." His face turned purple, Bourke-White later recalled, and the cords of his neck stood out. No one said anything. The train rolled on through fields of ripening wheat and young green oats.

Late in May the German press stepped up their campaign against the Czechs, referring to "intolerable provocations." Word came that German troops were mobilizing on the border; the Czech army followed suit. Although Bourke-White had not finished shooting, *Life* took what she had, combined it with the work of other photographers, and published a lengthy story on the crisis. Her five months in Czechoslovakia had yielded little pleasure of accomplishment. Instances of anti-Semitism were depressing, particularly to Margaret, who only after her father's death had learned that she was herself half Jewish. He had never spoken of his background, and in that time of widespread prejudice, the sudden revelation had shocked her. It was years before she made her peace with it.

Added to that were the pressures of working in a country where they were at the mercy of interpreters. Caldwell, often erratic and moody anyway, turned uncooperative and rude. Margaret felt that his hostility formed a barrier between them and their subjects. Nor was she pleased with her own work. There were photos of a Nazi storm-trooper training class in Moravia and a Nazi rally in Bohemia, but the majority were apolitical — shots of everyday peasant activities. They seemed to her superficial, lacking in depth and perspective. To a large extent she blamed Erskine. *North of the Danube*, the less-than-perfect book that emerged from this dual journey, was perhaps a harbinger of things to come.

As the Czechoslovakian crisis spun out that spring and summer, women reporting from American news bureaus in Europe were among

Nazi rally in Czechoslovakia, 1938.
MARGARET BOURKE-WHITE/*LIFE* MAGAZINE. © TIME INC.

the hordes of press to descend upon that hapless country. In May Virginia Cowles, now reporting for the London *Sunday Times*, had only just arrived in the Sudetenland with a colleague from the *Daily Mail* when a Nazi official tipped them off that the German army was preparing to cross the frontier. Cowles was astounded. That would mean war, she protested, and what about France's treaty with Czechoslovakia, England's alliance with France? Their informant shrugged. No one will fight for the Czechs, he said, an opinion supported by the 6,500 frenzied Sudeten Germans who packed a rally that night. But Germany indignantly denied any idea of marching, and the state of urgency cooled.

Back in London, Cowles found the average Englishman not much interested in fighting for the Czechs either. She joined Martha Gellhorn, now reporting regularly for *Collier's*, in an assignment to discover how the British were reacting to recent events on the Continent. After what she had seen in Spain, Gellhorn viewed peace as close to unsalvageable. But in England she found that speaking of war as a probability was considered "warmongering." Driving with Cowles through the Midlands to find out what ordinary people were thinking, she concluded that they were not doing much thinking. A woman in a pub opposite an armaments plant, asked if she had a gas mask, responded with a hoot of laughter. The director of a shipyard said that his firm was indeed building destroyers, cruisers, and battleships, but how they were to be used was up to the politicians. "We're on an island now, and the world is someplace else," Gellhorn mocked. "This is England and tomorrow there is probably a cricket match."

Cowles, with her patrician upbringing, was intrigued by Gellhorn's visceral reaction. "Martha was infuriated by the complacency," she wrote later. "The fact that the workingman in England was not stung to fury (as she was) by the treatment of his brothers in Spain or the doom of his brothers in Czechoslovakia struck her as shameful." The trip took on the character of a lecture tour as Gellhorn devoted less time to asking questions and more to soliloquizing on the danger Hitler posed to the world. At a Sunday afternoon tea in the Yorkshire home of Under-Secretary of State Lord Feversham, she complained that English people thought of nothing but racing and the weather. Their host, Virginia recalled, found it all very funny. "Fancy going round to the pubs and asking people what they think," he said. "You two are a couple of warmongers. Just trying to upset the country and stir up trouble."

If England appeared somnolent to Gellhorn that summer, she would have done well to accompany Cowles to Nuremberg to cover the annual Nazi Party congress. There was nothing sleepy about the Germans in Nuremberg. Virginia was impressed by the drama of that medieval city, especially at night. "The long red pennants, fluttering from the turreted walls of Nuremberg Castle, shone in the moonlight like the standards of an old religious war," she wrote; "the tramp of marching feet and the chorus of voices chanting the militant Nazi hymns had all the passion of an ancient crusade." It was already clear that Czechoslovakia was the object of the crusade. But for the time being, everyone seemed to be enjoying himself. Cowles reminded herself that these were not army men but ordinary workers who the rest of the year were bus drivers, garage mechanics, shopkeepers. This was their holiday, and they were making the most of it, eating sausages and sauerkraut and drinking beer and taking snapshots of each other. When questioned about the possibility of another war, they said no, no one wanted war, least of all Hitler.

One afternoon Cowles attended a tea that German foreign minister Joachim von Ribbentrop gave in Hitler's honor. The guest list consisted mostly of diplomats and delegates, but Cowles moved easily between the press and diplomatic society. She arrived at the Hotel Deutscher Hof at four o'clock to find the hall scattered with small tea tables, each with a card reading: Please Don't Smoke in the Presence of the Fuehrer. Besides the expected officials — Goering, Goebbels, Himmler, Hess — there were a dozen or so English visitors, most noticeably the Honorable Unity Valkyrie Mitford, with her shoulder-length blond curls and large blue eyes.

Unity joined Virginia at her table. A few minutes later the doors swung open, and as everyone stood rigidly at attention, Hitler came into the room and sat down. Glancing around, he noticed Unity, and Cowles saw his eyes light up, his face break into a smile, and his arm go up in the Nazi salute to her. Unity saluted back. A moment later Hitler's aide-de-camp came to their table and whispered that the Fuehrer would like to see Unity; would she please come to his suite after tea? She sent back an affirmative reply, and to Virginia's astonishment, Hitler suddenly appeared in better spirits, talking animatedly, laughing, and occasionally glancing in Unity's direction — showing off for her benefit, Cowles thought.

That evening she cornered Unity and asked her what Hitler had said. Would there be war? "I don't think so," Unity replied with a smile. "The Fuehrer doesn't want his new buildings bombed." Cowles pressed her further. What did they talk about? "Gossip," Unity said. Hitler liked gossip; it made him laugh. He had a good sense of humor, she said. He would do imitations of his Nazi colleagues Goering, Goebbels, Himmler — also Mussolini, which was the funniest. Sometimes he even imitated himself. He liked company, and especially excitement. "Otherwise he gets bored," she observed. It occurred to Virginia that Hitler might invade Czechoslovakia merely to relieve his boredom.

On her last night in Nuremberg, Cowles went with a correspondent from *Paris-Soir* to hear Hitler speak.

> The stadium was packed with nearly 200,000 spectators. As the time for the Fuehrer's arrival drew near, the crowd grew restless. . . . Suddenly the beat of the drums increased and three motorcycles with yellow standards fluttering from their windshields raced through the gates. A few minutes later a fleet of black cars rolled swiftly into the arena: in one of them, standing in the front seat, his hand outstretched in the Nazi salute, was Hitler.
>
> Hitler climbed to his box in the grandstand amid a deafening ovation, then gave the signal for the political leaders to enter. They came, a hundred thousand strong, through an opening in the far end of the arena. In the silver light they seemed to pour into the bowl like a flood of water. Each of them carried a Nazi flag and when they were assembled in mass formation, the bowl looked like a shimmering sea of swastikas.

The crowd grew silent when Hitler began to speak, Cowles continued, but the drums continued their steady beat. His voice thundered out into the night, punctuated by cheers from the multitude, some of whom swayed back and forth chanting "Sieg Heil" as if hypnotized.

Tears streamed down people's cheeks. The drums quickened their pace and grew louder, and Cowles, always so brave, began to feel frightened, as if they were actually in the heart of the African jungle.

When at last it was over and Hitler stopped speaking, she found that, inexplicably, the magic seemed to vanish. The small figure climbing back into his car looked dull and unimpressive. "You had to pinch yourself to realize that this was the man on whom the eyes of the world were riveted," she wrote, "that he alone held the lightning in his hands."

From her position as Berlin bureau chief for the *Chicago Tribune*, Sigrid Schultz was among the many correspondents who flocked to Berchtesgaden to report the first meeting of Hitler and Prime Minister Neville Chamberlain. In a strident and lengthy monologue, Hitler reviewed his plans for Czechoslovakia. Sigrid noted that his agenda had expanded from the mere annexation of the Sudetenland. Now he demanded all of Czechoslovakia.

All through September Schultz's byline dominated the front page of the *Chicago Tribune* and, via its press service, other American papers as well. If there was envy in the ranks, it probably went unvoiced, as everyone knew how favorably Colonel McCormick viewed his lady in Berlin. Meanwhile, that lady reported that at the second conference, Hitler increased his demands. The Czechs, backed by France, rejected them. Britain mobilized its fleet. Hitler issued an ultimatum ordering the Czechs to begin evacuation of the Sudetenland by 2 P.M. the next day, but then backed off and requested instead that Chamberlain come to Munich.

Chamberlain accepted the reprieve and went.

The itinerary of the prime minister was of particular interest to Helen Kirkpatrick who, along with Victor Gordon Lennox and Graham Hutton of the *Daily Telegraph* and the *Economist* respectively, had recently begun producing a weekly foreign affairs publication. The *Whitehall Letter* was sent to embassies in Britain and elsewhere opposed to the policies of Prime Minister Neville Chamberlain, and was cabled to subscribers in America. Having gravitated to London and severed her connection with the *Herald Tribune* European edition, Helen was able to give the *Whitehall Letter* her full concentration. Her take-home pay was negligible, but her inclusion in the triad of editors meant she was considered a serious writer, that her political acumen was recognized — i.e., that she was moving forward in the field of international journalism. (The same could be said of Virginia Cowles, whose unsigned *Sunday Times* articles on Spain were quoted in the House of Commons by Lloyd George until he discovered that the "eminent authority" was an American woman.)

Balanced on the roof of a parked car at Heston airport, Kirkpatrick had a clear view of the prime minister's return from the Munich conference. He stepped out of the plane, "a beatific smile on his face, waving a piece of paper in one hand, clutching his umbrella in the other," she wrote, and described the cheering crowds that lined the London road and packed Downing Street. "Tomorrow the war was to have begun," she continued, but no, here instead was Neville Chamberlain with a promise of "peace for our time." Did he really believe that? she asked herself. Did all the people who cheered so wildly believe it?

Young and idealistic, Kirkpatrick felt strongly about Munich. "The Czechs had one of the best armies in Europe at the time," she recalled later. "The British and the French had a pact that obligated them to go to their defense. The British sold out the Czechs." At the time Helen was covering for a friend, the diplomatic correspondent of the *Sunday Times*. "It gave me a marvelous insight into how news was manipulated," she said. "I worked very hard. I would see Roland de Margerie at the French embassy and then I would see Jan Masaryk, the Czech ambassador, and later I would talk to people in the Foreign Office, and anyone at Number 10 Downing Street who was available. Then I would put together the piece for Sunday's paper. . . . But I discovered that after I had done so, the editor would take it around to Number 10 and edit it to suit the Prime Minister."

From her room at the Hôtel Saint-Germain-des-Prés in Paris, Janet Flanner worked hard at capturing, with requisite *New Yorker* objectivity, French reactions to the events at Munich. Her own predominant response was relief. She had spent an anxious summer; after visits to Salzburg and Vienna, she had traveled with Noel Murphy along the Hungarian-Czechoslovakian border, where great concrete roadblocks and long stretches of barbed wire fencing portended imminent trespass. Back in France, she sat huddled by the radio at Noel's farm-house in Orgeval, comparing French, English, and German versions of Hitler's vacillating plans. When he announced German military occu-pation of the Sudetenland and France began to mobilize, they stocked up on staples like sardines, sugar, and brandy and stored gasoline in champagne bottles. After Munich they sorted and burned much of their correspondence and buried Janet's collection of gold coins and Noel's family silver. Not until the participants at Munich departed for home did they return to Paris.

In her Paris letter of October 2, 1938, titled "Peace in Our Time," Flanner described how the French press had learned details of the Munich meeting only after Prime Minister Chamberlain spoke before the House of Commons:

> Up to that time, Paris knew only that the problem of saving Prague had been replaced by the problem of saving democratic Europe . . . that communiqués communicated nothing since nothing was known . . . that war seemed imminent. Now all the French know is that there is peace. In their curious calm, they don't want to know anything else. It is the only thing worth knowing; that and the new knowledge which is exciting the whole population of Europe today — that statesmen can think everybody's way out of war.

Although she herself had never known war, Flanner shared the beliefs of her French hosts who had known all too much. She wanted desperately to believe there would be no war, and not only because of disruption to her own life. She viewed herself as a civilian writer who wrote on peaceful subjects, not a hard-nosed journalist who covered whatever came along and took all the risks that that entailed.

Always magnetized by the trouble spot of the moment, Virginia Cowles meanwhile decided to return to Prague, much to the distress of the young airport manager who had helped her board the flight to Paris only the week before and could not believe she was back. Neither could her buddies "Knick" Knickerbocker and John Whitaker; they greeted her as if she were an apparition. All the French and English correspondents had left the day before, they said. The frontiers were closed, trains no longer ran, phone wires had been cut. They hoped she'd brought enough clothes for a year, in particular more appropriate shoes than those little high heels she was wearing. In her hotel room that night she found a gas mask on the pillow and a card, "Compliments of the American Embassy."

On the afternoon that President Eduard Beneš was to broadcast to the nation on the results of the Munich conference, Cowles joined other foreign journalists in Knickerbocker's room overlooking the big square. A young Czech secretary came in to translate. The speech was little more than a matter-of-fact statement about the decision to partition the country. "Our state will not be the smallest," Beneš said in closing. "There are smaller states than we shall be." Cowles noticed that the translator was weeping too hard to continue. From the square below came the solemn music of the Czech national anthem, the people standing stiffly at attention as if they had not fully grasped the meaning behind the words.

About midnight Knickerbocker, Whitaker, and Cowles drove out of Prague on their way to the Austrian-Czech frontier to cover the crossing of the German army into Czechoslovakia. It was a dubious undertaking, but if her friends were going, she would not be left behind. At the village of Oberplan a crowd of Sudeten mountain folk — tough, wild-eyed, and armed — barred the way, and escorted them to the town hall. A heap of freshly murdered Czechs lay on the pavement. The Americans were led to a small upstairs room where their papers were examined by the local Gestapo; they were denounced as spies, sentenced to execution, then guarded with tommy guns until the arrival of the official agent from the Reich at dawn. The latter, impressed by the term "foreign journalist" on their passports, ordered their release. With "a great show of huff as outraged Americans," Whitaker wrote later, they then demanded, and got, an apology from the local Gestapo, after which that "cool little cucumber" Cowles demanded enough gasoline to get them back to Prague.

Later, in London, Virginia encountered Chamberlain at a small dinner party. During conversation in the drawing room afterward, she was brought up short by his question, "Tell me, did you find that the Czechs had any bitter feeling towards the English?" She was so astonished that she could not think at first how to reply, and it was a few moments before she could regain enough composure to describe the square in Prague, Beneš's speech, and the weeping people.

Martha Gellhorn also returned to Prague. She had been there in the spring, again in the summer, and now it was fall. Her "Obituary of a Democracy," which she wrote for *Collier's,* began:

> On all the roads in Czechoslovakia, the army was going home. You would see them walking in small groups or alone, not walking fast and not walking well, just going back from the frontiers as they had been told to do. Once in a while you would see a company, with its officer leading, marching along; but not the way an army marches to war. People would stand on the side of the road and watch them in silence.

There was more, largely on the futility of the country's brave preparations for a battle that never happened. Martha closed her piece with the leave-taking of Eduard Beneš and his wife to the citizens of Prague. "They stood along the curb and waited for this man who was a symbol of their state and their freedom," she wrote. "When he passed they bowed their heads as people do for the dead."

The following February, in Cuba with Ernest Hemingway, Gellhorn began a novel based on her Czechoslovak experience. In *A Stricken Field* the heroine, Mary Douglas, a long-legged blond American correspondent not unlike herself, free to come and go as she pleases, returns to Prague after the annexation and tries to reconcile it with the city she has known. Her colleagues inform her that concentration camps have already been set up in Czechoslovakia, that German Socialists, Communists, and Jews who had thought the country a safe haven are in real danger. Mary locates her friend Rita, survivor of an earlier camp, who has since managed to make a new life for herself. Rita asks her for help, and Mary responds in terms that Martha often used herself in a similar context:

> It's like war, Mary thought, people ask you to do something, there is very little time, they have to trust you because there is

no one else handy. . . . She knew she would always say yes, when she was asked for help, because she did not feel she had a right to her privileges: passport, job, love. She only felt she was lucky and lucky and luckier than anybody could be, and you had to pay back for that.

Like her fictional heroine, Gellhorn actively tried to ease the refugee situation. The frontiers had closed. New refugees coming into Prague from the Sudetenland "with wild eyes and stunned, exhausted faces" were given twenty-four hours to return. While Martha was in Prague, the League of Nations high commissioner for refugees paid a two-day visit and "didn't see a single refugee," she noted scornfully. In the novel Mary goes to his hotel (just as an outraged Martha had done) "and saw him and pounded the table as always and shouted and pleaded and explained." The commissioner agrees to try to obtain a stay for the refugees. Mary (again like Martha) escorts him about and makes introductions and argues her case, but it is hopeless. In the end there is nothing anyone can do.

The fictional Mary Douglas's week in Prague is over. She has failed to help the refugee situation or save her friend Rita. But she has given some good advice to a few persons and has found a way to smuggle an important document out of the country. The compassionate woman has won out over the merely competent writer, and that, Gellhorn seemed to be saying, was as it should be.

5

One Thought, One Holy Mission: Poland

By the spring of 1939 few correspondents in Europe believed that a larger war could be avoided. The question had become not "if" but "when," and for American women "how" — how to position themselves to ensure their right to remain and report the war when it happened. This was no problem for Sigrid Schultz, entrenched Berlin bureau chief for the *Chicago Tribune*, or Eleanor Packard, wife of UP bureau chief Reynolds Packard in Rome, or even Virginia Cowles, with friends in high places and herself firmly ensconced at the London *Sunday Times*. Dorothy Thompson assumed that her stature would guarantee her regular forays to the Continent. But Helen Kirkpatrick sought firmer journalistic ground under her feet than the *Whitehall Letter* provided.

This coveted stability came unsolicited from Bill Stoneman, London bureau chief of the *Chicago Daily News*, who knew her, valued her insights, and enjoyed her company. In her just-published little book *This Terrible Peace*, Kirkpatrick predicted that the present accord would fail, an assessment that provoked a furious response from Prime Minister Chamberlain's staff. Stoneman, however, was impressed. He was also shorthanded, and asked her to help out, hoping to negotiate temporary assistance into a permanent position. But Helen's talents were less obvious to Colonel Knox, publisher of the *News*. While London begged to hire her as a regular, Chicago held fast to its rule: No women on the foreign staff.

In the meantime Kirkpatrick watched the German takeover of the rest of Czechoslovakia in the spring of 1939. Appeasement died, she wrote, "a sudden, swift and agonized death. Chamberlain was angry, extremely angry with Hitler. It was a personal and bitter anger, for Hitler had wrecked all Chamberlain's plans, destroyed his chance of greatness, and forced upon him the alternative of retiring ignominiously or fighting." As Helen had warned in her book, Chamberlain's "peace for our time" proved a figment of his own imagination.

The one publication never shortsighted about hiring women on its foreign staff was the *New York Herald Tribune*. Had not Margaret Fuller served the *New York Tribune* a century before, and later Anna Benjamin the same? Now there was Sonia Tomara, already a valued member of the *Herald Tribune* staff, primed to become a major foreign correspondent.

Sonia Tomara, *New York Herald Tribune*

Sonia Tomara came from the Russian aristocracy. "A dark, rather mysterious young woman who wrote brilliantly" was how CBS's Robert St. John described her. Her childhood had been divided between her family's villa on the shores of the Black Sea and her aunt's estate near Moscow. She always felt herself plain, and grew up painfully shy, uncomfortable among women, happier in the male world of intellect and drive. Her primary influence was her father, a scholar and a rebel against the tsarist regime; her best friend was her gentle older brother, whose life she closely shared. When World War I prevented her from studying in England as planned, she insisted on enrolling at Moscow University to study chemistry.

With her father an unrepentant socialist nobleman, her mother's family liberal bourgeois, and her fellow students leaning toward Bolshevism, Tomara at first welcomed the Revolution of 1917. Having idealized the masses, she was bewildered by the violence, the lack of moral discipline, and the eventual rejection of all cultural values. That fall the Bolsheviks seized power. Her aunt's Moscow house was in the line of fire, and for a week Sonia was marooned inside. When at last she

Sonia Tomara, 1942.
AMERICAN HERITAGE CENTER, UNIVERSITY OF WYOMING.

ventured out, "blood was still running in the gutter and dead men lay in grotesque positions." The worldly goods of everyone of her class were confiscated, and food was scarce. Sonia, still in her teens, and her younger sister Irina decided to leave Moscow for the family home at Sukhum on the Black Sea, in spite of the civil war raging in between. Attempting to cross from Red territory to White, they were captured, imprisoned, and charged with spying. Sonia was condemned to be shot at dawn, but a sympathetic Red Guard had them released. It took two perilous months, much of it on foot, to get home. There she melted into the calm, still peaceful life until, restless "to plunge again into the thick of things," she left.

Her second odyssey was no less eventful. Working as an interpreter in a British military mission, Tomara watched the old Russian

Betty Wason with Leland Stowe in Norway, 1940.
BETTY WASON PERSONAL COLLECTION.

world — her world — die. In the years ahead she never saw anything worse than the civil war she witnessed then, when villages "passed from the hands of one party to the other, their inhabitants decimated by both, their houses burnt in reprisal, their harvest looted or ruined." She watched typhus spread among rich and poor alike, saw wounded men freezing to death and women carrying dead children, heard of punishment and torture at the hands of the victors — whoever the victors were — until at last the territory occupied by the Whites dwindled to nothing and all their people had to take ship and flee. It was then Sonia heard of the death of her beloved brother, one more casualty of the war. On March 20, 1920, on a coal ship with four thousand other Russians, she sailed into exile.

Her first stop was Constantinople, her second, Paris. In both cities she fell in love with married men, heady relationships followed by unhappy endings. In Paris, the work compensated. Jules Sauerwein, foreign editor at *Le Matin*, hearing of a desperately poor young Russian noblewoman who spoke French, English, Italian, German, and Russian, hired her on the spot. Before long the managing editor was including her in his midday conferences to report on current foreign

61

events. During her six years there, she also wrote on finance for the *New York Herald Tribune*, fashion for the London *Daily Express*, and politics for newspapers in Vienna and Constantinople. She saved enough to send for her sisters, and together they became part of a bohemian circle of young Russian exiles. In time her mother and once-wealthy aunt from the big house near Moscow came, too. With so many to house and feed, Sonia needed more money. Providence intervened, and in 1928 Leland Stowe, then Paris correspondent for the *Herald Tribune*, offered her a chance to write at double her previous salary.

When Italy went to war with Ethiopia, Tomara was sent to hold down the *Herald Tribune* desk in Rome. She reported Mussolini's balcony speeches from the Piazza Venezia and, in time, his victory speech from same. Later she traveled across the plains of Slovakia to the Sudeten mountains in Bohemia, sorting out for *Herald Tribune* readers the irreconcilable differences between the Sudeten Germans and the Czechs. After a stint in the home office in New York, she returned that summer of 1939 for a tour of Europe. On landing in France, she felt at once a sense of impending catastrophe. So many young men were in aviation uniform. She tried to reassure herself that France had the best army in Europe, but the thought kept recurring that the country was not yet fully healed from the last war.

At Strasbourg Tomara crossed over into the Reich. There she encountered German soldiers on maneuvers, "sun-burnt, steel-eyed men emerging from steel tanks, women smiling to them and the men waving and smiling back." It was an arresting picture. Somehow she doubted that these men thought it was France that had the best army in Europe.

In Berlin she consulted her friends from the Wilhelmstrasse. Hitler, they said, talked about nothing but Poland, read about nothing but Poland. He had changed since Munich, they told her; he paid no attention to his ambassadors or the communiqués they sent, the advice they gave. The newspapers screamed in big headlines about Polish atrocities against the Germans, exactly as they had done about Czechoslovakia the summer before. Hitler had only one thought, one holy mission: Poland.

Mussolini, of whom not much had been heard lately, found this gobbling up of territory far too one-sided. Three years had passed since his Ethiopian conquest, three years in which Hitler had annexed Austria and in effect Czechoslovakia, and Hitler was clearly not finished. The world might begin to think Italy a secondary power, or himself a minor leader. Facing Italy across the Adriatic was Yugoslavia, a large country with friends and protectors, where the consequences of a takeover were at best uncertain. But directly opposite the heel of Italy's boot was Albania. This small, backward country ruled by a nominal king would seem ripe for the plucking.

Eleanor Packard first heard the rumor of Italian designs over a bridge table in Rome. With her husband occupied as UP bureau chief, it was often she who dashed off for a firsthand observation of the latest trouble spot. In Prague for Czech army maneuvers the previous summer, for example, she had been standing next to William Shirer when a Skoda fighter failed to come out of a deep dive and crashed directly in front of them. The pilot and his observer were still alive when extricated from the mass of twisted metal. Shirer had been badly shaken, but everyone remarked how calm Packard remained. A woman correspondent could not afford to go to pieces, no matter what she witnessed.

With Albania in possible jeopardy, Eleanor decided to fly to Tirana, the capital. Cash was a problem: she and Reynolds had only sixty-eight dollars on hand, tucked at the entry on "money" in the *Encyclopaedia Britannica*. Because it was illegal to take funds out of Italy without special permission, she secreted most of that sum in her bra. She was glad of the assignment. Rome had become quiescent, and it was not for a steady dose of bridge that she had become a foreign correspondent. She much preferred to be *moving*, however slowly, and in Tirana where horse-and-buggy taxis clip-clopped to primitive hotels, that meant slowly indeed. She arrived to find an excited populace celebrating the birth of a son to King Zog and his young wife. On her third day she was awakened by the clerk from the American legation, informing her that the Italians had landed and she should proceed to the legation for safety. She brushed off that advice, but did check in regularly for progress reports. One disclosed the queen's escape with her baby son by ambulance to Greece, another the king's decision to go to the mountains to lead his troops. That, Eleanor reasoned, was only posturing; his troops had no arms of any consequence. As she anticipated, King Zog and the government were soon off to Greece as well.

The next day Packard watched Italian troops on shiny Bersaglieris roar into town. Opposition was minimal. The radio station and telegraph office were secured, leaving no way for her to send her dispatches. Italy resolved to legitimate this takeover without delay, and during the following week parliamentary delegates, preapproved by Italian officials, arrived from the provinces. Eleanor attended the session in the tiny opera house. Despite her shocked objection, she was frisked before entering — an official pawed through her pockets and handbag, felt her armpits for a shoulder holster, and otherwise carefully studied her silk-dress-clad figure from every angle. At the proceedings, officials announced that the Italian flag would fly next to the Albanian and that the crown (long missing) would be offered to the Italian king. The delegates accepted the inevitable. It had been a remarkably unbloody coup, but Packard hated the thought of another Fascist success in what seemed an irreversible progression toward war.

In Berlin that summer Sigrid Schultz was unearthing a prospective Nazi maneuver of the first magnitude. Her detective work was initiated by her doctor, Johannes Schmidt, also physician to party officials, who tipped her off about an astrologer whom he said Hitler had recently consulted. Schultz made her own appointment, but the astrologer's suggestion that the Fuehrer was planning some kind of rapprochement with the Soviet Union she found at first incredible. So much of Hitler's strategy was, always had been, built around opposition to Communism. On the other hand, if he had designs on Poland, it made sense that he would want advance assurance that the great power to the east would not rise in her defense.

On July 13, 1939, an article by "John Dickson" appeared in the *Chicago Tribune*, revealing that Berlin had sent negotiators to Moscow to discuss plans for Soviet-German cooperation. "The newest toast in high Hitler-Guard circles is: 'To our new ally, Russia!' " Dickson trumpeted. He conceded that cozying up to Stalin ought to discredit Hitler as a crusader against Communism, but "if Hitler says the wicked Red soviets are no longer Red nor wicked, the Germans will accept his word!" All this remained conjecture until August 21 when the *Chicago Tribune* first broke the story, under Sigrid Schultz's own byline, that

Foreign Minister Joachim von Ribbentrop had flown to Moscow to sign a nonagression pact with the Soviet Union.

Was Poland lost then? Virginia Cowles, in Rome that late summer of 1939 for the London *Sunday Times*, learned that Count Ciano, Mussolini's son-in-law, had returned from Berchtesgaden after conferring with Hitler. That news prompted rumors that a date for war had been decided, so when Virginia was invited by the Prince and Princess del Drago to join Ciano for lunch on the beach at Ostia, she accepted. Lunch on the beach with Ciano was always a comic affair, with waiters carrying trays of spaghetti and buckets of red wine along the sand.

Cowles avoided questioning Ciano outright about his Bavarian visit, but she knew he could not resist dropping a hint or two. After lunch he took her for a motorboat ride and, about a mile offshore, dove off the boat for a swim. When he surfaced, hair dripping over his eyes, he blurted out in his excellent English, "I bet you'd like to know what I talked to Hitler about." Virginia replied that she would indeed, particularly as she suspected Hitler had done most of the talking. The suggestion that Ciano had played a lesser role in the conference proved the wrong thing to say, and no more information was forthcoming.

They met again on the beach the following day. Dino Alfiero, minister of propaganda, was also there, and when an elderly man and his daughter, both in bathing suits, came along, Ciano and Alfiero rushed over to greet them. Prince del Drago rather pointedly did not. Cowles asked who the man was. "General Dlugoszowski, the Polish ambassador," del Drago said. "I would have liked to have clasped his hand and told him we would save his country for him. But alas, it's too late. We can't."

In her still unofficial role with the *Chicago Daily News*, Helen Kirkpatrick began to sleuth out the German scenario for war. She knew: one, that the summer-1939 German mobilization would reach its peak by August 15; two, that the Czechs had been ordered to deliver the harvest to Germany by the twenty-fifth; and three, that German agents were in Britain and Ireland buying copper, tin, and — yes — horses, all for immediate delivery. A German correspondent in London told her that she would be able to tell by August 20 if there would be war because, if so, arrangements for the Nuremberg rally, always held in September, would be canceled by that date. On the nineteenth Helen learned from a colleague in Berlin that firms with contracts for the rally had been quietly notified of its cancellation.

Later Kirkpatrick recalled her last weekend of real peace:

I spent it in the country, not far from London, in a luxurious house with eleven other guests. We swam, we played tennis, we rode horseback in Windsor Great Park, we gathered rather frequently around the cocktail bar, and we saw the latest films in a complete miniature moving picture theatre just next to the squash courts in one wing of the house. The company ranged from stockbrokers to film magnates, from movie actors to two other exceedingly depressing and serious newspaper people like myself. The whole atmosphere was slightly mad, tinged with the same undercurrent that must have pervaded the court of Louis XVI. "Après nous le déluge" might well have been the toast proposed in the excellent champagne we drank each evening.

On Thursday, August 31, 1939, Virginia Cowles flew into Berlin's Tempelhof airport to prepare a story for the Sunday edition. Grim rows of black fighter planes with white swastikas bordered the field, and she could make out antiaircraft guns on the rooftops. She sensed gloom and depression everywhere she went. At a press conference at the Foreign Office, the official spokesman fended off questions from the dozen reporters around the table. Shaking his head over and over, he repeated in a low, strained voice, "Ich weiss nicht." That morning, a colleague told her, the press chief had actually broken down and cried.

Afternoon stretched into evening. Everywhere there was anxiety, confusion, people speaking in hushed tones. The British ambassador left for a last talk with Goering, but no one expected a favorable outcome, and piles of luggage waited to go out on the diplomatic train when the signal came. The special flag indicating that Hitler was in residence flew from the chancellery on the Wilhelmstrasse, where a small crowd had gathered.

Cowles was awakened the next morning, September 1, by the tramp of feet on Unter den Linden below. Storm troopers lined the avenue. Hitler, she learned from a phone call to the desk, would address the Reichstag at ten o'clock. There was no time to call out the usual crowds of enthusiastic spectators; only a handful of Berliners watched Hitler drive past in the field gray uniform of the German army. His speech was short. He enumerated a list of atrocities he said the Poles had committed, and announced that, as of 5:45 A.M., German troops were "returning Polish fire." That afternoon Virginia expected to find a great crowd waiting outside the chancellery for Hitler to speak, but the crowd was small and Hitler stayed inside.

The previous Sunday, August 27, 1939, Sonia Tomara was winding up her six-week tour of Europe in Warsaw. She reported a football match between Poland and Hungary: thousands of spectators stood on the sidelines and cheered the Polish team to victory. But that night troops began moving out of Warsaw. Gas masks were distributed to the correspondents, and they were urged to leave the Hotel Europeiski, which was perilously situated between the General Staff building and the Foreign Office. Tomara reported that the government remained optimistic, relying on its ability to wage mobile warfare with forty regiments of mounted infantry, regular infantry, and a large air force.

On Tuesday, August 29, German troops moved into Slovakia. Poland's western boundary with Germany was already vulnerable, and now so was her southern border. Tomara watched thousands of soldiers leaving for the front; because there were not enough uniforms, many marched in civilian attire. She talked with women who were already taking over such home defense jobs as digging trenches in the parks, and who were heartened by avowals from France and Great Britain that they stood fast by Poland's side. When on Wednesday mobilization posters went up all over Warsaw, she noted that people read them silently, without emotion.

On Friday she was awakened by the ring of a telephone and the terse message of the *Paris-Soir* correspondent: "C'est la guerre." That day bombs fell on the bridges over the Vistula and the main railway station. Even for one who had experienced the terror of Russia's revolution and civil war, it was frightening. All communication was cut — a reporter's nightmare. Warsaw was the focus of the whole world's attention, and there was no way to send dispatches.

By nightfall it was quiet. A few heavily shaded lamps lighted the courtyard, and the correspondents dined as usual in the soft late-summer air. A press conference was called after dinner in a smoky upstairs room at the Foreign Office. Most reporters there spoke French, German, or English. No one spoke Polish. Tomara was the only woman present, and the only person speaking Polish and able to make sense of what was said. It was unclear when reporters could go to the front, or where the front was. There was talk of hiring a car, but no cars were available, and no reporter's papers were valid beyond the limits of Warsaw.

In contrast with the confusion in Warsaw, London on that first day of September 1939 was quiet and well ordered. The long-prepared-for evacuation of the children had begun. Helen Kirkpatrick reported how boys and girls assembled at their schools with gas masks on their backs, a small bag of clothes in their hands, and identification tags around their necks. Their mothers kissed them goodbye, much as if they were off to summer camp, except that these mums were unsure when, if ever, they would see their children again.

Parliament was summoned for six o'clock on September 2. Watching the ticker at the *Herald Tribune* office, Kirkpatrick hoped that if the news reached Chicago at the earliest possible moment, it would strike a point in her favor. She carried with her a cable to the *Daily News* drafted to include Britain's declaration of war. But Chamberlain did not make it easy. He spoke first of Hitler's "senseless ambitions" and of his own attempts at negotiation. Kirkpatrick waited for him to confirm her cable, to state that "Britain is at war with Germany," but no, there was to be an ultimatum instead. He would give Hitler one more chance. All aggressive action against Poland must be suspended and all troops promptly withdrawn or Britain would "without hesitation fulfill her obligations to Poland." To her dismay and disgust, Helen had to rewrite her cable from start to finish.

Hitler disdained to acknowledge the ultimatum. He did not order his troops, his tanks, or his planes to reverse course, and on Sunday morning, September 3, 1939, Britain and France declared war.

With communication out of Warsaw cut off, Sonia Tomara was not heard from again for nearly a week. By then the bombing was ruthless, air raid sirens screaming every two hours. Tomara and Cedric Salter of the London *Daily Mail* studied the map and realized that in four days the Germans had covered two-thirds of the distance to the capital. The Polish ministers asked Tomara to broadcast to the United States, and that night she did so, walking to and from the radio station in the blackout, its effect obviated by a full moon. She was exhausted on her return, and conscious as she fell asleep that the moon that played so charmingly on the windowpanes laid the city bare to imminent destruction. The air raid alert at dawn did not awaken her, and not until later did she learn that the German army was converging on Warsaw from three directions. She packed in fifteen minutes whatever she could carry in her knapsack, passing along suits, dresses, shoes, and her grandmother's ivory dressing set to a Russian maid at the hotel. Carrying her camera, typewriter, and gas mask, she slipped into a car with Salter and two other British correspondents. The Polish government had fled, and the reporters were following in their tracks.

Tomara and her colleagues came upon the Polish ministers in Naleczow, a health resort some distance south of Warsaw, where they camped in unoccupied villas and held meetings under the shade trees. An impromptu press conference was held on the shore of a pond. Swans glided with marked unconcern from one side to the other. "I saw high members of the Foreign Office confer at Naleczow in a whisper," Sonia wrote, "their faces gray after sleepless nights." At the provisional foreign office a Polish official rose to greet her, his face mirroring her own anxiety. Was her luggage packed? he asked, a question that under the circumstances amused her. The Germans, he said, had reached the Vistula, only fifteen miles away.

In her next dispatch, cabled from Rumania, Tomara reported the dwindling strength of the Polish army. Mere manpower was no match for motorized forces. The summer had been dry, and the German tanks rolled easily across the flat farmlands. Much of the country was occupied by the end of the first week of September; by the second, Polish troops were demoralized. Conditions were "distressing beyond words," she wrote — the army exhausted by rapid marches, entire regiments mowed down by machine-gun fire.

On September 15 Tomara crossed back into Poland, to the border town of Zaleszczyki, where members of the diplomatic corps had alighted after vacating Warsaw. They told stories of skies never free of German bombers terrorizing the people — not only bombing but diving low over roads and towns and machine-gunning troops and civilians alike. There was no food to be had anywhere, they said. Tomara described this final refuge as "a picturesque town with wide streets and pretty white houses buried among orchards." Flowers bloomed in the gardens. It was crowded: the British ambassador and his retinue were squeezed into three rooms, and the French ambassador was still hunting quarters. The foreign office shared a house with the press office, with cows and hogs in the courtyard and almost no press reports. "The population of the town is bewildered at all the government and diplomatic cars that have invaded the streets," Sonia wrote. "Most of the cars are covered with heavy dust and some have been riddled with bullets from German machine guns."

This bucolic respite was brief. Two days later, from the Polish-Rumanian border, Tomara filed her final report:

> September 17, 1939. This morning the Polish government learned that, with the Germans still attacking from the west, Russian troops had driven in from the east. It was decided that the fight could not continue against such a formidable array of armies. No resistance has thus far been offered to the Russian troops. They walked into Poland today without firing a shot and were seen marching side by side with the retiring Polish Army. It was learned here on excellent authority that the Russian move was made in full agreement with the German government.

Tomara stood by the Kuty bridge and watched the long line of cars crossing the river into Rumania. Only soldiers and persons with diplomatic passports were allowed across. Polish planes flew over in formation and landed at the airfield; the planes were requisitioned by the Rumanian military, but the pilots, wearing civilian clothes, left at once for France.

It was the end for Poland. That night the border closed. The war had lasted seventeen days.

6

Waiting for Hitler:
The Phony War

There is a maverick in every group, someone who looks at a situation from a different perspective than everyone else, and among the women reporting in Europe immediately after war was declared, that odd-woman-out was Janet Flanner. Unlike those who were doing their best to solidify their positions abroad, Flanner decided to return home. She had threatened this move twice before; each time the *New Yorker* had pleaded with her to stay, and she had relented. But this time she held firm. She was not a "news reporter," she explained. Her kind of writing required an openness to investigation and quiet surroundings for careful rewriting, for the weighing and judging of every phrase. This was not possible in a Paris where shops hid behind protective shutters, women carried vegetables home from market in their gas masks, and golden September days were punctuated by air raid sirens and trips to the shelters. As Hitler's armies advanced across Poland, Janet and her friends — Solita Solano, Noel Murphy, and Margaret Anderson, founder of the *Little Review* — sat mesmerized around the radio at Noel's farmhouse in Orgeval. At nightfall they walked in the garden, looked up at the stars, and wondered when they would all be together again.

All four women were American with American passports, but only Flanner and Solano, who had fled New York together nearly two decades before, contemplated return. Anderson would not desert her companion, the French singer Georgette Leblanc, who was suffering from cancer, and Murphy would not leave France and her work with Anne Morgan's organization American Friends of France, which J. P.'s daughter had started during World War I. That left the wrenching choice to Flanner. Quitting her Paris post did not mean resigning from the *New Yorker*, only shifting her position there, and returning to America with Solita did not signify a preference for her over Noel. But in honesty Janet had to acknowledge that she was abandoning Noel in a country now at war with a strong and malefic neighbor, with all the potentialities that entailed. How long America would remain neutral, how long Noel's passport would protect her, were questions no one could answer.

Indicative of Flanner's ambivalence was the fact that she paid the rent on her rooms at the Hôtel Saint-Germain-des-Prés through April 1940. She and Solano headed for Bordeaux, a city of transit for some fifteen thousand U.S. citizens and thousands more from other parts of the Americas seeking passage home. In what would be her last *New Yorker* piece from French soil for nearly five years, datelined Bordeaux, September 24, 1939, Flanner described the influx of weary evacuees, often low on money when long-expected ships never arrived. Few people had reservations; most simply went, registered, paid the fare, and waited. Flanner and Solano waited three weeks — not bad, really. Gertrude Stein wrote them to "come back to us soon," and Janet replied that she would, by January, only half believing it, and knowing Stein didn't believe it either.

Back in the United States, Margaret Bourke-White watched the progression of events in Europe with alarm. Those circled areas on the map of Czechoslovakia that the Nazi on the train had labeled "German territory" had become just that — along with the rest of Czechoslovakia, and now Poland. She and Erskine Caldwell had tried to arrange for their Jewish interpreter to emigrate to America, but were unsuccessful.

Ever since their return, Caldwell had been pressing Bourke-White to marry him. She was unconvinced. "Both much too used to looking out after ourselves," she noted at the time. "Can't help but feel that he wants me to change a lot." In fact, he both did and didn't — he wanted Kit, as he called her, to be a traditional wife focusing on *their* marriage instead of *her* career, but at the same time he was proud of her talent and accomplishments, and knew she would be miserable without her work. Fifty years later he would have been in company with other men in the same situation; in 1939 he knew none. But he knew that he loved her, and knew, or said, that he literally could not live without her. In February they flew to Reno where a marriage license could be obtained at moment's notice, as if once the decision were made, it had best be acted upon without delay. On the plane the bride drew up a prenuptial contract. Among its terms: all quarrels were to be settled before midnight, Erskine was to be polite to her friends, he was never to attempt to keep her from her work, and he must try to control his moods. The groom made no demands. Both of them wanted a child, or thought they did, and during the first year of their marriage they invented a fantasy child, a daughter whom they called Patricia.

By the fall of 1939, however, there was no hint of pregnancy, which to Bourke-White meant there was no reason for her not to take an assignment from *Life* to go to England. Great Britain was technically at war, although during that period of the "phony war," contact with the enemy was minimal. Bourke-White was excited about a recent breakthrough in news photography: a cable-photo system from London that enabled photographs to cross the Atlantic with amazing speed and accuracy. But she arrived in the capital to discover that *Life* already had two photographers in the area. They worked together on a photo-essay on the London blackout — worked night after night, often all night — but in the end only one picture of Margaret's was used.

In December 1939 Bourke-White left for the Balkans, widely expected to be Hitler's next target. From Rumania she reported that the populace was jittery. Cameras were all but banned. There was no way to photograph unobtrusively; to shoot unaccompanied by an official chaperone was to invite arrest. Moving on to Turkey, she found once again that another *Life* photographer had preceded her. Margaret began to feel that the magazine no longer appreciated her. She wrote her husband that she did not like squandering her time and talent, and Caldwell agreed. He was deeply jealous of the hold *Life* had on her, of the loyalty the editors demanded as a matter of course. He hated that she had written into their marriage contract that he was not to interfere with her assignments. She had been away five months, and he wanted her home.

She returned, and resigned from *Life*.

War broke out in earnest on April 9, 1940, when Germany invaded Denmark and Norway. No woman reporter was in either country, but as luck would have it, Betty Wason happened to be in Sweden, and she seized the opportunity as a gift from the Norse gods.

Betty Wason, CBS

Native of a small Indiana town and graduate of Purdue, Elizabeth Wason carved out a career in the middle of the Depression when a woman was lucky just to land a job. She began broadcasting in Cincinnati, moved on to New York, and after two years of working and scrimping, left in 1938 for Europe — with only the dubious encouragement of Transradio News to place stories on a "pay as used" basis.

It was a gutsy move for a young woman of twenty-six, barely five feet tall, fluent in no language but her own, who lacked contacts and had never done straight news reporting. In 1938 the place to go was Prague, so Wason went to Prague, and stayed on after the Nazi takeover to write of the formation of the new government. Later she accompanied Hungarian troops when they repossessed that piece of Czechoslovakia that had once been Hungary. She had the good fortune, or clairvoyance, to be in Rumania when the leader of the fascist Iron Guard, Corneliu Codreanu, was murdered, and in Rome during Neville Chamberlain's visit with Mussolini. Transradio News was pleased with her copy, but the paychecks were never quite enough to support her, and she returned home discouraged. After a stint on the New York daily *PM*, Betty determined to try Europe again. She booked passage, but before sailing dropped by CBS, where the news director suggested she see their correspondent William Shirer in Berlin. She did, and afterward checked in with him regularly.

That was how Shirer knew where to reach her when the Germans marched into Denmark and landed troops in Norway. His call was doubly welcome: nothing newsworthy was happening in Sweden, and

Wason was down to her last krona (about twenty-five cents). As the Germans bombed Oslo, the Norwegian king fled with his government and took refuge in a village. In short order Betty located a man from the Swedish legation who had evacuated with the royal party, and interviewed him. In her retelling of his story, the Swede happened to be standing by his car outside the house where the court and government were staying. Spying a German plane, he promptly blasted forth with his automobile horn.

> Down the road ran King Haakon, Crown Prince Olaf, the British and Polish ministers, and all the other government officials. They had to stand waist-deep in snow beneath fir trees while bombs crashed. . . . An hour later the second alarm came. This time the plane used machine-gun fire, and the court and visiting ministers fell flat on their faces with bed sheets, which they had yanked off the beds hurriedly in their departure, spread over them for camouflage.

CBS was impressed, and hired Wason as a stringer at a hundred dollars a week.

Her next challenge was to cross the frontier into Norway, where matters were not going well. The British, French, and Polish forces that landed along the coast to aid the Norwegians were ill equipped and defenseless against constant attack by air. On a daring sortie of her own, Wason managed to elude the border guards, cross into Norway, and hitch a ride on a truck across the mountainous terrain. Frightened, she experienced her first air raid, hiding in the woods amid the intensive bombing and machine-gunning. Later she managed to piece together a cohesive story from talking to wounded British soldiers, and was wondering how to return to Sweden to get it on the air when she ran across seasoned reporter and Pulitzer Prize winner Leland Stowe, now with the *Chicago Daily News*. With his melting smile and shock of white hair, Stowe could be very reassuring. Together they set out for Sweden, convinced they had enough material to prove that the Allies had irretrievably bungled the campaign. Hitching rides and, when the vehicles foundered in the snow, slogging along on foot, they reached the Swedish border, and Betty made it to Stockholm in time for her broadcast. Stowe admired her grit and spirit, and felt as bad as she did when atmospheric conditions prevented her broadcast from going through.

CBS proved less supportive than Stowe, however. In time there were complaints about her voice: too young and feminine, lacking the required authority. Would she please find a man to read from her texts? Wason felt betrayed, especially when the man she found, Winston Burdette, was offered a contract. But despite all her efforts and her very real success, there was no appeal — not with an almost entirely male company like CBS, not in 1940 when there was neither the fact nor the expectation of equality between the sexes.

The debacle of Norway's defeat in April 1940 sealed the fate of Prime Minister Neville Chamberlain. In Parliament for the debate, Helen Kirkpatrick reported that the Commons jeered him wildly, and that Chamberlain was shaken and gray. Candidates for the office narrowed to the foreign secretary, Lord Halifax, and Winston Churchill, then first lord of the admiralty. The lot fell to Churchill.

By then Kirkpatrick had been made "official" in the London bureau of the *Chicago Daily News*. On a recent visit to the United States, she had accepted an invitation to speak in Chicago. Before her talk she dropped in at the paper's home office. Foreign editor Carroll Binder, a strong ally, introduced her around. Later Helen recalled how editor Paul Scott Mowrer sat turning his pencil over and over. "I like your stuff," he said in his usual taciturn manner, "but we don't have women on the foreign staff." Their next stop was the office of the publisher, Colonel Frank Knox, who repeated the now familiar litany of exclusion. At that point Binder, no doubt frustrated, entered the fray: "Colonel, you know UP is trying to get her." This little fantasy was as much news to Kirkpatrick as it was to Knox, but it had the desired effect. "Well, we can't have that," the colonel said. "Let's have lunch." By dessert the matter was settled, and word went out to other women in the field: THE BARRIERS ARE NOT IMPREGNABLE!

When on March 23, 1940, Kirkpatrick sailed back to Europe on the *Manhattan*, she discovered Dorothy Thompson on board. Someone took a photo of them at the rail together, which Helen treasured because she admired Thompson. With her new legitimacy, Helen wanted Thompson to respect her, too, and she found it gratifying that in Rome the British minister gave a cocktail party for her. She could ask him to invite Thompson, and then take pride in being able to introduce her to Count Ciano, Mussolini's son-in-law. After years of diatribes against Hitler and the Nazis, Thompson was very much the grande dame of the interventionist viewpoint in America, and Kirkpatrick was pleased to appear a not inconsequential figure herself.

Thompson was about to set out on what she called "a swing around the hot-spot circle." In fact, she was not nearly so blasé as that term implied; she worried that she was getting in over her head, that the trip was being too frivolously undertaken. At the Vatican she begged Pope Pius XII to exert all his influence to keep Italy neutral in the coming conflict, but the pope only smiled. The Catholic Church, he said, was not so powerful as Miss Thompson thought, which she took as yet another indication of defeatism. From Rome she traveled to Ankara, Bucharest, and Belgrade, increasingly dismayed by the fatalism and resignation she encountered.

Sonia Tomara, who ran across Thompson in Bucharest that spring of 1940, shared her impression. Now serving as the *New York Herald Tribune* correspondent for all of southeast Europe, Tomara was responsible for reporting from Budapest to Turkey, and even made a tour through Ankara and Asia Minor into Syria and Palestine. Her bags were always half packed. Belgrade was her favorite city. The Simplon Express (London-Paris-Istanbul) met the Orient Express from Berlin there in the Yugoslav capital; cars from the warring countries merged into one train, and one could read the newspapers of both sides on the same day. In Belgrade correspondents stayed at the Serpski Kral, an old-fashioned hotel on the park with a porter who spoke a little English and always called Sonia "my lady." The bar was crowded with reporters and members of the Allied and American diplomatic corps; the German press drank elsewhere. Cy Sulzberger of the *New York Times*, Edward Kennedy of the AP, Sam Brewer of the *Chicago Tribune*, and Tomara all had rooms on the same floor and breakfasted together. She was also in touch with Italian newspapermen she had known in Rome. It was clear to her that none of the Italians in Belgrade liked their allies the Germans.

Austrians were different, however. Whenever Tomara was in Budapest, Heinrich von S., an Austrian who spent most of his time on his estate in northern Hungary, went to see her. They had met on a train between Vienna and Bratislava and discovered they had many interests in common. They belonged to enemy camps, but that was of little import in Budapest, Sonia said. They dined in fine restaurants and talked of the Europe of the past. And of the present — Heinrich brought her news of what was happening in Vienna, Germany, and Czechoslovakia.

In time Tomara moved along to Rumania. In Bucharest the bar of the Athenée Palace was the gathering place for correspondents. They were a sizable contingent, and apprehensive; a common pastime was mapping out avenues of escape in case of a German attack. The writing of dispatches became a science. There was no official censorship, but their phones were tapped, their desks searched, and copies of their stories scrutinized by the propaganda ministry. Those who made a slip were asked to leave the country at once.

Tomara was still in Bucharest when the Germans invaded Norway. She spent much of her time with Sam Brewer of the *Chicago Tribune*, Ed Beattie of UP, and Walter Duranty of the *New York Times*, hovering over the radio, following the course of the battle on the BBC. Listening as well to the German stations where broadcasts were all of Nazi victories, Tomara and her colleagues refused to believe the reports. Before long, however, they noticed that the same news they heard out of Berlin one day would appear on the BBC the next. The Deutschlandsender reports of German advances and Allied defeats were accurate; the BBC simply postponed the truth. Surrounded by many Germans there at the Athenée, Sonia and the others felt the shame of the Allied defeat.

In fact, Tomara found it a rather emotional spring. One day she and Cedric Salter of the *Daily Mail*, whom she had known in Warsaw, drove to the Rumanian-Soviet border and looked across at Russia. There wasn't much to see, but it affected her anyway. She knew it was the Communist government that had made the pact with Hitler, but still it hurt to think of her homeland allied in any way with the Nazis. The Balkans held many reminders of her past. The arrival of spring brought to mind other springs, and she yearned for more romance than was currently present in her life. She had good friends among her male colleagues, but most were either married or considerably younger than she. One of the latter was Derek Patmore, an Englishman who thought her "striking" and admired her "aura of delicate femininity" and quiet elegance. "Sonia could be charmingly Slav at times," he said. Once when they were having lunch together, she asked him abstractedly if he did not feel the need of falling in love during wartime. "Somehow," she mused, "it seems to help."

Dorothy Thompson would have understood. Her passion for international politics had stifled any romantic feeling remaining in her marriage, but she felt the void. From the farmhouse in Vermont, which in spite of their son Michael, now nine, they had not occupied concurrently for some time, she had recently written her husband, Sinclair Lewis: "Who knows? Maybe some time you might come home. . . ."

And had he done so, would he have found her there? A glancing encounter at best. From the "hot-spot circle" Thompson made her way to Paris. She was in her suite at the Hôtel Meurice on the morning of May 10, 1940, when the Germans invaded Belgium and Holland. France had already mobilized, and she followed the French army to the front on a highly publicized tour that included active participation with the artillery in an underground fortification on the Maginot Line. But it was the juxtaposition of war and love that most caught her imagination, and the story she wrote from a Paris railway station that same week, for her column "On the Record," served to remind her readers why it was she remained in the forefront of American journalism.

MAY 13, 1940 — The soldier stands face to face with his girl, his hands on her waist, under her jacket. The officer holds his girl by her arms. The soldier kisses his girl unashamedly. The officer kisses his girl with his eyes. None of the four speaks at all. . . .

The whistle blows. The officer holds his girl's cheek to his. The soldier kisses his girl on the mouth. Just once more!

Nobody watches any one else. No one pretends. No one is pretending anything.

"Kill a Boche for me, darling." Didn't they say that in the last war?

No one says a word about Boche or killing. Not a word. Not a flag. Not a salute . . . not an au revoir. They pull apart, and the men crowd into the cars. They wear good woolen uniforms and good thick boots.

They look through the open windows — a thousand faces, a thousand different faces, not one like another, not one common expression, not one replaceable face. Now, at last they smile, kindly, comfortingly, understandingly. The women and the girls stand together, but each alone, each surrounded by a little space of loneliness and separateness, each alone in her tears.

The train begins to move. The men wave. The women wave and weeping, smile.

No one calls "Vive la France!"

There goes France.

7

Fleeing France

Now, it was said, the great French counteroffensive would begin. Holland and Belgium had surrendered in the first week, but France would prevail. Meanwhile, refugees flowed southward from Belgium and Luxembourg into France, "two thirds of them women and children and many in rags," Sonia Tomara reported. She compared it to the exodus of White Russians after the Bolshevik Revolution, or that of the Poles the previous fall, but the numbers transcended those migrations. The American Red Cross estimated them at five million.

Tomara, back at the *Herald Tribune* Paris bureau, recorded their stories. In a babble of impressions, twenty Belgian boys relived how they had set out from Liège without saying goodbye to their parents and walked the entire distance to Paris. One woman had fled from a hospital with her newborn baby, leaving her six-year-old in the village with neighbors; when she tried to return for him, the village was already cut off. Most tragic was the woman who left Belgium with nine children and reached Paris with two, the others having been machine-gunned on the train.

The plight of the refugees was covered in the New York press too. Janet Flanner, at work in the home office of the *New Yorker*, saw a photograph in the *New York Mirror* of Noel Murphy among the volunteers of American Friends of France. Noel was helping Anne Morgan transport refugees who could not walk long distances — pregnant women and old men mostly. Flanner read of bomb fragments hitting the volunteers' cars, and worried. Later Noel wrote her of how in the Ardennes the Germans bombed the railroad station where she and

3,500 refugees had taken shelter, and how German fliers would dip down and machine-gun people on the roads. Noel described how she would have to pull her truck over and help the pregnant women — "all fainting and vomiting, poor women, you can imagine" — into a ditch. The situation was truly desperate, but she meant to keep on working as long as she could. She did not intend this as a criticism of her friend now safe in America, but it may have been hard for Janet not to take it so.

Meanwhile the battle went forward. In the north French troops were outnumbered two to one, and the RAF lost half its bombers operating over France. The only factor in the Allies' favor was Hitler's hesitancy on how to proceed. German panzer divisions, primed to push forward and wipe out French and British troops trapped at Dunkirk, were ordered to pause instead and repair their tanks while Hitler reviewed his options. Graced with those crucial hours and favorable weather, more than eight hundred British naval and civilian craft embarked on a massive rescue, spiriting some 338,000 men away to safety in Britain.

Virginia Cowles drove down to Dover to see the troops come in. "Hundreds of them filed through the docks, dirty and tired," she wrote. "Some had equipment, some had none; some were in uniform and some in an odd assortment of sweaters and slacks. Most of them seemed in high spirits and waved at the crowd clustered against the railings to cheer them. The English soldiers grinned self-consciously and made jokes to each other; the French soldiers blew kisses to the girls. I went back to London by train and all along the way Union Jacks were flying."

An American correspondent joined the influx of foreigners in Paris that spring. Despite the present threat, Mary Welsh found the city lovely after the gray English winter, and immersed herself in its sunlit, cosmopolitan charm. The closed-up shops and air raid drills that had distressed Janet Flanner seemed to her little different from those in London, while the English blackout was muted to a soft violet-blue in the French capital — less ominous somehow.

Mary Welsh, London *Daily Express, Life*

Mary Welsh was a practical woman; from childhood she had learned to adapt to the situation at hand. Her father was a lumberman, and she had spent summers following the Minnesota waterways on the family boat, young Indian loggers her frequent companions. When it stormed, she had waited it out on deck with the men, so the pervasive masculinity and wild tumult of war were a not unfamiliar ambience. Electing a career in journalism, Mary attended Northwestern, but was too eager to work in the field to stay for a degree. She took a job with a trade weekly, worked ten hours a day, six days a week, and at last moved along to the *Chicago Daily News* as a society reporter, the only position Colonel Frank Knox approved of for women. During her five years there she pleaded in vain for a foreign assignment, but the response was the same given to Helen Kirkpatrick — no women on the foreign staff. Welsh deliberated: should she remain at the *News*, which had taught her a lot, or try for a position in Europe? On a trip to London she met over tea with Lord Beaverbrook, publisher of the *Daily Express*, to no avail. But later, in Chicago and New York, he asked her to dine, and although she declined an invitation to join him on a trip up the Nile, she apparently wore down his resistance. He agreed to take her on at the *Express*.

A small, full-bosomed woman, Welsh was attracted to large men. At Northwestern she had married a tennis player, a tactical error soon remedied "without memorable hard feelings," she said. In London she tried again with Noel Monks, a gentle, oversized Australian with the *Daily Mail*, content to squeeze into her tiny Chelsea flat. When the British Expeditionary Force crossed over to France that winter of 1939–40, Monks went with it, and Welsh procured an assignment with the Royal Air Force in Normandy. English fliers were living comfortably in villages near the airstrips, she wrote, adding (perhaps a rumor) that one regiment of guards planned to import horses and hounds for some hunting.

In the spring the *Daily Express* sent Welsh to Paris in time to see the chestnuts blossom. Although by her own admission her "clothes, coiffure and savoir-faire were all untutored Midwest," she covered a

Mary Welsh, London, 1943.
UPI/CORBIS-BETTMANN.

showing of the latest collection at Lanvin's chic dove-gray salon. Edith Piaf, crooning wistful songs, was more to her liking. Welsh met with government officials, practiced her French, and learned how to get from her flat behind the Invalides to the Ritz bar by metro. She was determined to make the most of Paris while she still could.

Indeed, Paris remained an island of relative peace in a sea of upheaval. But one had only to read the communiqués in the daily papers, Sonia Tomara wrote, to see that battles were being fought where people used to motor for weekends — that is, two hours north by car. The nights might be soft and starry, but "Parisians look at the sky with one thought: Is the weather good for the Germans? Do bombing planes prefer clouds or a clear sky for their raids? Which way does the wind blow in case the Germans decide to use gas?"

And yet, she marveled, most people went calmly about their business, even their amusement. Theaters and music halls played nightly, restaurants were crowded, couples strolled in the parks. People thronged to the cinemas to be lulled by old American films, then jolted back to reality by newsreels of German bombings. Sunday, June 9, 1940, was hot, and Tomara watched cars driving south out of Paris on the only roads open to private vehicles. Many cars were topped with mattresses, a sign they were carrying families leaving the city and anxious to have a bed at their journey's end. But other cars returned to town filled with flowers, dogs, even children, in spite of the government's directive that all children under twelve be evacuated. In the Bois de Boulogne the swimming pools and tennis courts were crowded.

Sonia sensed it would be her last Sunday in Paris for a long time. She walked in the Tuileries Gardens in the morning when they were still deserted, sniffing the perfume of the lime trees. She studied the angle at which the towers of Notre Dame rose above the Seine. And at sunset, with the sound of guns pounding in the distance, she glanced down the Champs-Elysées and saw a "river of gold flowing from under the Arc de Triomphe."

Like Tomara, Mary Welsh felt the days winding down, felt she "was going nicely through the steps of a minuet in a house that was about to burn down." She scheduled another fitting with her dressmaker, lunched again with friends in the garden of the Ritz, and when her husband, Noel Monks, arrived in town from the front, drove with him to dine at an elegant restaurant in the Bois de Boulogne. That night brought the first faint thud of artillery. The next day the government fled Paris.

It was time to go. Already the roads south were clogged with sad, disillusioned Parisians. The Maginot Line had not proved magic after all; the great counteroffensive, long awaited, had not happened; the expected resistance had been a dream. Paris would not be defended, as its citizens had been led to believe, down to the last gray stone. It would not be defended at all. When news came that the government had departed without advising the civilian population what they should do, many panicked. Suddenly they too were refugees, like all those others trudging down from the north with vacant, expressionless eyes. Families mobilized whatever vehicles they could, stuffed them with blankets, pots, pans, and pets, and started south, toward what they did not know, only that it was in the opposite direction from the advancing German army.

Welsh and Monks left by train the same day as the government's withdrawal. They packed in twenty minutes, leaving behind, by Mary's calculation, two fur coats, twenty-seven sweaters, her grandmother's silver teaspoons, and various and sundry papers. She carried with her two changes of clothes, a tweed topcoat, a large bottle of Indiscreet toilet water, and her typewriter. At the Gare d'Austerlitz every car of the train was packed; when they managed to squeeze into one, Welsh found herself perched on her bag between the haunches of a spaniel dog and the knees of an elderly curator from the Louvre. At Blois, where they got off, seeking news to send back to London, they found the French information ministry sans information, and no way to send dispatches anyway.

Mary had had enough. Friends were driving to Biarritz. Noel might follow his own leadings, but she was joining them.

In London, Virginia Cowles had been following the censored version of news from France and trying to arrange permission to go to the front. Just when she believed herself successful, word came that the

86

Germans had crossed the Seine near Rouen. This placed Paris uncomfortably close to the front, and all flights were canceled. Unwilling to accept such a signal to remain where she was, Virginia grabbed the first available plane, mysteriously routed for "somewhere in France," which turned out to be Tours. She made her way by train to Paris. As her taxi driver searched for a hotel not boarded up, Virginia looked in vain for the defending army. When Franco laid siege to Madrid, she recalled, the city held out for two years. Where were the barricades, the troops? Where were her fellow reporters?

At last she located Walter Kerr, foreign correspondent for the *Herald Tribune*, and together they drove up the Champs-Elysées to the Arc de Triomphe. Three gendarmes stood in lonely vigil at the flame. Cowles and Kerr continued down Avenue Marceau, across the Pont de l'Alma, to the Invalides where fleets of taxicabs, an estimated five or six hundred, were lined up to effect the last-minute evacuation of government documents. At the Ecole Militaire they saw men carrying out file cases and loading them into vans. Only in the less affluent neighborhoods were the streets full of people. These, thought Cowles, were the people too poor to leave.

All day she kept her ears tuned, but a deathly quiet prevailed. At the Place de la Concorde they ran across soldiers plodding along. "Their faces were grimy and their clothes caked with mud," she wrote. "Two of them were limping, a third had a bandage round his head, a fourth was walking in his stocking feet, carrying his shoes. They were evidently stragglers who had got lost or deserted, and were making their way back to their homes. But there was no one to notice them. No one had time for soldiers now."

Cowles had to decide what to do. The German army was exactly seventeen miles to the north. Most of her colleagues had already left town, and no cars were available anywhere. Just when she thought she might have no choice but to remain for the occupation, Tom Healy of the London *Daily Mirror* appeared, driving a Chrysler. He agreed to take her with him to Bordeaux.

The only woman correspondent already a seasoned refugee, Sonia Tomara had been living with her sister Irina in a little flat behind the Etoile, a happy interlude that she could prolong no longer. After a farewell visit to their mother and aunt, two small figures dressed in black, Sonia and Irina and a Canadian doctor friend started out in a large car with enough gasoline to reach Bordeaux. But at the first hill the gears failed, and they had to pull off the road and wait out the hours until morning. Towed by a military truck to a garage in Fontainebleau, they learned that the car would require two days to repair — should there be a mechanic available, which there was not. Nor was anyone interested in towing the car further. They did persuade a young man with a truck, but no fuel, to siphon the gasoline from their car and take them to Orléans. Sitting on top of their luggage in the truck bed, they again headed south.

Now they were part of the dense caravan of fleeing humanity. The flight from Paris was the most motorized exodus in history at that time, and the hours were punctuated by noise and confusion, by the scrape of gears and the thick smell of petrol, by curses and despairing cries. The truck passed hundreds of nonfunctioning vehicles ditched by the roadside, and thousands of people whose only recourse now was to walk. At night the military commandeered the main route, and Tomara's crew had to make their way along dark country lanes, without lights because of the bombers.

They reached the Orléans railway station, only seventy miles from Paris, on the fourth day. "People lay on the floor inside and the town square was filled," Sonia wrote. "We piled our baggage and waited until daylight. There was nothing to eat in the town, no rooms in the hotels, no cars for hire, no gasoline anywhere. Yet a steady stream of refugees was coming in, men, women and children, all desperate, not knowing where to go or how."

The next day, pausing at Montbazon on the Bordeaux road, Sonia heard that the French government had relocated in Tours seven miles away, and set off alone to walk there. It was raining, and she carried her sleeping bag and typewriter. At last someone gave her a lift. In Tours she found the government gone, along with most of her fellow correspondents, but the wireless operator and censor allowed her to file her story before they, too, fled. That night there was an air raid, and as she listened to the bombs falling, she could only hope they were not aimed at the refugee-choked roads. "A catastrophe has befallen France," Sonia wrote. "Nobody knows how or when it will end. Like the other refugees, and there are millions of us, I do not know when I shall sleep in a bed again, or how I shall get out of this town."

Although Paris was declared an "open city" on June 11, 1940, and was entered by German forces on the fourteenth, many French clung to the belief that their armies would regroup and fight on. Churchill flew to Tours in a last-ditch attempt to persuade French premier Paul Reynaud not to make a separate peace with Germany. The prime minister returned to London with no commitment as to what course the French would choose.

Under those circumstances, Virginia Cowles and her party in the Chrysler were not surprised to find ordinary French citizens uninformed. On Sunday, June 16, they stopped in a tiny village café where the proprietress, a matriarch of seventy-eight, hovered over them. She was not depressed by the news from Paris, Virginia recalled. "All her life she had been troubled by the Boches, but in the end things always came right. She could remember the war of 1870, for she was eight years old at the time. In the war of 1914 her sons had fought, and today her grandsons were at the front." Cowles and her colleagues could not bring themselves to tell her that at that very moment the French cabinet was discussing whether France should capitulate.

In Bordeaux that Sunday thousands of people milled about the town, tired, tense, with nowhere to go. All talk was about the cabinet meetings in session. The word "armistice" began to appear in press reports, accompanied by categorical denials that France would ask for one. The evening communiqué informed reporters that Reynaud had resigned, that Marshal Henri Philippe Pétain, hero of the last war, would succeed as premier. Pétain was eighty-four years old.

Sonia Tomara reached Bordeaux with her sister in a truck packed with French sailors. On Monday she was in a café about noon — there was nowhere else to go if one had nowhere to sleep, she said — when word came over the radio that Pétain would speak. There was a dead silence. Nobody moved as in his old voice he spoke of his own sacrifice, of the heroism of the troops and the plight of the refugees. Then he said, "It is with a heavy heart that I tell you that we must try to stop the fight."

People looked at each other stunned. "It's armistice," a woman said. "It's defeat," a man corrected her.

Within a day or two most American and British correspondents left Bordeaux for England. Sonia Tomara remained to settle affairs for Irina, who was stateless, and to help the *Herald Tribune* Paris correspondent John Elliott, who was on crutches from an accident suffered at the front. On a straw-covered upper floor of a building they pounded out their stories. Tomara carried them to the censor, returning with food, which they ate with their fingers. In time, at the request of the *Herald Tribune*, she made her way through Spain to Portugal where she embarked for New York.

Well before then the others had congregated at Le Verdon, the port at the mouth of the Gironde, where the SS *Madura* lay in the harbor taking on hundreds of unexpected passengers. It was a perfect June day. Virginia Cowles described the white sand glistening in the sunshine, the tall pines bordering the beach, a hundred boats at anchor in the harbor. The *Madura* was a small British passenger-cargo ship that had left East Africa for England on what was scheduled as a three-week trip, but which already had lasted two months. The ship was almost within reach of the Channel when the order came for the captain to backtrack and pick up refugees at Bordeaux. Designed for two hundred passengers, the *Madura* had taken on eight times that many by the time it weighed anchor. Mary Welsh and Noel Monks shared an air mattress with another couple on the starboard side. Cowles, encamped on the top deck with the Fleet Street contingent, estimated there were some sixty journalists aboard.

Cars and other items had been abandoned at quayside, and each passenger was limited to one piece of luggage. The captain had had no opportunity to replenish the food supply, but adequate rations existed for a breakfast of tea and bread for all and a dinner of a little meat, some rice, and a potato. No submarines were sighted. When they put in at Falmouth thirty-six hours later, they were met by a troop of motherly women who passed out lemonade and sandwiches along with reassurances to the tired travelers that now they were in England, everything would be all right.

*   *   *

90

By June 25, 1940, hostilities had ceased. Under the terms of the armistice, France became a divided state: the north under German occupation, the south under putative French control. Premier Marshal Pétain set up office in the town of Vichy, a name previously connected with healthful waters and a thick potato soup, now to take on the connotation of collaboration with the enemy, disgrace. Vichy France was the France that sold out. But there was another France — some of it in Britain with General Charles de Gaulle, some of it primed to go underground. That would be the France that survived.

8

Braving the Blitz

The ink was barely dry on the armistice agreement of June 25, 1940, when the Germans sent their first bombers over England. The war came home to American correspondents that day; no longer need they fly in and out of various capitals seeking it. Facing England along the North Sea and Channel coasts were Norway, Denmark, Germany, Holland, Belgium, France, all under Nazi domination. It was chilling if one had time to ponder it, which none of the women did. Observing their British sisters with their daily courage, their proficiency in handling jobs long the province of men, they would have felt guilty admitting to leisure or fear.

Early summer 1940 was a time of settling in for the long haul, both physically and psychically. They were few in number by now, anyway: Virginia Cowles and Mary Welsh, just back from France on the *Madura*, Helen Kirkpatrick, who had remained in England, and Tania Long, come over from Berlin after the fall of Poland.

Tania Long, *New York Herald Tribune*, *New York Times*

Tania Long grew up in Berlin with her Russian-born mother and English father, who served as financial correspondent for the London *Economist* and the *New York Times*. As a brown-eyed child of eleven, Tania was sent to boarding school outside Paris; she loved Paris, and later continued her studies at the Sorbonne and the Ecole des Sciences Politiques. In Paris she met a young American. "I did everything too

Tania Long, London, 1941.
AP/WIDE WORLD PHOTOS.

early," she recalled, "got married at eighteen, had a child at nineteen." She found life in New York fascinating, American politics as well, but her conservative husband did not concur in her admiration for President Roosevelt. "I have to think for myself," she told him, but he did not see why. The marriage foundered, they separated, and Tania (by then an American citizen) needed a job. Journalism was the only profession she had observed at close hand, the only work that interested her. She had no real experience, but the *Newark Ledger* offered a low-level opening with promise of advancement. Tania hired a housekeeper to care for her son and took the job.

While over the next two years Tania grew to love reporting, she worried about her parents' welfare in Nazi Berlin. In the summer of 1938 she sailed for Bremen, but disembarked at Southampton to join her father who, although clearly ill, had gone to London to urge a strong stand against Hitler. After Munich the political situation appeared to normalize, and Tania sent for her son, but the family had barely settled down together in Berlin when her father died. At twenty-five she found herself the only wage earner for a family of three in a country she felt she knew no longer. Under Nazi regulations none of her father's estate could leave Germany, and Long realized that without it they could not get by in New York. They had no choice but to remain. It was then she learned that Ralph Barnes, Berlin bureau chief for the *New York Herald Tribune*, was looking for an assistant. The job required fluency in English, German, French, and if possible Russian; Tania had all the credentials.

She was grateful for the presence of Sigrid Schultz, although that old family friend appeared to have lost the gaiety and effervescence Tania remembered. Certainly the Berlin of 1939 was no longer the civilized capital of her childhood. "Hitler's storm troopers stood about on street corners glaring at people," she recalled. "On the night Hitler returned after the takeover of Czechoslovakia, there was a parade to the eerie light of flaming bowls of oil, with searchlights playing in the sky. The whole atmosphere was awful."

More ominous yet was that first night of the war, September 1, 1939, in Berlin. From the *Herald Tribune* office opposite Goering's air ministry, Long watched a modest crowd of townspeople standing solemnly in front of the chancellery. "People whispered to one another," she recalled. "There was no bravado. We all expected Armageddon from the skies. The first night we expected British planes would come; we thought the Germans would go after London. Instead they practiced their bombing by dropping bags of flour on Goering's

Air Ministry. We could hear them drop and see the white bags exploding." She and bureau chief Ralph Barnes had spent the night on the
floor of the office to be ready to handle the news, an unnecessary precaution as it turned out. There had been no news.

With the outbreak of war, Long sent her mother and little son on
to England and requested a transfer there herself. Accordingly, when
Ed Angly of the *New York Herald Tribune* asked for reinforcements for
the London bureau, word came that "a girl from Berlin" would arrive
soon. This was not what Angly had in mind, and he complained to
Raymond Daniell, London bureau chief of the *New York Times*. "Don't
let them palm off any second-raters on you," Daniell advised him.
"Besides, you don't want a girl. This is a man's job."

Daniell's attitude — that a "girl journalist" was automatically second rate — was the accepted one, but before Angly could head her off,
Tania arrived. Ray met her in the fall of 1939 at a cocktail party for correspondents going off to France, and ran into her again on the station
platform. Feeling guilty about his advice to Angly and depressed at
being left behind in England, he invited her to lunch. Across a small
table at the Savoy Grill they found they had much in common, including that both had once worked on the *Newark Ledger*. They liked the
same people, the same books, the same places in New York. They
laughed a lot. By the end of the meal, Daniell felt a lot better about not
going to France.

As he told the story later, Tania was soon the confidante of all his
troubles. When in the spring he came down with pneumonia, it was she
who bullied him into seeing a doctor and dropped by every day to check
on him. "She was the same with everyone," he said, clearly hoping otherwise, and indeed Long tried to keep things on a friendly basis. Besides
his position as head of the competition, Daniell had a wife and two children back in the States. By that time her own son was also there; after
sending him with her mother to Ireland where she could visit them regularly, Long worried that even Ireland was not safe and shipped them
on to New York. She felt it was the best solution, right in line with the
British government's plan to send several hundred thousand school-
children to Canada and the United States.

That summer of 1940, after France fell, Long and Daniell spent
more and more time together. Early bombings were concentrated on

airfields and coastal defenses, and with London still spared, they walked for hours through the parks or picnicked in the country. At the Café de Paris to hear an American Negro band, they sat on the balcony and looked down at the dancers, men and women of all ages in every variety of attire from evening to battle dress. That night the sirens began. No plane was sighted, and antiaircraft guns circling London remained quiet, but Tania felt the war closing in.

The most visible sign appeared over the English Channel where Royal Air Force Spitfires and Hurricanes battled the Luftwaffe's Messerschmitts, Junkers, Heinkels, and Dorniers almost daily. This uneven struggle (RAF fighter pilots were far outnumbered) became the core of what was called the Battle of Britain. Germany's aim was to gain absolute air superiority; for the British, it was simply to survive.

During August and September of 1940 Helen Kirkpatrick and Virginia Cowles often joined the press contingent at Dover. The town was only twenty cross-Channel miles from the nearest German air base, and the lobby of its Grand Hotel on the waterfront became the scene of heightened journalistic activity. Cowles noted the town's brave attempts at normalcy, the busy little roller skating pavilion next to the hotel with its gramophone blaring music out over the sea as if there were no war. But at any moment alarms might sound, and a red flag raised from Dover Castle signal pedestrians to take cover. As the music stilled, the faraway drone of planes could be heard.

In August Cowles and Kirkpatrick spent several days in Dover with fellow correspondent Vincent Sheean and David Bruce of the American Red Cross. They would climb to the top of Shakespeare Cliff about a mile from the town to view the battle. Later Cowles described the experience:

> In front of you stretched the blue water of the Channel and in the distance you could distinguish the hazy outline of the coast of France. Far below were the village houses glistening in the sun and the small boats and trawlers lying at anchor in the harbor . . . and above all this, twenty or thirty huge grey balloons floating in the blue, flapping a little like whales gasping for breath.
> You lay in the tall grass with the wind blowing gently across

you and watched the hundreds of silver planes swarming through the heavens like clouds of gnats. All around you, anti-aircraft guns were shuddering and coughing, stabbing the sky with small white bursts. You could see the flash of wings and the long white plumes from the exhausts; you could hear the whine of engines and the rattle of bullets. You knew the fate of civilization was being decided fifteen thousand feet above your head in a world of sun, wind and sky.

Kirkpatrick witnessed the great battle of August 15, part of Reich Air Marshal Goering's Operation Eagle, meant to designate a new and (he hoped) decisive phase of battle for the Germans. Many Britishers objected to radio broadcasters' reporting the event as if it were a prizefight, but in fact, Helen said, that was exactly how it appeared:

You have no feeling of carnage, such as you might have watching an infantry battle. Walking about on the cliff above the shore, with its rows of neat gardens below, under the warm summer sun and the bright blue sea beyond, with the butterflies fluttering about and the gulls making heathenish noises, it is impossible to feel that this is actually bitter war going on overhead.

After one such afternoon Helen and her colleagues took the late train back to London. Waiting outside the Dover station, they watched the approach of a new wave of enemy planes so low they could see their markings. One was hit by a tracer bullet and went down in flames. The train, when it arrived, was blacked out, but at each stop they got out for a moment to see "a searchlight combing the beautiful, moonlit sky."

By early September the big story was Churchill's warning that a German invasion was imminent. Virginia Cowles and her buddy "Knick" Knickerbocker drove down to Dover to be on hand for what was dubbed Invasion Weekend. Soldiers were instructed to sleep with their boots on, and people went to bed expecting to hear church bells toll the worst by morning. But nothing out of the ordinary happened. On Monday the boot order was reversed, and Knick and Virginia drove back to London. As later became clear, the Luftwaffe had not achieved the superiority Hitler considered a prerequisite for invasion, and a large number of barges, transports, and torpedo boats jammed into French and Belgian ports had been sent to the bottom by RAF night bombers and heavy gun bombardment across the Channel.

Instead of covering the arrival of German ground troops on English soil, the correspondents reported an accelerated Battle of Britain in the skies. On a typical day, Air Marshal Goering sent 1,300 planes against England. Britain had only 170 fighters to put into the air; by day's end 26 had been shot down, but once again the RAF had endured. This might have been thought cause for rejoicing, but the pilots were the country's idols, each one a national hero. Each loss was mourned. Earlier in the conflict Cowles, again with Knickerbocker, drove to the airfield where the 601 Squadron was stationed. She wrote of sitting at dinner with thirty "handsome and brave" pilots who, when they got the signal, were in the air in sixty seconds. A few weeks later she returned to find only three still there.

Cowles had a particular connection with the 601 Squadron. The unit had been formed some years earlier by young fliers of sufficient means to provide their own planes. The attendant glamour was increased by the rumor that the men gave their girlfriends the squadron emblem — a flying sword — set in rubies and diamonds. The previous fall Virginia had visited the 601st, not as a journalist, but as a friend of squadron member Aidan Crawley. She did not disclose whether she was the recipient of a flying sword talisman, or whether the plane Crawley piloted was his own — only that he was a Socialist candidate for Parliament and met her that day in his blue uniform with a thick book of economics under his arm. Crawley's plane was shot down over Libya early in the war, but he would survive, and wait out the next four long years behind the barbed wire of a German prisoner-of-war camp.

It was Cowles who first glimpsed the bombers heading for London. She and a friend had gone for the weekend to the country house of the elderly publisher of the *Sunday Dispatch*. The weather was warm and sunny that seventh of September 1940, and they were having Saturday tea on the lawn when a barely perceptible drone of planes grew to a deep full roar. "We made out a batch of tiny white specks, like clouds of insects, moving northwest in the direction of the capital," she

wrote. "Some of them — the bombers — were flying in even formation, while the others — the fighters — swarmed protectively around."
They counted more than 150 planes. The steady drone continued all
night; whenever Virginia woke up, she heard it.

Meanwhile in London, Mary Welsh and her husband Noel Monks
were at the movies when a notice appeared on the screen: "An Alert
Has Sounded. If You Wish to Leave, Walk, Do Not Run, to the Nearest
Exit." The feature then resumed. The sound of sirens could be heard
outside, but Mary and Noel remained in their seats. When they left,
they were surprised to find that all the buses and taxis had vanished, and
they were forced to walk the two miles home. "That night," Mary wrote
later, "began the Luftwaffe's long nightmare Blitz on London. . . . For
the succeeding fifty-six nights, without surcease, London shuddered
and burned."

The next day reporters fanned out to assess the damage. "For
nearly ten miles in the East End of London there was a scene of devastation today," Tania Long reported. "No wreckage looked alike. Here
three-quarters of a tenement had been blasted away, leaving an iron
bedstead dangling crazily from what was left of the floor. . . . There, a
block away, were the ruins of a Methodist church. Only three outside
walls were standing, and on first sight the whole had the graceful air of
an ancient Roman structure slowly crumbling to dust." Rescue squads
were still pulling bodies from the ruins, and everywhere she saw
people trying to dig out their belongings. Mothers trailed by children
were attempting to wheel perambulators top-heavy with salvaged
household goods to the riverbank, to ferry across to relatives or friends
on the other side of the Thames.

Those with a place to go were fortunate. Others, carrying babies
or small suitcases crammed with possessions, lined up at bus stops,
heading for makeshift shelters in the center of the city. By chance, Long
was dining in one of the large hotels that evening when a throng of the
newly homeless came in, seeking refuge in a few bare basement rooms
that the hotel had turned over to them.

As for Helen Kirkpatrick, she had gone downriver with the fire
brigade during the bombing. "It was both scary and fascinating," she
recalled. "The fires were huge, monstrous." Returning that night to her
flat in the West End, she could read a newspaper by the light of the fire

burning in the East End. "It lit the whole of London. And they used that to guide planes in and drop more bombs."

The second night, the bombing was more widespread. "London still stood this morning, which was the greatest surprise to me as I cycled home in the light of early dawn after the most frightening night I have ever spent." Helen had been with friends for dinner; they had ignored the early sirens, but "when the first screaming bomb started on its downward track we decided the basement would be healthier." All night they had moved back and forth. "Most of the time we felt that the entire center of the city had probably been blasted out of existence and we ticked off each hit with 'That must be Buckingham Palace — that's Whitehall.' " But the next morning when she cycled past those land-marks, each appeared solidly in place, as was her own house when she arrived there. Only later when she walked through the rubble and debris where the bombs had landed did she wonder how anyone who had been there could possibly be alive.

Before long every London correspondent had his or her own bomb story. Helen Kirkpatrick and Ben Robertson of the *New York Herald Tribune* went down to Cliveden at the invitation of Lord and Lady Astor to escape the London bombing, only to have a bomb fall so close to the house that it blew a car onto the roof. The windows of Tania Long's house were smashed, the shutters blown in, all the pictures knocked off the walls. Virginia Cowles was dining with a friend at Claridge's when the nearby John Lewis department store was hit. People who had come inside for shelter, as well as guests forced down-stairs in a variety of night garb, were warned to keep to one side of the lobby, as a time bomb had fallen on the other side and might go off at any moment. Cowles described how an elderly lady dressed all in black and followed by three other women descended the stairs, and the hush that fell over the crowd as exiled Queen Wilhelmina of the Netherlands and her ladies-in-waiting walked through the lobby.

Mary Welsh went down regularly to the workers' flats along the Thames to see how ordinary people were faring. They always wel-comed her with "a cuppa" (tea) and opinions on hot topics like rationing or evacuation to the country. East Enders were resigned to the former but firmly opposed to the latter. "Husbands and wives had been born and raised within a street or two of each other," Welsh explained, "and this was their territory. Nothing could lure them from their own private bits of London."

But staying put was chancy. More than once when Welsh visited, her friends took her to see the latest damage, and to speak with the newest homeless. The bombings were referred to as "incidents"; most distressing were the "incidents" in which people were buried, still alive, under the remains of their homes. Mary often went out before dawn and "hung around the edges of an incident" to watch the Welsh miners employed in the rescues. They removed the debris one brick or plank at a time, fearing to jar the support of persons perhaps still alive below. One morning near Paddington Station she was startled when a small boy of four or five, wearing pajamas, a sweater, and socks but no shoes, ran sobbing toward her. He clutched her knees and gasped, "My mum's down there, my mum's down there," until Mary sat down on a pile of bricks and held him, nuzzling his dirty hair with her nose and repeating, "It's going to be all right, buddy, it's going to be all right." An air raid warden came along to claim him, assuring her they would have his mother out soon, and that she was "not in too bad shape." That could be anything short of dead, Welsh thought, as she brushed herself off and headed for the *Time-Life* office. She might have stayed for the denouement of the "incident" had her employers expressed any interest in stories of this nature. They had not. Walking to work another morning, Welsh had passed a gray van with its back doors open parked near a heap of rubble which the day before had been a house. Several men were sliding canvas-wrapped bodies on litters into the van. "These were some of London's dead of that night," she wrote. "They looked nameless, and very still." She cabled a short piece on the gray van and its contents to New York. It was rejected — "too grim."

That kind of censorship irked Welsh, who believed the American public should be educated about war's reality. If she, a woman, could bear to go there, see it, and write about it, surely *Time-Life* readers sitting in their comfortable living rooms might be allowed to read about it.

In November 1940 both the *New York Times* and the *Herald Tribune* moved their offices into the Savoy Hotel, which meant it became more

101

than ever the focal point of the American correspondents' lives. There for dinner one evening, Helen Kirkpatrick realized that ten years had passed since her first visit. She recalled bright lights, glittering jewels and shimmering gowns, young debutantes swinging about on a gleaming floor, and a huge plate glass window reflecting the light into the Thames below. Now that window was boarded up, and guests moved on to safer rooms below where heavy curtains shut out the sound of the gun barrages. Men in uniform and women in tailored suits sat at little tables clustered cozily about the steel pipes. Puzzled, Helen asked the waiter if this had not once been the Abraham Lincoln Room. His expression did not change. "It is still the Abraham Lincoln Room, madam," he replied.

Most of the staff of the *Times* and *Herald Tribune*, including Tania Long and Ray Daniell, moved into the Savoy. Ray liked the arrangement there; he could no longer bear not being sure Tania was safe during a raid. They had known each other more than a year, had experienced normal, peaceful moments and times of great stress. A man and a woman who shared hard times were particularly vulnerable. After unwise marriages, and despite hardship to their children, Ray and Tania could no longer imagine life without each other.

Besides providing live/work space for their clientele, the management at the Savoy understood what hardworking people needed in an air raid shelter. Each guest had a normal upstairs room, and a mattress complete with linens "down below." There separate areas were designated for single men, single women, and married couples, and a little section was screened off for the Duke and Duchess of Kent when they were in town. There was a "snore warden" on duty all night who would gently shake an offender with "Sorry, sir, but you're snoring. Please turn over." Tania recalled a woman with lovely long blond hair who laid claim to a certain chair in the lounge; every night she sat there brushing her hair in front of everyone before lying back and going to sleep. Tania and Ray dubbed her Lady Godiva.

In time, however, they gave up going down to the shelter. Tania didn't like the rats running along the ledges high under the ceiling, and Ray snored and woke up one night to find the Savoy chef's hand pressed firmly over his mouth. He recalled how in the morning he would stagger up to his room and "there was the bed, crisp and fresh, with sheets unwrinkled and the coverlet drawn down invitingly." One night he was so tired that he didn't go "down below," and the next morning he was still alive, so he decided to take his chances, and Tania did the same. That placed her on the scene to report the direct bomb hits that severely damaged the Savoy, killing the former Belgian minister of war and another guest.

"When one hears bombs coming that close there is no time to do anything," she informed her readers. "In my own case I crammed deeper into the armchair, put my arms over my head, and prayed for the best. As one after the other the bombs hit, there was a groaning and creaking of the walls, the floor and the ceiling which, at one point, I thought was coming right down on top of me." When she dared open the door she saw the corridor thick with black smoke, and other guests, also shelter shunners, fleeing their rooms to spend the rest of the night "down below."

On November 16, 1940, the bombing moved northward. Beginning at dusk, the cathedral town of Coventry was battered and blasted by wave after wave of German planes dropping a million pounds of high explosives, sixty thousand of incendiary bombs. When dawn came at last, Coventry was unrecognizable.

Long and Daniell, driving through the blacked-out night, arrived to find the entire center of the city destroyed. The cathedral, one of the oldest in England, was an empty shell. Only the tower and spire still stood and the latter tipped dangerously. The beautiful half-timbered houses in the center of the city were demolished, and most of the streets impassable. They moved on to Birmingham and Manchester, which had also been badly hit. For four days Tania shuffled about through ashy ruins among distraught and grieving people. She hardly ate or slept — all the beds were given over to the bombing victims. She returned to Coventry on the day the victims of the attack there were buried.

Thin wisps of smoke still rose from the ruins of central Coventry today, and rescuers still were searching for further victims, as a thousand men and women silently watched their loved ones laid to rest in a common grave. The dead . . . now lie in plain pine coffins, placed end to end and tier upon tier in a deep, narrow trench hastily dug by steam shovels borrowed from a construction job.

There was nothing beautiful about this mass funeral. It was grim — as grim as the expression on the pale faces of the drably clothed mourners who had walked two miles in a drizzling rain from the city where they once had homes to the cemetery set among the fields. . . . The Bishop of Coventry led the brief services from a heap of muddy earth, his purple robes flying in the wind. The people stood below him, facing the common grave.

When the service was over, the people walked slowly along the length of the grave, casting their flowers on the pine boxes below. Death was anonymous — many of the victims were never identified — and there was nothing to distinguish one coffin from another. It did not seem to matter. The only decorations on the grave were a few rain-sodden Union Jacks, lending a vaguely military touch to the funeral, as if soldiers and not just ordinary citizens were being buried there.

The little group of women reporters in London during the Blitz contributed to a major shift in America's perception of Britain during that fall of 1940. Reaction to Prime Minister Chamberlain's appeasement policies had ranged from lack of interest to censure. But once the blunt-spoken, half-American Winston Churchill was in charge, once Americans read stories in the press of the daily horrors of the Blitz, saw photos of gutted buildings and dead civilians on the front page of their morning papers and heard the thud of bombs in the background of Edward R. Murrow's nightly broadcasts, the mood changed. The British were a brave lot after all, worthy allies in battle, should it come to that. As for American reporters who remained in London by choice — including the women, as exposed to danger as any — they were heroes all.

The following February, at the Front Page Ball of the New York Newspaper Women's Club, Kathleen McLaughlin of the *New York Times* paid tribute to "American women reporters now active on various war fronts." The women at home "envy their assignments and admire their achievements," she said, and proceeded to call by name each woman who had reported from the scattered battlefronts of 1940. Tania Long received an award as writer of the best news story of that year for her combined stories on the bombing of Britain, and Betty Wason was also singled out "for the daring and courage she had shown in her war coverage in Norway, Finland, Greece and elsewhere." The evening closed when guest of honor Eleanor Roosevelt asked all present to stand in a special toast to "those women war correspondents who are surely making, or helping to make, newspaper history in this critical period of civilization."

9

Working Under the Swastika

However harrowing it was to be in London during the Blitz, at least one was surrounded by friends. American correspondents in Berlin during 1940–41 lived among their enemies while being bombed by their friends. It was a not unwelcome paradox — but not easy, either, as Lael Tucker discovered.

Lael Tucker (Laird) (Wertenbaker), Time Inc.

Lael Tucker was the oldest of five children in a family of Deep South ancestry, where a Biblical name (Numbers 3:24) was nothing unusual, especially from a clergyman father. Like Mary Welsh, Tucker was impatient to get on with her life; she started college before graduating from high school, then left at eighteen to go to New York. Her goal was to be a playwright, but the income from that was worse than preacher's pay, so she took a job with the Theater Guild and wrote plays on the side. She had a vibrant personality and a husky voice that carried volumes. To hear her read a play was an arresting experience, but none of her own was ever produced. In time she abandoned the theater, joined the staff of *Fortune*, married fellow reporter Stephen Laird, and moved with him to Washington. There she filled in at *Time* when they were shorthanded, which entitled her to reporter status and to go along

Lael Wertenbaker, London, 1943.
PHOTO BY LEE MILLER. LAEL WERTENBAKER PERSONAL COLLECTION.

when Steve was sent to Berlin in 1940. Wives could accompany their husbands only if they were reporters themselves.

Even so, the road to Berlin was not without obstacles. The State Department considered the usual route through Lisbon too dangerous; Laird and Tucker would have to go the opposite way around, via Japan, Manchuria, and Russia. As it happened, the eastern route held far more perils than the western. In Manchuria, breaking their rail journey to spend the night in a town near Harbin, they came upon a surreal, nightmarish scene in the station — people clustered around a table, receiving injections from open pans of serum. Tucker managed to slip under a fence and cross the road to the Intourist bureau, but what she saw there was even more disquieting — the whole staff was masked, as in a medieval story. She must leave at once, they said. Grabbing luggage and making a dash for the tracks while eluding pursuing guards, Lael and Steve piled onto a waiting third-class train full of cackling chickens, a trade-off they minded not at all. At Harbin the truth came out: the area was subject to an outbreak of bubonic plague, which the authorities were trying to hush up.

The Soviets knew of it, however. When Tucker and Laird tried to board the Trans-Siberian Railway, their passports were confiscated and they were placed in quarantine with thirty missionaries on a railroad siding. Their clothes were taken away for disinfection, and they were issued cotton underwear, pajamas and dressing gowns, paper slippers, and toothbrushes. When after a week no one came down with the plague, their clothing was returned and they could begin the long journey across Russia to Germany. Lael always assumed that they had come upon a chance outbreak of that dread disease. Fifty-five years later she and the world learned the truth: the city of Harbin had been the site of a vast Japanese research project to develop weapons of biological warfare, including anthrax, cholera, and bubonic plague. In 1940 Japanese planes dropped bombs loaded with plague-infested fleas on nearby cities.

Knowing nothing of this at the time, Tucker and Laird tended to downplay all the fuss that delayed their arrival in Berlin until the fall of 1941. A dwindled press corps at the Adlon welcomed them with open arms. Still, Berlin took some getting used to. It was Lael's first experience with bombing, and at the first whine of the air raid alarm, she prepared to dive for the nearest shelter. The long-termers, however, were concerned only with whose room had the best view, and Lael, not wishing to be branded a coward so early, tagged along to the appointed window. Within a week she was leading the way. Life in Berlin was drab; one seized at any distraction. Besides, she said, they wanted Berlin to be bombed, and watched with grim satisfaction.

Not all the scary moments came from bombs, however. One night Lael stopped at a bierstübe to telephone her husband. A man came up behind her and grabbed the receiver out of her hand, growling, "You can't speak English here!" Startled, she turned to find herself surrounded by brownshirts. At first she was paralyzed with fear, but just as quickly fear dissolved into anger, and anger produced an adrenaline that initiated action. When the man put his hand on her arm, Lael burst into a stream of more fluent and profane German than she was aware she knew, then abruptly turned and stalked out. No one followed.

Still, Lael decided, it was like everywhere — some people were bad, some good, and for every crazy Nazi there was a German who remained quite sane. Many Berliners betrayed a grudging admiration for the RAF airmen who came from so far, hazarding antiaircraft fire and defensive fighter planes to unload their bombs and then return. When an RAF plane was hit, a gasp of horror rose instinctively from the watchers below. There was sympathy for the ordinary Englishman, too. Lael was heartened when one night after a movie a captured Allied newsreel was shown. Scenes of London burning from a night of bombing came on the screen. The audience, Lael said, was absolutely quiet. Then the prime minister appeared, inspecting the damage, and the German commentator shouted, "You're to blame, Winston Churchill, for all this." Again there was not a sound in the theater, except for one woman crying softly, "Those poor British people. Those poor British people."

Mixed emotions were not unusual with the correspondents either. From London Tania Long reported to the *New York Herald Tribune* of RAF bombers sweeping across Germany to attack Berlin. "A full moon lit up the sprawling city," one dispatch read. "The raiders circled high over the German capital picking out their targets . . . the large gas works on the Danzigerstrasse . . . the railway yards near the Tempelhof airport . . . the Lehrter Station just a mile north of the Brandenburger Tor." These were familiar landmarks to Tania; she had known them from childhood. She also knew that the gasworks on the Danzigerstrasse were in a poor section of Berlin, that a bombardier's aim was not always right on, and that the next day those women and children who survived would be sifting through the rubble for salvageable possessions just like in London's East End.

But Long lost all sympathy for the other side when her story was not of British bombs but of German torpedoes. One such concerned a Canada-bound ship torpedoed by a German submarine. A heavy gale was blowing at the time, and only a few of the lifeboats lowered onto the dark sea were able to stay afloat. Seven children were saved, Long reported — seven out of ninety children who only a few days before had said goodbye to their parents, just such a goodbye as she had said to her own son, now safe.

Sympathy for the enemy was not Sigrid Schultz's strong point either. In 1940, while still Berlin bureau chief for the *Chicago Tribune*, Schultz took on a second job. William Shirer had interviewed her one evening on CBS, and officials at the Mutual Radio Network heard the broadcast, were impressed by her grasp of Nazi politics, and hired her at once. Later they discovered there were drawbacks. Sigrid's information was superb, but her on-air delivery was often rushed, and she was known to stumble or break into giggles. But she was always there, often with stories no one else had.

Schultz and Shirer would broadcast sequentially, and late at night: news broadcasts were always live, and timed for the EST evening news. That placed them simultaneous with the RAF raids, which the two newscasters would watch from Rundfunk Haus with distinct pleasure. After their scripts were approved, they had to cross an open courtyard and descend a flight of steps to reach the wooden shed studio. One night, with explosions providing the only light and flak falling like rain, Schultz was hit in the knee by a piece of shrapnel the size of an egg. She stanched the blood and willed herself to ignore the pain during the broadcast, but it was maddening to hear later that bombs had knocked out the transmitting system just before she went on, and her broadcast was never heard.

Not long after that night, Schultz began preparations to leave Germany. Her instructions from *Chicago Tribune* publisher Colonel Robert McCormick were clear: if ever she felt herself in real danger, she should arrange to go at once. She had brazened her way through many difficult moments in her sixteen years as bureau chief, but recently matters had taken a definitive downward turn. There was reason to believe the Nazis were aware of her passing along some information, and she knew how adept they could be at rigging accidents. As it was, people set little traps — her neighbors, for example, always trying to catch her in an air raid infraction. In *Berlin Diary* William Shirer wrote that Propaganda Minister Goebbels wanted to get rid of her "because of her independence and knowledge of things behind the scenes," and added that perhaps no one else had revealed so much of what was really happening in the Third Reich.

After she put in for an exit visa, the Nazis found various reasons to delay her departure until pressure was exerted by the American embassy. Schultz never forgot her ride out of Germany on the night train to Basel early in 1941. Officials had warned her that if any more stories similar to those by the mysterious John Dickson appeared in the *Tribune*, they would know where they had come from. As it was, she carried several stories out in her head — such as the recent decision to do away with not only the crippled and handicapped and insane but others, ill but not incurable, because for every three sick persons, one healthy one was needed for their care. Hitler considered that a waste of national strength.

Schultz traveled through Switzerland, Vichy France, and Spain. Her shrapnel wound had not entirely healed, and in Spain she contracted a severe case of typhus. It was weeks before she could go on to New York.

Sigrid's old friend Tania Long also returned to the United States on home leave early in 1941. Tania had booked passage from Portugal on the *Excambion*; predictably, *New York Times* bureau chief Ray Daniell was also taking home leave and sailing on the *Excambion*. After eleven days of bad weather the ship, coated with ice, sailed past the Statue of Liberty into New York harbor. It was an emotional moment. Hungering for her little son, concerned about her mother, Tania could turn all her attention to them, but Daniell had the less happy task of convincing his wife that he was by now hopelessly in love with someone else, and wanted a divorce.

Back in Berlin, Lael Tucker and Stephen Laird were finding German censorship increasingly onerous. At first Tucker had reported the facts straight as they were offered, with just enough innuendo that an intelligent editor could read the truth between the lines. But an alert censor had caught on, and after that she was watched, which made her feel unsafe.

Sigrid Schultz had managed to get out before anything happened to her, but several other American reporters were spending time in jail — anywhere from a few hours to months. Everyone's telephone was tapped, and the Nazis were known to keep dossiers on all of them. Lael and Steve could not help but wonder what theirs contained. That spring of 1941 they filed for exit visas, and then waited ten anxious weeks for them to arrive. Not many Americans were left by then, and the few who were felt vulnerable. But the Gestapo always came at dawn, Lael said, so whoever made it to breakfast knew that he or she had one more day anyway.

By this time the Nazi flag flew over most of Europe, and where it did not, the reason was usually that Hitler, preoccupied with Britain, had yet to send in his army. Greece, for example.

Greece became Betty Wason's story. She had left Stockholm in the spring of 1940, after CBS replaced her with Winston Burdette, the man she had recruited to read her scripts when CBS complained of her "too-feminine voice." The Balkans were her next stop, but Betty did not enjoy living among people who viewed resistance to the Axis powers as futile. Besides, Burdette showed up there too, crowding her once again. A Harvard graduate and reporter on the old *Brooklyn Daily Eagle*, Burdette would later prove to have been a member of the Communist Party and a spy for the Soviets, but nothing of this nature occurred to Wason at the time. She moved on to Istanbul, city of intrigue. There she found herself under suspicion: the British thought her a Nazi spy, the Russians a British agent. The Turks believed that at the very least she was more than a reporter and asked her to investigate an Englishman they had doubts about. Betty refused, and left for Greece.

The war in Greece was a two-act drama: the first against the Italians in the fall and winter of 1940–41, in which the Greeks prevailed, and the second against the Germans in the spring of 1941, won by Hitler. Wason covered both for CBS and as a stringer for *Newsweek*. The Italian campaign took place almost entirely in Albania, where life at the front was harsh but the soldiers gallant and helpful. When regular transportation was unavailable, they found her room in the cab of a truck. She spent the night in an empty ambulance or sitting up on a crowded train, but usually she just laid her sleeping bag on the floor with the soldiers and her fellow reporters.

As winter advanced, Wason reported Greek soldiers returning from remote areas having gone four or five days without food. She described overcrowded frontline hospitals where men lay for days in their mud-soaked uniforms, where medical supplies were minimal and

Betty Wason, Athens, 1941.
BETTY WASON PERSONAL COLLECTION.

the casualty toll was rising. The planes Britain sent were far outnumbered. Always there was the nagging reminder that however successful the Greeks might be against Mussolini, the real question came down to what Hitler planned to do.

Hitler's plans did not become clear until the winter of 1941 was almost over. By then Wason had settled into press life in Athens, marred only by CBS's renewed insistence that she find a man to read her material on the air. A young secretary at the American embassy had been drafted. Betty was not happy about this, but at least "Phil Brown" (his radio pseudonym) had no designs on her job. They broadcast daily on events such as the arrival of British and Commonwealth land forces, including Anzacs, "tough Australians with wide-brimmed hats pulled rakishly over their eyes, New Zealanders with simple, easy manners who charmed the Greek girls." They also reported Greek hopes for

113

their Olympus Line defense — mountaintop fortifications dating back, it was said, to the ancient gods.

"Phil Brown" was not the only pseudonym in Wason's life. She had become romantically involved with a British counterintelligence agent, introduced as "Norman Smith" although in fact he carried three passports, "flipping through them so I could see the pictures but nothing else," she said. She called him simply "X." Early on, perhaps when he decided she was, after all, merely a reporter, he admitted that her name was on a list given him to investigate before he left England. He pointed out her "indiscretions" — mere adventures from her viewpoint — which had aroused suspicion in British intelligence circles. For a little while "X" was part of Betty's life. Spring was upon them. As Sonia Tomara had commented the previous spring, it helps to be in love in wartime.

On the first Sunday in April 1941 air raid sirens sounded continuously. Wason turned her radio dial to London to learn that Germany and Greece were at war. All day the streets were a frenzy of activity, but with evening a hush fell over the city. Betty heard the drone of approaching planes, saw them head for the harbor at Piraeus, and felt as much as heard the thud of bombs. Rushing to one of the various censors who had to approve her copy, she passed a group of Anzacs sitting on some steps. As the bombs fell, they began to sing, first "We're Off to See the Wizard," then "Coroido Mussolini," a boastful song about how the stupid Duce found he had made a mistake when he tried to conquer the Greeks. They had no song about Hitler.

Covering the German bombing attack on the outskirts of Athens was not easy. CBS requested five broadcasts between 2 P.M. and 3 A.M. for which six separate censors must approve the scripts. The on-air timing was exact to the second, like 11:46:10 or 18:48:15, at which moments Phil Brown would begin to read Betty's script, and she would sit nervously in an adjoining room, watching the second hand on the studio clock, "worrying about seconds while the world crashed around us," she said later. Afterward, from her terrace, she saw flashes from the bombs light up the pillars of the Acropolis. Each day she consulted maps posted at the newspaper offices showing the rapid German advance; people crowded around to stare at them in disbelief. The Luftwaffe was equally effective. Wason lived near RAF headquarters, and it seemed that every day another of her new flier friends was reported missing. On a day when eighteen British planes were shot down, Betty ran across one of the pilots in a cabaret. "The Germans are boasting it will take them only two weeks to reach Athens," she told him. He conceded that was probably right.

The Olympus Line broke; there were rumors that German troops would arrive in the capital on the Orthodox Easter, but they did not. Occasionally Betty's RAF friends came to see her, bringing canned goods to share for lunch along with stories from the airfields that she could use in her broadcasts. One flier volunteered to take her to Cairo in his Gladiator, but when he saw she was considering the offer, he backed down. "You had better not depend on me," he said. "Probably none of us will get out of here alive." Betty recalled that "X" had urged her to leave earlier, "because when the end comes, it will come in a hurry," but she had ignored his warning.

The end came on Friday, April 25, 1941. The censors were dismissed. There would be a "final broadcast" on Saturday, which had to be cleared by the military governor himself, a harassed man with little time to read a Greek translation of the script of an American woman's last broadcast home. But Wason was now recognized as a "friend of Greece," and people tried to help. In the early hours of Sunday morning she and Phil Brown completed their task with no assurance that the monitors in New York would be listening. Afterward, she went home to bed.

Awakened at seven by the sound of German artillery, she turned on the radio. A voice was advising the citizens of Athens to keep off the streets and to offer no resistance. Inexplicably, the Greek national anthem — the "Hymn to Liberty" — followed. When she looked out the window, she saw the swastika flying from the Acropolis.

The denouement to Wason's private Greek tragedy lasted about another month. Whatever the information the Germans had on her, they no longer allowed her to broadcast, which mattered little since nothing she wanted to say would have passed the Nazi censors. Every afternoon she served tea in her apartment; her RAF friends were gone, but her Greek neighbors would drop by with the latest rumors. Conversation revolved around obtaining food and the rampant inflation. Even when goods were found, few could afford them. Occasionally men appeared at Betty's kitchen door with a few eggs to sell, or a little cheese, which she would guiltily purchase, knowing that already there was famine among the poor. By June 1941 dying of starvation was not uncommon.

Her own situation was becoming precarious. Back when the foreign press could safely leave, she had incautiously remained — how could a professional journalist leave in the middle of a story? But it was crucial to get out before America became involved. After that, she would become a hostage of war. Only when German correspondents in the United States received orders to depart were the few American journalists still in Athens permitted to leave. Wes Gallagher of the AP, George Weller of the *Chicago Daily News,* and Wason flew out from Athens together on a regular Lufthansa plane. In Vienna they were detained as suspected spies until their identities could be verified. Shuttled through a succession of jails, they were then taken by train to Berlin under Gestapo guard. Weller and Gallagher were released, but Betty was held another week "for reasons never divulged except that the police wanted to know more about me," she said. At last Harry Flannery of CBS intervened, and the Gestapo allowed her to go.

Back in the United States and looking for work, Wason was once again rebuffed by CBS. They wanted you when they needed you; no other conclusion was possible. She turned to print journalism, and began a book about her Greek experience. Long before *Miracle in Hellas* was published (1943), America was at war.

10

Margaret Bourke-White Shoots the Russian War

When on June 22, 1941, the Germans tore up the nonagression treaty and attacked the Soviet Union, Margaret Bourke-White was there, overjoyed at finding herself in the hot spot at the right moment. Back with *Life* after her defection of the previous year, she was there under its auspices, in company with her husband, Erskine Caldwell, reporting for *PM*. The trip had not been easy. As Lael Tucker and Stephen Laird had discovered the year before, one approached Berlin and Moscow from the east — the Far East. Bourke-White and Caldwell flew with six-hundred-plus pounds of luggage (including five cameras, twenty-two lenses, three thousand peanut flashbulbs, and four portable developing tanks) from Los Angeles to Hong Kong. From Chungking, the wartime capital of China, they advanced in little hops, with successions of bad weather days spent in towns they had not known existed. Margaret estimated that of the month-long trip from Hong Kong to Moscow, only twenty-four hours were spent in the air.

After their arrival in Moscow early in May, however, the situation improved. Caldwell was much admired in the Soviet Union for his tales of class oppression in a capitalist society, and Bourke-White's two previous visits to Russia had produced pictures that accentuated what was healthy and positive in Communism. The usual barriers — to free movement, to cameras — collapsed before them. They could travel about, and Margaret could photograph, almost at will. Even when she happened into a church during a service and started shooting what most people thought no longer existed in that atheistic society, no one stopped her. But most of her photos — of students at their books, the editors of Pravda, a soccer game — lacked drama. War is nothing if not dramatic, and the German attack provided the scoop of a lifetime — an "opium dream" of an opportunity was how Margaret put it.

Stalin, a supremely secretive man, had chosen to ignore the plethora of intelligence reports warning that Germany was about to attack. By nature he accepted nothing at face value: Britain and the United States must have their own reasons for spreading such rumors, and Hitler was determined to provoke him. Stalin refused to provide the Nazis with like excuse of provocation. The nonaggression treaty with Germany had allowed him time to build up his military prowess and train new generals, most of the old ones having been executed in his purges. Time was Hitler's gift to Stalin; even when his informants in Switzerland pinpointed the exact date of the invasion, the Soviet leader forbade his troops to deploy to battle positions.

By special permission, Bourke-White and Caldwell were visiting the resort town of Sukhum (where Sonia Tomara had grown up) when news of the outbreak of war reached them. They spent the day driving with their translator from one collective farm to another to gauge the people's reaction. Soviet citizens knew nothing of the expectation of invasion. That the German army had taken up the offensive against them left them confused and anxious. Their assumed ally had proved false; who would side with them now? About dusk the Bourke-White party reached a large citrus cooperative on a hill. Loudspeakers were mounted in an orange grove, and a Russian translation of the speech Winston Churchill had made earlier that day in Parliament blared out of the amplifier. Great Britain, avowed the prime minister, would stand with the Soviet Union against their common enemy. Margaret saw tears of joy streaming down the farmers' cheeks.

The war was a month old when, in July of 1941, the Germans first bombed Moscow. Bourke-White joined the throng in the subway, but after that she and Caldwell got a "raid pass" so they could stay above ground — at the American embassy, for example. One night she climbed out of the ambassador's study window and set up her camera on the embassy roof. As she watched, searchlights beamed upward toward the oncoming enemy planes, and bombs began to fall. Suddenly she felt a kind of contraction in the atmosphere. Grabbing her camera, she climbed back in the window, dashed across the room and lay down, at which point every window in the house fell in. Glass rained down. Margaret's helmet and clothing protected all but her fingertips, which were cut by flying splinters. Shaken, she picked her way down the grand staircase in the blackness, where she encountered Henry Cassidy of the AP and Henry Shapiro of UP venturing up from the cellar. Before she left at dawn, she posted a note pleading that no one sweep up the glass before she could return to photograph it.

Hotels were off limits during raids but, having given up on the embassy, Bourke-White resorted to various subterfuges to stay in her room. Sometimes the alarm came just as she had started processing her photos. She would dive under the bed, hoping the wardens would inspect and be off before the film, soaking in a tub of chemicals, was badly overdeveloped. Too big to crawl under the bed, Erskine would crouch behind the sofa and pull the bearskin rug over him.

Bourke-White described her nightly postinspection routine:

> I would creep out on the balcony quietly so as not to attract the attention of the soldiers on guard in Red Square below, and place two cameras shooting in opposite directions so they would cover as much of the sky as possible. Usually I set two additional cameras with telephoto lenses on the wide marble window sill. . . . But I never operated all five cameras at once. My fifth camera I transferred to the Embassy basement. The possibility of being left without a single camera grew to be an obsession, so I took care to divide the risk.

Air raids affected people in different ways, Bourke-White recalled. One got hungry, or thirsty, or sleepy. As soon as the drone of the planes passed, she would drop off, right there on the windowsill beside her cameras. Then another wave of planes approaching would set off the antiaircraft, blasting her awake again. "I would start up to see the square below dancing with fireflies as the shrapnel tinkled down on the pavement. But as soon as the sound grew softer, I would be

back in slumber on the marble ledge, my cameras, set for time expo-
sures, still recording any streaks of light that might flash through
the sky."

Life accorded her the lead story in its September 1, 1941, issue: the
first photos of the bombing of Moscow released to the West. There was
Ambassador Steinhardt attempting to work in a sea of splintered glass,
the camouflage of Red Square, a downed Nazi bomber. Only three of
the dozens, perhaps hundreds, of night bombing photographs — a
sequence she had risked her life for — appeared. Perhaps in the end
they all looked pretty much alike.

In late July of 1941 Harry Hopkins, America's Lend-Lease admin-
istrator, arrived in Moscow as President Roosevelt's special envoy.
Bourke-White knew Hopkins from a Hyde Park photo session, and she
pleaded with him to arrange for her to photograph Stalin. Stalin had
not given interviews to, nor been photographed by, the foreign press in
years, but Vice Chairman Molotov, to whom Hopkins actually carried
the request, may have felt it politic to please Mr. Lend-Lease.
Permission was granted. Margaret put on her red shoes, tied a red bow
in her hair, and went.

A small red-carpeted elevator took her up to the second floor of
the old tsarist palace in the Kremlin. Just treat Uncle Joe like you would
anyone else, she murmured, trying to calm her nerves. Ask him to sit
down and chat. But when he actually appeared, stern and unsmiling,
she said nothing at all, and set to work at once under her camera cloth.
As the only other person at hand was the young interpreter, she started
handing him flashbulbs and reflectors to hold at this side of Stalin's face
or that. "Soon Tovarisch Litvinov was changing flashbulbs with a
single twist of the wrist as though he had done it all his life," she noted
later. "This amused Stalin and he began to laugh, and then I knew I had
the expression I wanted."

Bourke-White found Stalin different from what she had expected.
Shorter, gray and tired, "like a man who has been stout but has recently
grown thinner." He was wearing boots and plain khaki clothes, without medals, and his hands, she noticed, were wrinkled. Before she left
she summoned up her best Russian to tell him that on her first visit to
the Soviet Union, nine years before, she had photographed his mother.

Stalin made no response, but the young interpreter was impressed. "His very own mother!" he kept exclaiming.

Back at the hotel it was almost time for the nightly raids, and Bourke-White felt she could not risk developing these precious films in her hotel bathroom. With her chauffeur's help, she carried her developing tanks and trays of solution down the stairs and stowed them carefully on the floor of the car. The alarm went off as she reached the American embassy, and she set up her laboratory in a basement bathroom. One by one she processed the irreplaceable negatives. She could hear the boom of the battery guns as she worked, and the long shrieks of the bombs. The embassy steward provided pins for hanging up the wet negatives, an electric fan to help them dry quicker, soup plates for the print developer, and a dust cloth of a reddish color to wrap the flashlight in so she would have more control over the developing time. By dawn a complete set of remarkable prints was ready for Harry Hopkins to carry personally back to America.

Although one would never have guessed it from official newsreels or *Pravda,* by late summer of 1941 the war was not going well for the Soviets. The Germans had taken 300,000 prisoners around Smolensk and another 100,000 at Uman in the Ukraine. Odessa, on the Black Sea, was under siege. If the correspondents knew of this, they dared not write it. When Erskine Caldwell joined the other correspondents at the Narkomindel, or foreign office, where Vice Commissar for Foreign Affairs Solomon A. Lozovsky disseminated the latest official word, retreat was never mentioned. Erskine thought Lozovsky bore a distinct resemblance to Humpty Dumpty, and was amused at his colorful turn of phrase. The Germans were never merely "the Germans" or "the enemy"; they were "the bloodthirsty barbarians" or "Hitler's gang" or "the beasts of Berlin." Lozovsky was assiduous in refuting lies put out by the Nazi propaganda office and in matching German atrocity stories with more horrible ones of his own, always with the implication that the truth was more ghastly yet.

Still, anyone out for a Sunday stroll beyond the city proper could not help but notice men and women in the fields digging trenches and putting up tank traps. Moscow was being fortified.

*   *   *

121

Early in their Russian visit Bourke-White and Caldwell had struck a bargain with the Soviet authorities: if a trip to the front was arranged, they would be included. The editors of *Life* applied pressure at their end, too. Bourke-White's photos were important to Soviet-American relations, they informed Soviet ambassador Oumansky in Washington. This was almost certainly true. The House Un-American Activities Committee had long been hunting out domestic Communists, and until recently most Americans had lumped the USSR with Germany as "the enemy." Bourke-White's photos of Soviet men and women as a hardworking, patriotic people were helping to turn that negative perception around.

In mid-September the press bureau notified Bourke-White and Caldwell just before midnight that a week's tour of the central front would leave at 6:45 the next morning. Margaret was there early in her flaming red coat, which she turned inside out once they got to the firing area. The party included four other American and five British colleagues, one of whom was Charlotte Burghes Haldane, wife of the professor who had deserted Virginia Cowles in the trenches in Spain. In her book *Shooting the Russian War*, Bourke-White describes the others in some detail but never mentions Burghes's name, and only her left hand can be seen in a group photograph at dinner. Margaret preferred to leave the impression that she herself was the only woman present.

With a Red Army colonel and press censor in charge, the party set out in M1 sedans packed with hand grenades, bundles of food, and champagne. The first evening's meal provided every kind of delicacy, hot and cold, washed down with vodka, wine, port, or brandy. Fortunately, enemy planes did not arrive until the next morning. When they did, a torrent of bombs fell on the town, smashing all the glass in the hotel and wrapping a window sash around the censor's neck. Rushing out with her camera, Bourke-White found that particles of plaster and bricks hanging in the air made shooting difficult. Still, looking up was preferable to looking down, where the contorted bodies of a family of four lying dead in a nearby doorway unnerved her. Reminding herself that this was why she was there, she concentrated on light and focus, viewing her subjects through the lens of her camera as if they were an abstract composition. She congratulated herself later on her professional approach, but when she developed the negatives, she could not bring herself to look at the results.

More enemy planes followed them en route to Yelnya later that day. The road was a sea of mud — mud would prove the leitmotif of the week — and when their driver jerked to a stop and shouted for them to run for cover, they slithered through the mud toward a meadow. "We were lying in the largest patch of fringed gentians that I had ever seen," Bourke-White wrote later. "The gentians were at a level with my eyes, and over this blue border I watched three great curtains of mud rise into the air and hang there shimmering." She began picking flowers as an exercise in calm. The cars were covered with mire but undamaged, and soldiers tied boughs of trees to them. This leafy camouflage "made the war look like a back to nature movement," she quipped, "which in a way it is."

Smolensk, directly ahead, was still in German hands. They drove parallel to the front, and Bourke-White marveled at how, on approaching what looked to be an uninhabited little wood, they found that it lodged a whole community with telephones, dug-in tanks, and batteries. At field headquarters, while trying to ignore the continuous barrage of Russian guns directed over their heads, they sat down to a meal of quail, caviar, and champagne. During another picnic, equally dodgy, an accordionist appeared, and Margaret was pressed to teach the soldiers the latest American dance steps, despite her muddy slacks and earth-caked shoes.

Sleeping was a problem. The party lodged in tents or under thatched roofs, whatever served as shelter against the constant rain. One night they all slept together on the floor of a cottage, lying in ordered rows, their feet against the heads of the men below them. Erskine put Margaret's sleeping bag against a wall with his own by her side. She woke up once to see a sentry, bayonet in hand, guarding them by candlelight. In the mornings she got up early and slipped out to photograph whatever she could find in the grayness. The soldiers' faces under their dripping raincapes were varied — Ukrainians, Kazaks, Uzbeks, Siberians, Mongols. Using flashbulbs to augment the weak light, she would continue shooting until someone called out that it was time to get going, and admonished her not to hold them up *again*. Her sense of time was at odds with theirs. In the car Caldwell would produce some welcome tidbit salvaged from breakfast. Once, to her delight, it was the long drumstick of a goose.

At last they reached Yelnya. The armies had crossed and recrossed it in furious conflict; fifty thousand Germans were said to have died and been shoveled into their own trenches. The Russian loss was not divulged. To Bourke-White the battlefield called to mind the end of the world — a wasteland "as far as the eye could reach, channeled with trenches and littered with the remains of war . . . a torn sleeve, the piece of a boot, a tattered raincoat, a broken sword." With the brick chimneys often the only segments of houses left standing, she thought Yelnya had a skeletal aspect, but she noticed that its inhabitants were already drifting back, hoping to live there somehow, at least until the town should once again be lost to the enemy.

On the final day Bourke-White was preparing to photograph when she was informed that the cars were about to head back to Moscow. The rain had let up, and she saw that at last she could shoot a roll that had a chance of turning out well. How could she leave? In time she would learn to control her emotions, but that afternoon — after having slogged through mud for a week and seen little but rain on the other side of her lens — tears won out. They worked in her favor. A sympathetic Soviet colonel sent her colleagues off for one last champagne supper and commandeered some soldiers to help her.

Bourke-White and Caldwell set out for home a week later. They traveled in a British convoy across the Arctic Ocean and south to Britain, and then flew by clipper ship to New York. Margaret's photos from the Yelnya front would be her final scoop of the Russian war. Two weeks after that, with the Germans closing in on three sides, Stalin ordered that Moscow be evacuated.

11

Treading Water, Marking Time

The fall of 1941 was a time of waiting for an apparent inevitable. The war was two years old. Britain had suffered terrible bombing for more than a year, but except for the Lend-Lease program, America remained a silent partner. There were times when American reporters felt an unspoken reproach in the British attitude, and a consequent guilty response in their own. Correspondents on home leave found it difficult to reconcile their country's continued disinclination to enter the war with the political realities of Europe as they experienced them.

The sudden switch of the Soviet Union from "their side" to "our side" meant a new ally in need of American war materiel. Roosevelt's pledge of aid to the Soviets was hotly debated. From the conservative-isolationist point of view, the new enmity between Stalin's Russia and Hitler's Germany should be permitted to run its course, meaning if they wiped each other out, all the better. American military commanders worried about diverting equipment from U.S. troops, still inadequately supplied. Only gradually were Americans persuaded of the advantages of the trade-off: if our planes and guns allowed Russia to stave off the German army for even a few months, that army would be just that much weaker if our own soldiers were called upon to face it. And that "if" was beginning to translate as "when." By the fall of 1941, most Americans were reconciled to the near eventuality of war in their lives.

Dorothy Thompson was doing her best to promote that attitude. Her syndicated column, "On the Record," carried by more than two hundred newspapers across the country, had tremendous impact. Three times a week she hammered away at the necessity for America to enter the war. She regularly took her message in person to the White House, or telephoned, or smuggled notes to FDR in the pockets of foreign dignitaries whom she just happened to entertain first. Extravagantly pro-British, she compared the May bombing of Westminster Abbey, the House of Commons, and the British Museum to the destruction of civilization itself, and concluded in sonorous terms: "The Abbey stands, the Museum lives, the Commons meet. Because the human will cannot be broken."

That fall she crossed the Atlantic to satisfy herself as to the condition of her beloved ancestral land. The editor of the *Sunday Chronicle*, which carried her column, reserved three suites at the Savoy for a month and hired a coterie of secretaries to answer phones and mail and help arrange her schedule. This last was not easy. Besides obligatory

Dorothy Thompson consulting with (left) Czech foreign minister
Jan Masaryk and (right) Czech army general Miroslav, England, 1941.
UPI/CORBIS-BETTMANN.

visits to bomb shelters, munitions factories, hospitals, orphanages, and schools, Thompson addressed the House of Commons and "received" the leaders of the current governments-in-exile. At Plymouth she lunched with naval commanders whom, with American candor, she challenged to explain their badly botched campaign in the Mediterranean. Perhaps she asked the same of Churchill during the weekend she spent at Chequers; that conversation remained private, as did her tête-à-tête with the king and queen over tea at Buckingham Palace. On other days she joined Nancy Astor for lunch, J. B. Priestley for cocktails, H. G. Wells for dinner, and took in the cinema with Anthony Eden. Her departure was noted in the Court Circular. She was perhaps the closest America came to royalty.

Thompson's busy schedule left little time for fretting over the final breakup of her marriage to Sinclair Lewis. In a recent letter he had noted that they had not lived together for more than four years, and spoke of himself as "an unwilling ex-associate" held "in bondage." Dorothy was at first unmoved, but that fall she yielded and filed for divorce on grounds of "willful desertion." As she had done fifteen years before when Josef Bard left her, she immersed herself in work. "Good old routine," she had written then, "good old head that functions automatically at the sight of a newspaper." She was forty-seven and that head was crowned in white, but the newspaper as the driving force of her life went unchanged.

No doubt American correspondents breathed a sigh of relief when Thompson sailed for home and they had London to themselves again. They were not a large contingent, although recently increased by two when Lael Tucker and Steve Laird arrived from Berlin. Lael and Steve were surprised to find themselves much in demand socially. Everyone was curious to hear what it was really like in Berlin. They "sang for their supper," as Lael put it — and she had a way with a story. She might tell of a Nazi rally in which Hitler marched down the aisle repeating "Heil Hitler" every few steps, followed by Goering, "so fat he had to swing one leg around the other," Goebbels limping along, and the catatonic Hess. Or how in both Hamburg and Berlin the Germans had built a fake city out on the lake, with little streets and houses and lights, to decoy the bombers away from the city itself. Or how when she was in

Berlin she had the feeling that "the Germans did not feel in their hearts that they were going to win the war. They were always saying, 'We're going to win. We've won everywhere. How can we be defeated?'" But there was another side. "We'll win and win and win until we lose," a taxi driver she once encountered said.

What most impressed Tucker about London that fall was the breakdown of social conventions. She described sharing a compartment on a train with two white-gloved ladies who had never met before, and who were talking to each other about how extraordinary it was that they were talking to each other. Lael was also fascinated by people's attachment to their neighborhood air raid shelters in the Underground. Most shelters now offered bunks and artificial ventilation, and morning tea was served. But with fewer bombers over London after the Germans invaded Russia, there was talk of closing some of the shelters. The question of where to move if one's shelter closed was a serious one, Lael said.

Mary Welsh did a piece for *Life* that fall on British conscription of women. They might be drafted for anything from winding the long gelatinous strands of dangerous explosives to pitching hay and milking cows. The thrust of the article was the different types of young women in each of the separate services, and it was uncharitable at best. For example, the ATS (Army) attracted "hearty young women with chins" who wore khaki and slapped their thighs when they laughed; the Wrens (Navy) uniform was more flattering; the Waafs (Air Force) were the most datable. The Woman's Land Army consisted of vicars' daughters, little London manicurists, and Woolworth clerks — meaning, naive and dull. There was hardly a mention of the important jobs they were doing. Of course, it is possible that Mary included such particulars and that, considered boring by the New York rewrite staff, they were cut. Or perhaps she was not at her best that week. She appears not to have welcomed the addition of another, and very attractive, American woman to the Time Inc. London office. Mary was the only person Lael met who was not friendly.

There were those who thought Helen Kirkpatrick was not very friendly, or in any event was a loner who did not need female friends. On the contrary, Helen said, it was just that her social life revolved around her work. Everyone else in the *Chicago Daily News* office was male, and almost everyone she met in the course of her job was, too. This last was borne out by the diary she began to keep that fall, into which went observations that would have been censored out of her dispatches. The entries, reviewing the events of her day or analyzing the immediate state of affairs, had everything to do with her head and nothing with her heart. Her notations for the months of October and November 1941 indicated that, during her waking hours anyway, she was seldom alone. October 31, for example: that afternoon she met first with the British minister of economic warfare, just back from Washington, and later with the first lord of the admiralty. News of the sinking of the American destroyer *Reuben James* had just come in; it had been convoying British ships, she reported, and the admiralty now expected the Germans to go all out against the United States on the high seas. That evening she gave a dinner for Alexander Woollcott, who was in town; other guests included a married couple and half a dozen single men. Street musicians came in to play, and much brandy was consumed. It was a not untypical day in her life that fall.

In fact, Kirkpatrick's contacts made her enormously useful to the *News*. Unlike Virginia Cowles', Helen's roots were not upper-class; she would never be a familiar at Chequers, nor godmother to Churchill's grandson and namesake, as Cowles was, but her style and intelligence endeared her to many in the English aristocracy. Nancy and Waldorf Astor's Cliveden and especially Ronald and Nancy Tree's Ditchley were regular haunts of hers. The bombing of Pearl Harbor might have been less startling if she could have sent off to the *News* what she jotted down in her diary for November 29–30: "Went to Ditchley for the weekend. Ronnie who lunched at Chequers with the Churchills says that FDR talked to the PM Friday night and said war with Japan within a week."

When the imminence of the United States' entry into the war came up, the conversation always turned to the question of which Axis power was most likely to trigger the event. The British assumed Germany, Americans thought as often of Japan, and then there was Italy. Still in Rome, Eleanor and Reynolds Packard worried about the future. When the United States froze the funds of all the Axis countries, Mussolini did the same to American funds in Italy. In consequence, the news bureaus had no cash for their own salaries or to pay Italian members of their staff. Favorite restaurants and neighborhood shops allowed the Packards to run up tabs, but when permission was asked to withdraw money to pay the Italians who worked for UP, the government was unsympathetic. Good Fascists should not be working for American firms, they said.

By the fall of 1941 only a skeleton crew of journalists remained in Rome. The embassy promised that in the event of war they could leave on the diplomatic train. All very well, Eleanor remarked, *if* the Italians allowed it. In the meantime, Japanese nationals in Rome were being mysteriously overfriendly to those few American reporters left. On December 4 Japanese counselor Ando honored Japanese and American correspondents with a lavish cocktail party and buffet supper at his new home. Eleanor and Reynolds attended, unaware that similar parties were taking place wherever both Americans and Japanese nationals still resided, which was generally limited to Bern, Berlin, Lisbon, and Madrid. There was an abundance of food and liquor, more than Eleanor had seen in Rome for some time, and at the evening's climax Ando raised a glass of straight Scotch and toasted "the continued friendship of America and Japan."

12

China Hands

Europe was not the only promised land for a young American woman with journalistic ambitions in the 1920s and 1930s. There was also the Far East, specifically China — a vast but not unfriendly country, already home to thousands of American businessmen and missionaries and their families. They and their British counterparts made up the readership for English-language papers and journals often in need of staff, while U.S.-based newspapers and wire services hired stringers on a regular basis.

A small number of American women seized the chance. In the early 1920s, just out of her teens, Edna Lee Booker set out with a chaperone for China and nailed a job with INS and *China Press*. Before long she was striking out for the interior to interview powerful warlords, or reporting a civil war, or dodging shell fire to keep an appointment with Dr. Sun Yat-sen, concealed in a flotilla of gunboats on the Pearl River. By the late 1930s, married with children and writing for *Cosmopolitan*, she found herself scrambling off trains and into rice paddies to escape Japanese bombs.

Agnes Smedley, blue-eyed daughter of a part-Cherokee tenant farmer, was an established writer and journalist at the time of her arrival in China; she was also a passionate radical, friend of Emma Goldman and Madame Sun Yat-sen. Reporting first for the *Frankfurter Zeitung*, she shuttled between Shanghai and Hankow and spent seven months in Yenan, Mao Tse-tung's Red Army headquarters, where she taught Mao and Chou En-lai to dance. After the war with Japan began in earnest, she divided her time between canvassing for medical supplies and composing strongly partisan pieces for the *Manchester Guardian* and the *Nation* from the headquarters of Mao's New Fourth Army.

With her youth, style, and movie starlet looks, Helen Foster was Agnes Smedley's polar opposite. She arrived in Shanghai in 1931 with four evening gowns in her steamer trunk, and golf bag, tennis racket, and typewriter in tow. A stringer for the Scripps-Canfield syndicate, she prevailed upon seasoned reporter Edgar Snow to help her get a press pass; in time, she married him. Foster reported from Peking, Sian, and Yenan for the London *Daily Herald*, the *New York Sun*, and the *Nation*. In Yenan she crossed paths with Smedley, who thought her a political lightweight. Approaches differ. While in Yenan, Foster took down thirty-four oral histories of the Long March as told her by women survivors.

Then there was Peggy Hull, first accredited woman war correspondent following her World War I reporting in France. Hull came out to Shanghai accompanied by INS correspondent Irene Corbally Kuhn. They plus Booker, Smedley, and Foster were all in Shanghai when the Japanese first attacked in 1932. They covered the invasion of that port, the bombing of Chapei (the Chinese section of the city), and the subsequent "presence" of the Japanese military in China, as well as Chiang Kai-shek's policy of appeasement with Japan and his ruthless crusade against the Communists. All except Hull were still there to report the renewal of hostilities in 1937, which marked the start of the active Sino-Japanese War. Anna Louise Strong's arrival in 1938 could be said to complete the picture.

Well, almost. There was also the young and beautiful Emily Hahn, less a reporter than an adventuring writer, who after a year in the Belgian Congo went to China to visit a friend and stayed for nine years. During that time she worked on the *North-China Daily News*, for the literary magazine *T'ien Hsia*, and as an official correspondent for the *New Yorker* under the "Reporter at Large" designation. She lived her life as she chose. In Shanghai that meant a liaison with a married Chinese artist, and in Hong Kong with a British officer, also married. Her child with the latter was born just before Pearl Harbor and the fall of Hong Kong to the Japanese. With no way to send out stories, Emily concentrated on keeping her daughter and herself alive. In 1943 they were repatriated to America.

These were the early "China hands," the women who knew a China that ceased to exist after the Japanese wreaked general havoc on Peking, Nanking, Canton, Hankow, and a great expanse of the countryside.

Except for Emily Hahn, this little cadre of women journalists had all left China by the winter of 1941 when Carl and Shelley Smith Mydans flew from Hong Kong to Chungking. They flew with the China National Aviation Company (CNAC) over Japanese lines in the black of night, the only two passengers aboard the tiny plane, burlap bags of freshly printed Chinese dollars — soldiers' pay — strapped to the empty seats. The pilot navigated the Yangtze gorge to land on a sandbar in the middle of the river; except at flood tide, everyone arrived in Chungking in this manner. From the bottom of the gorge, one was transported by sedan chair up the almost vertical cliffside to the top. "Those poor men," Shelley lamented, recalling the coolies' leathered shoulders. "Never again."

Shelley Smith Mydans, *Life*

What one first noticed on meeting Shelley Smith was her natural grace. Dance had been part of her curriculum at Stanford, following a childhood on the Palo Alto campus where her father was head of the journalism department. After a brief career in West Coast theater, she took off for New York to work for the *Literary Digest* and then for *Life*, where she met Carl Mydans, a gifted, hardworking staff photographer. Mydans liked to tell how, emerging late one night from the darkroom, he found a beautiful young woman still in the "bull pen," her desk piled with sheets of paper scribbled with numbers. Her explanation, that she was balancing the budget for that week's lead story on federal expenditures, Carl found intriguing, and he liked the "exciting tones to her voice," as well. He was thirty, she twenty-two. Six months later they were married.

In September 1939, equipped with gas masks left over from the last war and money belts stuffed with a thousand dollars in small bills, *Life*'s first roving correspondent team flew to Europe to report defense

Shelley Mydans interviewing Indian troops, Singapore, 1941.
CARL MYDANS/*LIFE* MAGAZINE. © TIME INC.

preparations. The China assignment came six months later. Gaining access to the provisional capital of Chungking was not easy, but reporters for Time Inc. had little problem. Henry Luce was a close ally of Chiang Kai-shek, head of both the Nationalist army and the Kuomintang, the governing body of China. In China the phrase "Time-Life" was magic. One dropped it casually and closed doors opened, bumpy ways were made smooth — or as smooth as was possible in craggy, beleaguered Chungking.

Shelley Smith, starry-eyed at finding herself in China at all, was much taken with this medieval walled city of layered bamboo and mud structures poised high on a rocky promontory where the Chialing and Yangtze rivers meet. The wall dated back five hundred years to the Ming dynasty, and beyond it, as far as she could see, were rice paddies. Where once there had been no easy access, a motor road lined with stores and government offices and lit by electricity ringed the upper city, from where alleys dropped into the rank and congested poorer areas, lighted only by oil lamps. Shelley and Carl found walking the alleys a fascinating pastime. As a war capital Chungking's great advantage was its relative impregnability atop the soft sandstone hills from which caves had been carved for bomb shelters. Generalissimo and Madame Chiang Kai-shek lived there; so with less visibility did Chou En-lai, Mao Tse-tung's eyes and ears to official China.

Smith and Mydans moved at once into the government press hostel, a rough complex of two or three sizable buildings that included a stone one used for offices and two lines of cubicles constructed of mud and straw that when bombed could be easily rebuilt. Bamboo palings skirted with banana trees fenced it round. Shelley and Carl were allotted a single cubicle with a bed, table, and chair; floor and walls were of mud and wattle, the roof was thatch, the window without glass. Allergic to the charcoal used for heating, Shelley developed a rash, which she treated with a heavy white cream. Back home this might have caused her distress, but in China, a culture permeated by ghosts, her chalk-white face met with favorable regard.

Most of the occupants of the press hostel worked for Time Inc. Theodore H. "Teddy" White had come straight out of Harvard two years before to supervise the dissemination of news (i.e., propaganda) at the ministry of information (i.e., propaganda). Time Inc. noted his workaholic habits with approval and wooed him to their own staff; his job was to provide background information called "mailers" for stories to be written in New York. He joined Robert P. "Pepper" Martin, a UP reporter before *Time* took him on. Next to Martin's great size and physical prowess, Teddy looked like a gnome. Both men had been present at the saturation bombing of Chungking in May 1939 when thousands of civilians perished, and were considered "old hands," as was Tillman Durdin of the *New York Times*. Till and his young wife Peggy, born in China the daughter of missionaries, lived more comfortably in a mission. Peggy spoke fluent Mandarin and had taught school in Shanghai; she would later join the staff of *Life*.

The press hostel was also home to Jack Belden, an ex–wire services reporter, and Melville Jacoby, a China scholar and classmate of Shelley Smith's at Stanford, both of whom were, or were about to be, hired by Luce. The only permanent inhabitant of the press hostel not with Time Inc. was INS stringer Betty Graham. An attractive blonde with a wide smile, Graham had her own little hut in the hostel complex, built for her by Hollington Tong, vice minister of communication, out of deference to her unmarried state. She was what Emily Hahn called a "hardy Chungking perennial," meaning that she had worked for various organizations. Betty was in love with handsome Mel Jacoby, whom she followed about, much as she was trailed by an even more besotted Belden. Both she and Jack would be disappointed in love, but not in their profession; she would soon score a scoop documenting the Japanese use of poison gas, and Belden would become famous as General Stilwell's right-hand man and chronicler.

Not all American correspondents in China were in Chungking. Many preferred to remain in Shanghai, where life bore a semblance of normality, rather than subject themselves to Kuomintang suppression and Japanese bombs. The year 1941 was the third year of severe raids on the capital. After the horrific bombing of 1939, cavernous shelters had been dug out of the sandstone hills, and an elaborate warning system devised. Smith and Mydans found it uniquely Chinese. They watched in fascination as, at a main intersection, a soldier climbed onto a box in front of a large billboard painted with a map of western China. Spokes angled out from its center, Chungking, like the hands of a clock. Attached to the tip of the longest spoke were three miniature wooden airplanes which the soldier slid along toward Chungking, evoking a murmur from the citizenry, who then turned to stare at an empty flagstaff topping a building nearby. The first large red lantern hoisted up the staff served as a warning; the second was the signal for the populace to head for the tunnels.

The hours wasted waiting out raids underground did not add to the charm of the Chungking assignment. Nor did the damp, mosquito-infested climate, perennial murky gloom, rudimentary living conditions, scarcity of foods one dared eat, and limited number of fellow reporters, often depressed. "But Carl and I were young," Shelley recalled later. "We could view it as an adventure, even enjoy it, because we were young."

The adventure of China was exactly what Martha Gellhorn thought she wanted. Since her trips to Czechoslovakia in 1938, she had returned briefly to Europe late in 1939 to report the Soviet invasion of Finland. Otherwise she had been either in Cuba or in Idaho with Hemingway, whom she married in November 1940. It was soon after her wedding (if vows before a justice of the peace could be called a wedding) that she started angling for the trip to China. Her private and professional aspirations were focused there, although she later admitted that the Orient she hankered after was the one pictured in books from her childhood, not the reality. The hard part was persuading her new husband to accompany her. Scribner's had recently published *For Whom the Bell Tolls*, taken in part from their shared experience in Spain, and Ernest would have preferred a relaxing winter and spring in Cuba, but humoring his lovely new wife had its own priority. Her assignment from *Collier's* was to "report on the Chinese army in action and defenses against future Japanese attack around the South China Sea." What that meant in practical terms she had little idea.

In Gellhorn's mordant but highly amusing *Travels with Myself and Another*, she refers to Hemingway as "U.C." for Unwilling Companion, which he was throughout the six weeks or so (March–April 1941) of their visit. He settled down comfortably in Hong Kong, however, and acquired a coterie of blustery friends from local cops to retired thugs with whom he ate, drank, and told stories. These were not Martha's kind of people, and she was glad to escape to her first assignment: a story on the CNAC passenger-mail flight from Hong Kong via Chungking and Kunming to Lashio where the Burma Road began, and back again. From her vantage point in the seat nearest the pilot (there was no copilot), she experienced a baptism of the elements. On the first lap they hit a hailstorm; the windshield was a sheet of frost, elevator drafts lifted and dropped the plane. She thought she would perish from cold. On the next lap, the night flight to Lashio, downdrafts caused the plane to plunge thousands of feet in a few seconds, forcing them to fly at higher altitudes, where it was colder yet. Martha found the rest house at Lashio — a wooden shack with iron cots and a shower — "heaven itself," and was gratified that they traveled the Burma Road by daylight. "Beautiful hopeless country, jagged mountain after mountain and a brown ribbon of road," she wrote.

What she liked best, without doubt, was the camaraderie with the flight crew: squatting on the landing strip for a lunch of rice and tea, attacking a dinner of fried eggs and warm beer in a small Greek café in Kunming. Gellhorn adored adventure, and she liked associating with men who showed purpose and took chances. "I doubt if there were ever any other pilots like those," she wrote in her *Collier's* story. "They were immensely proud of their fantastic little airline. And I think they were in love with their kind of flying, the man and the machine off on their own against the Japs and the weather and the mountains and the landing fields." She seemed half in love herself, with the pilots, with their life.

By her return to Hong Kong a few days later, the CNAC junket had begun to contrast sharply with her husband's sedentary existence. To report a war was to go to the front, she reminded him, recalling Spain. Hemingway acquiesced. But this was *not* Spain, he reminded her, and this front was not a short walk from their hotel. The Canton front was closest; they would go there.

In Namyung they picked up two Chinese escorts — Mr. Ho, reasonably competent, and the good-natured Mr. Ma, who did his best to keep his charges happy in an unhappy situation. It was cold, it rained, there were mosquitoes. Gellhorn tried for objectivity in coverage, but the dark humor of their situation kept sneaking into her account. In an old Chevrolet they jolted along roads that could not be discerned as roads for all the boulders and rivers of mud. They boarded a rusty Chris-Craft towing a sampan on the North River and took roost among the coiled ropes on the sloping roof. "A line of men, women and children, like dark, straining statues, pulled the tow-rope of their sampan and slowly moved the heavy barge forward," Martha wrote. "They chanted to time their effort, and the sound came as a rising and falling wail across the water." With evening the mountains were silhouetted blue-black against the greenish sky. Still on their perch, they dined on rice and tea, with a little whiskey in hot water from their thermos for dessert. Hemingway fell asleep. Only Martha lay awake to count the times they ran into sandbars (five) before the tow rope wrapped itself around the propeller and they pulled into a mosquito-infested sampan village to wait out the night.

Gellhorn's introduction to "the Chinese army in action" came the next day in the form of a platoon of wet soldiers waiting for them on a mud bank. Stable coolies in large conical straw rainhats held the bridles of seven undersized horses and a normal one (for Hemingway), men and animals all shivering from the cold. The ground was "a mixture of grease and glue," Martha noted. "The rain came down in

Martha Gellhorn and Ernest Hemingway
on their way to the Canton front, China, spring 1941.
JOHN F. KENNEDY LIBRARY.

sheets. . . . The procession jolted forward in sodden silence. We were starting for the Canton front."

The problems intrinsic to covering this war were each day more evident to them both. For one, China was huge, which they had known but not appreciated; when eventually they reached the Seventh War Zone, it turned out to be the size of Belgium. The weather was consistently awful. Wet through, huddled beside a coal brazier, Gellhorn would take notes while with great enthusiasm a general regaled Hemingway with the details of his division. The war itself was stagnant. Although there had been thirty clashes on that front and two major Japanese offensives, the Chinese line had stayed the same. Each regiment remained in place and built up a life around the training ground and athletic field, classrooms and barracks.

Another problem was lack of sleep. Many nights were spent on plank beds, shivering in the wet clothes they had ridden in that day, listening to the hacking, phlegmy cough of their escorts. Tuberculosis was rampant in the Chinese army. Martha always remembered the single day it did not rain and they walked in the clear cold up and down gentle hills where peasants plowed their muddy fields behind water buffalo. But the people they passed were "stony-faced, exhausted by life, and also marred and scarred by unimaginable diseases." This was the reality of rural China. "Soldiers always look like sad orphanage children," she jotted down in her notebook. They were inadequately clothed, housed, and fed, like the peasants they lived among.

At last they reached the front, "to the extent that the Chinese had their machine guns on these hills and, three kilometres away, the Japanese had the same," Gellhorn reported. Special maneuvers were scheduled. She and Hemingway watched through field glasses as Chinese troops simulated an attack on the Japanese positions. That night there was entertainment. Seated on chairs beside the general, surrounded by eighteen hundred squatting troops, they watched a series of plays presented by the Political Department. It was buffoonery pure and simple, as inauthentic as the morning's pretend attack, but the audience laughed and applauded, and the honored guests found themselves laughing, too.

On the following day they turned the horses back toward the river. Gellhorn rode, she recalled, in the rain, with her head down like her horse, both of them nodding wearily. At their last stop, the 189th Division headquarters, banners of welcome awaited them along with a grand farewell lunch of local delicacies. Hemingway was called upon to respond to many toasts with yellow rice wine. No reporters — perhaps no other foreigners — had ever come there, Martha mused, and she could understand why. The front was simply a place where two armies lived closest to each other. They built their barracks and schools and trained their troops. The soldiers on both sides were completely cut off: there were no furloughs home and hardly any mail, which could not matter, since how would illiterate peasant parents write a letter, or their illiterate sons read it, anyway?

Late that spring of 1941 another American journalist arrived in Chungking. Annalee Whitmore traveled from California to Hong Kong by freighter, and then caught the usual CNAC night flight over the Japanese lines. Nothing was ever quite "usual" with Annalee, however. As a child she had watched her father build and then race planes; she described these private spins to the CNAC pilot, and he (who had flown the Prince of Wales around the world) invited her to copilot, which had the advantage of putting her next to him rather than back with the money bundles. Whitmore was dark-haired and pretty, with a quick mind and a stimulating presence; no doubt the pilot found her at least as exotic as the prince. In an attempt to prolong the encounter, he made an unscheduled landing at Kweilin to show her the famous pointed hills. It was dark, the little plane got stuck in the mud and had to be dug out next morning, but eventually it sailed back into the sky and then jolted down again onto the little sandbar landing strip in the middle of the Yangtze.

Annalee Whitmore Jacoby, *Liberty*, *Time-Life*

By the time Annalee Whitmore, another Stanford graduate, came out to China, she was already a flourishing screenwriter, the youngest in Hollywood, cowriter of the hit movie *Babes in Arms* (Judy Garland, Mickey Rooney). MGM rewarded her with a seven-year contract, and a golden career seemed in the offing. But Whitmore had not been editor of the *Stanford Daily* for nothing, and she found the prospect of seven years of Hollywood fluff when the real world was falling apart unendurable. What she really wanted was to go to China. The *Reader's Digest* agreed to send her, but she failed to get the requisite permit from the State Department. Then word surfaced that Mel Jacoby was back from Chungking. Annalee remembered Jacoby from college — nice-looking but standoffish was what she recalled. Perhaps he would know how permits were obtained.

At the bar on Wilshire Boulevard where they arranged to meet, Whitmore at once recognized that this elegant, assured, darkly handsome man was no longer the quiet student of her memory. Jacoby was not only attractive and, as it happened, wealthy, he was also knowledgeable about permits: it was all a matter of providing a solid reason for going to China. Henry Luce was looking for a Chungking representative for United China Relief, Jacoby said, and John Hersey, whom

Annalee Whitmore with Melville Jacoby, the Philippines, 1941.
WALLACE KIRKLAND/*LIFE* MAGAZINE. © TIME INC.

he knew from Chungking, had been sent west to find the best person
for the job. Mel arranged for Annalee to have dinner with Hersey, after
which, as Mel predicted, Hersey recommended that Luce hire her for
United China Relief. Whitmore had her entrée to China, and to her
delight Jacoby was about to return there himself. To be where Mel was
had assumed high priority with her. She saw him off on the Pan Am
Clipper; coincidentally, or perhaps not, Henry and Clare Boothe Luce
were also aboard. Somewhere between San Francisco and Hong Kong,
Jacoby was hired as a correspondent for *Time*.

In Chungking, Whitmore worked directly for Madame Chiang
Kai-shek, who fortunately for the new representative of United China
Relief had gone to Wellesley and spoke perfect English. She was a dom-
inating presence. It amused Annalee that Madame felt herself above the
law, even laws she herself had devised, but she was no more arrogant

than the movie moguls Annalee had known in Hollywood, and she grew rather fond of her. Perhaps because Betty Graham, still pining after Mel, lived at the press hostel, Annalee did not move there. Instead she settled into the seedy but romantic Chialing House, and it was there that she and Mel had dinner every evening — until she moved into the mission compound, which had a better chef, and they dined there.

Whitmore was conscientious about her work with United China Relief, but all her friends in Chungking were journalists, and she may have hoped that in time Luce would move her, too, into the Time Inc. fold. She was careful to give Madame Chiang no cause to complain.

Reporters from magazines with wide American readership always visited Generalissimo and Madame Chiang Kai-shek. Shelley Smith and Carl Mydans went, so that Mydans could photograph them for *Life*. "Being a radical young person, I had her down as a dragon lady," Shelley said later. "And him likewise. She was beautiful, immobile in her face, but they came across, in Carl's pictures, too, as very hard people."

Martha Gellhorn's reaction was much the same after she and Hemingway were invited there for lunch. Madame was still beautiful, she recalled, charming to Ernest and civil to her. The general, straight-backed and impeccable in his plain gray uniform, talked of articles that appeared in the Western press to the effect that the Communists' armies were necessary to the war against Japan. They were not, Chiang insisted. Gellhorn was not taken in. She felt instinctively that "these two stony rulers cared nothing for the miserable hordes of their people." Never one to mince words, Martha asked Madame outright why China did not take care of the lepers, forcing them to roam the streets and beg. Furious, Madame declared that the Chinese, humane and civilized unlike westerners, would never lock their lepers away from other mortals. Ernest, Martha recalled, acted with perfect decorum, saving his laughter until they had departed.

Both couples, however, were impressed by Chou En-lai. Smith and Mydans went to the tiny room where he sat writing reports in brush stroke for Mao in Yenan. Although Carl's photographs depicted Chou in a frayed suit and unshaven, Shelley recalled him as very good-looking. Perhaps it was his clear eyes under heavy arched brows. Gellhorn also recalled his "brilliant amused eyes," and that they laughed at the same jokes. For the first time she felt at home with a Chinese. They knew little about him at the time, she said, but "he sat in his bare little room, in his nondescript clothes, and he *was* somebody . . . the one really good man we'd met in China."

At the request of the home office, Mydans, Smith, and Mel Jacoby visited the Yellow River front. It was a saga they never forgot. They planned to fly to Lanchow, travel by bus over the Six Dishes Mountains to Sian, then go on to the front by horseback. On paper it sounded reasonable, even fun. Martha Gellhorn would have assured them it would be neither.

A large crowd of Chinese also waited for the bus that bright morning in Lanchow. They huddled protectively around their collection of bedrolls, basketed chickens and ducks, and small valises. When at last the bus — a high, square, wooden affair — drove up, they poured inside. Those who could not enter fast enough by the door climbed through the windows, pulling their belongings after them and occupying every inch of space. The Americans watched helplessly. Fortunately, a plump young man in the uniform of a minor government official arrived, informed them (in English) that he had been sent to see them safely to Sian, and explained the situation (in Chinese) to the other passengers. Room was made for them.

The bus soon reached its top speed of fifteen miles an hour, and streams of fine dust sifted upward through cracks in the floorboard, covering everyone with a kind of cornmeal yellow. At one point the gasoline tank dropped off, and the other passengers, nodding deferentially, indicated that Mydans and Jacoby were the ones to fix it. Later it was also up to them to knock out the spark plugs, clean them, and pound them in again. As the day wore on, other repairs were made, and the next day was the same. Only when they had to produce their identity cards at a government checkpoint did their fellow passengers learn they were journalists — not, as their escort had indicated, American fliers come to fight for China, and a nurse.

Shelley remembered the whole expedition as horrendous. There was tea of a muddy variety, but hardly anything to eat. At a village headquarters they mounted little Mongolian ponies and trotted along behind an artillery regiment. She could not keep up, fell off her pony, and hit her head. When she came to, an old woman was standing over her. The crone led her to a nearby cave and wiped her forehead with a damp and filthy rag, meant as a kindness. At last the others came in search of her. At the Tungkwan city gate, they dismounted and followed a shoulder-high communications trench to an outpost where the Yellow River makes a hairpin bend. There they gazed across at the Japanese, who obligingly lobbed a few shells across.

Although she did not know what to expect, Shelley had thought there would be *some* kind of action. There was none.

Martha Gellhorn and Ernest Hemingway left China in April 1941. Martha was glad to leave, and not only because she had developed "China rot" on her hands and had to smear on a vile-smelling ointment and wear big cotton gloves. China had quite simply overwhelmed her. She admitted that Hemingway had been more game, even gallant, considering that it was she who had dragged him there — "nagged him into this horror journey" was how she put it. She had matched him in Spain, where courage and endurance were the standards of measurement. But China was a whole different world. So many people, so little food, so much disease. Her U.C. "saw the Chinese as people, while I saw them as a mass of downtrodden valiant doomed humanity," she said.

They parted in Rangoon, where even Martha, who loved heat, suffered and Ernest was like a "beached whale." He flew home, but she had two more stories to do — Batavia in the Dutch East Indies, and Singapore. Carl and Shelley recalled seeing her there. The city was highly civilized, and Martha blossomed. Her hands healed, her hair was clean and shiny blond again. She dined out in lovely homes where "the legendary silent-footed Oriental" waited table and fresh caviar was a staple. Two Scots regiments were stationed at Changi, and you could drive out to hear retreat on the bagpipes at sundown before cocktails at the officers' mess, and later "watch the moon rise over Singapore harbor and all the tiny black islands on the flat, moonlit sea."

Of the other Singapore, where the Chinese, who comprised three-quarters of the population, lived — the Singapore of tin mines, hovels for the miners, and kampongs on rubber plantations — Gellhorn wrote little. It was perhaps too close a reminder of the China she had left.

By fall 1941 most American reporters were leaving Chungking. It was almost impossible to circumvent the censorship, and besides, action was moving elsewhere — to the British harbor at Singapore and the American air bases in the Philippines. Mydans and Smith were posted in Manila now, investigating the island defenses for *Life*; Mel Jacoby was also there, sending "mailers" to *Time* and broadcasting for NBC. Back in Chungking an air raid flattened the press hostel, after which the bombing faded. The Japanese, too, were occupied elsewhere.

In November it was rumored that Japan was planning an attack, probably soon, probably on the Philippines. Mel Jacoby sent a message to Annalee Whitmore, still in Chungking; come to Manila and marry me, it read, but come *now* — later will be too late. Annalee resigned from United China Relief and with two baby pandas in tow, a gift from Madame Chiang Kai-shek to the women of America, flew CNAC to Hong Kong and took the China Clipper to Manila. The wedding took place at once, with Carl and Shelley as best man and matron of honor, and the bride in "a wild little nylon knit with palm trees and ukuleles on it," she recalled. Honeymooning at the Philippine mountain resort of Tagatay, the newlyweds fed and photographed the baby pandas in Annalee's care before placing them on what would prove the final clipper ship to fly out of Manila.

On the last day of November 1941 the two couples attended what was billed as the biggest American social event of the year — the annual celebration of the Army-Navy football game. Long tables had been set out on the lawn and a giant scoreboard erected, but the Time Inc. contingent noted that many chairs remained empty. A major alert prevented most navy men from attending, and the usual play-by-play account fell through when broadcasting was cut off. There was music, but few people danced. By early morning, when news sifted through that in Annapolis Navy had won, officers in Manila had been called to their posts and ships had quietly sailed off into the night. Later Shelley and Carl recalled how people just sat there at the tables, looking out over the dark sea where, somewhere, the Japanese fleet was moving, and now their own as well.

13

Facing the War
That Is Our War Now

Today we speak of "before Pearl Harbor" and "after Pearl Harbor" as if those words were not a place but an event, like the Boston Tea Party. To Americans they signify the beginning of their war, but they have other connotations, too — a grave national error, for example, or a dark smudge on the myth of invulnerability. Pearl Harbor has become a mark on our national time line rather than a spot on the map; Americans not yet born when the Japanese bombed the U.S. Pacific base there can rattle off the date — December 7, 1941 — but have only a vague notion of where it actually is.

This same lack of geographical savvy was present on that Sunday when Americans around the world first learned that the Japanese had bombed a place called Pearl Harbor. It was home port to much of the nation's fleet of destroyers, battleships, and cruisers, but its location was a mystery to farmers in Kansas and journalists in Europe alike.

In London on December 7 the first reaction to the news was bewilderment. Mary Welsh was dining with her husband, Noel Monks, in a Park Lane restaurant when a friend from the *Daily Express* stopped by their table. "A naval base somewhere in the Pacific," he said in response to their blank looks. In their flat on Marylebone Road, Lael Tucker and Steve Laird heard about it on the nine o'clock news. "I hadn't the faintest idea where Pearl Harbor was," Lael said later. "Everybody was phoning and asking, 'Where the hell is Pearl Harbor?'" Helen Kirkpatrick, a houseguest at one of the great country houses outside

London for the weekend, recalled that the company gathered there was "flabbergasted." She drove back to London the next day and had supper that night with American ambassador John Gilbert Winant, whose conviction that democracy would triumph over Fascism was a welcome change from the defeatism of Joseph P. Kennedy. They listened to Churchill on the BBC. "[He] sounded tired," she confided to her diary, "or else very tight."

Eleanor Packard was in the UP office in Rome when the urgent cable from New York came in. She informed the American press attaché, who set up a "war council" in his hotel suite; Eleanor phoned them with the latest from New York as it arrived. At Monday morning's weekly press conference, she politely inquired if the Italian government had any comment on the actions of its Axis ally at Pearl Harbor. Italy had none.

Although the outbreak of war had long been anticipated, Americans in Rome were unsettled by the news. The expatriate poet Ezra Pound dropped by the Packards' to talk it over. An admirer of Fascism and personal friend of Mussolini, Pound lived with his English wife and daughter in a small house in Rapallo on the Italian Riviera. He had been broadcasting against Roosevelt for nearly a year. He said he thought war between Italy and America inevitable, but he intended to stay. Reynolds reminded him that he would be branded a traitor if he did so, and that he would do well to stop praising Fascism and keep quiet. Pound replied that he believed in Fascism, and gave the Fascist salute. Yes, he was paid for the broadcasts, but very little, and that was not why he did them, he said, rising indignantly to pace about the room. He did them to save the American people.

Eleanor and Reynolds had known Pound years before in Paris when he focused more on poetry than on politics; they thought the lack of appreciation he had received in America for his dozens of volumes of prose and poetry had embittered him. He knew that at home he was regarded as a failure and an eccentric. Italy didn't treat him as a failure. So he stayed.

By Wednesday, December 10, it was clear that Mussolini would line up with Germany and Japan and declare war against the United States the next day. The Packards were deep in discussion with other

149

correspondents at the bar of the Foreign Press Club, with Japanese reporters doing their best not to hear any remarks derogatory to Japan so they would not feel obliged to respond, when German press chief Baron Wolfgang von Langen came in and announced that German correspondents in America had been arrested. Yes, Reynolds said, and the same was true of American reporters in Berlin. He knew that Italian reporters in the United States had also been taken into custody, but left that unmentioned. Still, it was a reminder not to dawdle. Excusing themselves, Reynolds and Eleanor returned to the UP office, locked the door, shoved all the files and documents into a tin wastebasket, burned them, and threw the ashes out the window. At home that night, they burned letters from anti-Fascist friends, which, if found, could have been used against them.

Eleanor lamented the break with ordinary Italians she had known through the years. They had exhibited none of the fanaticism of their German allies, but had remained unfailingly polite and helpful. At breakfast the next morning the cook and maid were both in tears. Why would Mussolini declare war on the United States? America must be half Italian, they had so many friends who had gone there. At the office, where Reynolds paid the salaries to date of the staff, several men turned their heads away as they shook hands, embarrassed at their emotion.

At one o'clock Eleanor and Reynolds locked the office and made their way, skirting the crowd of thousands, toward the Palazzo Venezia. Many men were in Black Shirt garb, and Mussolini, when he appeared on the balcony, was wearing the same. In a scene out of a Laurel and Hardy movie, he was followed by the German ambassador, who towered above him, and the tiny Japanese ambassador, whose delicacy was in sharp contrast to Mussolini's paunchy form. He spoke briefly, pausing after each sentence to allow the professional cheering squad to do its duty. The applause was amplified by loudspeakers, but Eleanor noticed that most people were silent. Italy's alliance with Nazi Germany and imperial Japan had never been popular, and the shouts of "Duce! Duce! Duce!" at the end were theatrical but lacked feeling. The passivity of the demonstration marked the first open protest against Mussolini that Eleanor could recall.

As they turned to leave, a White Russian colleague, whom they knew to speak excellent English, addressed them in Italian. Had they heard, he remarked in an impersonal tone, that the Italians were arresting American correspondents? It was all the tip-off they needed. Grabbing a taxi, they directed it to the American embassy and, once there, made a run for it straight through the line of carabinieri. Other American reporters were arrested that same afternoon. About midnight the Packards had a bite to eat and then left the embassy, having concluded that some reasonable arrangement would likely be made, and it was perhaps best not to appear to be avoiding arrest. They were escorted to the stone gateway, and had just stepped out into the darkness when two men joined them with the gruff message: "We have orders to take you to the Questura."

The Philippines lie on the far side of the international date line, so when Japanese bombs rained down on Pearl Harbor on Sunday, December 7, it was Monday, December 8, in Manila. Mel and Annalee Whitmore Jacoby lay asleep in their room at the Bay View Hotel, and Carl and Shelley Smith Mydans in theirs. When Carl heard the swoosh of the morning paper pushed under the door and opened his eyes, the headlines were exceptionally large and black. Shouting to Shelley, he jumped out of bed, grabbed the paper, and read aloud: "PEARL HARBOR BOMBED. WE ARE AT WAR WITH JAPAN."

Correspondents in the Pacific knew very well where Pearl Harbor was, but the residents of the Bay View were nonetheless dumbfounded. No one had thought Hawaii within reach of Japanese bombers; everyone had expected the Philippines to be the first object of Japanese aggression. In fact, Japanese planes bombed Clark Field outside Manila within hours of Pearl Harbor. After the attack, with Carl occupied elsewhere, Shelley interviewed members of the New Mexican National Guard who had manned the antiaircraft guns. The score was all in Japan's favor. Although the pilots had been ordered into the air when news of Pearl Harbor first came through, they failed to encounter the enemy, so returned for lunch. American planes were thus wing-to-wing on Clark Field when the Japanese bombers arrived. *Life* printed Shelley's story of two sergeants in their early twenties who had never fired at a live target before that day:

We just got in position when pursuits started coming over us. I was down on my knees behind the sandbagging at the gun when I got hit . . . if I'd been six inches further over, I'd have got it. It felt like a red-hot wire going right under my arm and past the forearm. I looked down and saw some blood and it felt hot a minute. But I didn't have time to think about it, just wiped the blood off and kept firing. . . . We were just a bunch of little kids out there when we started. We didn't know what it would be like. We had no officers — our second lieutenant was still at lunch — we sergeants were the only ones there.

If Shelley considered inserting a few obvious questions into the story — such as, did the U.S. military think the Japanese held the American lunch hour sacrosanct? — she squelched the impulse. They would never have seen print anyway. General Douglas MacArthur, the man in charge in the Philippines — like General Chiang Kai-shek, the man in charge in China — had the perfect confidence of Henry Luce.

Annalee Whitmore, now attached to *Liberty* magazine, set out after stories of her own. That night, looking out the windows of the Bay View into the blackness, she watched "searchlights cutting the sky into parallelograms." With dawn came the air raids. At first the alarm system malfunctioned, and she and Mel lay clutching each other in the darkness as the thud of bombs came closer. The roar of planes seemed to shake the room, and from the window, in the direction of Nichols Field, they watched a patch of red spread through the sky. In the morning they learned that all the forts and airfields around Manila had been hit.

Whitmore sent off her stories in "cablese," i.e., lacking obvious words any editor could supply, and *Liberty* printed them verbatim.

Friday, December 12. Manila's tenth air-raid alarm on. Bombed day before yesterday, night before that, day before that. May be again any minute. Can still look across bay and see fires.

We're used to hearing shots now. Don't even stop to wonder if they're snipers, antiaircraft fire, automobile backfires. Hospitals overflowing. Enlistment stations jammed with volunteers. Taxis, gasoline, even film requisitioned by army. Many stores padlocked — rest shut down at four. Nothing on streets after sunset except tired volunteer wardens and few groping cars, headlights painted out. All light globes removed; chandeliers yanked down. We live with packed bags in world of blindness at night once we leave dim hotel lobby.

Rumors run riot — Japanese landed on Luzon, marching here; parachutists at large; fifth columnists on air-raid-alarm staff; water supply poisoned. Eleven people rushed to hospitals violently ill after drinking tap water. All sent home in perfect health. Nerves. . . .

Schools closed. Bloody railroad bombings began. Drugstores had no more bandages, iodine. Hardware stores empty except for clutching crowds around flashlight counters. Our grocery taped and padlocked beneath sign, "Cheerful service to all." Favored buyers admitted after speakeasyish whispered conference. Frenzied buying inside — half shelves bare. Drove by evacuees sitting patiently on small bundles of belongings, waiting to be picked up by Red Cross trucks.

Hotel boys painted windows of bathroom thick dark green. That night we used it, with one feeble medicine-cabinet light, for our office. Our doorman joined navy; our lavandera fled to provinces with laundry; hotel boys deserted; menu shrank. "What to do in case of poison-gas attack" posted in lobby. . . .

Next day it really came — a little before noon, when cracking of antiaircraft guns started from every direction — drone of engines — air-raid siren. Twenty-seven planes directly overhead, very high, in perfect formation. A dogfight began. One plane down, crashed in distance. Bombs spurted in big semicircle of white, gray, black smoke columns. Geysers of water rose and fell in bay, leaving two ships burning. . . .

Mydans, Smith, Jacoby, and Whitmore were four of some 3,500 American civilians in the Philippines. At first that was reassuring — surely the United States would not abandon so many of its citizens — but what their government *could* do was less clear. The inadequate defenses that Shelley and Carl had noted in the fall proved just that, but the editors at *Life* missed the import of that message. They liked Shelley's story on the two National Guard sergeants defending Clark Field, they cabled, and how about a story of Americans on the offensive? Something like the stories coming in from MacArthur's headquarters about heroes in the air, and such. Shelley was amazed that they thought an offensive still possible in Manila. Censorship was tight, so she simply cabled back: "Bitterly regret your request not available here." Her cable hit the Time Inc. office like a bomb; only then did the editors perceive that America was in real danger of losing the Philippines.

In fact, denial was general, even among the correspondents. Some conjectured that perhaps Japanese troops would bypass the capital. Had they not landed on Luzon nearly two weeks before, and still not been seen in Manila? But Annalee was present at USAFFE (U.S. Army Forces Far East) headquarters on the morning of December 22 when the daily communiqué was passed out, indicating that eighty enemy warships and transports had been sighted off Lingayen Gulf, headed for shore. The invasion is upon us, she thought. What shall we do now?

Christmas morning was quiet. Shelley and Carl opened their presents beside a tiny tree in their room at the Bay View, while in the courtyard below a Filipino serenaded them with "God Bless America." Mel and Annalee had Christmas dinner — turkey, a bottle of champagne — with Clark Lee and Russell Brines of the AP. A phonograph scratched out old songs. Brines asked Annalee to dance, and Lee took advantage of the moment to warn Jacoby that events were moving fast; it was time to fold up and get going. "Especially you," he said. "You are on their blacklist for your work for the Chinese government in Chungking."

Both couples were faced with a dilemma. They had seen Clark Field and the naval base at Cavite knocked out in the first few days, seen squadron after squadron of Japanese bombers blast the old walled city, seen the centuries-old Santo Domingo church go up in flames. From private sources they also knew that as Japanese troops landed outside Manila, American-Filipino forces were retreating into Bataan, the thirty-mile peninsula stronghold along Manila Bay. Immediate action was called for, but how should they act? Should they try to leave Manila — an initially dangerous but, if successful, surely preferable course? Or should they join other civilians in almost certain internment? Shelley, always mindful that someone else might need a place on a boat more than she, leaned toward staying. Besides, a boat she and Carl considered leaving on had been blown up in the harbor, which gave one pause. Annalee, with her determination, her predilection for decisive moves, favored escape. If Mel's name *was* on a Japanese hit list, she thought, surely escape was the better course.

On the last afternoon of the year, Carl, Shelley, Mel, and Annalee, along with AP reporters Clark Lee, Russell Brines, and Ray Cronin, collected in the Jacobys' room at the Bay View. Mel had located a captain who was taking a freighter to Mariveles, on Bataan, that night. Clark Lee announced his intention of going. Carl assessed the plan as too risky and opted for internment for Shelley and himself. Cronin and Brines, whose families were also in Manila, chose the same course. Jacoby could not make up his mind; in the end it was Annalee who said, "We're going, Mel." With that settled, they proposed a farewell drink together, only to discover that the women, having heard stories about the effect of alcohol on Japanese troops, had poured all the liquor down the sink.

At ten-thirty that night the captain picked up his passengers and drove to the docks. The U.S. military had dynamited the oil storage tanks, and flames leapt toward the sky. By their light the four scrambled onto a tug and from there to a small freighter, which promptly backed out into the bay and headed toward Bataan.

At dawn on January 2, 1942, Carl and Shelley watched Japanese troops enter Manila, riding up the boulevards on bicycles and tiny motorcycles, little flags with the rising sun on their handlebars. The city "lay ringed by fire waiting for the conquerors," the Mydans team wrote later in *Life*, and continued, "The river was ablaze, and the bay, dotted with the hulks of sunken ships, was scummed with thick oil. As the smoke condensed in the thunder clouds above us, it rained black rain."

Orders were issued that all non-Filipinos were to collect whatever they could carry, including food for three days, and gather at a central point. Shelley and Carl hid Carl's cameras on the off chance they might see action anytime soon. Crammed with other Americans and their possessions in the back of a truck, they set off for the deserted University of Santo Tomás, arriving at the great dusty compound at sunset. The main building was overflowing with anxious men and women and crying children. Numbed, the couple walked along the concrete hallways, peering into barren classrooms — concrete floors, plastered walls, a blackboard, all lit by a single bare bulb. Sleeping quarters for men and women were separate. They found a spot for Shelley on the floor of a room with thirty other women.

The next morning, after coffee contributed by those who still had coffee, the internees began to organize themselves. Their captors appeared to have forgotten them. Luckily, their Filipino friends had not; they came to "the fence" — an area near the gate where the yellow concrete wall and barbed wire stopped — with food, clothes, and bedding. The only food the prisoners had during the first week came in that way, thrown over the eight-foot wall. Once in those first few days a man with a German accent, standing in front of Shelley in the food line, mentioned that he had been interned before. All within hearing were interested. It was during the First World War, he said. He was a German citizen caught in Canada on business when hostilities began. There was a German community in the area; all in it were interned, and he with them. Certain that it was a temporary measure, they kept telling their Canadian guards that in just a few more days they would surely be released.

"And how long were you there?" someone asked.

"Till the end of the war," he replied. "Four years."

On Bataan Annalee Whitmore and Mel Jacoby thought of their friends, whom they knew to be at Santo Tomás, and wondered who had after all made the better choice. Some 83,000 American and Filipino soldiers, plus 26,000 civilians, were crowded on the peninsula. All were on half rations; by mid-March, when on President Roosevelt's orders General MacArthur left for Australia, the garrison was down to one-third rations.

At least she had a job to do, Whitmore thought, although only a few of the stories she and the other five reporters wrote passed censorship for transmission. The military situation was dire, the isolation total, the prospect of reinforcements every day more bleak. There could be no Dunkirk here, she noted. Where would the boats sail to? There was no rear to send to for supplies. It was a war without a rear. It was a war "with Japanese on all sides, long-range guns in all directions, planes overhead everywhere." No relief. No escape.

In an article for *Liberty*, Whitmore compared the world of the

USAFFE on Bataan and Corregidor to "a subdivision of hell." At night she was assigned to a bed in the navy tunnel on Corregidor; by day she visited the wounded in the hospital tunnel, or crossed over to Bataan with Jacoby. The soldiers on the front line had gone through weeks of constant attack — dive bombings, machine-gun strafings, and shrieking, blasting shells that shattered bodies. One had to see it to understand what a machine-gun bullet could do to a human leg, she wrote. The men she talked to had not taken off their shoes for fifteen days. "All night they hope for daylight because of snipers; all day they hope for night so the waves of enemy planes will stop." But they were holding, and they thought they could continue to hold "until help comes." Annalee did not say when, or how, they learned that help would not be coming.

One day she and Mel drove along a bumpy dirt road to Bataan Hospital #2. They found "admissions" under an old bus roof supported by four bamboo poles. Bombs landed close enough to shake the tent operating room. Annalee spent a lot of time with the medical teams; with wounded constantly coming in and malaria and dysentery rampant, they were always understaffed. She selected several nurse's reports and edited them for *Life*, heartbreaking accounts of shrapnel wounds, gas gangrene, and malaria, with all anti–gas gangrene serum gone months before and no more quinine for malaria either. Then the Japanese bombed the hospitals themselves, leaving the nurses with their own share of shrapnel wounds.

The "subdivision of hell" became a little more bearable after the bombing let up and the Jacobys moved with Clark Lee into a little house on Corregidor. At night they would sit in the blackness, watching the flash of artillery on Bataan and debating how to get out. By mid-February it was clear there were no plans to relieve the Philippines, but it occurred to them that if they — reporters who had been on the scene — could just get their story out, perhaps they could persuade those in power otherwise. Chances of survival for those who remained looked slim.

Again it was Mel who found a boat and made arrangements. On an afternoon late in February he and Annalee sat in an army vehicle on a Bataan road, waiting. Through the omnipresent film of fine dust they could see the great Mariveles Mountain, the last line of defense. At the arranged time they moved toward the shore, passing the clearing in the trees where caribau mules were slaughtered for meat for the troops and a bakery was turning out the next day's supply of bread. They drove slowly through a civilian refugee camp where thousands of Filipinos lived out in the open. At dusk Clark Lee joined them. Their boat appeared out of the gloom and they boarded, carrying light packs and wishing they needn't to take anything from hard-pressed Bataan. At a bridge they picked up several Englishmen. Then they moved off, slipping through the minefields, out into open sea.

The journey was in two parts. The first boat traveled almost entirely at night, lying to by day in whatever sheltering inlet could be found. It took them only as far as the island of Cebu, where for days they awaited the arrival of another craft. They took turns standing watch; Mel and Annalee would share each other's at night, long hours during which they could sit close, feel the soft breeze through their hair, and whisper their hopes and feelings to each other. At last a second, much larger boat appeared which to the little group seemed their only hope. The *Doña Nati* only barely evaded a Japanese warship as it hurriedly put to sea, and several times detoured to avoid distant vessels feared to be Japanese. The run through the Surigao Strait was the most dangerous part of the trip. "There was always a tight feeling in our stomachs," Annalee said, recalling how she sat on deck filing her nails over and over again. Twenty-two days after leaving Cebu, the waters were at last safe, and the little crew sighted the port of Brisbane ahead.

14

Women Behind Walls: Manila, Siena, Shanghai

For women the prospect of capture by an invading force is unnerving at best. Gwen Dew, a freelance reporter for the *Detroit News*, who was in Hong Kong in December 1941 when it was taken by the Japanese, acknowledged knowing the danger she faced, but said she had thought only in terms of being injured or killed. Had she seriously considered capture, she might not have remained. Hong Kong and other points accessible to the Japanese army in China bore the brunt of the violence — rape, torture, general slaughter — that marked the initial onslaught against British and American enclaves. The forces that invaded Manila three weeks later came directly from Japan. Hoping to win the Filipinos to their side, they were more orderly and controlled.

Nineteen forty-two began a period of internment for American civilians on a scale never before envisioned. In Japanese-occupied Asia — the Philippines, Indochina, and large areas of the Chinese mainland — thousands of American men, women, and children, who had no common denominator except their citizenship, were incarcerated. In the United States later that same year, other men, women, and children — legal immigrants and their American-born offspring — were also confined to camps for the duration; the common denominator there was that all were of Japanese extraction. Their internment was billed as a "military necessity" against potential sabotage, no instance of which was ever proved. Rather, it was a misdirected act of retribution against a people from a land whose leaders had outwitted the

Americans at Pearl Harbor and evicted them from the Philippines. Then, too, internment allowed their neighbors to acquire cheap the farmlands these immigrants had made so productive. The physical hardship of American civilians in Japanese camps was undeniably worse, but the mental anguish of the hundred-thousand-plus internees in America —branded "Japs" when they had thought themselves loyal Americans, and forced to abandon thriving careers and flourishing farms to live in crowded shelters behind barbed wire for the war's duration — was arguably greater.

The Japanese storming through southeast Asia designated English, Dutch, and American civilians living there "enemy aliens." In much of the West there was another category, "friendly enemy aliens," which allowed journalists, businessmen, professors, and the like, to be held in "polite confinement" until an exchange with their opposite numbers could be arranged. No tradition of "polite confinement" existed in the East. Other camps were far worse than Santo Tomás, where except in the sleeping quarters the men were not separated from the women and children and there was little overt violence. But never did the experience resemble "polite confinement."

It is often the case that when danger threatens, even when the risks are apparent, people do not heed and leave while they still can. Journalists are a special case: the story, and the glory, belong to those who stay. Neither Carl Mydans nor Mel Jacoby gave serious thought to quitting Manila until the choice had narrowed to hazardous escape or internment, and although the Smith and Whitmore families may have urged their daughters, both in their mid-twenties, to return home while they still could, those daughters, reporters themselves as well as wives, did not consider that option. Both experienced the intensified romantic feeling and marital connectedness that danger elicits. Both loved their husbands deeply.

If there was anything Shelley and Carl Mydans found to be grateful for at Santo Tomás, it was that from the beginning the presence of their Japanese captors was minimal. The internees were left to organize their own lives. Structurally the buildings were in serious disrepair, but little by little plumbing was fixed, lighting improved, and schools arranged for the children. A communal kitchen was organized to prepare meals for three thousand. Medical facilities, including dentistry, were set up, and religious services scheduled. An executive committee was created to deal with infractions of the rules and interpersonal problems, and to mediate with the Japanese hierarchy. That hierarchy cared little about what went on inside as long as no one escaped outside. One night three young British seamen went over the wall. They were captured, returned to camp, beaten within hearing of all, and carried off to be executed. A few selected prisoners, taken along to witness the event, returned to spread the word that, should anyone else escape in the future, his roommates would be held responsible.

After the first few weeks, life settled down to a contest between tedium and nerves. Hunger was not yet the problem it would be later. Sometimes the women would amuse themselves by writing out the recipes of wonderful concoctions they (or their cooks) had once made. There was little opportunity for creative cooking at Santo Tomás. Shelley worked in the kitchen picking weevils out of the cracked wheat, which was breakfast, and shavings out of the rice, which along with perhaps a little stew, sometimes sardines or duck eggs, and occasionally a spinachlike vegetable called "peachi" was dinner. Only children and pregnant women got three meals a day. Shelley also worked in the hospital, as did Carl, but even after they had done their jobs and their laundry, there were hours left to fill. Classes in French, Spanish, mathematics, and music appreciation were arranged. Mydans taught a course in photography, without camera or film, and wrote for the camp newspaper *Internews*. In the evening a baseball game might be organized, or there would be phonograph music on the front lawn. The best time-filler was stories. Somebody would tell a good one, and then you could think about that when you were trying to go to sleep. But for Shelley and Carl, accustomed to moving about at will in their job, there was no forgetting the walls and the shut-in feeling. They often walked around the compound together at dusk, Carl in his khaki shorts and open-neck shirt, Shelley in her gathered skirt and white shirt, bobby socks, and blue tennis shoes. It was their time to talk privately together.

Not surprisingly, illness was frequent at Santo Tomás. Toothache. Itchy skin rash. Dysentery. Dengue. Mosquito-borne dengue fever swept the camp. Dengue was also called breakbone fever, because that was how you felt when you had it, your bones ached so, Shelley said. In an effort to shield the smaller children from such afflictions, they and their mothers were assigned their own building with a private kitchen and screens on the windows. The hospital, another priority, occupied the building that had been the geology lab, with missionary doctors and nurses for staff and untrained people for aides. There was not much in the way of drugs, but there were real beds, cots anyway, instead of just mats on the floor. When Shelley came down with appendicitis, she was allowed to go out of the compound for surgery at Philippine General Hospital with a good Filipino doctor. There was no general anesthesia available, but there was still novocaine, which worked very well, she recalled.

Plain old nerves were another problem, especially for the women. One doctor, a good listener with a reassuring manner, served as a kind of lay therapist. A woman could go to the hospital (if there was a bed free) for a little rest cure — a few days of not sharing a room with thirty other women, of bathing more privately than standing under a spigot shower with up to six other women in the communal bathroom. A quiet breakfast. Some women were rocks of Gibraltar, but others were needier.

For journalists, one of the hardest aspects of internment was knowing nothing of what was going on in the outside world. Every few days rumors about the war surfaced and were batted about the compound. At first they concerned the imminent landing of Allied troops, although it soon became obvious that that was wishful thinking. All through January and February, Shelley and Carl watched Japanese bombers heading for Bataan and wondered about the Jacobys. Was it really only three months since their wedding, since the four of them stood together, young and purposeful Americans in a friendly land, free, carefree even? When Bataan fell, families from there were brought to Santo Tomás, but Mel and Annalee were not among them. The new arrivals said that MacArthur had left by boat for Australia and American troops had retreated to Corregidor. From the camp you could hear the guns on Corregidor, strong for a while, and then every day less until there were no more guns, and word circulated that the Allies had surrendered. Almost everyone in the camp had a husband or fiancé or brother or friend on Corregidor.

Then along would come a new rumor — good, bad, indifferent. The same people were usually the carriers of such nuggets of information; it allowed them a measure of importance for a few days. One morning later that spring, on his way to "the fence" on the chance that a Filipino friend might have sent some food, Mydans was stopped by one of the regular rumormongers. Had he heard the news? the man asked. Carl tried to ignore him, but the man was insistent. "Have you heard the news? That *Time* and *Life* photographer, Carl Mydans, was killed in Australia. Killed in a plane crash with General George. Spanish friend of mine down at the fence just told me. Got away from the Japs and made it to Australia and then went and got himself killed there."

Mydans hated this man, the way men in prison can come to hate one another. "That's one you're wrong on," he heard himself saying with a kind of vicious triumph in his voice. The man erupted in a furious shouting — what did he know about it anyway? — and Carl was about to tell him, cut him down to size, when he stopped. It came to him in a rush what had happened; he and Jacoby had been confused before. He must find Shelley and tell her. Mel and Annalee had gotten out, had made it to Australia, but now Mel was dead.

So little real news seeped into Santo Tomás that its inhabitants had no idea if there were other camps for other civilians in other parts of the world, and whether other American reporters were incarcerated there. They assumed that in European countries Allied correspondents were promptly and politely exchanged for their counterparts on the Axis side. Certainly Eleanor and Reynolds Packard had never worried much about remaining in an Italy soon to be their enemy. Their Rome was a civilized place, a city sure to preface the term "enemy alien" with "friendly," and on the night they dashed for cover into the American embassy, they were almost embarrassed to find that none of their fellow reporters felt such action necessary. The Italian police arrested all seven of them, but promptly sent Eleanor home, and although Reynolds and the others spent some hours in jail, they were soon transferred to a former brothel for safekeeping. By New Year's 1942 the seven — joined by Teddy Lynch, J. Paul Getty's wife, who had been studying singing in Italy — were taken north to Siena and installed in the Excelsior Hotel.

This was truly "polite confinement." The Americans took their pick of available rooms and an extra one for a "club room." They were loosely guarded when they left the hotel to go to a restaurant or the movies, or to shop in the little antique stores in town. They ate as well as other inhabitants of Siena, better after they began bicycling about the countryside, buying contraband eggs and butter from the farmers. Visits to the zebra-striped cathedral and the art galleries inspired a craze for charcoal and crayon drawing. In the evening there were billiards in a nearby café and Ping-Pong. When weather permitted, they played tennis. Their appearance on the court with brand new tennis balls sent up from the embassy caused a sensation — Italians had not seen a new tennis ball in years.

Their constant preoccupation was bridge. They all played; one or more games occurred nightly in the club room, often for high stakes. Enforced leisure was not easy, and the concentration required by bridge helped keep shaky interpersonal relations from deteriorating further. Except for Eleanor and Reynolds, who suited each other very well, none of the remaining correspondents had really been friendly before. Confinement did not improve matters, but bridge helped keep them bearable.

For Americans in Italy in 1942, news from the outside world was depressing. The Italian papers were full of Japanese victories, and although Herbert Matthews of the *New York Times* wrote out summaries of what news he gleaned from the BBC, it was hardly more optimistic. Winter passed. Spring in Siena proved beautiful. In May the Americans learned they were to return to Rome: the exchange was on. That night they celebrated, auctioning off their crayon and charcoal drawings to each other, and applauding Dick Massock of the AP in his imitations of soon-to-come Returned War Correspondent Lectures.

In Rome several Americans whose fate they had not known joined them. Harold Denny of the *New York Times*, captured in the Libyan desert the previous November and since shifted from place to place, arrived with a long white beard. Padre Woolf, rector of St. Paul's Protestant Episcopal in Rome, had been arrested while discussing Thanksgiving Day hymns with his organist; he had been accused of espionage, tried, convicted, and imprisoned. The American ambassador called it an old trick for the sole purpose of making a "blue chip" of him: in the event of a trade, a number of ordinary "white chip" Italians in the United States could be traded for him. In the end Padre Woolf cost thirteen white chips. He was relieved to see his compatriots in Rome, having been told the American embassy had already gone and left him behind.

The last diplomatic train left on May 13, 1942, for Lisbon. On the railroad platform the carabinieri ignored the presence of their own foreign-office personnel and passed out names and addresses of relatives in the United States for the reporters to look up. Not until they were on the train, however, did the idea of "home" begin to take root in their collective consciousness. As many as could jammed into the compartment of the third secretary, also a guitarist, to sip brandy and sing "Carry Me Back to Ole Virginny" and "Home on the Range." The mood was one of relief, verging on giddy.

They reached the Spanish border late the next afternoon. Because the railroad tracks in Spain and Portugal were of a wider gauge, the passengers had to climb down from the Italian train, trudge across the border with their belongings, and clamber onto a Spanish train on the other side. Unknown to them, news of their progress preceded them. At Barcelona, which they reached about midnight, Eleanor was touched to find Spanish reporters whom she and Reynolds had known when they covered the Civil War waiting to shake their hands and wish them well. In Madrid the next afternoon the UP bureau chief brought two bottles of his best sherry down to the station to toast their release.

The train was held up in a small town near the Portuguese border. It was dinnertime, and children crowded up to the dining car windows, begging for bread. When the diners passed some out to them, their shrieks brought what appeared to be the whole town. There had always been beggars in Spain, Eleanor recalled, but never whole towns of them. The train crossed into Portugal early the next morning. Portugal was a neutral country, but the Packards knew that if something went wrong with the *Drottningholm* — the Swedish diplomatic ship returning from the United States with their Italian and German counterparts — the train would be halted, perhaps turned back. Not until they reached Lisbon, where when they dismounted British reporter friends rushed up to shake their hands, did it finally sink in that they were free.

By September 1942 Shelley Smith and Carl Mydans were also on the move. As it happened, among the people interned at Santo Tomás back in January were a number of American women who had fled Shanghai with their children and were caught in Manila when war broke out. They had petitioned to be allowed to return to Shanghai, but by the time arrangements were made and a boat sent for them, most had changed their minds. How could they know what awaited them there? Santo Tomás was bad, but perhaps Shanghai was now worse. What if their boat — Japanese, of course — encountered American submarines? Or what if, in their weakened condition, they or their children did not survive the rough voyage?

Shelley and Carl also worried about these matters, but they were aware as well of the prison camp psychosis which makes the greater outside so strange and frightening that familiar territory within, no matter how bad, appears preferable. Then, too, an old retina condition in Shelley's eye had been acting up. There were, or had been, good doctors in Shanghai. Perhaps chances of repatriation were better from there, or perhaps escape to Free China. These were the considerations that led to their being part of the little group — baggage tied into bundles, best clothes hanging loosely from their bodies — that piled into an old U.S. army bus and, with a mixture of joy and trepidation, left Santo Tomás behind.

The *Maya Maru* was a small freighter converted into a troopship merely by installing wooden shelves in the hold for beds and cooking vats on the well deck for a kitchen. Three privies on planks had been lashed to the railing so that they extended over the side. Shelley could not imagine the American navy considering such conditions remotely suitable. Because the ship had to zigzag to avoid minefields, the trip lasted a very long two weeks. On their side, the Santo Tomás group tried to keep the same discipline they had practiced in the camp; on the far side Japanese soldiers with their Formosan women lounged about, playing games and making love. A group of Hindus — men in loincloths, women cooking on charcoal stoves, children picking lice out of each other's hair — acted as a kind of buffer. From down below came the whinnies of a herd of thin, nervous horses captured on Bataan, many with the U.S. Army brand on their flanks. At night cockroaches moved along every surface; even worse were the rats, sniffing out food anyone tried to hoard.

Paradoxically, Shelley recalled, the humans easiest to tolerate were the soldiers. They had nothing against the Santo Tomás contingent, and smiled and bowed as if they were all at the Imperial Hotel in Tokyo together. At times she found it hard to view them as the enemy. One particular encounter always stayed with her. She had arisen one morning while it was still dark to go up on deck and try to wash a little at the spigot. As she was brushing her teeth, some soldiers came along to brush theirs. They crowded around, jostling each other, and as she hurried to finish, by accident she spit right into a soldier's toothbrush cup. She straightened up at once, bowed, and apologized, and the soldier bowed in return. As they stood there in the half-light bowing to each other, Shelley experienced one of those moments of recognition that sometimes occur on a battlefield but are unexpected on a crowded, vermin-infested freighter. She saw a young man from some Japanese village, or perhaps a farm, who had done nothing to her or probably any other American, who had no better accommodations on this ship than she had and was fed the same food in the same portions, who was polite and unthreatening — and yet was the enemy. Whenever she relived the scene, she always hoped he had survived the war.

After two long and painful weeks, the *Maya Maru* landed in Shanghai. The city seemed to Shelley remarkably unaffected by the war. She was surprised to find the streets clean and orderly, hotels and restaurants busy, and well-fed westerners living — outwardly anyway — much as they always had. Those American women and children from Santo Tomás who had braved the trip were able to return to their old homes. At the Palace Hotel where the Mydanses were quartered, an elderly Chinese man waited upon them — "turned down our sheets in the evening and drew our baths and would have laid out our evening clothes had we had any," Carl said.

Six months after their arrival in Shanghai, this pleasant life came to an abrupt end when all British and Americans were interned. Their baggage was loaded into rickshas and deposited on the lawn of an earlier bastion of American commercial success, the Columbia Country Club. Shelley and Carl found their own belongings meager compared with those of the old China-hand families who had lived much of their lives in Shanghai, but lavish in contrast to a few down-on-their-luck types whom none of the establishment families had ever seen before, but who were now part of their circle because they, too, possessed a U.S. or British passport.

The Mydanses were assigned to a camp within the walled ruins of the old China University in Chapei. Rations were inadequate and deficiency diseases developed, but the group was fortunate to have as a member an American missionary from North China who improvised a kind of primitive grindstone at which eight men spelled each other, Carl recalled, "walking the grindstone round and round by the staves like plodding Missouri mules." By grinding soybeans, they produced soybean milk, an essential addition to their nutrition. Shelley's eye problem was aggravated by the poor diet, but she was allowed to go regularly to a clinic for treatment, and in fact managed to remain outside the camp much of the time.

The day came when news of the first repatriation reached the Chapei internment camp, and on the bulletin board appeared a list of internees scheduled to be exchanged. Never had Shelley and Carl felt more vulnerable than when they inched through the crowd to check the names; never had they felt such relief as when they found their own there. All around them were people whose names were absent, to whom it was awkward and painful to talk after that. Not until the morning the buses came through the gate did the departure become real, to those going and those left behind, but many of the latter followed their luckier compatriots to the gates, singing "God Bless America" with great bravado. Even after they could no longer see them, Shelley and Carl could hear their voices.

The once French, now Japanese freighter *Teia Maru* waited in Shanghai harbor, its first stop. Accommodations existed for seven hundred; by the ship's final stop, more than twice that number were aboard. They filed on from Stanley Prison Camp at Hong Kong, from Santo Tomás in Manila, from Saigon. Emily Hahn, who had managed to escape internment but not malnutrition, came on at Hong Kong with her little daughter. Everyone looked shrunken and aged. It took days of no fences and wide horizons before they began to feel like individuals again.

Shelley and Carl were strongly affected by the trip. As they approached the neutral port of Mormugao in Goa, where the exchange would take place, they became depressed and anxious. It was, Carl wrote later, a kind of fear that life had gone on and left you behind, that people had forgotten you, that your job wouldn't be waiting for you and your life was finished. So when on the twenty-sixth day they passed a few small fishing boats and the long empty dock area came into view, they could not work up any enthusiasm. Tugs pushed the boat broadside against the dock. There below they could make out a little knot of people waving and shouting, but they saw it all in a fuzzy sort of way until a voice beside them broke through their trance. "It's you they're calling, Shelley. Right below. They're calling you and Carl!"

Only then did their eyes focus on the little group of men in khaki bush jackets and shorts. Suddenly they recognized them — those were old friends down there, journalists like themselves, waving their sun helmets and laughing, *expecting* them. And just as suddenly, Carl later recalled, he and Shelley were themselves again.

15

Learning the Rules, Dressing the Part

In London in 1942 women correspondents found there was an upside and a downside to America's entry into the war. Their new position as declared allies of the British made their lives easier, particularly after hours when one shopped in half-bare markets or dropped by the local pub. The downside was that where before American reporters had moved about freely, now there were rules. Instructions were issued, directives dispersed, permissions required. Authorization became obligatory for things that one had done of one's own accord before. Authorization came from the new command structure: European Theater of Operations, U.S. Army (ETOUSA, or just ETO), created in Washington by Chief of Staff General George C. Marshall and headed in Europe by General Dwight D. Eisenhower. Now every reporter and photographer moving into the war zone had first to be accredited to a particular branch of the service (usually the U.S. Army) so that the War Department could keep track of them.

The next step was to put accredited war correspondents into uniform. As yet there were no ready-made uniforms for women (the Women's Auxiliary Army Corps was in the formation stage), but practicality suggested an officer jacket and two skirts — khaki for everyday and "pinks," really a warm gray, for dress — plus khaki shirts, ties, and cap. Pants, cut slightly slimmer than the men's, were soon added. Helen Kirkpatrick, Mary Welsh, Lael Tucker, and Tania Long set off at once for Savile Row to have their uniforms tailor made. They were soon

Women war correspondents in London (left to right): Mary Welsh, Dixie Tighe,
Kathleen Harriman, Helen Kirkpatrick, Lee Miller, Tania Long, 1942.
NATIONAL ARCHIVES.

joined by two INS reporters — Dixie Tighe, famous for her blunt language and flamboyant life style, and tall, engaging Kathleen Harriman, who also reported for *Newsweek*, but left London to accompany her father, presidential envoy Averell Harriman, to Moscow.

The insignia designating "war correspondent" had its own evolution. Initially, it was a green armband (green signified noncombatant) with the letters WC on it, but when this prompted too many jokes in Britain, it was changed to a single C for correspondent and P for photographer. Soon these were supplemented by a neat patch reading War Correspondent — rectangular over the left jacket pocket and circular on the cap.

Uniforms were important as identification. Correspondents held the rank of "captain"; the rank was theoretical, assigned to allow them leverage should they be captured by the enemy. If this happened, as it did to several male reporters, and they were in uniform, they would not be viewed as spies by the enemy, and would later receive captain's pay for time lost. But more important from a woman's point of view was that a uniform made her look professional — equivalent to her male

171

Mary Welsh interviewing AEF troops, Northern Ireland, 1942.
MARGARET BOURKE-WHITE/*LIFE* MAGAZINE. © TIME INC.

counterpart in similar attire — and indicated her role in the United States Army.

That army reached the British Isles only seven weeks after Pearl Harbor, and remained part of the British landscape until well after the end of the war. Helen Kirkpatrick and Mary Welsh were at a not-to-be-named port in Northern Ireland to cover the arrival of the first troops of the American Expeditionary Force (AEF). Writing for the *Chicago Daily News*, Kirkpatrick described how hundreds of workers from the dock area gathered to welcome them, and how women and children lined the country lanes over which they marched to their various camps. Mary concentrated on the nuts and bolts of daily existence for the Yanks, as they were called both in Ireland and in *Life*: the Nissen huts, elongated igloos of corrugated iron in which they would live; their food, which came directly from America; and the dance halls they planned to build at various crossroads across Northern Ireland.

These troops were the beginning phase of a virtual deluge of Yanks and accompanying tanks, trucks, jeeps, housing, and supplies that poured into the British Isles. By summer the AEF was deemed ready

Helen Kirkpatrick with King George VI and Queen Elizabeth.
HELEN KIRKPATRICK PERSONAL COLLECTION.

for a visit from King George and Queen Elizabeth. Helen Kirkpatrick, already acquainted with the royal couple, accompanied them as they toured field hospitals, examined pontoon bridges, reviewed artillery and infantry units wheeling past to the strains of Sousa marches, and watched light tanks roar over the hills and motorcycle patrols fire tommy guns at a moving target. It was a cross between a Wild West show and a hometown carnival.

At the king's request, fifty-four American privates joined Their Majesties for lunch around a great horseshoe table. Helen described the menu which began with roast beef and concluded with cherry pie and coffee from outsized mugs that made the queen laugh — perhaps because everything that day was outsized by English standards. Later Their Majesties were tucked into jeeps and driven to the top of a small mountain where, seated comfortably under a large tent, they viewed a simulated "battle for the North Ridge." Tea was served, along with American doughnuts made on the spot. Kirkpatrick summed up the day as a royal success all round.

After a nine-month home stay in the United States during most of 1941, Tania Long and Ray Daniell were planning their return to England. The New York offices of the *Herald Tribune* and *Times*, respectively, had kept them busy, but it had been a difficult time for both. In London during those months of the Blitz it had seemed clear — a young divorced woman (with a child in America) meets a man (with a wife and two children in America). Thrown together by the vagaries of war, they hold and comfort each other as bombs rain down around them. In time they return to the States to put their lives in order — a new order satisfactory to all concerned, they hope. But however possible that may have seemed in England, it was much less so in America. Even after Ray's wife at last agreed to end a marriage that had been troubled long before Tania came on the scene, there were still the children. In America the children, silent until now, proved to have voices. They spoke outright how they felt, protested, or withdrew in tears. Tania's son felt displaced by this stranger in his mother's life, and abandoned when she told him she planned to return to England. It was the war, she told him; war separated families; but this was less obvious to a child in the winter of 1941–42 than it would be later, and he knew no one else whose *mother* had gone away to war. Tania was torn by divided loyalties. She could, she supposed, remain in the New York office of the *Herald Tribune*, but she knew how unhappy she would be there, reporting civic affairs with the world at war and Ray in London braving the dangers alone. No, she had made her decision.

After Ray's divorce came through, they were married. News of Pearl Harbor reached them on their honeymoon in Pass-a-Grille, Florida. It was a warm Sunday afternoon, they came back from fishing, and there it was — confirmation of the long expected, and a message that the *New York Times* requested Daniell's return ASAP. So much for honeymoons. In New York, Long transferred her allegiance to the *Times*; both agreed that it would be inappropriate for her to work for her husband's rival, and Daniell was returning as head of the *Times* London bureau. Even had he been a mere reporter, Tania would not have suggested that he switch to *her* publication. No woman would have done that in 1942.

Back in England, in charge of acquiring material and writing pieces for the *Times Sunday Magazine*, Long went down to Dover to report on how the town was coping with bombing raids. She found a whole new system of deep tunnels and connecting passages honey-combed through the famous cliffs. Deep in the interior were kitchens equipped to feed the entire town, open areas where dances were held on weekends, and a hospital complete with operating rooms for the wounded. There was a bunk for every man, woman, and child; many families went regularly into the caves at night to avoid having to do so before morning anyway. Some children could not remember ever sleeping anywhere else.

She had saved her son from that disrupted existence, Tania thought, even as she recognized that he might very well have preferred it.

During her 1941 sojourn in America, Tania Long could not help but notice an unexpected twist in the national mood, and the strong approval now enjoyed by that God-forsaking, capitalist-denouncing country Soviet Russia. Although the embattled Britain of 1940 had been accorded high marks for endurance, by mid-1941, with British troops concentrated in Libya and Egypt and losing most of the battles there, Americans had begun to question both their ability and their motives. Saving the British Empire was not an American priority, which was probably the reason why nearly half the Americans polled in an OWI (Office of War Information) survey, asked if they thought Britain was doing all it could to win the war, replied in the negative. The same question in reference to the Soviet Union, however, brought a ninety percent "yes." From the American point of view, Russia's total immersion in the war was admirable, and no one believed that more heartily than Margaret Bourke-White. Judging the United States much too comfortable for a nation at war, she looked back with longing on her Soviet venture. That spring of 1942 she asked for an assignment overseas. Her editors at *Life* requested that she be accredited to the U.S. Army Air Force, and the Pentagon agreed on condition that they have first claim to her photographs. With much fanfare the Army War College set about designing her uniform, which emerged looking not very different from what the women correspondents in London were already wearing.

As for Erskine Caldwell, he was not happy about his wife's choice of career moves. They had bought a house in Arizona and still talked, or he did, about having a child. While Bourke-White was on a lecture tour, he took a well-paying job in Hollywood and lined up one for her, too. But Margaret had no desire to go to Hollywood. During wartime a photographer's job was to be where the real action was. That summer she received her orders to go to a secret American air base in Britain.

The United States had recently sent over thirteen heavy bombers — big fast B-17s that could cruise at high altitudes and thus safely be sent out on daytime raids. Bourke-White was there to photograph their first mission, and *Life* gave the story seven pages. Photographically, it was not very interesting. Most of the shots were of men — meteorologists, intelligence officers, duty officers, navigators — conferring with each other or with the bombing crews before and after the flight. The intent was to give the reader a sense of the experience of a B-17 in action, but as Margaret was not allowed up in the plane herself, the heart of the story was missing.

Still, she enjoyed herself and was delighted when one of the bomber crews asked her to christen their plane. An elaborate ceremony was arranged, employing a small band with a piano on the runway. The weather and the Germans both cooperated, and a glowing Bourke-White brought the bottle of Coca-Cola down hard on the nose of the plane. "May the *Flying Flitgun* bring to the enemy the devastation its godmother has brought to the Ninety-seventh," quipped the commanding officer, Colonel J. Hampton Atkinson, in this, his initial encounter with that "godmother."

At first no reporters were allowed on the B-17 bombing raids, but once that rule changed, Bourke-White worked hard to get permission to go. She was never refused outright, but on the other hand, when a permission did come through, it was always for a man. Of the first two reporters who went, only one came back, but that did not deter Margaret from continuing to try.

Charles Wertenbaker, widely known as "Wert" in his post as foreign editor at *Time*, arrived at the London office that spring of 1942, and Lael Tucker was assigned to show him about. Lael had never met him, but she had been cabling him stories for several years and, like many *Time* reporters, depended on him as a perceptive, open-minded editor. Wert had a sense of her, too; her analyses were at times politically ingenuous and her preconceptions uncritical, but he believed what she sent was as truthful as she could make it, which he knew was not the case with every reporter.

Wertenbaker was forty-two, twice divorced, and contemplating a third marriage, and Tucker, thirty-four, was married to one of his own reporters, Stephen Laird. The Lael-Wert relationship thus began quite innocently, turned mildly flirtatious, and then suddenly grew serious. One day they deserted a Ministry of Information tour in Liverpool "to see the things we wanted to see, which were the same things," Lael recalled later. Another day she took him to Dover and, after viewing the installations, introduced him to three schoolgirls she had come to know. The girls clustered around her, giggling at their inability to understand Wert's Virginia-accented English. Later Lael wrote that they first looked at each other with love across those dark, blond, and red heads. And when on the grass at Oxford he solemnly pronounced that he was a very lucky man, that seemed to settle it.

Except, of course, for Steve. Lael had known her marriage had problems, but she had thought it would improve with time. She had not expected it suddenly to be engulfed by a far stronger force. Nor had she anticipated getting pregnant. But Wertenbaker was indeed lucky. Laird, who had long admired him, rejected the role of outraged husband. Only Steve's uncompromising decency, Lael admitted later, kept a tense emotional situation from turning ugly. They had shared a lot —the bubonic plague scare in Manchuria, the long trip across Russia, the anxious year in Berlin. "It was hard leaving Steve," she said.

That summer Laird remained quietly in London reporting for *Time.* Lael went home and filed for divorce. In due time Wert returned to the New York office, they were married, and their son was born.

Besides having to follow directives, obtain permissions, and seek authorization for even minor activities, women correspondents during the war found their customary easy movement between Britain and America obstructed by a certain Mrs. Shipley, head of Immigration and Naturalization. It was Mrs. Shipley's belief that women had no business exposing themselves to danger in a war zone, and to that end she began to pick up their passports when they returned home for what they had planned as a brief visit. Unless they first obtained an ironclad guarantee of an exact return date, women could find their home leaves extended indefinitely.

Sonia Tomara ran afoul of Mrs. Shipley when she arrived in New York after the fall of France in the summer of 1940. Tomara's plan was to stay the prescribed time to become an American citizen and then return. Meanwhile from the home office of the *New York Herald Tribune* she turned out regular analyses of events in central Europe. But Tomara was a twenty-year veteran; to her, reporting was not just a job, it was her whole identity. And Mrs. Shipley was blocking the delivery of her new passport. Having observed Margaret Bourke-White's much publicized accreditation to the Army Air Force, and the ease with which her former colleague on the *Herald Tribune*, Tania Long, returned to England for the *New York Times*, Sonia realized that it was all a matter of who you knew.

So she went to Helen Rogers Reid. Reid had brought Dorothy Thompson to the *Herald Tribune* and was responsible for its having more women on the editorial staff than any other daily in the country. Throughout her long life Reid acted on her belief that women, married or not, should work and be economically independent. That, like her advocacy of women's conscription for military service, was antithetical to Mrs. Shipley's views, but Reid had, a colleague once said, "the persistence of gravity." In no time Tomara was accredited, her new passport issued, and her assignment to the China-Burma-India theater, known as CBI, assured. By mid-August 1942 she was off.

Sonia's first dateline read "Somewhere on the coast of Africa," and although she could not be more specific, she did inform her readers that whereas eight months earlier there had been nothing on this spot, there were now living quarters for sixty-odd military and technicians, a well-equipped hospital, and a mess hall serving food imported from America. There was an airfield, but no road to the interior. The base was surrounded by jungle, and the nearest town, reached only by air, was sixty miles away.

With the rainy season over, Tomara reported, the weather on the coast was delightfully cool. Palm trees bent in the wind. One can imagine her leaning against one, looking out to sea, exultant.

16

Women On Trial: North Africa

In the fall of 1942 American troops landed along the coast of North Africa and engaged in their first ground offensive. Early successes freed Algiers for U.S. Army headquarters and, impelled by the need for clerical personnel, Eisenhower secretly requested that a newly trained contingent of the Women's Auxiliary Army Corps be sent there instead of England. For its part the War Department conceded that female members of the press might go along to report WAAC activities. And as a Washington reporter who had been covering their training, and an old friend of Oveta Culp Hobby, head of the Wacs, Ruth Cowan was a natural for the job.

Ruth Cowan, Associated Press

The daughter of a mining prospector of limited success who died when she was still young, Ruth Cowan had a childhood that was sparse of funds but even more of stability. Her mother moved her about at whim until, in her teens and anxious to live and go to school among people familiar to her, Ruth elected to remain behind in San Antonio. "I'll perch someplace," she recalled thinking, her terminology reminiscent of the chickens she had cared for during her mother's Florida citrus farm tenure. Her first perch during high school was a convent, her second a large civic-minded family who took her in as a surrogate

Ruth Cowan equipped for battle reporting, 1942.
<small>SCHLESINGER LIBRARY, RADCLIFFE COLLEGE.</small>

daughter. Blond and blue-eyed, she had acquired an air of independence that amused people, she said, but which developed out of her conviction that she had no one to fall back on.

After graduation from the University of Texas at Austin, where she worked in the state library to support herself, Cowan took a job on the *San Antonio Evening News*. She had a desk in the city room, the only woman there. It was in the city room that she learned how to find the news angle of a story, how to write a lead, how to call in a story — collect, of course. "I covered everything I found uncovered," she joked later. Then she turned to freelancing and covered the 1928 Democratic convention for the *Houston Chronicle*. A United Press official saw her there, was impressed, and hired Ruth B. Cowan as R. Baldwin Cowan, but she lost the job when the main office discovered she was a woman. R. Baldwin was not one to give up easily, however, and she soon signed on with a somewhat more enlightened Associated Press. She worked in the Chicago office, again as the only woman, throughout the gangster years of the 1930s, covering the trial of Al Capone along with more benign events such as the 1933 World's Fair. She was strict, almost hard on herself. Whenever possible, a story should be a scoop, but in any event each story should be well written and a little unusual. When asked to write a story again, she would write it again. No complaints.

In 1940 Cowan was transferred to Washington. There she quickly became a regular at Eleanor Roosevelt's weekly women-only press gatherings, as well as covering White House social events and Washington cultural events. On Sunday, December 7, 1941, Ruth was one of the few AP reporters in town, so she covered the Washington aftermath to Pearl Harbor too. In 1942 she added the Women's Auxiliary Army Corps training to her schedule, and that fall, hearing that her Wacs were going overseas, presumably to England, she applied to accompany them. The AP was willing, even agreed to a clothes allowance for wool pants and long winter underwear. Then in December a story came over the teletype that five Wacs had been torpedoed off the coast of North Africa. Ruth stared at the story. She knew that a small WAAC contingent had already gone to England, and she also knew that General Eisenhower had requested a second detachment. And where was the general now? North Africa.

Cowan's first reaction was to ponder, half philosophically, half emotionally, whether she wanted to get that close to war. But her reporter instinct dismissed that question almost at once, and she filed a new application to the War Department, which read in part: "It is presumed that the WAAC are going to England, but nevertheless, the Associated Press desires that Ruth Cowan accompany them wherever they may go." The AP chief signed it, and Cowan personally delivered it to the brand-new Pentagon building. There she was subjected to a small and not unfriendly interrogation by the chief of the war intelligence division in the War Department's bureau of public relations. "So you want to go to war?" he asked her. He was regular army, a colonel, but Ruth happened to know he had once been city editor on a Salt Lake City newspaper. Was she athletic? he asked. Did she like camping? (No to both.) Was she afraid of firearms? (She was.) Could she keep a secret? She must always be very careful, he stressed. It would be most unfortunate if a leak in military security were traced to a woman. (She promised to keep all secrets.) One thing more. "You won't be very comfortable. Things will happen you won't like. Do you think you can take it?" Ruth thought she could.

After that Cowan began the process that would become familiar to all women setting out as war correspondents over the next few years. Once her accreditation came through and she suffered through the inoculations — tetanus, typhoid, typhus (typhus in England? Ruth mused) — she received a small green folder of identification, called an "AGO card" for having originated in the Adjutant General's Office. Wac uniforms were ordered; in time a package arrived containing two officer jackets, two skirts, pants, half a dozen shirts, ties, and a raincoat (nothing warm enough for England in midwinter, she noted).

On January 2, 1943, Cowan reported to the troop movements division at the New York port of embarkation in Brooklyn. Almost instantly she was confronted with army red tape. Did she have her orders? She had no orders, no one had mentioned orders, but (God be praised) her name was on the sailing list. Did she want to pick up her equipment while there? It had not occurred to her that she would require "equipment." Of course, she replied, and was taken to an upper floor of a huge warehouse where, yes, her name was on the list sent up from the War Department. She was issued a helmet, a musette bag, a fatigue outfit, green coveralls with white hood, gloves that had been treated for gas, insect powder, sunglasses, mosquito netting (for the river Thames? she wondered), a canteen, and a gas mask, which a bemused sergeant taught her how to use. His chuckles were understandable. It was still new for Wacs to go overseas, and now here was this bewildered blonde who didn't know enough to carry her new belongings downstairs, "thereby violating another rule for women in war," she noted later. "Carry your own weight. Don't expect men to be gallant."

The staging area before embarkation was Camp Kilmer, New Jersey. Cowan had been told to pack her musette bag so she could live out of it for a month, and to keep in mind that she would be carrying it on her back. A Wac officer helped her. In went three shirts, pants, underthings, socks, cold cream in a tin tube, powder, lipstick, anti–gas attack salve, and two small bottles of self-apply bleach (out of the dozen she was taking — Ruth fully intended to remain a blonde throughout the war). A few days later, in a crowded army transport, part of a huge troop convoy, she put out to sea.

In the meantime Margaret Bourke-White, languishing in England, was desperate to go to North Africa. It seemed to her she had done all she could with the air force in Britain; now much of it was moving down to Morocco and Algeria, and the action would be there. She needed new challenges, new successes to prove to herself that she had done the right thing in trading her marriage for her career — which was what she had done in rejecting the Hollywood job her husband had arranged and taking an assignment to England. Her reflections were private ones. *Life* reporter Lincoln Barnett, who occupied the hotel room next to hers and ate with her often, had no idea she and Caldwell had separated. Perhaps she sensed that her male colleagues might not have sanctioned her decision.

Military protocol did not permit Bourke-White to request that *Life* send her to North Africa, so she set about persuading the U.S. Army Air Force still in England that they would need her there. This caused a problem because the magazine already had a photographer in that combat zone, and two from the same publication were not allowed. A highly competent and unhappy male photographer had to be evicted before Margaret could go in. If she knew this, she chose not to dwell upon it. The assignment came through, although the air force decreed that flying was too dangerous and sent her with American and British nurses in a large convoy. She was assigned to the flagship, formerly a pleasure cruise boat, along with six thousand troops, four hundred nurses, five Wacs (the very ones that attracted Ruth Cowan's attention on the teletype), and several women from General Eisenhower's staff, including Elspeth Duncan, a tall, handsome Scotswoman, and his spirited Irish driver, Kay Summersby.

War is heavy with best-laid schemes that gang agley. If the air force had sent Bourke-White off to North Africa in the *Flying Flitgun*, she would have arrived promptly and safely. As it was, she endured five days of violent storm and gales, and then worse. "Down in the trough you felt you would never see the sky again," she wrote in her autobiography. "Up on the peaks, you caught a second's flash of other ships bobbing like celluloid toys." Through it all, lifeboat drills took place on schedule two or three times a day, the poor sick nurses grabbing at the guide ropes strung along the decks as they made their way to the lifeboat stations.

Once in the calm Mediterranean everyone breathed a sigh of relief. But this was premature. Trouble lurked under those still waters. Bourke-White packed and repacked her small musette bag, meant to contain soap, extra socks, and concentrated chocolate. In the penultimate packing her small Rolleiflex and some film displaced the socks and most of the chocolate, and in the final one her beloved Linhof, with the five most valuable of its twenty-two lenses, went in too. She and two newsmen obtained permission, should an enemy attack occur, to cover the action from the base of the bridge. They were among the few aware of the submarines following them.

In her story "Women in Lifeboats," which appeared in *Life*, Bourke-White described the sensation when the torpedo awakened her — not so loud a crash as she might have expected, but suggesting that the contact was a fatal one. She tore into her clothes, put on her greatcoat, grabbed her life belt, helmet, and musette bag, and flew past two lines of troops filing in perfect order up from the hold, one turning to starboard and the other to port. Pausing under the bridge, she realized that the nighttime sky would not provide enough light for pictures. This excuse allowed her to make a dash for her boat station, relieved to find that the nurses were only beginning to board and she could take her assigned place in the order.

There was a problem, however. Lifeboats on the port side were flooded with splash from the torpedo, and crew members were discussing whether they would stay afloat. Bourke-White noticed two of the nurses trembling uncontrollably. Her own mouth felt terribly dry. "This must be fear," she thought, realizing she had no idea what was going to happen to her. "There's a fifty percent chance you will live. There's a fifty percent chance you might die." This was true of all of them, she thought, but some people seemed to have a hidden well of courage, like the two Wacs who, when their lifeboat became overloaded, stepped out of line with a cheerful "Oh, of course, we can't all go," and watched it lowered without them.

In her piece in *Life*, Bourke-White wrote of her astonishment at finding herself in the lifeboat with water up to her hips.

The sea, which from above had looked so calm, rose up against us wave after wave and began beating us back against the side of the ship. Our crew strained at the oars. There was so little space left in our crowded boat that we started singing, bending our bodies in rhythm to give the rowers room to move their arms. Just as we had created a small margin between ourselves and the big ship, down came lifeboat No. 11 with its load of British sisters. Its crew had been unable to replace the plugs properly and it filled to the gunwales. A couple of dozen sisters were washed over the side. Some of them were carried immediately back into their flooded boat on the next wave. Others started swimming toward rafts which were tossed from the upper deck.

At that point, the rudder on Bourke-White's boat broke, the oarsmen needed help rowing, and everyone wearing a helmet took it off and started bailing. Many were seasick from the boat tossing about, but at least they had a boat. Already the dark sea was filled with people struggling to hold on to rafts. One raft drifted in their direction, and they pulled the young woman riding it, who had broken her leg, into their boat. The nurses held her tight to keep her from bouncing with each swell. Margaret never forgot a voice off in the blackness crying, "I am all alone! I am all alone!" They tried to steer their rudderless boat in her direction, but the voice grew fainter and then stopped altogether. As the rowers, too, became seasick from the constant swell, they were spelled at the oars by the less squeamish, including Margaret and the "splendid Elspeth Duncan," the best rower of all. With time, survival began to appear likely. A raft of soldiers drifted by, and no fewer than nine young men were transferred into their already overcrowded boat. Later another lifeboat approached with three heavily loaded rafts roped to it. Nurses in the boat passed lighted cigarettes back to the men on the rafts. Somebody started to sing "You are my sunshine, my only sunshine," and others took it up. People felt able to joke a little.

The moon sank, large and golden, into the sea. For a while only stars lit the sky, but as Bourke-White watched, puffy clouds on the horizon picked up the light of dawn. As soon as she could, she pulled out her camera and mounted the gunwales of the bobbing boat to photograph her fellow passengers. A British flying boat overhead spotted them, and they waved back wildly. Not far off a destroyer from their convoy began picking up survivors, and before long they too were aboard. In the general relief they learned that only two soldiers had died, although a number of nurses had suffered twisted ankles or broken bones. People felt in their pockets to confirm what had made it through: Margaret had her Rolleiflex and her Linhof, Jeanne Dixon (Ike's secretary) her prayer book, and Kay Summersby her lipstick.

Bourke-White concluded her piece in *Life*:

> I climbed again to the gun station. Far over on the horizon our mother ship was still afloat. She was listing much lower to port now and destroyers were taking off all the troops that were left. The hundreds of survivors on our destroyer watched the mother ship disappear in the distance. She had meant something very special to all of us. She had stood by us through 60-ft waves and 70-mile-an-hour gales. When wounded she had held up until the last living man was removed from her decks. Our destroyer picked up speed now and before the day was over we sighted the purple hills of Africa.

In the heady emotion of stepping onto solid land, the importance of lost clothes and cameras faded to insignificance. She was alive; she was whole; she had met the challenge of a truly frightening experience without panic; she had her photographs and vivid recollections for a story for *Life*. Not for the world — let alone for Hollywood — would she have traded that.

In contrast to Bourke-White's England-to-North Africa voyage, Ruth Cowan's trip all the way from America in the early weeks of 1943 proved uneventful. She and Inez Callaway Robb, an INS reporter from New York who had joined her, were in the mid-Atlantic before the Wacs were informed that their destination was not England but Africa. No one seemed to mind. Everyone was determinedly roughing it, Cowan reported, fourteen to a cabin in bunk beds, no sheets, pillows, or hot water — no fresh water at all except for drinking. They wore their army fatigues day and night, and never left their rooms without life jackets. Despite several U-boat alerts, the convoy reached Algiers without incident.

There was plenty of "incident" awaiting Cowan in Algiers, however. The head of the AP office, Wes Gallagher, had not been consulted on the subject of attaching a woman reporter to his unit. A recognized misogynist, he suggested that when Cowan's ship returned to the United States, she should be on it. Robb's welcome at INS was warmer, but both women had trouble with General Robert McClure, U.S. Army public relations officer, who was all wrought up about women reporters in a combat zone. Ruth thought she had put the "no women" rules behind her long ago, and was distressed to face the same prejudice again. She did not really mind, she said, eating alone in her room in Rabat when the press corps dining room steward refused to serve her on the grounds that it was a stag mess. Exclusion was practiced in some Washington press circles, too. Harder to take was the cold-shouldering by Gallagher, his refusal to assign her any stories or afford her transport to the WAAC area. But she had ferreted out her own news before, and would do so again.

Still, Cowan could not resist one act of protest. At the wireless office she wrote out a telegram to a good friend: Mrs. Eleanor Roosevelt, 1600 Pennsylvania Ave., Washington, D.C. She knew the first lady strongly supported her present undertaking, but now Ruth cautioned her to desist. "Don't encourage more women to come to Africa," the wire read. "The men don't want us here." The wire never left the country, as Cowan suspected it would not, but word of it got around, and the atmosphere around military personnel improved. It would not look good for a friend of the commander in chief's wife to be treated shabbily while trying to do her job, no matter what one's private opinion on the wisdom of her having been given that job.

The home offices of AP and INS expected a variety of stories from their women correspondents, and Cowan and Robb did their best to comply. Although they traveled together much of the time, their stories were surprisingly dissimilar. Robb's were breezy anecdotes of the American soldier's life overseas, lighthearted and optimistic in tone. Her reports from an evacuation hospital made no mention of nurses being tired or injuries serious; she recorded the joking banter of the young patients in the ward, the kind of thing considered reassuring to the folks back home. That may have been the directive given her. If so, it was unfortunate, because it lent her reporting no weight, as she herself must have been aware.

Cowan's pieces had more depth and texture. Her readers, if not exactly on the battlefield, at least knew they were behind the lines of a recognizable war. One day Ruth visited an evacuation hospital in an open valley high in the Tunisian mountains. It was marked by a great white cross made of sheets spread out on a field and held down by rocks. The campaign was not going well, and American forces in the area were retreating. The surgical hospital farther to the front had been disbanded, Ruth reported, and their evac hospital had become frontline. "I never thought women could live a life so hard as that of these nurses," Cowan wrote. It was bitterly cold, and while some of them had small oil stoves in their tents, others did not. They slept two to a tent on army cots, and heated water for bathing and laundering in discarded biscuit tins. On duty they were always neatly dressed in their blue seersucker uniforms, blue sweaters, and traditional white stockings, shoes, and aprons. Ruth's account was one of many paeans to American nurses during the war.

Margaret Bourke-White experienced none of Cowan's difficulties with military authorities in North Africa. When her clothes went down with her ship, Major General Jimmy Doolittle, commander of the Twelfth Air Force, North Africa, loaned her some of his, and had her flown to the Ninety-seventh Bomb Group air base on an oasis in the Sahara. Romantically dubbed the Garden of Allah, the oasis was in fact swept by stinging sands, hot by day and cold by night. Its few buildings were in ruins from regular bombing.

But for Bourke-White, the Garden of Allah was her reward on earth after her recent troubles. The Ninety-seventh was her own bomb group from England, and its commanding officer the same Colonel J. Hampton Atkinson present at the christening of the *Flying Flitgun*. Shortly after her arrival at the air base, the tall, lean, and good-looking Atkinson was promoted to brigadier general, affording Margaret an excuse to give a party in his honor. This not very subtle sign of her feelings inspired like sentiments in the new general, and before long they were openly sharing quarters. As her biographer, Vicki Goldberg, noted: "In the evening, when the entertainment was over, she left with

Margaret Bourke-White attired for a bombing mission, North Africa, 1943.
MARGARET BOURKE-WHITE/*TIME* MAGAZINE.

the general, while every man there dreamed of what it might be like if she had left with him." The liaison provided delicious gossip for both military headquarters in North Africa and *Time-Life* offices in New York. Neither the general nor the photographer cared. He was the captain of the football team and she was his sweetheart — welcome tonic for a woman whose ex-husband had just taken another wife, one half his age, and hers.

Besides, there was her work, and as Bourke-White observed, "You can do one of two things: put your mind on your work, or worry about what people are saying about you. The two do not mix." When General Doolittle asked if she wanted to go on a bombing mission — an opportunity still rare even for male photographers — she did not hesitate. It was the obvious next challenge in her skyrocketing career. With cameras loaned by the signal corps, she practiced for a week how she would operate inside the big B-17. The severe cold would necessitate electric mittens, making everything that much more difficult. On the hot desert floor she donned layer after layer of flying apparel, plus an oxygen mask, and rehearsed manipulating the cameras in and out of the best shooting spots in the plane's interior.

Later Bourke-White wrote that she did not recall having given a thought to the fact that the expedition into which she was putting so much effort was a mission of death. Perhaps she could not afford to consider that her target might include human beings, even civilians, any more than that her plane might be hit and she not return. The flight, she wrote, had "its own equipment, its own rules, even its own morals." The Flying Fortresses set off at dawn for El Aouina airfield near Tunis. In the lead plane, Bourke-White began at once to photograph the crewmen at their positions, including the bombardier when he went back to pull the safety devices from the bombs. As the plane gained altitude, they donned oxygen masks. A portable oxygen bottle allowed Margaret to move about, from the waist gunner's port to the radio gunner's hatch, until the moment they were over the target and she heard the command "Bombs away!"

After her plane had unloaded its cargo, banked, and turned, it began a dipping and weaving evasive action to avoid the antiaircraft fire from below, offering her a variety of angles to shoot from. Her involuntary squeals of delight came through over the interphone. With no little amusement the crew heard "Oh, that's just what I want, that's a beautiful angle!" followed by "Hold me this way so I can shoot straight down." For a woman who began her career shooting from the protruding beams of skyscrapers, the flight was a consummate experience.

The mission, too, was a success. Indications were that as many as forty German planes had been destroyed. *Life* gave her story seven pages, and included a small picture of the photographer in all her flying regalia. The caption called her "the first woman ever to fly with a U.S. combat crew over enemy soil." This was true. Not true was their claim that all the planes had returned intact. Two Flying Fortresses had gone down, two crews had not returned, but *Life* did not think its readers needed to know about that.

The American military must have wished they could obscure their own setback so easily. The retreat Ruth Cowan had reported on the southern Tunisian front was not checked, and as the Germans continued to advance, all nonessential Americans were ordered to leave the area. Cowan and Robb knew that "nonessential" included them. In the company of four officers, they headed for the rear in a courier auto that soon broke down, leaving them to pile their bedrolls, knapsacks, and typewriters at a fork in the road and take turns thumbing a lift. Eventually a colonel managed to secure a weapons carrier that could be spared long enough to take them to the nearest town, where they spent the night, hopping a ride in a transport the next morning.

In March 1943 Robb returned to the United States, and Cowan left North Africa for England. It could not be said that their participation in the North African campaign had been a success. This may have been partly the fault of their inexperience with the military, but surely far greater blame lies with their superiors who could have aided them if they had chosen to. Wes Gallagher's silent treatment of Cowan was humiliating — unforgivable considering that she had been employed by the AP for twelve years and was there under its auspices. General McClure never became reconciled to either woman's presence. When their negative attitude on women reporters was questioned, both men claimed it was the personalities of these particular women that was the problem. In 1943, that was still an acceptable thing to say.

17

Touching Base on Five Continents

Among women in any field at a given time, there will be one or two who possess "star quality." Their work is their signature; they are true originals. Around them hangs the aura of the exotic. Dorothy Thompson was such a person. Another was Lee Miller.

By early 1942 Elizabeth Lee Miller had been living in England for nearly three years, working as a photographer for British *Vogue*. Although most of her friends were British, she regularly encountered American journalists, including women who now were in uniform, looked very smart, and carried cards allowing them to shop at the PX (post exchange) for items unobtainable anywhere else. Why should she not do the same?

Lee Miller, *Vogue*

Lee Miller grew up in Poughkeepsie, New York, the only daughter in a close and loving family, but two events in her early life shattered an otherwise normal and happy childhood. First, she was sexually molested at the age of seven by the son of family friends, and from that experience contracted venereal disease. The cure for that before the age of penicillin was terrible for a child to endure. In an effort to keep the psychic scars at a minimum, her parents did their best as she grew up to persuade her that sex and love were only minimally connected, that sex was an insignificant part of life. The second event occurred when, as a teenager out rowing one day with her first real boyfriend, she sat helpless while in the space of a few moments he either fell or jumped overboard, suffered heart failure, and died. Lee reacted with mounting rebellion against the incongruities of life. Expelled for "unsuitable" behavior from one school after another, she was at last sent off with two spinster ladies to Paris. In no time she had ditched her chaperones and taken charge of her own future.

Miller's deepest emotional bond, perhaps ever, was with her father. When he feared her emancipation might go too far, he went to Paris and brought her home. She entered the Art Students League in New York, by chance met Condé Nast, and began to model for *Vogue*. Barely twenty, tall and blond with pale blue eyes, she had a kind of detached beauty perfectly suited for the clothes of the period. Edward Steichen photographed her often. So did others, including her father on her weekend visits home. He had become enamored of stereoscopic photography, and his secret passion was nudes. Lee posed for him, cool and unselfconscious. Taking off her clothes in front of a camera, her family, friends, was natural to her.

Miller returned to Paris with the goal of becoming a photographer herself. She approached Man Ray and asked to become his pupil; before long she was his lover as well, but it was the work that was important. She learned fast, took her own apartment and studio, set up a darkroom, and won assignments from top fashion houses like Schiaparelli and Chanel. She continued to model, and on the side starred in Jean Cocteau's film *Blood of a Poet*. At twenty-five Lee returned to New York where, assisted by her brother, she achieved remarkable success in portrait photography, then threw it up to marry an Egyptian twenty years her senior and move to Cairo. Egypt, however, proved confining. With her husband's blessing she spent several carefree, hedonistic months traveling in the company of Roland Penrose, who had introduced surrealism in Britain. In the south of France, Picasso painted her with a sunny yellow face, smiling green mouth, and breasts like the sails of ships. She returned to Egypt, but in the summer of 1939 her husband accepted the inevitability of a divorce. Miller left Egypt to travel again with Penrose. They were in Antibes with Picasso and Dora Maar as war clouds loomed, and just made it to a Channel port when Hitler marched into Poland.

Miller rejected advice to return home, and remained with Penrose in England. She joined British *Vogue*, but "Brogue," as it was known, virtually ignored the war. Lee photographed throughout the Blitz and, in collaboration with Ernestine Carter and Edward R. Murrow, published *Grim Glory: Pictures of Britain Under Fire*. In fact, the pictures were less grim than they were poetic and surrealist. But with *Grim Glory* as evidence of her ability, she applied in 1942 to the U.S. Army for accreditation, and was accepted.

The great advantage of a uniform and an AGO card, Miller discovered, was access to areas that were otherwise off limits. She began with an upbeat story on American nurses, followed by a piece on Wrens in training, and another on ATS (Auxiliary Territorial Service) women who operated a searchlight battery in north London. On these last two she worked with David Scherman, a young *Life* photographer. They were immediate buddies, sharing the same irreverent humor and devil-may-care attitude toward danger. Lee had barely completed her shots of the beaming young ATS women in their heavy anoraks and boots when the battery came under enemy fire. Another night she and Scherman went down into the London Underground air raid shelters to photograph sculptor Henry Moore, who regularly went to sketch the people there.

The compatibility Miller had with Scherman was all too absent when *Vogue* sent her on a job with Cecil Beaton. Lee thought Beaton conceited and, worse, anti-Semitic. One rather boozy evening she molded a small wax figure of him and stuck it with pins. When word came next day that he was on a plane that had gone down, she was filled with guilt; she had meant only to wound him, she said, not kill him. In fact, she had done neither. He had not been a passenger after all.

Lee Miller's photos during 1943 corroborated the resumption of full-scale German bombing, and Mary Welsh, returning to England from home leave in America, was startled at the gray faces and general weariness of her friends. All U.S. publications allowed their reporters regular, if infrequent, home leave. It was a time to rest and visit families, but also to get reacquainted with the home office. It was always a shock to reporters when they returned from the safe, privileged U.S.A. to the hardships of the war theater. While hardly comparable to the Blitz, the renewed bombing of London was a lot more disruptive than Mary had expected. Her earlier nonchalance vanished; when the Hyde Park guns let go during a dinner party nearby, she found herself shaking uncontrollably.

Welsh and her Australian reporter husband, Noel Monks, who had been in the Pacific theater for most of 1942, were reunited in New York at Christmas. In London after the New Year, they found that the long separation had left both of them changed, and neither seemed inclined to address those changes. His leave over, Monks was sent to North Africa, and word drifted back about a pretty woman often seen with him. Mary shrugged. London was a Garden of Eden for a single woman, she said, apparently including herself in that category.

After her joyful resumption of the profession of foreign correspondent in the summer of 1942, Sonia Tomara, *New York Herald Tribune* reporter for the China-Burma-India theater, had moved on to winter at an American advance outpost in the Naga Hills on India's eastern border. The natives there had no alphabet and wore only loincloths, men and women alike, which had taken some getting used to. By the following summer, 1943, Tomara had continued her easterly course to relatively civilized Chungking. A new Japanese offensive was pressing westward — perhaps only to seize the rice harvest, but possibly with intent to seize the capital, as they had the old capitals of Peking, Nanking, and Hankow. Tomara stayed in the press hostel, and in the evenings, when the light inside was too dim to read by, she sat with other correspondents in the courtyard and talked of escape alternatives, just as she had done in Warsaw and Belgrade and Paris in the first year of the war. One could always flee over the old caravan trails, she said, although her colleagues preferred the Marco Polo route through Central Asia. In fact, that was the only land route still open, except for a circuitous course through Russia.

But the Japanese advance fizzled, and early in August 1943 Tomara left Chungking. Leaving felt a bit like treason, she said, because the city

196

(From left) Robert Pepper Martin, Madame Chiang Kai-shek, Sonia Tomara, and
Brooks Atkinson, *New York Times*, Chungking, 1943.
UPI/CORBIS-BETTMANN.

had suffered so much. She moved on to the headquarters of the
Fourteenth Air Force in southern China, where the monsoon season
was in full swing, and where, when weather permitted, she hitched a
ride in a bomber raid over Hankow. Scrunched down in the nose with
the bombardier-navigator, she watched the shadows of the other planes
on the ground below, and the bombs falling in clusters onto the airfield.

Tomara spent a month with the Fourteenth U.S. Air Force
Forward Echelon. Every day she watched shark-nosed P-40s zoom into
the sky on their way to bomb more airfields, destroy more Zeros, blast

harbors as far away as Hong Kong. "You do feel the war here at this airfield," Sonia wrote. "When a mission goes out, your heart is twisted with anxiety."

Other women were on the move to other continents that summer of 1943. Helen Kirkpatrick went down to North Africa. Word of General McClure's resistance to women in a combat area had sifted back to London, and Kirkpatrick began by treading very lightly around the Algiers press corps, but no one voiced an objection to her presence. From Allied headquarters on July 10, 1943, she forwarded dispatches on the invasion of Sicily, only three miles from the Italian mainland, by British and American forces. Within a week or two she reported that General George Patton's troops had reached the capital, Palermo, and were poised to pounce on Italy itself. Italy's withdrawal from the war might come sooner than anyone expected, Helen suggested. Indeed, in August Mussolini was arrested, King Victor Emmanuel was restored to the post of commander in chief, and Marshal Pietro Badoglio became prime minister. Badoglio was the very man with whom Eleanor and Reynolds Packard had shared a car during the Italian advance to Addis Ababa seven years before. Now he initiated secret negotiations and in September 1943 surrendered Italy to the Allies — which did not, however, mean that Italy was out of the war. German forces remained firmly entrenched there.

That same fall Carl and Shelley Mydans were on the final lap of their journey home. The Japanese attack on Manila, the long months in the Santo Tomás and Shanghai internment camps, were behind them. At the neutral port of Mormugao, Goa, the Swedish exchange ship *Gripsholm* tied up beside the *Teia Maru*, and passengers filed slowly off one ship and onto the other in two great semicircles, one well inside the other. It was startling how the Americans and Canadians, thin and brown in their ragged clothes, Chinese straw hats on their heads and bundles and baskets in their arms, looked more Asian than the well-fed Japanese wearing the latest American styles and carrying shiny American suitcases. As they started up the gangway of the *Gripsholm*, Carl and Shelley paused for a moment to watch them, but then, as Carl wrote later, "hands reached out to help us aboard, someone said, 'Come on home,' and our composure crumpled and everything went out of focus."

Almost immediately they were offered a nearly forgotten delicacy — ice water in little paper cups. As they started across the deck, a tall American approached, introduced himself as a State Department representative, and held out to Carl what he passed off as "this old thing that I've never been able to work myself and I thought you might like to borrow for the trip home" — a camera, complete with film. "I saw him take a camera in his hands for the first time in nearly two years and watched his eyes light up," Shelley wrote later to an editor at *Life*. "His fingers curled around it automatically and he started right off on the job."

The trip home, via Rio de Janeiro, lasted six weeks. As Mydans's photos show, it was a recuperative time of food, rest, vitamin pills, and new clothes distributed by the Red Cross. But as the warm waters of the Caribbean gave way to the cold, choppy sea off Cape Hatteras, anxiety set in again. They had been gone so long. Could they regain their lives?

On the morning of December 1, 1943 — almost two years since the bombing of Pearl Harbor and the Philippines — the *Gripsholm* sailed into New York harbor. On deck Carl and Shelley watched the tips of skyscrapers rise above the fog. They were met first by officials, then by tearful family and friends, but what they later treasured most was the *Life* reporter they knew from the past, in full war correspondent attire, greeting them "with a wonderful casualness and saying, as though we'd never been away, 'Better hurry. They're waiting for you back at the office.' "

In the months that followed Shelley and Carl Mydans picked up their lives with little difficulty. Both received their delayed accreditation, and Carl was assigned to a European post. Shelley planned to stay home, write a book, and join him later. On a soft April evening they stood at Penn Station saying goodbye — a picture Carl had shot many times — but when the train pulled away, he felt strangely unsure of himself. "As I headed back to another front in another land," he wrote, "I was suddenly aware that so much of the strength I had always thought was mine, was Shelley's."

18

Slogging Through Italy

In October Margaret Bourke-White flew into Naples soon after its capture by the U.S. Fifth Army. There was not much left of the city. Allied forces had bombed it through August and September, and the occupying Germans had blown up everything in the harbor before they withdrew, including the city water system. American troops entered to discover mines ready to explode at the flick of a light switch or at some arbitrary moment perhaps still a week away. Bourke-White found hundreds of families who had lived in caves for more than a year, hiding first from Allied, now from German bombs. There was no shortage of subject matter for her camera, but the pictures were not pretty.

She was in Italy on sufferance. After her return home from North Africa earlier that year, she contacted the families of dozens of soldiers she had come to know during her time with the Ninety-seventh Bomber Group. Margaret carried messages from GIs to their families, even telephoned wives, mothers, and girlfriends to report on the general well-being of a loved one. But when her editors at *Life* approached the air force about her return to the war zone, they found that the top brass had no interest in sending her back. General Eisenhower charged that she had maneuvered herself into that bombing mission with the Ninety-seventh; he had known nothing about it and had not condoned it. Bourke-White "evaded PRO regulations, violated security and broke rules in other ways," *Life* was reminded. Still, the military could not argue with the fine publicity her story had brought to the bomber command, and other branches of the armed services had requested similar attention. The army relented, and authorized a photo series on the engineering corps; less chance for violating rules on the ground, they said.

In *Purple Heart Valley*, the book she wrote about her time in Italy, Bourke-White included photographs of the Naples harbor with its sunken ships, ghostly wrecks of buildings, and hungry children picking among the wreckage. She described how a thorough job of mine clearance had to be completed before the electricity could be turned back on, so that with the act of throwing the main switch, no hidden mines or time bombs would be activated. When the day came, a radio truck crisscrossed the city warning people to take to the hills. Margaret photographed the flood of ragged civilians carrying chairs, pots, babies — whatever was most important to them. She had cameras focused on buildings all over town, ready to catch any part of the city that might start to blow, but when at noon the main switch was thrown, nothing happened. Army officers went into the buildings and calmly turned on the light switches. Power had returned. The people came down from the hills.

One side of her life in Naples that fall went unmentioned in *Purple Heart Valley*. Six months had passed since Bourke-White said goodbye to Brigadier General "Hamp" Atkinson of the Ninety-seventh Bomber Command; they had corresponded for a while, but were no longer in communication. In Naples, in need of a military pass from counterintelligence, Margaret applied to the commanding officer, Major Maxwell Jerome Papurt — Jerry to his friends, Pappy to his men. It was Papurt's job to assess individuals quickly, and he did. When Bourke-White gave her name and occupation, his face lit up; he was full of praises for her work.

Unlike the tall, lanky Hamp, Jerry was stocky, bespectacled and prematurely gray, charming and gregarious. He was also married, but that position was shaky, he implied — not so big a hurdle as to stop him in his pursuit of Margaret, which began at once. If he was a womanizer, he was also much more: at home, a university professor of abnormal psychology and director of a home for delinquent children; in the army, head of counterintelligence and the object of intense loyalty from his men. He admired Bourke-White's dedication to her work and was fascinated by her zest for life while surrounded by death. As for her, she was chastened by the difficulty *Life* had had securing permission for her to return to the combat area, and was on her best behavior. There were two Margarets. The one with a camera in her hand could be a demon, but the other one — gay, full of fun — could brighten drab army life immeasurably. In the evenings she and Jerry did those little romantic things they might have done in peacetime, like singing (off-key) together, or dancing in a leaky old ballroom. Within a month he was begging her to marry him. He had, he said, written to ask his wife for a divorce.

But when the main action moved north to the mountainous area below Cassino, Bourke-White packed up her cameras and moved with it. She was quartered in a monastery with fifty monks. Her cell opened out into a vaulted corridor, like scores of identical cells inhabited by the brothers; at night she could hear them pattering about, visiting each other. The fourteenth-century cloister seemed unaffected by the war raging all around it, and she appreciated this island of sanity in an otherwise crazed world. The engineers camping in the neighborhood appreciated it, too, especially for the hot water available there in the mornings for shaving. They would drift into the central courtyard, fill their helmets and prop them up on the balustrade. "Buon giorno," the friars would say, passing by with their kettles, and the lathered Yanks would reply in kind.

Bourke-White could not very well wash in the courtyard, so by previous arrangement the CO would walk over early each morning, knock at her door to awaken her, then continue down the hall to a large stone cell fitted up with primitive plumbing. When it was empty, he would call out, "Coast's clear!" and stand guard while she was inside. Her grooming completed, he would escort her to the senior officers' mess tent for breakfast, after which the corporal assigned as her aide would load her cameras into a command car and climb in front. With Margaret and an officer in back, they would be off to that day's destination to inspect, and photograph, the engineers at work.

Their route one morning encompassed a newly completed Bailey bridge that spanned a gorge and was positioned so deep in the ravine that it could not be seen by German marksmen across the valley. The Bailey bridge was a wonder of invention; assembled in sections on one side of a river, it was then pushed across, some distance above the water, until its extremity found a safe landing spot on the far side. Bourke-

White's party crossed the bridge and arrived at the work site; she took her pictures, and was about to begin a K-ration lunch when shelling was heard in the gorge behind them. The colonel and the photographer went to investigate.

At the stretch of road before the bridge, they came upon men standing motionless in ditches, crouched behind big rocks, or lying flat in the shelter of an old ruined wall. Another shell whizzed across and sent a truck up in flames. The colonel slammed the jeep to a stop, and they made for the nearest ditch themselves. From its high protective side Margaret took pictures as the shells landed all around them. During a pause the jeep made it back to the work site, but the shelling continued all afternoon. The Germans seemed determined to knock the Bailey out; Bourke-White was all too aware that if they did, she could not get back to the monastery, and if they did not, she would have to cross that bridge while they were still trying. When the time came and they approached the bridge, they found it still in one piece, and they crossed without incident. A large open area on the far side was also within enemy range, but again nothing happened. Margaret was just beginning to relax when they hit a bottleneck. Bottlenecks were scary because they made for sitting targets, and as feared, a shell sailed over their heads. When traffic resumed, they saw ahead two soldiers lying on either side of the road, so quietly that Margaret thought they were asleep. Jeeps and trucks flowed steadily between them, and only when their own car reached that spot was she jolted into awareness: one man had lost half his head, the other his face.

Bourke-White returned exhausted to her cell. In short succession the nightly ritual of two knocks on her door was repeated: first, an engineer and amateur photographer who had appointed himself to collect her mud-caked boots and leggings each evening and return them to her washed and dried in the morning; second, the CO come to escort her to the "plumbing." Back in her dark cell, Margaret crawled into her narrow cot, and if she could ignore the flashes of light in her window, the barking of distant guns, and the image of a dead GI on either side of the road, she too might sleep.

A quiet monastery cell, however primitive, would have seemed a lovely respite to Helen Kirkpatrick that fall of 1943. After covering action in North Africa, Corsica, and Malta for the *Chicago Daily News*, she continued north into Italy and joined an American mobile surgical unit on the Volturno. November was a month of constant rain and mud. She lived with the nurses in a tent; the latrine was "walled" by blankets, the top open to the elements. Hospital beds and operating room were also tented, and the enemy was just over the hill. A Japanese-American Nisei division in the area fought magnificently, leading to heavy casualties, and the wounded of both sides were brought in there. The staff was shorthanded, so when Helen was not actually writing her stories, she was helping out. "Amputations didn't bother me — I could tolerate anything as long as I didn't see the face of the man," she said later. "It was then that the casualty became a person."

She had been there only a few weeks when a message arrived: she was to return immediately to Algiers. Her publisher, Colonel Frank Knox, had assumed the post of secretary of the navy, and was in consultation at Allied headquarters there. Still in her combat boots, Helen flew back across the Mediterranean, and barely had time to wash up and put on a clean uniform before she was whisked off to a fine villa where stewards in white jackets were passing around cocktails. It was not easy to go to a cocktail party straight from the mud of the Volturno, the wounded men and exhausted nurses, Kirkpatrick discovered. She hoped Knox would ask her about Italy, but he had not recalled her for conversation. He wanted her to return to London at once. Helen protested, but the colonel was firm. There were things she would need to do in London, he intimated, and made it clear the discussion was over. Early in December she went.

That same month, December 1943, Sonia Tomara covered the Teheran Conference for the *New York Herald Tribune*, then moved on to Allied headquarters in Algiers. From there she, too, turned her attention to Italy, a country that bore little resemblance to the one she had known nine years before when Mussolini was riding high, ordering troops into Ethiopia, shouting from the balcony on the Piazza Venezia that Italy must assume her rightful stature among nations. The Italy of the winter and spring of 1944 had no stature at all — it was overrun by foreign troops. Pushing up from the south were American (including African- and Japanese-American), British, Canadian, New Zealand,

Indian, Free French, French Moroccan, and Polish regiments. Facing them from the north, grudgingly relinquishing a village here, a mountaintop there, were the Germans.

Tomara began the New Year of 1944 with an optimistic assessment: the American Fifth Army was only six miles from Cassino, which was seventy miles from Rome — how long could that take? As it turned out, with frigid weather conditions and fierce enemy resistance, achingly long. Near the end of January, when she reported the landing of thousands of Allied troops at Anzio, only thirty-two miles from Rome, it was hoped that real progress might be made. But again, nothing was easy. Tomara's dispatches revealed that two days after the Anzio landing, nine German divisions — a hundred thousand men — moved in for counterattacks. Advance there, too, was slow and cautious.

Margaret Bourke-White's final Italian assignment, early in January 1944, was to do a series on the medical corps. She began with the Thirty-eighth Evacuation Hospital near the ridge of hills that bordered the Cassino valley. It was hard to photograph such suffering close at hand, but the surgeon encouraged her: it was important for people at home to know what their boys were going through. Her first subject was a young soldier with a hole in his throat and chest and a wound in his stomach; to keep him from drowning in his own blood, the surgeon was siphoning it out from his lungs through a tracheotomy tube and returning it to him through intravenous injection. Margaret thought it impossible that he would recover, but she was assured that he would. The photos *Life* selected gave folks back home a close-up view of their wounded GIs, but the dominant perception was one of mud. Nurses emptied pails of water from leaky tents and slithered through a morass of slime to the "powder room." A convalescent private waded to the mess tent in muddy boots. All were models of cheerful endurance — *Life*'s kind of Americans.

More dramatic were the photos taken at the Eleventh Field Hospital. By chance her arrival there coincided with an attempt by the Thirty-sixth (Texas) Division to make an assault crossing of the Rapido River as part of a plan to open up Highway 6 to Rome. The Eleventh fought in front of the American heavy guns and within aim of German guns controlling the heights. On Margaret's first night a number of shells landed in the hospital area. One shell scored a direct hit on the mess tent. The electrical system went out.

In *Purple Heart Valley* Bourke-White described how she and her aide made their way to the operating tent where work was continuing by flashlight. She photographed the doctors and nurses in their surgical gowns, muddy boots, and battle helmets attempting to repair the young bodies. At intervals a warning whistle or scream would break the quiet and everyone would drop to the floor, only to jump up and go back to work the minute the bang of the exploding shell was heard. Casualties kept pouring in. Blood supplies ran low; members of the hospital staff began volunteering theirs, and truck drivers were called in to give a pint before hurrying back to work again. Margaret photographed one recipient, a soldier from Texas with two crushed legs. He would not be one of the successes: in the early hours of the morning he begged the nurse to cover the feet he no longer had, whispered, "I'm so cold," and died.

"Watching death so close before my eyes," Bourke-White wrote, "I had forgotten the wholesale screaming death being hurled from the mountaintop." The shelling began again, and back in the nurses' tent the exhausted women spent the rest of the night rolled in blankets under their cots. Next morning Margaret accompanied a medic to an ambulance relay point where more wounded were waiting. As the jeep headed out toward the enemy-held mountain, the sun broke through the clouds. "Everything was so still, so pure," she wrote, "it seemed impossible that from this same mountain such hell could have gushed forth the night before."

The American assault lasted for three days, and a thousand Texans died. Her assignment finished, Bourke-White returned to Naples. Major Jerry Papurt was still there; she had spent several weekend leaves with him, and he never ceased assuring her of his love. They talked of her next trip to Italy, the war's end, a life together. Then she got on a plane and flew home. Her negatives and notes routinely traveled to the Pentagon in an army pouch and were developed there by the signal corps, or by *Life* technicians under military supervision. Only those that passed censorship went on to New York. Unaccountably, the pouch containing the film of her time with the Eleventh Field Hospital vanished. The less dramatic evacuation hospital negatives were there, but not the ones of medics operating in battle helmets by flashlight, nurses diving for the floor at the burst of a shell, a young Texan receiving blood transfusions in both arms. Bourke-White, who had risked her life to get those shots, stormed about the Pentagon, but they were simply gone. She always thought of that loss as her wound, and Papurt's letters about how she had become a legend in Italy, how stories of her courage were being told and retold, only partially consoled her.

That fall and winter of 1943–44 Martha Gellhorn left her disgruntled husband behind in Cuba and returned to the war zone. She went first to England, then moved down to Italy. Although she made repeated attempts in her letters, she could not persuade Hemingway to join her. He insisted that scouting for enemy submarines off the Florida coast was more important, but Gellhorn did not believe that was the real reason. One explanation for his reluctance was that he had mythologized his earlier war experiences in France and Spain and was now a prisoner of his own myth. Also, although he was only forty-five, it was not a trim, energetic forty-five. At thirty-five, Martha had recently completed a new novel and was ambitious to resume her war correspondent career. "I would give anything to be part of the invasion and see Paris right at the beginning and watch the peace," she wrote him from England.

By February 1944 she had made her way to Naples, where she arranged to accompany a French transport officer returning to the French sector of the front. In an open jeep, the wind blowing snow and hail in their faces, they circled up a mountain. "The French held these mountains and opposite them, on higher mountains, were the Germans," Martha reported in *Collier's*. "The mountains to the right were occupied by the Poles, and to the left, around Cassino, were the Americans."

In March Gellhorn moved over to the American sector, where she ran into her old friend Virginia Cowles. For more than a year Cowles had served as assistant to American ambassador Winant in London, but she missed reporting and had recently returned to journalism. Aside from a visit she had made to the Hemingways in Cuba early in 1942, Virginia and Martha had seen little of each other. Now, just as they had done in Madrid during the civil war in Spain, they visited a hospital together. With her remarkable ability to picture a scene in such detail that the reader felt he was there, and then put that scene in a larger perspective, Gellhorn wrote:

> It smelled of many things, of men and dampness and old blankets and ether and pain. . . . War, which is such a large and incomprehensible and impersonal affair, becomes very personal indeed inside a hospital, for at last it is reduced to its basic materiel, the human body. You speak to the wounded who look at you, assuming that they may want company. You try not to let your own health shout down at them; and you try to keep your face and your voice clean of pity, which nobody wants.

When they returned to their jeep, Cowles remarked that at least it had been nice and warm in the hospital. What more was there to say?

Still in Algiers that winter of 1944, Sonia Tomara envied her female colleagues like Gellhorn and Cowles in the war zone. From press communiqués at Allied headquarters she described how the Germans had again failed in an attempt to dislodge the Americans from the Anzio beachhead. Put another way, that could be interpreted to read that the Americans had failed in repeated attempts to advance inland from the beachhead. As for Cassino, although it was hardly more than a ruin, pockets of German troops remained in rocky hideouts above the town, firing away with their mortars.

At last, in April 1944, Tomara left Algiers for Italy. She celebrated Easter with two hundred soldiers of the American Fifth Army clustered around a makeshift altar high on a rocky ledge. They had climbed the hill before sunrise while the mist still lay below them, careful not to step off the narrow path for fear of mines. Beneath them was the great Garigliano valley; on one side Sonia could see a thin strip of sea, and on the other, through the haze, the mountains. Thick-trunked olive trees sported silvery leaves, and wild anemones peeped from between the rocks.

The Germans were no more than four hundred yards away. Occasionally shells whizzed over the heads of the men, but for the most part it was still. An army chaplain of German background from

Nebraska, speaking into a microphone, welcomed both Catholics and Protestants of the German army and wished them a "joyous Easter." Loudspeakers wired to the microphone carried the sound to mountain dugouts and low into the valley. The chaplain read from the twenty-eighth chapter of the Gospel According to Saint Matthew, first in German, then in English. A little camp organ had been hauled up on muleback, and a nurse from the evacuation hospital sang an Easter hymn and "I Know That My Redeemer Liveth" from Handel's *Messiah*. Then the Catholic chaplain said mass, while the Catholic soldiers knelt and received communion. At the designated time, the service was over. The big Allied guns resumed firing. It must have been an emotional morning, even for hardened soldiers on the line, but as usual with Sonia, the writing was spare and the drama underplayed.

Later that spring she reached Cassino. "At last I've seen with my own eyes the front I've been writing about," she reported to the *Herald Tribune*. She traveled the southern front, observed the enemy's positions, listened to the whistling shells and learned to distinguish a departing from an arriving one. She visited American, British, New Zealand, and French troops, and sat at lunch as the guest of a French colonel with a Polish officer on one side, an American on the other, and a Scot in kilts directly across. As a Russian-French-American herself, she was impressed by the internationality of the campaign, while unsure of Allied success. "No invader has ever taken Rome from the south," she reminded her readers. Hannibal had learned that the hard way, as had the Hohenstauffens, and Napoleon. "After seven months of campaigning on Italian ground we are still bogged down. And it tears your heart as you drive through ruined hill towns or see a two-thousand-year-old Roman bridge destroyed by bombs."

One night at the front Tomara watched as the full moon through the narrow silver leaves of olive trees lit up "thousands of brown tents camouflaged in groves and thousands of brown trucks rolling up and down the road. In daytime you could see shells piled in neat rows under blooming peach trees, and tanks seeking cover behind the walls of a peasant's pink house." She described the devastation of the Allied line:

> It begins in the marshy Garigliano plain, once conquered for cultivation, but which will have no harvest this summer. It is

209

cratered by shells, and the roads through which we have to carry supplies are repaired at night and covered with metal net to permit trucks to pass. Beyond the plain are hills, whereof we hold only a few. . . . I have visited Ornito, where dugouts cling to the rocks and where the men are short of water, which must be hauled by mule. On the crest the Germans are twenty yards away and every time we hurl grenades queer shadows creep in the darkness over the rocks. They may be Germans' or ours. Both sides need prisoners for information and this is the way to get them.

As for Cassino, Tomara concluded, it was all one had heard of it, and worse. The plain below it was dead, the earth shriveled; the once picturesque little villages approaching the town were heaps of rubble. Sonia saw one wall of a church still standing, bells rocking gently, but there were no people to call to prayer. Many of the olive trees were cut cleanly in two. Cassino, when she reached it, was hidden by smoke. It seemed to be burning, she wrote, "yet nothing is left there to burn. Guns thudded continuously. Our own shells passed over our heads. The roads were deserted."

For Allied troops and the press that covered them, the Italian campaign had another year of rain and cold and mud to go, but for women reporters there were none of the internal obstacles encountered in North Africa. In Italy the women took care of themselves, even when living with the nurses placed them between their own heavy guns and the enemy. Margaret Bourke-White's little foray across the Bailey bridge under enemy fire, and a risky jaunt into Cassino that Martha Gellhorn attempted in company with several male colleagues, remained undetected by the higher authorities. In truth, the battle for Italy provided about as much danger and discomfort as any reporter of either sex would want to cope with. The real conflict between military discipline and the goals of the press would come with the Normandy landings ahead.

19

New Women Come Over for Overlord

Early in 1944, in anticipation of an imminent cross-Channel invasion and campaign in northwest Europe, code-named Overlord, newly minted American women war correspondents set out for Britain. Editors of major newspapers, impressed by stories under feminine bylines in the *New York Herald Tribune* and *Chicago Daily News,* began to consider whether they perhaps had been neglecting an important angle of war reporting. Local papers boasted a high circulation among women whose husbands or sons were overseas, but military strategy and tactics made the average woman's eyes glaze over. What these women wanted was news of how their men were doing. Martha Gellhorn's assertion that the basic materiel of war was the human body was exactly how most women thought of it.

Accordingly, editors who a year before had summarily dismissed the idea of sending a woman to cover the war were reassessing their position, and wire services that had thought token female representation adequate were beginning to see advantages to having a woman in each area of combat. Competition was a factor, too, in cities like Boston and New York with rival local papers: when one hired a woman on its overseas staff, the other knew its readers would demand the same. The trend was far from universal, however. Editors on small or more traditional papers still relied on picking up a woman's story from one of the news or wire services.

Space does not permit an accounting of all the American women who came over to Europe between the fall of 1943 and the end of the war. The five included here arrived before the Normandy invasion, and are representative in that all were serious reporters, anxious to prove that they could carry out their mission and that their editors' faith in them was not misplaced.

Virginia Irwin, *Saint Louis Post-Dispatch*

Perhaps the most determined was Virginia Irwin of the *Saint Louis Post-Dispatch*. A midwesterner, she was a successful feature writer who covered a wide field, everything from marriage and divorce (both of which she had tried) to opera, theater, national political conventions, and Hollywood (vacationing there one summer, she returned with twenty-one columns). Her articles were fast-paced, funny, provocative. After Pearl Harbor she added serious pieces about women's role in the war, and was sent to WAAC training areas to gather information first-hand. In the summer of 1942 she traveled across the country interviewing manufacturers, plant managers, and women workers for an eleven-part series on women in the war industries.

Irwin had requested assignment as a war correspondent early on, but the *Post-Dispatch* relied for war news on wire and syndicated news services. They had no plans to maintain any war correspondent, certainly not a woman. Virginia was not one to give up easily, however, and in mid-1943 she asked for, and was granted, a leave of absence to join the American Red Cross overseas. The ARC operated more than fifty "clubs" throughout Britain; they provided meals, recreation rooms, and anywhere from five to several hundred beds in hotels appropriated for the duration. Irwin was first assigned to a large club near an airbase (where the young fliers referred to her, age thirty-six, as "Mom") and later moved on to London. Needless to say, stories regularly made their way back to the *Post-Dispatch*.

By early 1944 when that newspaper first seriously considered sending its own war correspondents to Europe, such appointments were harder to arrange. Some areas were virtually closed — Italy, for example, where only replacements were accepted. Accreditation could be slow; security clearance seldom took less than six weeks. There was the problem of "priorities" in getting a reporter passage. But the *Post-Dispatch* requested, and the War Department approved, accreditation for two correspondents, one of whom was Irwin. Her proximity to the action was a major reason for her selection, which surprised her not at all. It was all part of her plan.

Lee Carson, INS

Had there been a prize for glamour, it would have been shared by Lee Carson and Iris Carpenter. An INS Washington reporter for several years, Carson had been labeled the capital's "best-looking woman correspondent" by *Newsweek*. She had a perfect oval face, shoulder-length titian-hued hair, well-arched eyebrows, and a pinup girl figure. Army khaki hid her curves, but the skirt fell just over the knee, and a woman with long and lovely legs had an advantage. Lee was regularly accused of crossing hers and batting her lashes to get a story, but that

Lee Carson, London, 1944.
UPI/Corbis-Bettmann.

was the standard complaint of male reporters when a beautiful woman was part of the competition.

Whatever the faculty at Smith College thought they had prepared Carson for, it was not a job as "stunt reporter" for the *Chicago Daily Times*, which she took right after graduation. Her first assignment was to report an automobile race from behind the wheel of a contending vehicle, regardless of the fact that she barely knew how to drive. She lost the race but won attention and, before long, a post as White House correspondent for INS. As would become clear when she went through three jeeps in a week in the Ardennes, the nerve she displayed in that race never left her. Nerve was a valuable commodity in war reporting, for men and women alike.

Iris Carpenter, *Boston Globe*

A reporter who would share the Ardennes experience with Carson was an Englishwoman who signed on with the *Boston Globe*. Iris Carpenter, daughter of a wealthy movie magnate, started out at eighteen as a film critic on a small publication and then moved on to Lord Beaverbrook's *Daily Express*. Blond and blue-eyed, with near perfect features, she looked more like a film star than a journalist. After she married and had two children, she resigned her position to give more time to her family, but with the outbreak of war, priorities changed. She was summoned by the Ministry of Information and put to work broadcasting for the BBC. Her husband, at the time of the retreat from Dunkirk, piloted the family yacht back and forth across the Channel, retrieving soldiers. During the Blitz, five German planes were shot down over the family estate in Kent, and part of her own house shattered.

Before long Carpenter discovered that more than her house was shattered. Her marriage was in similar disarray. "My husband had found another woman," she said later. "If he wanted somebody else, then that was that. I went to war and forgot him quite deliberately." It was the stiff-upper-lip response to a not uncommon wartime occurrence. Like others before her, Iris saw that work would be her salvation. She settled her children with her sister's family and moved up to London. With the demands of the BBC, the Ministry of Information, the London *Daily Herald,* and now the *Boston Globe,* there was little time for brooding.

Colonel Barney Oldfield, Ninth Army press officer, who saw a lot of Carpenter once she reached the Continent, remembered her as a gracious, sympathetic person who put her troubles behind her. "She could get interviews from anybody," he said. "She was so svelte, animated, and, well, gorgeous. In all that mud and drabness, she made men who saw her think they were dreaming, and if they weren't, they started to do so."

Marjorie "Dot" Avery, *Detroit Free Press*

Both Marjorie Avery, known as Dot, and Catherine Coyne came to Europe with a straightforward, adaptive approach to war reporting.

Marjorie Avery, London, 1944.
DAVID E. SCHERMAN/*LIFE* MAGAZINE. © TIME INC.

Avery's journalistic apprenticeship consisted of a year covering fashion in Paris for the *New York Herald Tribune*. From there she moved to the *Detroit Free Press*, where she reported for, then served as editor of, the women's page. She was small and slim with a helmet of sleek, honey blond hair and an addiction to crazy hats. Her position placed her close to Detroit society, where she developed the tact and forbearance requisite for one in frequent contact with the grandes dames of the auto industry. In private life Dot was known for her soirees and her expertise with exotic curry dishes and delicious salads. It was a pleasant midwestern life, and her colleagues were surprised at her decision to trade it in for a war correspondent post. The *Free Press* hierarchy was much opposed, but they agreed to a six-month trial, beginning in the fall of 1943. Avery's column, "London Diary," would appear on the women's page, and she should approach her work with the aim of providing a light complement to the "important" stories written by *Free Press* male reporters or taken from the wire services. Avery didn't mind. Her strength was in feature stories. She would comply with grace, write as they desired — just let her go.

Catherine Coyne, *Boston Herald*

The last to arrive, in the spring of 1944 only a few weeks before D Day, was Catherine Coyne. Coyne had graduated from Boston University in the same class as Spanish Civil War reporter Frances Davis and *Life* photographer Carl Mydans. "The brightest and most fun-to-be-with of them all" was Carl's memory of her. If Catherine was more fun, it was perhaps because she was more relaxed, less driven than others in the field. Tall and slender, with dark hair and blue eyes, she broke into journalism by writing for a trade paper in cemetery monuments. She later applied for a post as a stringer for the *Boston Herald*, and in time was added to their regular staff. It was a leisurely career progression.

Coyne was possibly the only woman whose war correspondent post simply fell into her lap. At a time when the list of applicants was already lengthy, the *Herald* managing editor bluntly asked her one day how she would feel about covering the war. Iris Carpenter's stories had

Catherine Coyne, London, 1944.
<small>CATHERINE COYNE PERSONAL COLLECTION.</small>

already begun to appear in the *Globe*, and the *Herald*'s female reader-ship was asking why they, too, could not have a correspondent of their own sex. Coyne was startled at the query, but answered in the affirma-tive, which prompted a second blunt question: how soon could she go? Passage was said to be unavailable, but perhaps could be arranged if she could leave at once. In New York the passport bureau was persuaded to cut its waiting time, the British embassy came up with a visa, and Lord & Taylor provided a uniform. In two days she was off.

She traveled on the flagship of a convoy with four USO women and five thousand soldiers. "There was nothing glorious about going off to war," she wrote in her first dispatch to the *Herald*. "The pier was gloomy, almost deserted, as groups of pack-laden soldiers marched all

Ruth Cowan, Normandy, 1944.
SCHLESINGER LIBRARY, RADCLIFFE COLLEGE.

through the night toward the gangplank that was the bridge between the safety of home and the uncertainty of war on foreign soil." Coyne knew it was those very pack-laden soldiers that her readers wanted to hear about, and about this beautiful ship that was their first home-away-from-home, with its scrubbed deck and vast kitchens. The problems of serving so many meant there were only two meals a day, she wrote, and while she and the USO women sat down with the officers, the enlisted men ate from their mess kits, standing.

On the third day out a message was delivered from President Roosevelt. "It was received soberly," Coyne observed, "for it pointed out that 'never were the enemies of freedom more tyrannical, more arrogant, more brutal.'" But except for those few moments when the men pondered the words of their commander in chief, they were seldom serious. She described them always laughing and joking, coltish, forever locking arms and legs for wrestling, and as she wrote she imagined how their mothers and grandmothers would be smiling and nodding in recognition.

With the invasion of the Continent in the offing, the arrival of new women correspondents did not escape the attention of the old hands, who for the most part adopted a wait-and-see attitude. They were too busy themselves to pay much attention. Helen Kirkpatrick, for example: when Colonel Frank Knox, her boss on the *Chicago Daily News* (and now secretary of the navy) had mysteriously sent her from Italy back to England, it was to take her appointed place on the correspondents' committee to plan press coverage for Overlord. There were four on the committee — three men, for magazines, wire services, and radio, and Kirkpatrick for newspapers. Her presence there was a signal honor. The committee met once a week with SHAEF (Supreme Headquarters Allied Expeditionary Force) personnel, including censors, and discussed how many reporters could be accommodated in the first wave of the invasion, how copy would get back to press headquarters, what kind of censorship they should expect. It was not their job to select the correspondents who would go in the first wave, nor was it their decision that none would be women. That unpopular call was made by the top command.

Planning for Overlord itself took place at the old St. Paul's School with General Eisenhower in charge and General Omar Bradley as the number two American. Helen, it was noted, moved among generals and journalists alike with enviable ease and charm.

The same month that Kirkpatrick returned to England from Italy to assume her new post, November 1943, Martha Gellhorn arrived in London from Cuba. She took a room at the Dorchester and applied for her official war correspondent credentials. The subjects of her stories for *Collier's* ranged widely: the daring flights of RAF pilots; how the poor children of London were faring during this long war; Polish refugees.

Both she and Helen Kirkpatrick wrote stories at that time from interviews with men who had slipped out of Poland and made their way to Britain. Helen's informant was a key man in the Polish underground who to her surprise spoke fluent English, which he said he had learned from British prisoners of war who had escaped from their camps and were living with members of his network. Gellhorn interviewed three Poles for her story; only one was Jewish, but all described the horrors that the Jews were suffering there.

The first, whose farm had been confiscated by the Germans but who remained there as a servant in preference to being deported elsewhere, described how German soldiers had made a group of Jews dig their own graves nearby, and then had shot them in the village square. "We have seen everything," the man said.

The second Pole, a student when the war started, told Gellhorn he had been sent to do forced labor in East Prussia, but had jumped from the train. Back in Warsaw he had changed his appearance, his name, and his papers. The underground sent him all over Poland, so he had seen more than most people — the breeding farms, for example, "where selected Polish girls are kept so as to augment the great Aryan race." As for the German policy of extermination of the Jews, he had nightmares, he said, after he saw the cattle cars with Jews of all ages packed into them, forty-six cars with 130 persons per car. They just ran the train twelve kilometers outside of town. It took the people inside seven or eight hours to die.

Gellhorn's Jewish informant had been in the ghetto in Warsaw. Before the war he had been a lawyer and an official at the League of Nations, but he had gone back to Warsaw and lived in the ghetto until, near the end, some Poles helped him escape to France because of his particular usefulness. She recorded his story of the ghetto, of the ten-foot-high wall, how the Jews were not allowed to go out to work but forced to live off meager rations. Hunger, cold, lack of sanitation, then typhus, and no medicine to combat it. Young German soldiers prowling about, taking potshots at anyone they saw, as if they were rabbit hunting. And finally, the decision of the remaining Jews to fight back, perceiving that although the Allies would get there sometime, it would be too late for them.

"Poland seemed dreadfully far away, dark and silent," Gellhorn concluded her story, "but these men . . . speak for the silenced millions of their own people." As for herself, she was making sure they were heard, heard in safe, comfortable America where too many people did not want to hear, or believe, what was happening in a faraway, dark and silent land.

Gellhorn's interest in Poland had been noted by Mary Welsh, who recalled a cocktail party given for Martha in which she "had devoted her entire attention to a couple of Polish pilots." Welsh, who took her socializing seriously, had not approved. She was a regular at the over-populated and often raucous weekends at Time Out, the Time Inc. home-away-from-home in Buckinghamshire. William Walton, another *Time* reporter who shared an office with her, said she was very gay that winter and spring, had given up on her marriage, and had a string of beaus, including a very ardent general who competed for top dog with Irwin Shaw, reporter for *Stars and Stripes* and *Yank*. All were married, but Mary's husband Noel Monks was in the Pacific, and the men's wives a long way off in America.

Another man was about to enter Welsh's life. Ernest Hemingway was not only married, he was the husband of a colleague. After her winter in London and Italy, Martha Gellhorn had returned to Cuba to make one last attempt to pry him loose from what she saw as his dissolute life, and get him to Europe. Perhaps she hoped that if they were reporting the same war, even if not always together as in Spain, some of the companionship of that time might be restored. Hemingway at last acquiesced, but in his anger at her for forcing the issue, he asked Martha's editors at *Collier's* to take him on as a combat correspondent, knowing that they could not refuse, and that it would limit her chances at the front. He acquired air passage for himself only, leaving her to recross the Atlantic on a slow freighter loaded with dynamite.

Welsh was lunching with Irwin Shaw at the popular White Tower in London one warm spring day when Hemingway stopped by the table and asked to be introduced — he didn't actually say "to this fine woman who looks so devastating in her sweater," but his old friend Shaw knew that was what that glance meant. He also knew that although he had competed quite satisfactorily with the general, the famous novelist was out of his class. Not long afterward Shaw learned that in spite of the fact that Mary's husband Noel had just arrived in London on leave, she had moved with a woman friend into the Dorchester Hotel, ostensibly because of its "roof of lovely thick concrete." Hemingway was also staying at the Dorchester. Late one night after a cocktail party, he visited the two women in their room, and as they lounged on the beds with the lights off and the windows open to the blacked-out London night, he proposed. "I don't know you, Mary," she recalled him saying. "But I want to marry you. . . . I want to marry you now, and I hope to marry you sometime. Sometime you may want to marry me." Welsh reminded him they were both married. "You are very premature," she murmured, somewhat lamely.

A few nights later, returning from a party at which everyone had drunk too much, the car in which Hemingway was a passenger went head-on into a steel water tank, and Ernest head-on into the windshield. He suffered a concussion and required many stitches at a nearby hospital. Mary brought him spring flowers and spoke soothingly. In contrast, Martha, when at last she reached England and visited him in his hospital room, was critical of the drunken orgy that had brought about his mishap and laughed at the size of the bandage. His injury was in fact serious, but after two weeks on a freighter with explosives and without lifeboats, Gellhorn could not dredge up much sympathy. When he began his usual taunting, she cut him short. She had had a long time crossing the Atlantic to mull over his endless, crazy bullying, she told him. She was through. She stalked out and, back at the Dorchester, took her own room some distance from his.

Most women correspondents were not even aware of these mad goings-on. They searched out stories by day, wrote and filed them, caught a bite to eat somewhere, tried to get back to their digs before the blackout, and often as not went to bed early. The coming invasion weighed heavily on their minds. They knew that troops had begun to collect in the great marshaling area along the south coast, but that was all they knew, since only reporters accompanying the troops could go there. Iris Carpenter slipped in because she had family there, but then she had to stay. Once you were in, you couldn't get out again, nor could you communicate with anyone beyond the barriers. Not until later could she send dispatches describing the lovely verdant spring, the stacks of ammunition sheltered by hedges covered with May blossom, the road signs topped with myriad colored disks and code signs of units hidden nearby. The camouflage was effective. "Woods and hedgerows were spiky with guns and jammed tight with vehicles," Iris noted. "Towns and villages bristled with men and armor and equipment. Yet from the air southeast England looked unmenacing as Maytime."

Accompanying the Red Cross doughnut girls, Carpenter saw the trucks "ready packed and waiting, snugged down under the trees." She was surprised at the outward lack of anxiety in the soldiers. When the order came, the men clambered into their vehicles, cursing the weight of their ammunition belts and most of all the long hours of waiting until their convoy could meander its way, as Iris wrote, "to a coast so tight-jammed with craft that the feat of walking on the sea would have been no miracle."

20

D-Day

"At about 4 a.m. on June 6 my military friend rang to say, 'Take the curlers out of your hair and get going,' " Mary Welsh wrote later. "I had no curlers but I got going."

It had come at last, this day for which the preparations of three nations over two years' time were finally coming to fruition. Expectations for April, and again for May, had prompted a kind of invasion anxiety that by June was bordering on frenzy. It was open knowledge that the date for an amphibious landing such as this one was governed by abundant daylight, the weather, and the tides; the readiness, or unreadiness, of the troops was a factor about which no one in the press would have dared speculate. Dawn came early in June, allowing preinvasion bombardment, and the early morning low tide needed to spot obstacles on the Normandy beaches was present from the fifth to the seventh of the month. On Sunday night, June 4, rain poured down along the coast and winds were high, but by Monday morning there were signs of clearing. From the standpoint of the fliers, and particularly the paratroops, the weather was far from perfect, but the decision was Eisenhower's to make, and he decided it would do. He spent that evening mingling and talking with young paratroopers of the 101st Airborne, their faces blackened and heads shaved. Until the very early hours of Tuesday, June 6, not one had ever dropped into combat.

Awakened that cold, gray morning with the notification of D Day, the women correspondents were immediately aware of an undertone of excitement, a sense that their lives had shifted into a higher gear. In their dispatches they were limited to reactions on their side of the Channel, but images from the far side kept intruding into their heads. They knew that even as they set out for the Ministry of Information, tens of thousands of infantry were pouring off assorted landing craft, making their way through the surf, and possibly a rain of fire as well, to the French shore. They worried that although many British and some Canadians were veterans of earlier battles, among the Americans only the First Division had seen combat. Most GIs were as yet untried — "unblooded," as the term went — young, and probably scared. So were the thousands of paratroopers dropped into France in the dark of the night. Yet the women could not but think that this long awaited invasion *must* succeed. So much preparation had gone into it, so much equipment, so many men — if it failed, surely the outcome of the war itself was in jeopardy. It was a possibility not to be entertained.

Helen Kirkpatrick, who from her position on the correspondents' committee to plan press coverage of Overlord was familiar with that preparation, sat in the bureau chief's chair at the *Chicago Daily News* that morning. She was the only one on staff to remain in London. "The correspondents who were going with the troops were down in the south," she recalled later. "The rest of us — we didn't know until it happened. We heard planes, just hordes of planes. The sky was black with them."

In the first of several dispatches she would send off that day, Kirkpatrick wrote:

> The first landings today were made on the Normandy coast of France at 6 a.m. (11 p.m. last night, Chicago time). Landing craft continued to disembark initial assault troops up through 8 a.m. . . . First reports indicate that mine-sweepers had effectively cleared long lanes for the convoys to go in and for bombardment ships to get into position for naval shelling of the beach and enemy coastal artillery. Behind them, on a 20-foot tide, came small craft, followed by Seabees. Planes that dropped airborne troops returned with very light casualties. No great German air strength had been noted up to 9 a.m.

Marjorie Avery's dispatch to the *Detroit Free Press* was more personal. "I was fast asleep, dreaming I was riding on top of a freight train in Australia," she wrote, "when violent knocking at the door announced a phone call. Calls also were announced to the rooms on each side of mine, across the hall and immediately above. It was SHAEF with a message to proceed at once to a designated place. Ten minutes later, with my eyes half shut, I was on the street." At the Ministry of Information she found her fellow reporters — American, Canadian, and British — various of whom confided that they had not washed, shaved, or brushed their teeth, and weren't sure what clothes they were wearing.

Catherine Coyne had received a similar call, but when she walked into the Ministry of Information, she was asked first thing for her SHAEF papers. When she told the officer she hadn't been "SHAEFed" yet, meaning that her accreditation had not come through, he would let her no further in, but when she started to leave, it turned out that she couldn't go out either. By default, they allowed her to stay. "I guess I was looking lost," Catherine recalled later, "because Dot Avery called me over to sit with her. She said, 'I've ordered you breakfast.' And that's how we became very good friends."

Martha Gellhorn was also there in that "great guarded room," as she referred to it, "with a good percentage of the world's press watching the clock." An English officer came forward to announce that in five seconds the first communiqué would be given to the world, and they could leave. "Go!" he said, and everyone raced out as if fleeing a fire. Martha had hired a car, but when she told the driver the invasion had started, he didn't believe her. "I'm on twenty-four-hour duty when the invasion starts," he said defensively. "They'd have told me if it was starting. They wouldn't start it without calling me."

By D Day plus one, news had sifted back from reporters on the scene, and not all of it was good. Against minimal resistance, British and Canadian troops had waded ashore onto the easterly beaches labeled Sword and Juno and Gold, while the Americans had encountered little trouble landing on Utah to the west. But between Gold and Utah was Omaha, a stretch of shoreline subdivided into smaller beaches called Dog, Easy, and Fox and protected by a crack German unit firing relentless volleys from the steep cliffs onto the struggling American forces below. The few men in the lead company who reached the beach could do little more than try to rescue the wounded still in the water.

Attack plans were of necessity jettisoned; survival became the only real-istic objective.

Later Iris Carpenter attempted to record the landing as men who were there had described it to her:

> Wherever troops hit France on those Omaha beaches — Dog, Easy, and Fox — they took terrific punishment, as, feet slipping in the shifting sand, men stumbled through gray wave caps which raced over them to slap them down with their too-heavy equip-ment, toss them on the beach, suck them back, toss them on again among the nightmare of jumbled equipment, smashed boats, drowned and broken bodies. . . .
>
> "Easy Red" was a small beach at the mouth of a wooded gully. . . . Gun emplacements laced the slopes on each side, with summer villas converted into pillboxes. Woods were tunneled under and fortified so the Germans could and did fight their way back through them for miles without ever having to come into the open. . . .
>
> From the sea the view was as unmenacing-looking as the Normandy landscape. . . . Only [later] it became visible — vis-ible as a wall of fire so withering that it cut men down in drifts which will forever haunt the memories of those who had to fight their way in over them.
>
> One of the big tank landing ships attempted to beach — there were only ten allowed on all the Omaha beaches on D-Day because that was all we dared risk losing — finally made shore as a machine gun in the cliffs above chattered while the big doors in her bow yawed slowly open. When, eventually, the first tanks debarked, the drivers cried and vomited as they had to drive over the bodies of their buddies.

The dispatches women correspondents filed that week reflected their own activity, and were without question less dramatic. On D Day plus one Catherine Coyne hitchhiked, in company with three other reporters, to an invasion base town on the south coast. The dock area seemed at first glance a spectacle of confusion, but gradually they divined an intricate traffic pattern at work. Ships that appeared about to collide, didn't. They walked along the quay, passing vehicles crowded with American soldiers sitting quietly, smoking or munching chocolate bars or just staring into space. Within a few hours they would be on one of the craft there in the harbor, and a few hours later in France. What were they thinking, Coyne wanted to ask, but regulations did not permit conversation.

That night Marjorie Avery went out to a C-47 carrier station. "Great formations of gliders rose in the air," she wrote, "circled low over their home fields, then floated off toward the French coast. . . . " The sky was completely blanketed by C-47 cargo planes towing small light American cargo gliders, four abreast." A courier pilot described for her how, flying low in his tiny Piper Cub, he saw above him gliders strung out all across the sky, their red, blue, and green lights glowing, while below him were "crowds of people standing in the streets of towns, and workers in the gardens and farmers in the fields, all standing like statues, looking up."

At headquarters, where Dot went to wait for the C-47s to come back, everyone was exhausted. She described a Waaf going back and forth with trays of sandwiches and coffee, trying to keep people awake. Men found that if they so much as sat down, their eyes closed. The colonel, called to the telephone, was discovered asleep with his head on his desk. A desultory game of billiards went on through the night, although the players kept changing as people wandered in or were called away. Through it all, RAF pilots sat by the fire, waiting for the last planes to return.

Ruth Cowan had formed a connection with an army field hospital on the south coast. Now she stood on the dock of a military port marshaling area to watch the first American dead of the invasion, along with nineteen survivors "picked up at sea," brought off returning minesweepers. A young British sailor with fixed bayonet stood at the head of the gangplank, while rifle-bearing American soldiers in blue armbands marked "security" lined the wharf, barring anyone without proper credentials. A tall American with a CIC (counterintelligence) armband whispered a few words to a Wac press relations officer, who approached Cowan. "I've been told to tell you that if you attempt to talk to anyone getting off the ship you will be shot," she said. Ruth assured her she would not.

A minesweeper eased up to the dock. The ship's officers descended to the foot of the gangplank, and the first survivor strode down, a young man wearing the pajamalike two-piece white wool suit given to men picked up at sea. Others followed: this one seemed very tired; that one stumbled. Willing hands helped them into a waiting truck. A man dressed in borrowed navy gear and holding tightly to a small leather case stopped to shake hands with the ship's officers. As Cowan watched, another minesweeper eased alongside the first, and three survivors descended its gangplank and climbed into the truck, which then drove off. Only after that did the British sailors carry out the first litter, covered with canvas. "Then as gently as though the soldier were alive and able to feel pain," Ruth wrote, "British hands . . . shifted the burden to the Americans. Four litter bearers took the stretcher away to an ambulance."

That action was repeated eight times.

The invasion was barely under way when a few of the cannier women began to devise ways to bend the rules and get closer to the action. Lee Carson managed that on D Day itself; while all the others cooled their heels at the Ministry of Information, she went out to an air base and found a group commander who found a pilot who found her a seat on a plane. She knew it was a risk, but she would chance it. Her aerial view of the attack was as comprehensive as any that came in that day, and perhaps first as well.

On D Day plus one, or maybe two, Martha Gellhorn crossed the Channel in a hospital ship. It was a daring act, against all regulations. She simply went down to one of the ports, boarded, and hid in the lavatory until the boat was under way. In her story "The Wounded Come Home," she did not mention this stratagem, focusing instead on the trip across — the "snowy white" ship with its "many bright new red crosses painted on the hull and painted flat on the boat deck," and the six nurses who had scrubbed walls and floors, made beds, and prepared all the supplies. She wrote of the difficulty of taking on the wounded in rough seas from a landing craft, and of the water ambulances that churned off to the beaches and came back full. From two o'clock in the afternoon until seven the following evening when the ship docked again in England, the nurses were absorbed in caring for the wounded. "They had to be fed, as most of them had not eaten for two days; their shoes had to be cut off; they needed help to get out of their jackets; they wanted water . . . it seemed to take hours to pour hot coffee from the spout of a teapot into a mouth that just showed through bandages." Besides such menial tasks, there was the constant administering of blood and plasma and oxygen and sedatives.

Gellhorn helped wherever she could, but when an opportunity arose to go ashore, she seized it. This was, after all, her real purpose in making the trip; she was a reporter, not a nurse. She climbed into the motor ambulance with the stretcher bearers and they headed through the dusk for the Normandy shore, hoping to pick up more wounded "before the dangerous dark cold could get into their hurt bodies." She was out to get the story that no other woman — and not many men — would get.

When the motor ambulance could go no closer, Gellhorn and the stretcher bearers waded ashore in water to their waists. They stumbled up a road being scooped out of the cliff and walked the narrow mine-free path between white taping to a tent with a red cross on it. There a couple of grimy but polite young American soldiers were directing trucks transporting the wounded to the beach. Martha's crew helped unload the stretchers into an LST (landing ship, tank), where they all sat immobile until a tide change allowed the water ambulances to pick them up. A German air attack provided some danger and diversion. As it turned out, all the wounded on Gellhorn's run were German prisoners, which effectively canceled out any Yank hero angle to her story. Some readers might have questioned why injured American boys on a hospital ship were held up extra hours while a water ambulance went back to shore for Germans.

Martha's *Collier's* story ended with the ship's return to the Channel port, but her personal story did not. The army press office took a dim view of her excursion to Normandy in open defiance of the rules. She was arrested, confined to an American nurses' training camp outside London, and told she could go to France with the nurses when they were ready. Gellhorn quickly tired of this arrangement. Abandoning her passport and credentials, she climbed over the fence and hitched a ride to a military airfield, then another on a flight to Naples. She had already written Hemingway a note, having been told that he was livid on hearing she had reached France when he, although he had crossed the Channel in an LST on D Day, had not been allowed ashore. She wrote that she was off to Italy, adding, not very subtly, that she preferred reporting the war to hanging around a London hotel.

The next woman correspondent to step onto French soil was Iris Carpenter. By D Day plus four a tiny landing strip had been laid out along the terrible stretch of beach at Omaha. It was so short there seemed not an inch to spare, either for landing or taking off, but ammunition and medical supplies had to be flown in, and the wounded flown out, so it served. Iris crossed in the same plane with reporter Cornelius Ryan, who would later immortalize the events of June 6 in his book *The Longest Day*. Ryan moved on into Normandy. Carpenter was restricted to the airstrip.

But even there lay a story. The great bay, like blue velvet, was littered with hundreds of ships — battleships, yachts, tugboats, barges — each with a silver barrage balloon swaying protectively above its deck. Alighting from the little plane, Iris was confronted with the sight of several dozen medical corpsmen gingerly poking about with spades, excavating bodies that had been hurriedly buried in the white sand. Long rows of sticks marked the temporary graves; from each hung a small canvas bag with that soldier's dog tags and personal possessions inside. Now the army was recovering its dead, unwrapping each body from whatever scrap of blanket had been used as a cover, slipping it into a clean white shroud, and carrying it up the hill to the new cemetery where men were digging fresh graves in the earth. Iris thought that if only those officials rejoicing at the lower-than-estimated casualty figures could walk on that little hill, they would feel less smug.

Although Carpenter flew back to England with a load of badly wounded soldiers, most casualties returned by water. On D Day plus five Marjorie Avery stood on a narrow pier on either side of which an LST was moored — one loading troops and equipment for France, the other, having just come back, about to unload its wounded. It was the latter that captured her attention:

Some of the men who made the first assault on the coast of France have returned.

Some of them tell stories. These are the ones who walk off the ships with head, arm, hand or shoulder bandages. They tell of the battle as each saw it, of waves beating on the sands, of murderous cross-fire on the beaches, of shells exploding in air, of pain and fear, of grotesque details that leave impressions when death is all around.

Some joke and say that they're going back. Some, too dazed to smile, tell you stories in dull voices. They are eager for human contact and want me to write down their names for the papers. They ask how the war is going in France, just as I asked them. None knows.

Some of the men coming back aren't talking. They are carried off the ships on stretchers, bits of their clothing lying pathetically across their blanketed figures. A few look at the sky with unseeing eyes. Some are coming back who will never talk again. Their stories are finished. They come off the ships last, still figures covered with blankets and loaded like their dying brothers into waiting ambulances.

Barrage balloons ride nervously over the big blue LST boats docking at this port. The job of unloading has been going on all morning and will go on all afternoon. It is a slow, painstaking task. The port and the men who are doing the work are very quiet. There is no break in the stillness except for sudden shouted orders which are muted by the sounds of the surf. . . .

As the ambulances roll up from the wharves to the main road above the harbor, they meet another convoy coming down — a long line of men and tanks and trucks. The men who move into war are as silent as those who are coming out.

This was the story that at last moved a happy Dot Avery off the women's page and directly onto page one, column one, of the *Detroit Free Press*.

As if in retaliation for the invasion, Hitler chose D Day plus ten to launch a new weapon at England — a pilotless, jet-propelled rocket-projected plane, twenty-five feet long with a sixteen-foot wingspan, operated by an automatic pilot device set before takeoff. Trailing orange fire as it spun low over London rooftops, and at some unforeseeable point dropping to the ground and exploding, it was variously referred to as a robot, buzz bomb, doodlebug, or V-1 (as opposed to the soon-to-come V-2). "There was something macabre about this wholly mechanical enemy and about the idea of being killed by an insensate, innocent machine," Mary Welsh said.

Tania Long reported from London that people had gone back to sleeping in the shelters again, and that normal life during the day was difficult. You thought very hard before taking a bath, she said, because you couldn't exactly run naked and dripping into the hallway of the Savoy to avoid the glass, which was what you were supposed to do when you heard the bomb's final cough before it zoomed downward. She and Ray had bought a little house outside London, but the drive to it was unsettling now, and its doors and windows had been blown out the first week.

Catherine Coyne was in a Red Cross club in London when a voice over the public address system warned that a "gas buggy" was headed their way. Catherine hit the floor with the men. "The infernal machine seemed to be buzzing down upon us," she reported. "Suddenly its broken rhythm ceased. There was an awful silence. The sailor beside me beat his fists against the floor and muttered, 'Crash, you bastard, crash!' " It crashed, but not on them, and Coyne noted that after the initial relief, you felt guilty, because what missed you might, say, have toppled the wall of a day nursery. But she also felt relief, almost exhilaration, to be sharing some small part of the danger daily experienced by the troops in France.

Helen Kirkpatrick felt it was important that American troops in England were learning firsthand how it was to live in a bombed city. Touring London, she was reminded of the old Blitz days. "There were streets where, for several miles, the entire populace seemed engaged in sweeping away glass," she wrote. "School children were being evacuated again, boarding trains in the railway stations, wearing the same tags and carrying the same small bags and seen off by the same half-tearful, half-relieved parents."

Meanwhile, in Normandy what had begun (except at Omaha Beach) as an early success soon reverted to sustained and bitter combat. The area was a network of high banks and tight hedges, far easier to defend than attack, and the Germans clung tenaciously to each hedgerow. German forces in the vicinity of Calais, where Hitler had predicted the main invasion would occur, sped to the aid of their compatriots and were holding the line. The battle for the port of Cherbourg lasted five days; the city of Caen, which General Sir Bernard Montgomery had expected to take on D Day, was not captured until six weeks later. The Allied advance slowed to a crawl.

It was against this reality that women correspondents in Britain conducted their own campaign to get to where the war was. By late June the military had reached the point of arranging trips for them. Ruth Cowan and Iris Carpenter went over together in an LST. Their orders were for the beachhead only. Cowan had expected to be gone no more than thirty-six hours and hadn't even taken a clean shirt; it was eight days before she got back to London. Carpenter interpreted the term "beachhead" to include Cherbourg, now in Allied hands, and took off for there. She was court-martialed for this indiscretion, but the American officer present stood up for her. It was deemed a fuzzy area, and her professional future was saved.

Other women correspondents flew to France and back on day or overnight trips, some of them several times, but by D Day plus one month still none had gone to stay, and all were letting the army know how unhappy they were about it. They had been told they would go when the nurses went; well, the nurses had gone. The Red Cross workers had gone. The battle for France was moving ahead. If something were not done soon, the battle for France would be over, would be won, and *they* would still be in England.

21

Trekking North from Rome

But not all women correspondents that summer of 1944 were primed to go to Normandy. When Martha Gellhorn, confined to a nurses' training camp in England as punishment for her hospital ship jaunt, further disobeyed orders by bagging a lift to Naples without papers, travel orders, or PX card, it was because she saw no other course open to her. Italy offered more options. There the war slogged along on several fronts; she could avoid American jurisdiction by attaching herself to the French, Poles, Brits, or Canadians. Besides, women correspondents in Italy were battle-savvy. No wave of novices had been sent there, for whose sake veterans like herself had been handed a list of dos and don'ts that straitjacketed their talents, Gellhorn huffed. In Italy she could get on with her job.

Eleanor Packard would no doubt have agreed had her opinion been asked. She and Reynolds were back in Italy, in charge of the UP office in Naples. Anzio and Cassino were old news now, and just before D Day, as the last German troops fled through the northern gates of the capital, the U.S. Fifth Army had entered Rome from the south. The Packards rode with them, past throngs of Italians heading toward the capital on foot, their voices a joyous roar. The Piazza Venezia, when they at last reached it, was jammed. Through a deluge of white flowers Eleanor looked up at the balcony where Mussolini had so often stood. Reminded of that December day in 1941 when he had declared war against the United States, she half expected his short, bull-like figure to reappear.

The figure that did appear on a balcony that day was Pope Pius

XII. From the great square in front of Saint Peter's, Eleanor heard him offer thanks for the sparing of Rome; she was part of the sea of humanity that fell to their knees in a single great rippling motion. As a Catholic, she had always defended the pontiff against the charge that he was sympathetic to Fascism. Now, learning that he had harbored dozens of escaped Allied fliers and prisoners of war at the Vatican, she felt vindicated.

After the ceremony, at an audience especially for journalists, Pius XII glimpsed what facing the media in the postwar world would be like. Gone was the decorum of the past. As he spoke in his excellent English from the dais, photographers scrambled about in mad gyrations to get the best angles for their pictures, jumping up beside him, popping their flashes almost in his face. A newsreel camera ground away. Old-timers in the press stood red-faced with embarrassment, Eleanor doubly so because she was already breaking protocol by appearing in army garb, meaning pants. Circling the long room afterward to speak with those present, the pontiff drew up short when he reached her, and she felt obliged to explain how when you move with a fighting army a skirt is not useful. She had not anticipated the present occasion. His holiness forgave her with a smile.

Later that week, traveling with an army patrol, Packard underwent the unsettling experience of being taken for a spy. The road to Volterra had been blown up by retreating Germans and the town could only be reached by a two-mile climb. Her physical condition not what it once was, she stopped off at the first available café for a little rest. As she told the story later, she ordered a glass of wine and was at once surrounded by excited villagers wearing patriot armbands. She spoke to them in Italian, and when some of them switched to French, so did she. Three GIs heard her and asked if she were a French ambulance driver. No, she replied in English, she was an American correspondent. That brought on a shower of questions "by a tough old Partisan looking like Mr. Underground himself," and she became aware of a ring of hostile faces.

It was then that Mr. Underground pounced. "Have you heard there is a German woman hiding in Volterra?" he asked. In fact, Eleanor had heard that, but thought it unwise to say so. Several ugly examples of mob psychology crossed her mind, along with the disconcerting thought that a spy always carries a complete set of fake papers. One of the GIs, who had been conferring off to one side, approached her. "Ma'am," he said, "can you prove you are what you say you are?" Packard was indignant, but when he suggested that she was unlikely to get out of there unless she could, she produced her passport, War Department accreditations, vaccination certificate, New York checkbook, and PX card. It was the PX card that convinced the GIs. They huddled with the Italians, and suddenly suspicion melted away. Apologies were made, amidst laughter, and wine was poured all round. "We'd never seen a woman correspondent so close to the front before," one of the GIs explained. "It just didn't look right."

Allied forces continued to nudge the Germans northward, and in July Martha Gellhorn, who since her piece on Polish refugees had felt a natural affinity with the Poles, attached herself to a squadron that called itself the Carpathian Lancers, all its members having escaped Poland over the Carpathian Mountains. They had fought in the Western Desert and at Tobruk, had helped take Cassino, and were now moving up the Adriatic coast. In their prewar lives many had spent time in prison — German or Russian. All they talked about, Gellhorn reported, was the Russian army advancing across Poland. They listened to news broadcasts with agonized concern, although how the British were doing in Florence, or the French in Siena, or the Americans in Pisa was of no interest to them, and Normandy could be the moon. Only Poland was important; they worried that, once there, the Russians would never leave. Martha tried to reassure them, but after talking with a twenty-two-year-old whose father had died in a German camp, whose mother and sister had been sent to a labor camp in Russia, whose brother was simply missing, no one knew where, she realized how naive her thinking was. "I belong to a large free country and I speak with the optimism of those who are forever safe," she conceded.

The war in Italy was at a sluggish stage. The Germans were retreating northward, nothing urgent, and the Poles, in convoy on the roads, were keeping pace. "We moved the next day and every day after that," Gellhorn reported. "It was great fun, like being gypsies or a small-town circus." Her troubles with U.S. Army protocol and with her hostile, bullying husband seemed a long way off. In the evenings the

237

Lancers camped and sent out scrounging parties to local farms to buy geese or ducks or rabbits before soldiers from other squadrons could grab them. It was hot and dusty, and they were glad not to have to fight just then. The whole regiment spent Saturday night trying to get clean, and the next morning appeared at the little local church. The chaplain celebrated the mass "rather shyly, as if he were taking someone else's place," Martha wrote. "The villagers came too, old women and young women, with lace scarves on their heads and rosaries in their hands." The soldiers' clean brown faces were quiet and respectful, and when they sang their national prayer at the end, their rich, sad voices "carried out through the open door of the church into the sunny fly-ridden village."

In August 1944 Eleanor Packard took on the role of UP bureau chief in Rome while her husband Reynolds went with the troops. In the first of a long series of dispatches printed verbatim on the front pages of many American papers, she reported the Allied invasion of southern France on August 15:

> The U.S. 7th Army, comprising American and French troops, stormed eight miles into Toulon against weak German opposition today, while thousands of sky-borne troops struck far inland to throw a solid block across the path of enemy reserves moving down on the beachheads.... Unopposed by the strangely dormant Luftwaffe, hundreds of gliders and transports streamed boldly across the French coast before nightfall.... Giant naval rifles of the Allied fleet, firing over the heads of the advancing Americans and French, devastated the Nazis' inland defenses.

In succeeding dispatches Packard described the fall of the great naval base at Toulon and, in rapid succession, Grenoble, Avignon, and Nice. On August 28 the cities of Toulon and Marseilles were liberated.

The invasions of southern France and of Normandy could not have been more different. On the Channel coast the armies fought desperately for every foot of ground with heavy losses, while on the languorous Riviera the troops splashed ashore virtually unopposed and moved forward against minimal resistance. At the culmination of a mere two-week operation, the French Forces of the Interior (FFI) took it upon themselves to seize Bordeaux. That news must have struck a poignant note with those women correspondents — Sonia Tomara, Virginia Cowles, Mary Welsh — who had been in that city when news came of France's capitulation some four years earlier.

The Allied command in Italy read with envy of the Franco-American "prance across France," as some called it. The U.S. Fifth and British Eighth Armies were preparing to attack the Gothic Line, the German army's major line of defense across Italy. Still avoiding the former body, Martha Gellhorn attached herself to the First Canadian Corps of the latter. She was shocked by how the "lovely range of the Apennines" had been altered almost beyond recognition. Not only had the Germans dynamited villages, but they had laid barbed wire in the gravel riverbed, along with "never-ending mines: the crude little wooden boxes, the small rusty tin cans, the flat metal pancakes which are the simplest and deadliest weapons in Italy." In the hills themselves concrete machine-gun pillboxes were concealed, and tank turrets with long 88-mm guns. It was this armored trap that the Eighth Army faced, and Martha identified with the common soldier whose job it was to break through. "It is awful to die at the end of summer when you are young and have fought a long time . . . and when you know that the war is won anyhow," she wrote.

It would hardly seem possible from Gellhorn's description, but the Canadians found "a soft place" to penetrate, although, she wrote, "if you have seen one tank burn with its crew shut inside it you will never believe that anything is soft again." For the reporters watching from the hill opposite, the first day's battle was spread out in miniature:

Suddenly you see antlike figures of infantry outlined against the sky; probably they are going in to attack that cluster of farm-houses. Then they disappear, and you do not know what became of them. Tanks roll serenely across the crest of a hill, then the formation breaks, you lose most of them from sight, and then in what was a quiet valley you unexpectedly see other tanks firing from behind trees. On a road that was quite empty and therefore dangerous, because nothing is more suspect at the front than the silent places, you see a jeep racing in the direction of a town which may or may not be in our hands.

The next day the correspondents crossed the river and drove along that "dangerous" road. The remnants of the battle, no longer in miniature, were all too real. Still, the Gothic Line had been cracked, the crack would be widened, and armored divisions could now advance to the Lombardy plain. The battle for Italy was that much closer to the end.

Before that summer's end, Margaret Bourke-White returned to Italy. U.S. Army personnel still had her tagged as "temperamental" and "inclined to ignore orders"; her request to cover the Normandy invasion had been denied. But with many in the press having deserted Italy for fresher fields, her application to return to that forgotten front was granted.

Besides her determination to continue her career as a war photographer, Bourke-White was anxious to renew her connection with Major Jerry Papurt, the counterintelligence officer with whom she had formed a relationship in Naples exactly a year before. They had been writing ever since. In the spring Papurt had left Italy for England, then crossed over with the invasion to France. After that Margaret knew nothing until her convoy docked at Naples and a close friend of his met the boat to tell her that Jerry had been wounded, then captured by the enemy and confined in a German POW hospital. She was distraught. Thin blue V-mail letters, written before his capture, continued to be forwarded to her. She could not write to him, but the Vatican had set up a system for delivering messages to prisoners of war. There was a ten-word limit, and no guarantee anything would get through. Bourke-White's message was only eight words: "I love you. I will marry you. Maggie." She never knew whether he received it. Later that fall she learned that during an Allied bombing, the hospital received a direct hit, and Major Papurt was among those killed.

After his death, his personal effects, probably not on his person when captured, were returned to his wife, Maxine "Mackie" Cohen Papurt, in Columbus, Ohio. Along with a Swiss Army knife, assorted pendants, and a couple of U.S. Army gold leaf major insignias was a simple black leather wallet made by Mark Cross and embossed with

"Maxwell Jerome Papurt, United States Army." In the place for photos there were three: a white-haired man, no doubt his father; a dark-haired woman, not beautiful but with wide-spaced eyes and a warm half smile, his wife Mackie; and a headshot of a young and lovely Margaret. Tucked into another section were a pair of more contemporaneous photos of Margaret and a tiny, much folded note dated "Naples 1943," reading "My Darling: I have only one thing to give you this Christmas Day and that is my love. But it is yours. Maggie."

A half century later Margaret Wolf, Maxine Papurt's niece, brought me this little collection of items. She affirmed that her aunt had known nothing of Bourke-White's existence until the packet from the U.S. Army arrived. There had been no letters asking for a divorce, as Papurt had told Margaret. There had been no indication in his letters home that anything was other than normal. Was Maxine heartbroken then at learning the truth? The answer to that was probably also in the negative, Wolf said. Mackie adored her husband, as did everyone — he was so vibrant a personality, so warm and full of, well, sex appeal. Perhaps there had been indiscretions before, or perhaps, knowing him well, she had given him leave to be not-so-literally faithful. There were no children, but the family was a close-knit one and she was quite sure that, after the war, her husband would have come home to her. She felt so confident of this, in fact, that when Bourke-White's final book on the war, *"Dear Fatherland, Rest Quietly,"* was published in 1946, Maxine Papurt proudly showed the book and its dedication — "for M.J.P. who died too soon" — to all her friends.

During that fall of 1944, the Time Inc. office in Rome wrote the home office in New York of a changed Margaret Bourke-White. "During the month she's been in Italy she has worked quietly and graciously," they reported, and praised her "considerate approach." If they knew of the grief behind her submersion in her work, they did not say.

22

That Summer in France

It was mid-July 1944 before women correspondents crossed the Channel to stay. They went mostly in pairs or small groups, attached either to a Wac contingent or a field hospital; the army was not about to float them free if it could help it. The rules were laid down by SHAEF: women reporters were not to visit the press camps, were not to go farther front than the nurses, were not to leave a hospital or Wac area without permission from the CO. Jeeps and drivers were not offered to them. While the men's stories were censored on the spot, the women's would go by ordinary field-message service back to London, by which time (as an exasperated Iris Carpenter pointed out) they often made no sense, because there was no chance for the writer to bridge over what had been censored out.

Some women rebelled against these restrictions right from the start. Carpenter believed she was at least as competent to handle Normandy as most male correspondents. Lee Carson felt the same, and certainly Helen Kirkpatrick had no intention of allowing herself to be unduly constrained. Other women, especially newcomers unfamiliar with the Continent and those who spoke little or no French, were content to go slow. They had seen the wounded brought back; they knew what a mine could do, or a sniper, or an enemy shell, and they were aware that reporters too died in the war. Some had been cautioned by their editors to take care — major risks were not expected of them. Later they would push at the barriers; for now it was enough just to get their bearings, to seek out and write their stories.

Marjorie "Dot" Avery, Catherine Coyne, and Virginia Irwin fell generally into the go-slow category. They crossed over to France with the first Wac contingent, dressed in Wac garb of woolen underwear, olive drab pants with waterproof canvas leggings, sweater, field jacket, boots. They carried the regulation gas mask, helmet, folding spade, two musette bags, and a portable typewriter. The spade was for digging a foxhole should the need arise, and the second musette bag for their writing supplies. Coyne was so weighted down when she stepped out of the taxi at the London rendezvous point that she toppled over backward onto the sidewalk. "It was terribly humiliating," she recalled, "the way I went to war."

The group moved from truck to train to truck again until at last they reached the troop marshaling area, a camp hemmed in with barbed wire. The Wacs were allowed to mingle with nearby troops, young enlisted men with shaved heads also waiting to cross to France. It would be their last day resembling normal life for a long while. They played some hilarious coed softball, Coyne reported, but mostly they just sat on the grass and talked. "Talk American," the homesick GIs begged, so the Wacs did — about their hometowns and movies they'd seen and music they liked. A few soldiers went into a nearby field and picked bouquets of brilliant poppies, daisies, Queen Anne's lace, and gorse, and the Wacs filled their seasickness bags with water to keep the flowers fresh.

Their cross-Channel transport was more like a cruise ship than a troopship. Irwin thought it incongruous, considering how they were all dressed, but she delighted in her private cabin and the turbaned Indian waiter who brought around lemon squash. They dined from china plates set on pristine tablecloths; there were pressed sheets on the beds, and real eggs and bacon for breakfast, items they would only dream about for a long time to come. Their arrival next day — July 14, 1944 — fell on Bastille Day, and the Wacs went ashore marching in step and singing the "Marseillaise" because this small part of France was free again. American soldiers on the beach watched them with open joy.

It was late but not yet dark when the party arrived at the apple orchard near Valogne. Except for the lucky few who had ridden in trucks with the equipment, they had marched the distance and were tired. Avery, among the marchers, described wild, desolate beaches dotted with pup tents "that looked like the sand-houses prairie dogs make" but were occupied by soldiers who crawled out to cheer and wave. Their way coursed through tiny ruined hamlets where houses had no roofs and windows no glass. Thick dust settled on their clothes and hair and faces until at last they came to a peaceful green orchard with tents set up among moss-encrusted trees.

For an undetermined time this would be home. Avery, Irwin, Coyne, and British reporter Judy Barden each pulled a canvas cot from the pile, retrieved her bedroll, and arranged her own area in the shared tent at the foot of the Wac stockade. An eight-holer latrine was positioned nearby. Each woman carried water for washing in her helmet and learned to take an entire bath out of it. There were intruders: bantam hens scratching for worms, snails that had to be removed from one's boots in the morning, an occasional cow, even humans. They were once

Virginia Irwin, Marjorie Avery, and Judy Barden, Normandy, 1944.
NATIONAL ARCHIVES.

awakened by Dot, "whose voice," Catherine said, "even at two o'clock in the morning had a blond loveliness about it," asking conversationally, "Hello, who are you?" of three tired army officers who had walked up from the beachhead and, quite lost, were peering into the tent.

On sunny days the women correspondents set up a folding table and chairs under the apple trees and wrote their stories in the soft-scented air. The weather did not always cooperate, however, as on the evening the four tentmates were invited to dinner by the camp colonel. It had rained all day, the ground was saturated, the women were muddy and disheveled, but then so was the colonel. Although dinner was served as usual in the open field, a tent had been set up, and there were tin plates and cups instead of the usual mess kits. Everyone was very social, and the women slogged home in good spirits. It was still raining, and very dark in the tent with the flaps down. Just as they were trying to go to sleep, a great slithering noise was heard, the stakes pulled out of the ground, and half the tent caved in — a fitting conclusion to their first week in France.

The Channel crossing was in some cases a test in itself. Tania Long and *Woman's Home Companion* reporter Doris Fleeson went on a Liberty ship and were stalled for three days by fog. They passed the time on deck mending torn signal flags. Tania had spent her schooldays in France, and she expected to feel emotional at returning, but she later recalled how they were met by "such a mechanical, well-organized operation that not a tear would rise to my eyes. There were soldiers doing traffic duty, their arms going up and down, signaling. They sent out a tiny boat for Doris and me, and we had to climb down a rope ladder, which was not steady at all and slapped against the boat. I had my typewriter in my right hand and kept getting my fingers pinched. The soldiers were yelling, 'Throw it down, lady, throw it down!' but I didn't dare. Or else they'd say, 'Jump! Why don't you jump?' and I'd look down, and it would seem like a mile. We finally got there, but it wasn't at all the return I had expected."

The two women were assigned to different areas. Long asked why she could not stay at a press camp (just to see what the answer would be), and was informed that the press camps had no women's latrines and they weren't about to dig any. Instead, she spent two weeks in a little tent at the edge of a field hospital. Initially she thought she could never sleep with her tin hat on, but she soon discovered that with shrapnel raining down from the sky, she could not sleep with it off either. As London editor of the *New York Times Sunday Magazine*, she had planned to confer with other *Times* reporters and encourage them to write pieces for the magazine, but that was impossible with no access to press camps, no car or driver, not even a telephone. She was able to write only of wounded soldiers at one hospital at one little spot in the woods. Still, the battle lines were very close. Tania saw a lot of the war in those two weeks.

Sonia Tomara had come north from Italy and, in company with Rosette Hargrove of Newspaper Enterprise Association (NEA), headed for Cherbourg. They dropped in to a little shop run by two sisters. Tomara had not been in her beloved adopted country since June 1940; this was her first conversation with ordinary bourgeois. The sisters were at first suspicious of the unlikely combination of American uniforms and Parisian French, but other townspeople came in, and the little store was soon full of people interrupting each other, everyone trying to explain how it had been to live under German occupation for four long years. Deeply sympathetic, Tomara could only think of her own family in Paris, holding on somehow for those same four long years.

Late in July, Lee Miller packed her cameras and thirty-five rolls of film and boarded a plane for Normandy to do a hospital story for *Vogue*. Coming in low to land, she recognized the walled farms and austere Norman architecture, but much was unfamiliar, like the pockmarked terrain and a huge new cemetery just up from the beach with the un-Gallic name of Omaha. The same incongruity of nomenclature struck her when driving: signposts at the crossroads juxtaposed French villages — Marigny, Saint-Jean-de-Daye — with code names of army units like Missouri Charlie and Vermont Red.

Miller's first objective was the Forty-fourth Evacuation Hospital. Her mind worked on a visual plane, so that her story developed into a series of word pictures, brought into focus by her photos. She wrote of rows of tents with their "sloping, dark, swaying roofs, the swishing grass floor, and the silent wounded," and compared a ward for severe abdominal wounds to "a jungle of banyan trees, a maze of hanging rubber tubes swaying in khaki shadow." Later she moved on to a field hospital closer to the front. The tempo was quicker there, and the staff even more tired. She wandered about asking questions, taking care to warn the surgeons each time she used her flash.

One morning, sitting four in a row in the latrine, Miller asked the off-duty nurses what they planned to do with their free time. One had decided to sleep all day in her pink satin nightie and wool socks, another thought she would wash everything she owned plus herself, and a third had in mind to look up a boy from her hometown in ward two. Lee photographed them lying on their cots in the sun, pretty even in their army-issue long johns. She enjoyed their company, but she preferred that of the GIs, who smoked and cussed at the same level as herself; she thought they were without exception wonderful, an affection that was roundly returned. The chief surgeon took her along to a collecting station near the front, housed in a row of pretty gray cottages with roses and hollyhocks blooming. The wounded, brought by ambulance from the battalion aid stations, were carried directly into the flower-papered drawing room where wounds were re-dressed, splints applied, and plasma administered. Lee photographed it all; she felt it incumbent upon herself to educate the readers of *Vogue* who, she was convinced, thought of "the wounded" as brave, clean-shaven boys in freshly laundered uniforms, only a little bloody. On the contrary, she wrote, they were "dirty, dishevelled, stricken figures."

At a nearby airstrip, en route back to England, she watched as planes lined up to take on the wounded. One at a time they taxied up to the loading area, the wide double doors were flung open, and from a group of waiting ambulances twenty-four litters were off-loaded, lifted directly into the cabin, and locked into the three-level decks. A nurse and a surgical technician checked in each patient, the doors swung closed, the plane moved off, and another one took its place. Each turnaround took exactly twelve minutes.

Lee Miller flew out herself a little later, climbing into the rain with her notes and precious film. The editors at *Vogue* were overwhelmed when they received the story; it was not at all the quiet picture piece they had expected. They ran it in full, and editor-in-chief Audrey

Withers often spoke of it as "the most exciting journalistic experience of my war." As for Lee, she was hooked. All she could think of was how soon she could go back.

Iris Carpenter and Ruth Cowan started out at the Fifth General Hospital outside Carentan. Cowan, whose admiration for American nurses had only increased since her experience in North Africa, had requested exactly that assignment, but Carpenter saw it as being "farmed out" and was not happy. There was yellow dust everywhere. There were jumbo-sized lizards and relentless mosquitoes. There was the strafing — "the German way of saying goodnight" — and the flak. The choice for reporter and nurse alike was whether to lie with her helmet over her face and hope the rest of her would survive, or to stumble out and hunch up in her slit trench behind the tent for the night. Later Carpenter wrote about the "tent talk" that she shared with the nurses when a heavy night kept them from sleeping. They told her of the restlessness that ate at them when nothing seemed to offer stability, when they met so many men and saw so many things that they could not afford to think deeply about. They described the fatigue that made their bones ache to the very marrow. Iris could not help but think that this was only the first month, and how would they hold up through all the months ahead?

It must have seemed to both women that the words "war" and "wounded" were synonymous. If there was glory in battle, they saw little of it. When after a dogged defense of the crossroads town of Saint-Lô the Germans at last surrendered it to the Allies, Carpenter and Cowan went there to find devastation beyond describing, although Iris was determined to try. For her the surreal composition of a dead American soldier lying under a fuchsia bush in full bloom at the gateway to a villa, with a large white rabbit hopping about him and a donkey grazing near his boot, expressed the futility of the war, at least for those who had to do the fighting. It was not as if this GI had been defending his home, or even his homeland, she pointed out. The few yards of earth he had died for meant nothing to him. Orders had been given, and "over the top of the hill he had gone, through the villa grounds, crawling on his stomach . . . finally making the gateway, to peer carefully through, ready to rush across — to take a few yards of vital, precious main road. And for those few yards that could never benefit or matter much to his own country, or to those dear to him and to whom he was dear, he had to die."

Carpenter's view was substantiated by the carnage of the next few days. The American Nineteenth Corps was advancing at a good clip along the Normandy hedgerows, but was paying for it. The field collecting post that she and Ruth visited was jammed, even though the casualties stayed only long enough to be given plasma, oxygen, and a rough dressing on their wounds. Combat strain was beginning to tell, Carpenter reported: "As the ambulances slid to a standstill, men would lurch out of them with no mark of battle-hurt, but gray faces, often streaked with tears." She noticed that the medics were especially gentle with these men. Iris revered the medics, many of them conscientious objectors, "working always under fire and often against greater handicaps than any combat soldier."

That evening the two women, headed for Carentan, hitched a ride on an ambulance as far as the crossroads near Saint-Lô. As they looked anxiously skyward at some planes they could not identify, a nearby MP shouted for them to take cover. A piece of wall — all that was left of the town jail — afforded slight protection from the German bombs suddenly falling all around them. The final stick of bombs fell very close, showering them with debris and, although she did not realize it until later, shattering Carpenter's eardrum. They had just brushed themselves off when a command car drew up. The officers inside were highly incensed that two women in American uniform would have to thumb their way back to their quarters. They were war correspondents, weren't they? Where was their jeep? Where was their driver? Cowan just smiled at them. "But we're *women* correspondents," she said, as if that naturally explained their lack of all the usual amenities.

The best thing about this assignment from Carpenter's point of view was her partnership with Cowan. "Ruth was a straightforward person who took everything in its natural course," she said later. Iris always thought her friend was feeling more than she said aloud, as she was herself, but the natural reticence of the upper-class Englishwoman and the acquired protectiveness of the American for whom life had not been easy meant that, for the most part, they kept their thoughts private.

* * *

Helen Kirkpatrick was one of the few women the army allowed to go off alone. In July 1944, after she was relieved as bureau chief of the *Chicago Daily News* London office, she went in to see Eisenhower. She mentioned the buzz bombs. "It's not safe in England," she told him. "Send me to France." Ike laughed, and the next day she had her orders. At her request she was assigned to General Marie-Pierre Koenig's French Forces of the Interior (FFI), although she spent the first few weeks at General Bernard Montgomery's headquarters in Bayeux. Montgomery was known for refusing to allow women reporters with his troops. Helen did her best to avoid him.

If she did not exactly experience the glory of war, Kirkpatrick at least saw a less depressing side of it than most of the women. At the end of July, General George Patton's Third Army, which had crossed the Channel in spurts and under great secrecy, began an advance south through Brittany toward the Loire. Calculating their probable route, Kirkpatrick and several British reporters set out after them, only to discover that finding them meant getting stuck in the middle of a crawling convoy. Just as they cut out of line in hopes of making better time, they saw a jeep with three stars bearing down upon them. An irate General Patton leapt out and launched into a lecture on the negative effects of getting out of line when in a convoy. Shamefaced, Helen and friends crept back into place.

On August 3, Patton's forces attacked Rennes, the capital of Brittany, and that night the Germans withdrew. Kirkpatrick joined several other American correspondents driving toward the liberated city along a road lined with excited French. Their enthusiasm was contagious. "Our jeep had to be emptied three times of flowers that filled it, surrounded it, and threatened to bury us," she reported. "Our helmets were covered, our road was strewn with magnificent blooms from gardens for miles around." In one village a delegation of little girls presented an enormous bouquet to *la dame américaine*. That night the reporters camped with the troops in a wheat field. Kirkpatrick recalled that the sky was a brilliant red from the fires of burning bridges. They spread out their bedrolls, and in the morning there was a bottle of milk, a loaf of bread, and a wedge of butter, left by a grateful farmer.

The next day the American infantry marched into Rennes, the American reporters with them. People cheered and clapped and cried.

A beaming Helen strode along with Jean Marin, a handsome, six-foot-three Breton with a big cross of Lorraine on his uniform, whom she had known when he worked in London with de Gaulle. In the Place de la Mairie tension was high, the townspeople having pounced on some collaborators and brought them to the square. "Resistance men, tough and dirty, with their Sten guns slung from their shoulders, were all that prevented the crowd from tearing them to shreds," Kirkpatrick reported.

She went with Marin and a few of the resistance men for lunch at what had been the town's best restaurant. Its windows were shattered and there was no water, gas, or electricity, but a little cold ham had been discovered, along with bread, cantaloupe, and a great deal of champagne. Events moved so fast, Helen could hardly believe that only two days before, German troops had still controlled the town. At a ceremony that afternoon she stood on a balcony with Marin who was being roundly cheered. Nearby, astride a dormer window, a man took out his bugle and began to play the "Marseillaise," and as Helen recalled, everybody sang "while we just stood there with tears streaming down our faces."

Experiences like these are the perks of war, but aside from Kirkpatrick, they had so far been reserved for the men.

By August 1944 Germany's Atlantic Wall was crumbling. Patton's troops had taken the entire northern coast of Brittany except for the little seaside town of Saint-Malo, which had been reported captured but was in fact only partially so. What was left of the enemy force was commanded by one Colonel von Aulock, a relic of the old Reichswehr, holding out on an island citadel while in the town solitary armed marauders and snipers lay in wait, unaware how far behind their own lines they now were.

That was Saint-Malo's situation when Lee Miller grabbed at a chance offered by army public relations to photograph the work of a civil affairs team whose job it was to ease the town's return to normal life. When she discovered that army PR had been misinformed and the battle was still in progress, she could hardly believe her good fortune. She knew the rules against women in combat, but surely no reasonable officer could expect her to back off now. On that assumption, she remained. The troops were delighted; when she got out her camera, men jumped to find her the best vantage point, even when that meant driving her about in full view of enemy guns. From a bedroom window in a tiny hotel down on the beach, she photographed Old Saint-Malo still smoking, a fort where several hundred French civilians were being held, and the Ile du Grand Bé fortress from where most of the shooting originated. Her guide thought that should be adequate, but Lee was after more. "I had the clothes I was standing in, a couple dozen films, and an eiderdown blanket roll," she gloated. "I was the only photographer for miles around and I now owned a private war."

For the next few days Miller dashed about from one vantage point to another. At night she spread out her eiderdown wherever it looked safe. Photographing an air attack in which smoke belched upward, "mushrooming and columning — towering up, black and white," she was unaware that the mushroom was in fact one of the first uses of napalm. When the film was developed back in England, British censors promptly confiscated that section of it.

On the occasion of the first Allied attempt to take the citadel, Miller watched a platoon of soldiers creep down to the rocks by the shore and then climb single file up the steep approach to the fort, while a second platoon crouched among the rocks waiting their turn. The tension was palpable; her own arms and legs ached from projecting into the struggle, which became all the more real when German shells landed just above her window. She saw the platoon leader hit by enemy fire, and the men behind him begin to retreat, scrambling along and finally "oozing down the escarpment and sliding down the path they had so painfully climbed."

A new assault was planned for the next afternoon. Miller's friend the *Life* photographer David Scherman arrived, and they sat in easy chairs in front of a hotel window facing the citadel, eating K-rations and waiting. Just before three o'clock a patch of white appeared. There was frantic telephoning to try to stop a formation of P-38s scheduled to bomb momentarily, and Lee saw an American captain with a white flag and an interpreter running toward a cluster of German officers outside the fort. Another American officer followed, and together they spread scarlet boundary markers on the ground to signal the pilots not to bomb, that the fort had surrendered. It was too late to stop the first plane, but those that followed saw the markers and veered off. With Miller and Scherman in close pursuit, the major in charge raced along the causeway to the tunnel entrance at the back of the fort. Vanishing into the tunnel, he reappeared escorting the tall figure of Colonel von Aulock — pale, monocled, Iron Cross around his neck, camouflage coat over his uniform. The flash from Lee's camera prompted him to shield his face with a gray-gloved hand. Directed into a waiting jeep, he stood to shake hands with each of his aides before he was driven away.

Later Miller went through the tunnel into the fort. Hundreds of men had packed their bags on very short notice, and she took note of the general disorder: clothes strewn about, empty bottles, photographs and letters, loot taken from French towns. The wounded were lying on litters outside the hospital corridors, waiting for transport. The resident Reichsdoktor assured his captors that in return for what the Germans considered clean fighting on the American side, the tunnels were not mined. It was perhaps the most gentlemanly battle of the war.

Lee retraced her steps and crossed back over to the town. Reporters were gathering "like vultures for the kill," she recalled, and were amazed to see a woman correspondent already there. The army would be similarly surprised. Since her pictures had to pass the censors, there was no way to hide what she had been part of. Even should the army admit responsibility for her presence in Saint-Malo, for her to have remained in what was clearly a combat zone violated the terms of her accreditation. What her fate would be she did not know, but Miller felt strongly that in all spheres of life men and women should have the same opportunities, and she would not have hesitated to do the same thing again.

By mid-August 1944 the activities of the Wacs and nurses in Normandy offered little in the way of fresh copy, and most of the women had moved on to Brittany, and its capital, Rennes, to report the return of General Charles de Gaulle to France. Although he had assumed almost godlike status among Bretons who had risked their lives to hear his broadcasts from England, they were divided about his political expectations. Some felt the leadership should go to those who

253

had remained in France and suffered the hardships — not that life in blitzed and buzz-bombed England had been a picnic.

De Gaulle slipped into the country unheralded, but word got out, and his drive down from Cherbourg was marked by cheering crowds. When next day it was announced that he would speak from the Hôtel de Ville at noon, throngs of people began filing into the square despite a heavy rain. The scene was almost theatrical, Catherine Coyne wrote. "Drawn up in front of the city hall, standing stiffly at attention with new American carbines over their shoulders, was a company of the French Forces of the Interior, shabby civilian youths from the resistance movement who looked like characters out of novels by Dumas." Men and women were pressed so tightly into the square that they could not raise their umbrellas, while hundreds waited on the roof of a partly bombed-out building.

Standing bareheaded in the pelting rain, de Gaulle intoned words of old-fashioned declamatory French. "Great is our emotion at being here in free Rennes in Brittany, which is victorious . . ." he said. "Great is our emotion at being on a piece of French soil on the road to victory towards freedom and grandeur." Oddly, he spoke of this great emotion in a cold and expressionless voice. Iris Carpenter felt he was much moved by being there, and held himself in check for that reason. Coyne thought that with so much emotion permeating the very air, it didn't matter. "The crowd started shouting and screaming at the conclusion of every phrase," she said. At the end, before anyone could applaud, he ordered, "Sing 'Marseillaise.' " He sang the first phrase himself, and the rain-soaked crowd joined in.

Other women correspondents had varying impressions of that day. Sonia Tomara wrote of how deliriously happy everyone seemed. Carpenter thought they were disappointed by de Gaulle's failure to mention the part they had played during the four years of oppression. Afterward, Virginia Irwin seized the opportunity to go out onto the balcony from which the general had spoken; she leaned over, and the crowd looked up and cheered, "Vive l'Amérique!" Coyne recalled descending the stairs from her room on the top floor of the press building and smelling "something awfully nice," which turned out to be Lee Miller, there under house arrest for her actions in Saint-Malo. "She was rubbing eau de cologne all over herself because she'd been bitten by fleas," Coyne said later. "I told her calamine would be better, and gave her some of mine."

Helen Kirkpatrick did not return to Rennes for de Gaulle's visit; instead she went to the just-liberated Mont-Saint-Michel, a rocky isle in the Gulf of Saint-Malo which had become the correspondents' R&R. The photographer Robert Capa was there, as were Charles Wertenbaker (Lael's husband) and Bill Walton, all of Time Inc., plus Ernest Hemingway and Irwin Shaw. Hemingway was recovering from yet another accident — while riding a motorcycle with Capa, he had leaped into a ditch to avoid a German antitank gun, hit his head against a boulder, and suffered a second concussion. Helen thought him dogmatic, always talking about military strategy as if he were a consultant to the generals, but good company nonetheless.

Afterward, driving up the Cherbourg peninsula with Walton, she pointed out an inviting little beach, and Bill said they *had* to go for a swim, never mind that neither of them had suits. They took off their uniforms and ran into the water, Helen in her khaki Wac underwear but "looking very statuesque," Walton reminisced a half century later. Their presence attracted a small crowd, which made reemerging onto the beach a little embarrassing, but Bill said that he for one had never had a better swim.

Back in Bayeux, Kirkpatrick joined the French Second Armored Division at Ecouché. She was surprised to find that there was no mess; each section had its own *popote*, built a fire, and cooked for itself. At night, listening to the BBC, they could tell that the Americans were closing in on the capital. "These Frenchmen were going out of their minds wanting to get to Paris," Helen said. "We all were. And finally the order came."

23

Liberating Paris

All the women could talk of that month of August was the expected advance on Paris and whether they would be a part of it. They could not have known that American troops themselves came close to missing the action; that Eisenhower, fearing a loss of eastward momentum, would have preferred to bypass the capital. But the fate of the city hung too delicately in the balance. Hitler had ordered that in the event of German evacuation, Paris be left "a pile of ruins." This was a course General Dietrich von Choltitz, head of the occupying forces and guardian of his own historical reputation, was reluctant to take. He quietly let it be known that he would need an Allied force to surrender to, and he would need it *soon* — before Hitler realized that he was procrastinating and sent in the Luftwaffe.

Ike sent out the order to General Philippe Leclerc's Second French Armored to advance on Paris. Helen Kirkpatrick, camping with that division outside Ecouché, said that when word came "everybody fell into line and we just went hell bent straight across that French plain." It was raining, and Helen rode with John Reinhart, an American liaison officer with the French, in a captured German jeep with no top or doors and water sloshing back and forth. In climbing out at one point, she slipped and broke her toe. It was after dark when they reached Rambouillet, the designated rendezvous point, and they camped in a pasture. "To tend to one's needs hopping on one foot in mud was quite a feat," she recalled.

Kirkpatrick found Rambouillet full of PR men, censors, and correspondents, the most prominent of whom was Ernest Hemingway in his Papa Soldier role. He was surrounded by a band of what she kindly referred to as his "scouts" (others termed them "ruffians" or worse), whom he had shaped into a partisan force to scout the approach to Paris. (In a dispatch he wrote at the time, Hemingway admitted that General Leclerc seemed unimpressed with his reconnaissance activities, no doubt true.) Leclerc had decreed that only French forces would go in the next day, Friday, August 25, but in the end the French captain guarding the Porte d'Orléans could not buck the American opposition and gave way. Charles Wertenbaker and Robert Capa told their driver to swing in behind a passing armored car — which turned out to be General Leclerc's own — and entered exactly at 9:40 A.M., claiming to be the first among the correspondents.

Kirkpatrick's party had spent the night in a little bistro just outside the city. "I will never forget the next morning coming up over the hill and there below was Paris, white and shining in the sun," she recalled. "Our driver was as excited as we were." They crossed into the city that afternoon with a column of French tanks. Snipers still haunted the rooftops, but cheering Parisians lining the streets were not to be robbed of their victory, even when gunfire up ahead forced a brief retreat. Kirkpatrick's little band were ushered to the *mairie* of the sixth arrondissement where the honorary mayor of Paris, Henri Boussard, age seventy, received them with tears coursing down his cheeks. From the windows she gazed at the Saint-Sulpice Church rising majestically in the afternoon sun. "The Germans are still holding out," Helen wrote, "but Paris is free. Its freedom is heady and intoxicating."

Sonia Tomara rode into Paris on a weapons carrier, an arrival that doubled as a homecoming. She had left the city four years before, on a warm June day in 1940; there had been no tanks under the trees in the Bois de Boulogne then, she recalled, no barricades in the streets or burned-out cars like now. "My heart was so tense," Tomara wrote of her return. "For four years Paris had been a forbidden city immersed in legends brought over by refugees or by agents of the resistance. Now I was on its pavement once more . . . and there was the house. It took me a second to run up the three flights of stairs, and here were my folks, just a little older, a little thinner than when I had left them."

As Tomara soon discovered, Paris had been liberated from within

257

before the Allied armies ever arrived. One of her first stories from the capital was on the mechanics of that uprising: how the FFI laid their plans from a hideout in the vast underground sewer system, how liaison agents (many of them women) stole German guns, how on the prescribed day shots were heard and barricades went up all around Paris. Ordinary citizens seized their moment of reprisal, their chance for revenge, and settled the fate of their enemy in whatever way came to hand.

Lee Carson of INS reached Paris with the Fourth Infantry Division, by jeep. It was the first time anyone in authority had seen her for two weeks. An order had been out on her ever since she had gone to Normandy on a "facilities tour," linked up with several (male) reporters, and vanished. Lying low, she could not send out any stories, not even the one in which she took sole charge of six German soldiers offered up by local resistance forces, but she was never in real danger until she arrived in Paris. There, standing in the shelter of a building with two FFI men, trying to figure how to cross the street while avoiding snipers, she was approached by a dark little man with a bundle of Oriental rugs. "Madame want to buy a beautiful rug very cheap?" he asked, and started to roll them out onto the pockmarked sidewalk for her inspection when a sniper's bullet got him and he collapsed right onto his rugs.

A near miss like that was exactly the kind of experience SHAEF was trying to avoid for its women reporters. Carson knew this, and after two weeks incommunicado, she was apprehensive as to what kind of welcome she would receive at the Scribe, the hotel reserved for correspondents. Major Frank Mayborn, the first SHAEF PR man to arrive, was just checking in when she appeared in the lobby. He was aware of the order to apprehend and return her to London, but was so glad to see her alive and well (having had adequate time to consider the alternative) that he ignored all else. Lee was doubly lucky: her appearance was also witnessed by another early arriver — publisher and principal owner of INS, William Randolph Hearst Jr.

Mary Welsh reached Paris that night, having driven down with a major she thought much too cautious and pokey, but she was "deliciously, deliriously back in real France," and never had she seen so many people on the roadsides or such unbridled jubilation. The major dropped her off near the Hôtel Scribe. "In the noisy, happy dusk, I was propelled from one to another group of roistering, singing, shouting unburdened Parisians, hugging and kissing me and my knapsack when they saw my uniform," she wrote later. "The city had gone crazy with rejoicing. Everybody was eighteen years old, free of shackles, bursting with joy."

Next day, when Welsh dropped by room 31 at the Ritz Hotel, she found Monsieur Hemingway and his buddies ("scouts," "ruffians") cleaning rifles and sipping champagne. Hemingway was giving a lunch for a select group: Helen Kirkpatrick and her jeep partner, John Reinhart, Charles Wertenbaker, and Irwin Shaw. Welsh, on assignment, and perhaps not happy about the combination of Hemingway, Shaw, and herself at an intimate function, did not attend. The menu was sparse except for the alcohol, but the company was jovial. Over brandy Helen mentioned that she and Reinhart were about to leave for the victory parade. Hemingway tried to dissuade them. "Daughter," he said, assuming his Papa mode, "sit still and drink this good brandy. You can always watch parades but you'll never again celebrate the liberation of Paris at the Ritz." But Kirkpatrick had other reasons for being in Paris that day besides sipping brandy and listening to Hemingway pontificate.

Even so, she could not have guessed she would witness one of the most dramatic moments of the liberation. With all Paris and its suburbs converging on the center of town, she and Reinhart could not get near the Arc de Triomphe, so turned back to Notre Dame where a Te Deum service was to be held. French tanks were drawn up around the square, and people thronged toward the cathedral, which was already filled with families of FFI men who had died during the battle for Paris. Helen came across Robert Reid of the BBC, and they established themselves at the entrance just as generals de Gaulle, Koenig, Leclerc, and Alphonse Juin, who were leading the procession, arrived.

"The general is being presented to the people," Reid began his broadcast, when suddenly a splattering of shots rang out and piercing screams were forever registered on tape. People pushing to get into the shelter of the church trampled and disconnected his microphone. By

259

the time it was reconnected, de Gaulle and the others were progressing in measured steps toward the waiting cardinal and monsignor at the altar. From her pivotal vantage point Kirkpatrick described the scene:

> The generals' car arrived on the dot of 4:15. As they stepped from the car, we stood at salute and at that very moment a revolver shot rang out. It seemed to come from behind one of Notre Dame's gargoyles. Within a split second a machine gun opened up from behind the Hotel de Ville. It sprayed the pavement at my feet. The generals entered the church with people pressing from behind to find shelter.
>
> I found myself inside in the main aisle, a few feet behind the generals. People were cowering behind pillars. Someone tried to pull me down. The generals marched slowly down the main aisle, their hats in their hands. People in the main body were pressed back near the pillars. I was pushed forward down the aisle.
>
> Suddenly an automatic opened up from behind us — it came from behind the pipes of Notre Dame's organ. Other shots rang out and I saw a man ducking behind a pillar above. Beside me FFI men and the police were shooting. For one flashing instant it seemed that a great massacre was about to take place as the cathedral reverberated with the sound of guns. There was a sudden blaze and a machine gun sprayed the center aisle, flecking the tiles and chipping the pillars to my left. Time seemed to have no meaning. Spontaneously, a crowd of widows and bereaved burst forth into the Te Deum as the generals stood bareheaded before the altar.
>
> It seemed hours, but it was only a few minutes, perhaps ten, when the procession came back down the aisle. I could only stand amazed at the coolness, imperturbability and apparent unconcern of French generals and civilians alike who walked as though nothing had happened. General Koenig, smiling, leaned across and shook my hand. I fell in behind them and watched them walk deliberately out to their cars. A machine gun was still blazing from a nearby roof, and one could hear shooting all along the Seine.

Various theories were later put forward as to the purpose behind the assault, but none was ever proved. The next days were quieter.

Kirkpatrick went over to the *Chicago Daily News* office at 21 Rue de la Paix; old editions of the paper were piled by the door as delivered after the staff had left the city more than four years earlier. Edgar Mowrer's last piece was on his desk; when Helen picked it up from the gray blotter, the surface underneath was green. The office was on the top floor, and the concierge had convinced the occupying Germans that nothing was up there. Now the Germans had been evicted from the city; Kirkpatrick opened the office, and within hours the *Chicago Daily News* Paris bureau was functioning again — with herself as bureau chief.

With Paris pronounced safe that August of 1944, the women correspondents at the press building in Rennes were released. They traveled the route to the capital with mixed emotions. Catherine Coyne wrote of German soldiers "sprawled in hideously awkward death across the shoulders of the road or flung like waste on the green fields"; Marjorie Avery reported shelled houses, burned-out tanks, occasional bands of dispirited Germans walking the road under guard. On a happier note they passed French farmers shoveling the soil back into foxholes no longer needed. Their entry into Paris lacked the earlier crazy emotionalism, but the roads "were still avenued with cheering people when we drove in," Iris Carpenter noted in her broadcast for the BBC, although her shattered eardrum, memento of the crossroads at Saint-Lô, prevented her from hearing herself speak. Lee Miller was in time to photograph the barbed wire barricades at the Place de la Concorde and the sandbags near Notre Dame. "I arrived exhausted by my share of millions of handshakes, the embraces of grandmothers, of French sharpshooters and bevies of French girls," she reported to *Vogue*. "I was the 'femme soldat.' Small use to say I was just a journalist. . . ."

Virginia Irwin and British reporter Judy Barden took a roundabout route through the suburbs of Paris in an attempt to see if they could locate a fellow correspondent who had crossed enemy lines and not returned. They were traveling in a jeep with a driver, following a sign that read "Paris — 15 km" and snaking their way confidently among Allied trucks, when a blinding flash and explosion sent them diving to the ground. When they dared raise their heads, it was to see two dead Germans and another one badly injured only five yards away. Sensing a downturn to his career if anything should happen to his passengers, their driver decided to backtrack to the nearest village. Irwin had never laid claim to courage and was "shaking like an aspen leaf," Barden wrote, especially when they approached the town and saw no American flag. The first Americans to arrive, they were exuberantly kissed and hugged and cried over, their jeep heaped with flowers, tomatoes, peaches, and cognac. The driver's face was plastered with lipstick and Virginia declared she had kissed the whole village. When at last they reached Paris, it was almost anticlimactic.

Tania Long drove down from Cherbourg with her husband, Ray Daniell, through Chartres — "lovely but dead, with no water, light, gas or food," Long reported. The crowds became thicker as they neared Paris. Every Allied vehicle that passed, "whether a gigantic tank or a modest little jeep, was individually cheered by the joyous French," who appeared to have relinquished all normal activities "to stand in the street hour after hour to shout and wave and yell and throw bouquets." Tania felt she could not absorb it all, and it was not until the next day that the enormity of it hit her. She was sitting in a café on the Boulevard des Capucines — a spot she remembered well from her years at the Sorbonne — when behind her an accordion struck up the "Madelon," at first softly, then with increasing volume. Suddenly the emotion that she had suppressed almost without knowing it welled up inside her, and tears poured down her face.

On arriving in Paris, the women went directly to the Hôtel Scribe, already overflowing with correspondents. Jeeps, trucks, and army cars lined the adjacent streets, and a hotel attendant guarded the door against anyone not in uniform. In the lobby khaki duffel bags and bedrolls lay in heaps topped by gas masks, and the current guests were as likely to be in field clothes with mud-caked boots as in proper attire. The first floor was consigned to the press offices; in a couple of rooms with bare tables censors worked all day and much of the night, and couriers came and went with their distinctive bags. In the transportation room the beds were pushed against the wall to make room for the cans of precious gasoline, which were doled out as cars were assigned to correspondents; it doubled as a mail room, with thin V-mail envelopes spread out more or less alphabetically on the red eiderdown

Hôtel Scribe after the liberation of Paris, 1944.
PHOTO BY LEE MILLER. © LEE MILLER ARCHIVES.

quilts. The correspondents' mess, featuring K-rations, coffee, and champagne, was next to the kitchen in the basement.

Once she had settled in, each woman had her own priorities. Ruth Cowan's was to recover her blondness. Having discovered that the 203rd General Hospital was scheduled to move to Paris, she had herself transferred with it — or as far as the suburb of Clichy where it was to occupy the modern Raymond Poincaré Hospital. While army doctors inspected the blue-tiled operating rooms and a delouser "big enough to drive a jeep into," Cowan looked for the beauty parlor. She found it next to the barber shop, both in shambles, but the proprietors had returned. Ruth was their first customer. They applied a little of this and a little of that, she recalled, Charles using a single kettle of water for the wash, while Henriette with her many-pronged dryer executed the set. At the end of three hours, Cowan said, "I not only matched my passport and credentials, but I had my courage and glamour restored." These were not unimportant commodities in liberated Paris.

Lee Miller, who had left so many friends in France, was in her element. *Where* were they, and *how* were they, these artists and dancers and writers she had not seen for five years? First of all, Picasso, whom she found at his studio: they fell into each other's arms. He declared her to be the first Allied soldier he'd seen, and looking so different from the gaudy portrait he'd painted of her that summer in Antibes that he'd have to do another. He tried to show her everything he'd been doing in that first morning. There was little to be had at the corner bistro for lunch, but Lee had K-rations to contribute, and of course there was wine. After a glass or two, talked out for the moment, they sat and held hands and cried.

Catherine Coyne wanted nothing so much as to *experience* Paris. Delighted by the Gallic enthusiasm after the stolid Normans and phlegmatic Bretons, she set out in a buggy drawn by an ancient horse, but was soon persuaded by GIs in a passing jeep to join them instead. Americans in a jeep were sure to find themselves surrounded by an emotional crowd at every traffic stop. "Even I, conservative Boston spinster that I am, came in for my share of kisses," Coyne quipped. When they stopped for lunch, Parisians congregated, insisting that the liberators join the liberated in an aperitif. Toast followed toast, succeeded in turn by a magnificent lunch of delicacies hoarded for years for this moment.

Later Miller and Coyne shared accounts of their day, and Catherine so loved Lee's story about visiting Picasso that Lee took her friend along to meet him. Coyne thought the painter looked like a Prudential Insurance collector, but she laughed at the way Lee ran into his arms and he picked her right up in the air. They joined other artists for lunch, Catherine regretting her less-than-fluent French but managing to follow the conversation. Afterward, in Picasso's studio, she found words to be unnecessary. One needed only to look. She was most intrigued by the tomatoes he was growing in tins as subjects for a series of small paintings.

Another day Miller invited Coyne up to her room at the Scribe for

Picasso with Lee Miller, Paris, 1944.
© Lee Miller Archives.

a drink. Catherine remembered later that Lee's friend and fellow pho-tographer David Scherman was there, and that Lee was excited because she had just received a cable that Roland Penrose, with whom she had lived in London, was coming to Paris. "Suddenly she took off all her clothes, right there," Coyne recalled, "and said, 'I'm going to go have a good clean bath for this!' and Davy took me by the arm and said, 'Come on, let's you and I go get our drink.' " Scherman, who had wit-nessed Lee disrobing many times, did not remember this particular incident a half century later, but "Spinster Coyne" never forgot it, and for her the words "Lee Miller" and "liberation" were forever synony-mous.

Lael Wertenbaker wanted desperately to come to newly liberated Paris. The previous spring she had left her baby son with her mother and rejoined her husband in London. Of course she missed the baby, she said later, but his grandmother was an excellent substitute, and Wert was not the kind of husband you wanted to leave loose out there. The problem was that Lael had come over rather suddenly, without waiting for her accreditation to the army, and now Wert was in Paris and she was back in London, still waiting. The solution emerged in the form of General John Clifford Hodges Lee, known as Courthouse Lee (or alternatively as Jesus Christ Himself Lee because of his conspicu-ous religiosity). Head of Services of Supply (SOS) and later deputy the-ater commander, Lee was responsible for the mechanics of getting the main corps of the army to the Continent, a massive undertaking. As Lael remembered it, a PR man from Lee's retinue came to Wert and said, "I want my general on the cover of *Time*," and without batting an eye Wert replied, "I want my wife in Paris." A little trade was arranged, and in quick-step time there was General Lee on the cover of *Time*. Lael was in uniform in three hours, a not-too-well-fitting one right off the rack, and was provided phony papers and told not to go near the PX, which as yet was nonexistent in Paris anyway. She flew over in Elliott Roosevelt's plane and was never questioned. She could work, send cables, write stories, and six weeks later when her papers at last came through, so had the PX, to everyone's satisfaction.

Most of the women did at least one article on the Paris fashion scene, and a few covered every show, which miraculously materialized only a few weeks after the liberation. Marjorie Avery interviewed Lucien LeLong, famed fashion designer and president of the syndicate of Paris couturiers. LeLong compared his position to someone who for four years had walked a tightrope with no net under him. In 1940 he had been informed that the entire fashion industry would be moved to Berlin. He objected, explaining that fashion cannot be ordered, but must emerge as the free creations of the designers. The German officials seemed nonplussed at that idea, and nothing happened.

Throughout the occupation, Avery reported, women's fashion had been an expression of dissent. German uniforms were gray-green in color, so nothing green was worn. When the situation was at its darkest, women began wearing increasingly wide crazy hats, until a visiting general decreed a maximum on width. After that hats climbed to absurd heights instead. LeLong told Avery there were regulations on the width of skirts, too, and that the Germans wasted a lot of time crawling about the floors in dressmakers' establishments, trying to prove an infringement of the rules.

With Parisians still in a celebratory mood, it only gradually became apparent that there was a dark side to postliberation Paris. Early in September the French announced that during the four years of German occupation, an estimated 75,000 persons had been shot by the Germans, which came to about fifty per day. This figure did not include those who died of torture, an area in which the extent of the Gestapo's activities was only then beginning to emerge. A torture chamber on the grounds of the French ministry of aviation had been discovered, and there were others, too — on the Rue des Saussaies, at 84 Avenue Foch, and in the suburb of Chatou. Reporters were invited to come see for themselves; not all women had the stomach for it, but Sonia Tomara, Helen Kirkpatrick, Catherine Coyne, and Martha Gellhorn, lately arrived from Italy, were among those who went.

The horror of it was almost too much to take in, much less write about. The little "tour" began at the Gestapo's main headquarters on the Rue des Saussaies. One could see the tiny bath room "where they say prisoners were plunged for an hour into water almost at freezing point," Tomara reported, and then revived, to begin it all again. Above was the room where electric current was used. In another prisoners were placed against the wall, virtually crucified while beaten. At the rifle range at Issy, the little group saw three macabre poles standing. "The prisoners were attached to the poles by the neck and the Germans shot at these live targets with blunt bullets which tore the flesh horribly," Tomara wrote.

"When you first go into the chamber you disbelieve everything," Coyne wrote of Issy.

> It is like a movie set, and you tell yourself human beings cannot treat other human beings the way men and women were treated here. . . . It is a long room, a separate concrete building erected by the French as a practice range for its air force. The floor is of soft white beach sand. . . . The posts are chewed near the top, chewed by whizzing bullets fired into the heads of blindfolded men and women by Germans lying on their bellies on the wooden platforms there. . . .
>
> Execution was not swift and merciful. There is proof of torture in the front portion of the building where the concrete wall is covered with gray matting, a soft asbestos-like material used to deaden sound. . . . Into the soft matting of the walls are pressed handprints, prints of hundreds of hands that scarred the material with tearing, clasping fingers. They look as though tortured prisoners tried to claw their way up the wall, tried desperately to hang on by digging their sweating hands into the soft material. . . . There are hundreds upon hundreds of those prints . . . some small enough to be the prints of women or boys.

Coyne also described the vents from which jets of steam were sprayed on the prisoners — victims burned alive with steam. Those who were tortured seldom came out alive, because the Germans did not want them to talk of what had happened.

Helen Kirkpatrick visited one of the exceptions — a French-woman, a member of the underground, who had somehow lived through her torture. A large, solidly built woman, she moved with difficulty as both her shoulders had been broken and then healed without having been set. Her right arm and left leg were nearly paralyzed. Dark brown stains on her wrists indicated how deeply the manacles had cut into her flesh, and the burned soles of her feet were healing, although they still looked "like underdone beef," Helen wrote. After her interrogators decided that perhaps she did not know anything after all, they had dropped her off at a hospital, where she was fed but received no medical aid until "on the 32nd day Paris was liberated and so was she."

Martha Gellhorn went to look at the underground passages at Ivry, one of the old fortifications of Paris. Young men from the FFI — they seemed like children to her — conducted them inside. The French had stored ammunition and explosives in the great dank tunnels that the Germans in turn used as prisons. "They simply locked men and women there in the wet unending dark until they died, or until it was time to torture or shoot them," Martha wrote, describing the central tunnel with its hard mud floor, wet with seepage from the stone walls. There was no light anywhere. Rooms opened off passages, and it was so cold that in half an hour one was chilled to the bone. In places there were embers from small fires, and charcoal had been used to write on the walls "as if, dying, a man or a woman felt the fierce need of leaving some word or cry in this black silence."

There was also a cemetery at Ivry, handily so. Two rows contained the graves of some nine hundred men shot by the Germans, often for no reason other than terror tactics. The graves were unmarked, but family members could come and ask the cemetery keeper if the name of their father or husband or son was on his list. If it was, and if it was possible, the guardian would show them the proper mound so they could keep flowers on it. He said that no other graves were so covered with flowers as these.

Gellhorn also visited the fortifications at Romainville where people were burned alive in great ovens, gradually, from the feet upward. "It is impossible to write properly of such monstrous and incredible and bestial cruelty," she wrote, adding (as if hyperbole were itself inappropriate), "But since there are more torture chambers in and around Paris than you can conveniently visit in a week, this place, too, is probably not remarkable."

At one site Martha visited there was a thin little book of the last letters of those killed. One, she reported, was from a boy of eighteen, who like most eighteen-year-olds could not believe he was going to die. "And you, Mama," the letter went, "Maurice told me you had been to the Kommandantur. How tired you must be. Above all, take care of yourself and do not get sick because of me. Really, Mama, all is not yet lost."

The torture chambers of Paris were the first glimpse the women had of the horrors they would find revealed in full in the concentration camps some seven months later. Only a few wrote about them, indicating that perhaps only a few visited, but they all heard about them, and it could not but color their thinking, and their expectations of what lay ahead.

Some women correspondents remained only briefly in Paris; others stayed on longer. Martha Gellhorn was glad to be back in Paris again, but her visit was colored by Hemingway's presence and their mutual animosity. One evening he insisted she have dinner with him, and she complied, hoping to discuss the divorce she had determined upon. Instead, he brought along his soldier buddies and then insulted and mocked her throughout the meal. The young men were embarrassed, and Gellhorn fled as soon as she could manage it. A sympathetic Robert Capa found her in tears at four o'clock in the morning. As Capa told the story, he brought up the subject of Hemingway's liaison with Mary Welsh and suggested Martha call the Ritz and ask for Mary. Hemingway would probably answer, he said, and when he did Martha was to tell him she knew all about him and Mary and demand a divorce. According to Capa, Martha made the call, and it all happened right on cue.

If Gellhorn did not already know about her husband and Mary Welsh, she was one of the few in Paris so uninformed. "Mary and I live at the Ritz. You might as well do it in style," Hemingway informed his first wife, Hadley, in correspondence the following spring. For Welsh, those early fall days of 1944 were dominated by the progress of their relationship, which was often rocky. Hemingway wanted to be sure that by going from one war correspondent wife to another, he was not about to repeat his current situation: a wife who favored her career over her marriage and preferred reporting in the field to staying at home with him. But Mary's career was important to her, too, and was not to be relinquished lightly. She wanted to make very sure of her man. She and Noel Monks had grown apart, but she had never known him other than gentle and considerate. Hemingway was that only occasionally. He drank too much and was subject to wide mood swings. One night Marlene Dietrich met them for dinner in the Ritz dining room, and Ernest brought along several officer friends. Champagne flowed, and before long the men became drunk and offensive. One of them insulted visiting Congresswoman Clare Boothe Luce — wife of Mary's boss — at a nearby table. Furious, Mary excused herself and went upstairs, only to find that another of Ernest's buddies had vomited all over her bathroom. Hemingway, returning later, accused her of insulting his friends, and when she retorted that they were "drunks and slobs," slapped her face. "You poor coward!" she baited him, dancing about the room. "You poor, fat, feather-headed coward! You woman-hitter!" Handing him his clothes, she pushed him out the door. It took many apologies, and many emissaries in Ernest's defense, before peace was restored.

For most of the women, however, Paris was an exciting, joyful interlude. Sonia Tomara spent happy evenings reunited with her sister. Helen Kirkpatrick kept the *Chicago Daily News* bureau going, and Tania Long and her husband Ray Daniell reopened the *New York Times* Paris bureau and hired a pretty young cousin of Tania's as a bicycle messenger. In the late afternoons they sat on the terrace of the Café de la Source and talked with the waiters of the hardships of the recent past and their hopes for the future. Lee Miller continued to make the rounds of her friends — the poet Paul Eluard and his wife Nusch, Jean Cocteau, Colette — and to photograph fashion shows for *Vogue*. Marjorie Avery reported the arrival of the Wacs and their sweet innocence in that sophisticated town. And Lee Carson interviewed Paris hepcats, who had kept the jitterbug and boogie-woogie alive and well during the occupation, and delighted in the bistros and nightclubs where "jerking, jumping, hair-in-eyes GIs reign as supreme monarchs." All that and so much more was liberated Paris.

24

Crossing the Siegfried Line

Their sojourn in Paris provided war correspondents with an unexpected bonus: it threw male and female reporters together at the Hôtel Scribe, most notably in the correspondents' mess in the basement. In Normandy and Brittany women had not been permitted in the press camps, and with SHAEF so concerned about their safety, mixing had been minimal. Longtime reporters such as Sonia Tomara, Helen Kirkpatrick, and Martha Gellhorn had by default more male than female friends, but the majority of women now covering the war had arrived on the Continent in the last year to find themselves cloistered with their own sex by regulation. After Paris, however, SHAEF appeared to recognize that the initiation period had passed, and that attempts to extend it further would be difficult to enforce.

The front expanded rapidly that fall, with American forces fanning out across northern Europe in five distinct army groups — the First, Third, Seventh, and Ninth Armies and the Twelfth Army Group. SHAEF would have preferred that women correspondents remain well to the rear of the advance, but the women knew their publications and wire services expected them to follow the action along with their male colleagues. As a result, although the rule prohibiting women from combat areas remained absolute to the end of the war, it was variously interpreted. Once enemy ground forces had retreated, women reporters tended to consider the area "ex-combat," never mind a few last incoming shells and tardy snipers haunting the side streets. Frequently a lucky woman met up with a CO who was keen to cooperate on a story that would play up his outfit's performance under fire and was not particular about who wrote it. The European theater was expanding, and ambitious women were learning fast how to bend the rules.

Virginia Irwin, reporting for the *Saint Louis Post-Dispatch*, was a case in point. She was unabashed in her preference for the company of men over that of women, which she felt she'd had enough of in the apple orchards of Normandy and the press hotel in Brittany. Somehow she contrived to be attached to the command post of the Nineteenth Tactical Air Command of the Ninth Air Force. Headquarters, located in a pine forest by a landing strip cut through a grain field somewhere in France, was commanded by General Otto P. Weyland. The six-foot-two towheaded Weyland with his cowboy stride and continuous good humor was exactly what Virginia thought a general should be, but it was "the boys" who captured her heart. Her visit, scheduled for three days in mid-September, lasted well into December. This was not what the PR officers at SHAEF had in mind, but Virginia was adept at dodging their all-points bulletins for her return. Although the *Post-Dispatch* could seldom locate her either, they printed her stories in full, often on the front page, and were pleased she was so close to the front, particularly as their other (male) reporter had reached Europe too late for an assignment to France and could file his stories only from England.

In mid-September three airborne divisions — the American Eighty-second and One-hundred-and-first and the First British — parachuted and glided into Holland. This surprise attack by the greatest airborne armada ever attempted up to that time was clearly newsworthy, and the Eighty-second's commander, the charismatic thirty-seven-year-old Lieutenant General James Gavin, suggested that reporters cover the action. Martha Gellhorn, Marjorie "Dot" Avery, and Catherine Coyne accepted the challenge.

In her story "Rough and Tumble" for *Collier's*, Gellhorn, who struck up a close friendship with Gavin, reported how the Eighty-second flew in formation over the Channel, then dropped by parachute or glider onto the Dutch countryside. Their mission was to take and hold the steel-girded bridges at Grave and Nijmegen, which were heavily defended. Gellhorn related how this was accomplished, in part by acts of bravery that seemed almost suicidal. Her admiration of the raw courage of the Eighty-second pervaded her story. "They do not boast when they say that where they fight, they fight without relief or replacements and that they have never relinquished a foot of ground," she wrote. "Men who jump out of airplanes onto hostile territory do not have dull lives." As with the CNAC pilots on the China-Burma route, Martha felt a visceral connection to men who took such risks.

Nijmegen, which remained precariously exposed for weeks, was the subject of another story, "Death of a Dutch Town." Martha reported on the dangers and hardships to civilians who coped with the daily allotment of broken glass, always sweeping it up "in a despairingly tidy way." She also explained why one never saw any Jews in Nijmegen. Already she had documented the fate of Europe's Jewry, a concern she shared with her friend Eleanor Roosevelt, in a number of stories, beginning with Prague in 1938. She was lucky in her choice of periodicals: the editors of *Collier's* never flinched from printing her revelations. Nijmegen's Jews had been deported to Poland, she wrote; she then described in considerable detail the tiled "baths" that were in reality gas chambers.

Dot Avery and Catherine Coyne drove up to Nijmegen with two male journalists they had come to know at the Scribe in Paris — Flem Hall of the *Fort Worth Star-Telegram* and Ervin Lewis, broadcaster for Station WLS, Chicago. The trip was unsettling. "The battles had been recent ones," Dot noted, "and I got a fresh view of the aftermath: bricks and debris tumbling into the streets of clean little Dutch towns. Dead bloated cows with stiff legs outstretched in a sort of dumb protest. Freshly dug graves. A few still unburied Germans lying like heaps of rags. The smell of decay." Her first act on arrival in that border town was to fulfill a vow to cross the Siegfried Line onto German soil. In the cool fall sunshine, she and Coyne walked over that fabled line of demarcation on the grounds of a hotel that German officers had only just abandoned. Some admiring paratroopers took their pictures, while solemn-faced blond children trotted behind them, nodding when they spoke, but saying nothing themselves.

A major from Baltimore invited Coyne to accompany him to the command post of a parachute regiment. They arrived in time for supper, and were just having coffee when a thunderous roar was heard.

"You're lucky," the colonel in command told her, "you'll get a good show." Officers ushered her to a top-floor dormer window, which provided an excellent view of enemy planes dropping flares over the command post. The great bridge, their target, was silhouetted cleanly against the moonlight, while flares on the opposite shore started fires that turned the velvety sky a pale pink. Catherine was particularly impressed by the pattern of orange tracer bullets, pellets merging to form a great wall of fire in the sky:

> There was about it constant beauty, constant movement, a kind of grace. . . . Certainly nothing could get through that steadily moving wall of fiery bullets! Then the planes roared in. The flares, the moon and the tracer bullets made it as light as day. I leaned out the window to get a look at the planes silhouetted against the sky.
>
> The ack ack batteries went into action. Great puffs of black exploded high in the air. You could feel the concussion in the very air you breathed. Then I was aware there was no air in front of me to breathe. Just a hot sensation of emptiness that passed quickly. The building vibrated. When it happened I don't believe I was aware of sound. Then I knew, even without recognizing sound, the planes had dropped their bombs.
>
> They didn't get the bridge. The ack ack stopped. The tracer bullets disappeared into nothingness. The flares burned low. . . . Most of the bombs on that run landed in the river. One was close enough to damage one of our supply sheds and killed a soldier. All the glass in the windows on the two lower floors of our building was blown out. . . .
>
> Major Ireland suggested we take advantage of the lull to get back across the river. We got into his jeep, drove carefully through the moonlight dusk to the bridge, then dashed madly over it to the other side. It was a cold starlit night. I tried not to think of the boy who had been killed. The major sang phrases from popular songs — he did not seem to know a whole song — probably to keep up that daredevil attitude that characterizes the paratrooper. "Doesn't this remind you of football weather back home?" he asked. . . .
>
> As we rode through the quiet streets of Nijmegen, we heard the faint rumble of planes. They were returning. The cold

starlit sky was changed again into a pattern of dazzling orange and golden light. The air was rent with the explosions of flak and of bombs. Now it did not seem so beautiful, for we could smell the burning homes. We could smell charred and burning wood, first the hot smell, then the acrid odor of water having been poured on the fire; then we could smell the bombs and the tracer bullets — they smell just like old-fashioned fireworks.

In the faint light we could see silent Dutch families standing close to their dignified and substantial homes looking skyward, silent.

Coyne's experience was indicative of how a woman could fall into a dangerous situation through no design of her own and emerge with a story that might have cost her her life.

The Allied hold on the bridges at Nijmegen and Grave allowed General Eisenhower to order the U.S. First Army to begin the attack on the West Wall, a string of fortifications running roughly along Germany's western boundary. Both Iris Carpenter and Lee Carson had managed to attach themselves to the press corps of the First Army, which meant that despite previous acts of insubordination on the part of both women, SHAEF was sufficiently impressed by their cool heads and competence to permit them a trial run. Carpenter had spent much of her time in Paris in the hospital receiving treatment for her shattered eardrum. Quantities of sulfa drug had alleviated the need for an operation, but the ear specialist insisted she receive more treatment. Watching other correspondents moved out of Paris, Iris had begun to fear the war would be over before she caught up with it again. When she heard that the Ninety-first Evacuation Hospital was scheduled to go to Germany, she convinced her doctor that she could continue treatment while moving with it.

The city of Aachen, on the far side of the West Wall, was the First Army's objective. Hitler's command that it be defended at all costs was countered by an Allied order to surrender under threat of destruction. In the ensuing American bombing, only the cathedral was spared. It rose from the rubble with the altar where Charlemagne had been crowned still intact. Entering the town on the heels of the victorious

Americans, Carson and Carpenter were struck by the sudden reversal of realities. Until now, civilians in combat areas had been liberated by Allied successes; beginning with the defeat at Aachen, civilians were among the conquered. Those who had not evacuated as ordered had only an unsympathetic American army to turn to for help.

There were moments when both women must have stopped to marvel that they were actually reporting from Germany with the U.S. First Army press corps. But if they thought their inclusion would prove seamless and without conflict, they soon learned otherwise. Most male reporters were delighted to have such "good-lookers" as daily company, but a few viewed them as competitors out to use their sex for advantage. Their new situation also exposed the women to what Carson called "the wolf in correspondent's clothing." She noted that "when it became glaringly apparent that I was not having any, thank you, knighthood in full flower withered quick."

So, apparently, did common sense. The GIs adored Carson, who represented that almost-forgotten other world of the "American girl." Lee would try to get them to laugh and relax. In Aachen she found herself one evening "with a bunch of red-eyed miserable doughs" in a house under enemy sniper fire. They found a phonograph that worked, a bottle of wine and some eggs, and decided to have a party. Lee was happily dancing with every GI there when a male correspondent wandered in, took in the scene, and left in high dudgeon. "How can you work against a dame?" he protested. "There she was dancing with these guys and getting a helluva story. Can I dance with GIs? Can you? Course not. But that's the way a dame gets stories." Carson's response — that dancing with weary soldiers was strictly extracurricular — was brushed off with a shrug.

Janet Flanner returned to Paris from New York that fall of 1944 in her old role of *New Yorker* correspondent. The progress of the war had left its mark on her, even from a distance. A friend, the photographer Horst, had approached her the year before to compose a text for a book of his photographs of the 1930s, and Janet had indicated her willingness, but now she wrote to tell him she had changed her mind. Included in the book were a number of Parisian society figures rumored to be collaborators, and Flanner shrank from being in any way associated with them. Horst offered to remove the most flagrant offender, the Vicomtesse de Noailles, but Janet stood firm. The photographs were as beautiful as ever, but the times had changed.

Flanner flew from New York to London, where she found life much altered. The house she had often stayed in before the war had vanished. The blackout took some getting used to. She bought a uniform and field jacket, an electric heater, and a bicycle, and moved on to Paris, where she deposited everything at the Hôtel Scribe and took the first train for Orgeval. That much was the same, she noted, recalling all the times she had taken that train before the war, when she and Noel Murphy had meant everything to each other. Except for a relatively brief period when the Germans interned resident Americans, Noel had lived out the war years on her farm in Orgeval. It was raining as the train pulled into the little station. Janet saw Noel waiting on the platform with her bicycle, noticeably thin and stooped, but smiling. The meeting was more complicated for Janet: it was she who had abandoned her friend five years before and had gone to live safe and well-fed in America. Worse, she had abandoned Noel emotionally: much of that time had been spent with a new friend, Natalia Danesi Murray. Flanner knew that Hemingway had mentioned this fact to Noel, but in those first days at Orgeval, the name Natalia hung in the air between them unspoken.

After that initial visit Flanner spent part of each week with Murphy on the farm and part at the Scribe in Paris. She often saw that "splendid Helen Kirkpatrick" and renewed her old friendship with Hemingway, always on his best behavior with her. Together they attended a literary party at Sylvia Beach's apartment — old friends from the days of Beach's Shakespeare and Company bookshop. Flanner wanted to make it clear that she had discarded her prewar apolitical stance. She knew that the half snobbish, sardonic humor of her previous writings was wildly inappropriate now. "Paris is still a mass of uncoordinated individuals, each walking through the ceaseless winter rains with his memories," Flanner wrote in her first "Letter from Paris," December 15, 1944. At the Scribe, where everyone knew she was Genêt of the *New Yorker*, she was alternately sharp-tongued and sentimental, and the only white-haired woman there.

*   *   *

During this time, General Patton's Third Army was gradually encircling the town of Metz, and Iris Carpenter (on leave from the First Army) arrived with John Arthur Bockhorst of News of the Day newsreel service and Johnny Morris of *Life* magazine to cover its surrender. With German forts up in the hills still shelling the town, she had no business being there, but there she was, and not about to turn back. The road in ran directly between two German forts and, crouching down in the jeep as they came within range, Iris could feel prickles on the back of her neck. At the river's edge they were obliged to abandon the jeep for a just-completed infantry footbridge.

Their progress took on the quality of one of those "home free" games children play on summer evenings in backyards across America. They would edge warily along, hugging a building, peeping around its corner to jump back, peep again, and then race across. On reaching the railway line, they crouched by a shed in somebody's back garden, each in turn crossing the tracks and scrambling up the far bank.

At the command post they crowded into a jeep with half a dozen other correspondents and set off for the cathedral. Parking the jeep in the town square, they were inching down the narrow street that circled back of the church when their driver, not four feet from Iris, was shot in the hand. Another correspondent dashed up to warn them of snipers ahead. They turned back, the driver less concerned about his injury than about Iris's future. "If SHAEF hears about Carpenter being in this show, they'll discredit her so fast it'll make her head swim," he said. She was advised to write her story without mention of having been present at the cathedral, and her companions swore they would deny ever having seen her there.

Late in November 1944 Sonia Tomara, attached to the press corps of the Seventh Army, moved into Alsace. Traveling by jeep along the Strasbourg corridor, she could hear the artillery of a fierce battle going on in the Vosges Mountains. "The American 100th Division is cleaning the Germans out of the Vosges," she reported to the *New York Herald Tribune*. "I used to go skiing there before the war. There is no snow now, but all the valleys are flooded and streams have swelled into big torrents." Fortunately, conditions were just as bad for the enemy, who were surrendering by the thousands. All along the road they passed groups of bedraggled Germans in field gray. Sonia recalled Hitler boasting that he had annexed Alsace to Germany forever. For the troops in field gray, "forever" had not lasted very long.

Tomara was there to report the day the French Second Armored and the American Seventh Army infantry entered Strasbourg, capital of Alsace. One could walk through the streets, she wrote, although there was still some shelling. Always when entering a cathedral city, reporters went first to that great stone edifice to see whether it had survived the Allied bombing. Here all the stained glass was gone, but the wonderful exterior sculpture still intact. Sonia found it strange to be back in Strasbourg. She had first been there as a child, before 1914 when it was German, then later when it was French, and finally just before this war began, when she crossed the Kehl Bridge on foot between the Maginot and Siegfried Lines. After that, with the fall of France in 1940, Alsace and the province of Lorraine to the north had reverted to Germany. But now, by the New Year of 1945, they would be French again. Sonia marveled how people could live in so topsy-turvy a world.

A week later, in the town of Saverne, she attended the parish church to hear the first sermon delivered in French since June 1940. The joy of it was in sharp contrast to what followed. That afternoon Sonia and several colleagues went forty miles by jeep to Struthof, a small-scale concentration camp at the top of a mountain banked by forests of dark fir. It began to snow as they wound their way upward and entered through an electrified barbed wire gate. Here were many dark green sheds, and their guide, a member of the FFI, led them to one in particular. In the first room was "a sort of stove to make gas — the FFI man did not know what gas," Sonia reported. "A pipe led to another small room without light. There were eight rods running parallel under the ceiling and attached to them were hooks, such as butchers use for meat. When Struthof was in operation, men and women were attached to these hooks, and the gas arrived through the pipe opening."

Tomara had visited places of torture around Paris, but this was the first time she had seen anything like a gas chamber, although word of their existence had circulated for some time. The one at Struthof appeared small and primitive, but as yet she had little basis for comparison. It was not known how many people died there, only that 6,000 people could be accommodated at the camp at one time, and the ashes of 1,665 women were carefully stored in earthen urns like flowerpots. Those prisoners still alive when the Germans began their retreat had been taken back across the Rhine with them.

Night came early that time of year, and it was getting dark as they completed their tour of the camp. Tomara felt the wind lash at her; her feet were numb with cold, and her heart, she said, was frozen.

Each woman experienced a different war. Dot Avery and Catherine Coyne, for example, were surprised to find that there was a social life east of the Siegfried Line. Was it because of the rain and mud, which were constants, and were more bearable in company? Or because American men at the front would find any excuse to spend a little time with American "girls." Avery and Coyne were visiting an area of "static warfare," which meant that the infantry was holding — that although there was shelling, usually at regular times of the day, neither side was moving forward, for reasons not revealed. Instead the men spent time improving their foxholes and, whenever possible, their meals. In static warfare, the men were fed twice a day from chow wagons that brought the food in hot insulated vessels; otherwise they ate cold K-rations.

Avery and Coyne had been invited to lunch at battalion headquarters, and it was clear that K-rations were not on the menu. Over a small wood-burning stove a captain was frying potatoes in a big skillet into which he tossed some very tender-looking meat. When Dot asked what it was, he replied that his sergeant had been "attacked" by a deer the day before and, by way of defending himself, had brought back venison for lunch. As for the stove, it had been "found" all alone by the roadside. And the Rhine wine? Also "found." An unexpected treat for the two correspondents.

Back on the Luxembourg side soon afterward, Avery and Coyne were invited to a dinner party, once again made possible when another deer "attacked" yet another American soldier, this time a general's aide. The two-star general was host. After a day in the rain and mud of a section of the Siegfried Line, the general's aide picked them up, presented each with an American Beauty rose, an anomaly in those surroundings, and drove them through the wet blackout to the house that served as headquarters. In the long white modernistic living room, their host and another general and a colonel stood before the fireplace to greet them. Clean shirts were the only fresh apparel the women had found to put on; they had brushed their pants and field jackets and scraped their boots as best they could, but the sole feminine touch Catherine was able to come up with was a piece of mottled green parachute cloth given her by a paratrooper which she wore around her neck. In contrast, the officers were in dress uniform complete with campaign ribbons, highly polished boots, and insignia that glowed in the firelight. The opportunity to dine with American women was rare, and they had dressed in honor of the occasion.

Over dinner Coyne and Avery entertained their hosts with a humorous description of their life with the Wacs in Normandy. The men laughed uproariously. More dramatic was the brigadier's story of capturing a notorious German general. The German had at first declined to surrender to a general with only one star, but was informed that "captured," not "surrendered," was the operative term. Arrogant even in defeat, he came out of his bunker sixty feet underground leading a beautiful dog. He looked at the line of grim GIs facing him, then up at the sky. Patting his dog, he commented, "Ah, this is no time for warring. The hunting season is just beginning."

The rain beat against the windows, while inside the Americans lingered around the fire, sipping wine and talking — spinning out what was for all of them a very special evening in an otherwise crazy war.

25

The Battle of the Bulge

In early December 1944, SHAEF reversed itself and granted Lee Carson and Iris Carpenter full accreditation to the First Army. This may have come in response to pressure from INS and the *Boston Globe*, neither of which had another correspondent with the First. Sonia Tomara had already received full accreditation to the Seventh Army, but SHAEF made it clear that these were to be considered special cases, not an opening of the dike through which many more would soon flow. Such accreditation guaranteed them a seat in a jeep, the opportunity to attend briefings and examine maps and eat in the same mess as the men, and the right to submit copy as soon as it passed the censor rather than waiting until the men had sent theirs.

The unresolved question was how far forward they were to be allowed to go. For the record, the camp commander noted: "They can go wherever their reporter's conscience drives them — same as the men do — and if they get a beat on the story and scoop the pants off the men, it's all right with me." Privately he was more restrained. "Now don't go making it harder for yourself than you need," he warned Iris and Lee. "Remember, you're going to be no darned good to your paper if you get hurt, and you'll be one hell of a big embarrassment to me."

Fifty years later Carpenter recalled that when she and Carson met at First Army headquarters and press camp in Spa, Belgium, they began by disliking each other intensely. Then one evening Lee returned to the press camp, saw that Iris had been detained, and phoned the *Boston Globe* contact to inform them that Carpenter's copy would be coming and to hold for it. "I thought that damned decent of her," Iris said. "We grew to like each other very much."

For nearly two months the First Army had been attempting to take the Huertgen Forest southeast of Aachen — attempts that not only had failed but were proving more costly in casualties than any single objective so far, except for Omaha Beach. Men were dying at far too high a rate, and it seemed to Carpenter that her daily trips to the front were increasingly more harrowing. About ten o'clock one night, after completing a story she was sure the censors would cut to bits and thinking that perhaps now she might wash her face and comb her hair and get something to eat, she was confronted by the redheaded First Army operations officer. He suggested that although she could not write about it yet, it might be a good idea to go down to the crossroads in the forest where the entire drive was then held up. That was a tip she could not ignore, and the next day they went there together. In a cottage in a forest clearing, the division commanding officer described the difficulties — swampy pine thicket on either side of the causeway, pillboxes, thickly mined and booby-trapped terrain. He had lost almost a whole regiment there already, he said, and added, "I don't like the way the Germans are holding so hard in this neck of the woods. It wouldn't surprise me to find them breaking out of here any time in such force we'll get the shock of our lives."

That was what Iris Carpenter and operations officer Russell "Red" Akers — a man to whom she gave little thought at the time but would one day marry — heard about noon on Friday, December 15. Eighteen hours later the commanding officer's prediction came true. German forces broke out of those very woods, and the Battle of the Bulge began.

The term came from the large protuberance the German army carved into Allied territory before they were stopped. The heart of the battle took place in the Ardennes, a wooded plateau averaging two thousand feet above sea level and covering parts of France, Belgium, and Luxembourg. Hitler's plan was to sweep through what he correctly saw as a weak spot between the American First and Third Armies to Antwerp, retaking Brussels on the way. The element of surprise was virtually complete, and the American position was further endangered by infiltrators: English-speaking Germans dressed in American uniforms, carrying American weapons, and driving American tanks and jeeps.

When the Germans began to march, before dawn on December 16, Lee Carson and Iris Carpenter were asleep in the Hôtel Portugal near First Army headquarters in Spa, directly in line with the main thrust of the attack. The only troops there were a few armored cavalry, a couple dozen MPs, engineers, jeep drivers, cooks, and censors, all of whom were issued arms. The briefing in the press camp was short: "The Germans have broken through at several points. The situation is extremely fluid." Walking back to their quarters afterward, Carson and Carpenter passed frantic citizens hammering shutters over their windows.

Almost at once the American lines broke. Eisenhower ordered an armored division from the Ninth Army to the north and another from the Third Army to the south to proceed immediately to the Ardennes. But it took time for them to arrive, during which four divisions of the First, one of them new to battle, took the offensive head on. The day was chaotic. The men were not used to retreat. The skies were gray, the snow was gray, and billowing gray smoke rose from fuel pumps purposely set aflame.

On the morning of the eighteenth, three wire service reporters — Jack Frankish of UP, Bill Boni of the AP, and Carson, who jeeped together — drove to see how the situation looked from a forward command post near Monschau. "Retreat in the face of Germany's smashing counteroffensive on the Luxembourg-Belgium frontier today is a new experience to the battle-tested doughboys of the American First Army," Lee began her story, then continued in rapid-fire prose: "The Germans are roaring up nearby roads in their Tiger tanks, zooming down from the pink-streaked winter skies to shower our frontline positions with streams of hot lead, and tearing the world apart with their heavy artillery barrages." She had talked with a private from New York entrusted with carrying a message to the command post from his unit, which had been surprised that morning by nine Tigers rolling down the main street of the little village where they were billeted. "Those German tanks came right under the windows of the houses we were staying in," Lee quoted him as saying. Since his unit had nothing to fight tanks with, they had fled.

In her story, Carson did her best to put a positive slant on the day's events. She wrote of Yanks "ensnaring scores of Germans," "hammering back," "blunting the German spearheads." But she also reported what sounded much more ominous — enemy tanks roaring in "to unleash a withering fire." The nearby town of Malmédy was endangered. "Nazi penetration in the Malmédy area . . . remained the enemy's most successful thrust," Carson noted. "German tanks in this vicinity were reported roaming the woods unchecked."

Iris Carpenter and her jeep buddies set out for Fifth Corps headquarters at Eupen along a road of hairpin turns bordered by pines. There is no more beautiful country in the Ardennes, but they had more on their minds than scenery. At one point an armored car headed out in front of them. "Better stay close behind," the driver said. "This road is lousy with parachutists." At Eupen the general was curt. Where had they come from? By which road? They'd best get back to Spa while they still could, and they shouldn't dawdle there either. First Army headquarters was pulling out.

Seven times on the return trip low-flying Luftwaffe obliged them to hit the ditch. As they approached Spa, they came upon bumper-to-bumper trucks loaded with supplies, including gas and ammunition from a huge Allied dump, all retreating westward. Their fellow correspondents were stripping the press camp, piling maps and personal belongings into trucks. "Keep my room," Iris told the sobbing proprietress at the Portugal. "I'll be back soon." On the way out of town people waved them goodbye, and when they passed the schoolhouse, the children were lined up singing "The Star-Spangled Banner."

On December 20, four days into the battle, Carson first reported that the enemy was shooting American prisoners. In an incident occurring near Saint-Vith, German troops ambushed a supply and medical convoy, disarmed an unspecified number of GIs, marched them into a field with their hands above their heads, and opened fire. She also reported a more extensive massacre said to have taken place on the second day of battle:

A field artillery battery, supply troops and medics, numbering about 150, were moving south on a road in the vicinity of Malmédy. At a fork in the road the convoy saw tanks at a short distance dotting the woods on either side of the road. As the tanks opened fire, the Americans leaped into ditches. An ambulance trailing the convoy was fired on. Two wounded enlisted men were dragged from it, loaded on a tank by the Nazis and taken off down the road.

The others were rounded up, disarmed and robbed and then marched to a nearby clearing, lined up in ranks and searched again. . . . Then the killers in the tank, parked some 50 or 60 feet away, opened up. The wounded crumpled and others, pretending to be hit, fell with them. Machine-guns on the tanks continued to fire into the writhing mass. The Germans kicked their way through this bloody tangle and answered the cries of wounded for help with pistol shots.

Carson's dispatch was an early, bare-bones account of what became known as the Malmédy Massacre. Later, when the site was recaptured, victims were tagged and photographed where they had fallen in the snow. Eighty-six Americans lay dead; four survived to tell the tale. The photographs would later be used as evidence at the Nuremberg trials in the prosecution of the German officer in charge.

During the first week of battle, the First Army press camp moved twice. From Spa it retreated to a chateau near Liège, but when this was shelled until no glass was left in a single window, they relocated to a hotel in Chaudfontaine only just abandoned by headquarters.

"We were very much a family," Iris Carpenter recalled. That night they sat around, family style, discussing the advisability of continuing to go to the front. The boundaries had become so fluid that nobody knew which areas were held by the enemy and which by the Allies, or, for that matter, which apparent GIs were in fact Germans. UP's Jack Frankish, jeep companion to Bill Boni and Lee Carson, thought he wouldn't go out the next day unless the picture cleared. "I've got a wife and a couple of kids," he said. "I guess I owe something to them as well as to my job." Lee and Bill said they understood, but thought they'd go anyway, and in the morning they left without Jack. They were gone all day. It was December 24, and Lee, with her big heart and her loyalty as much to the GIs as to INS, was determined to do what she could to make the day a little happier for them. "I spent Christmas Eve on the line," she wrote later. "The poor guys tried to make a Christmas for me. I ate fruitcake until it hung out of my ears. Everybody had fruitcake from home and I had to eat some of everybody's. They all gave me something from home — food, soap, aftershave lotion — or wine they had taken from somebody's cellar. I had to take it. But about one a.m. we had a tank attack and a hell of a bad time thereafter."

Carson and Boni did not make it back until the next day. In their absence German planes, perhaps thinking the hotel at Chaudfontaine was still occupied by headquarters, bombed it. Colonel Andrews, the camp commander who had warned Lee and Iris not to "go making it harder for yourself than you need," suffered a fractured skull and was sent to a base hospital in England, where he died. Jack Frankish was killed outright.

Although Lee Carson and Iris Carpenter remained the only women to experience the Battle of the Bulge from the start, other women attempted to cover it in its later phase, which gravitated around the market town of Bastogne. By December 23, 1944, Marjorie "Dot" Avery and Catherine Coyne — who seemed to have no problem following the action, usually in the company of friendly male colleagues — had made their way to Belgium and were advancing with the troops. Which troops they could not say. "The convoys were huge, fantastic, noisy parades — if you did not look at the young faces beneath the heavy steel helmets," Coyne wrote. Holly and mistletoe adorned the netting of those helmets, and the Belgians, who counted on these young men to save them from another Nazi invasion, cheered them on.

All that the reporters knew of the Belgian town of Bastogne was that it was at a road junction in an area where few crossroads existed, and its capture was essential to the success of Hitler's undertaking. At one point German troops came within two miles of the town, but halted there until morning. This proved their undoing. During the night the 101st Airborne, driving headlong the hundred miles from Reims in open trucks, reached Bastogne and joined forces with the battered

Tenth Armored. After that, and though surrounded and outnumbered three or four to one, they repelled attack after attack and held the town. Dense fog kept planes grounded, and supplies were dangerously low when, on the twenty-third, the clouds broke. By noon the blue sky was filled with silver C-47s dodging German ack-ack to hover above the town just long enough to drop their precious containers of food, clothing, blood plasma, gasoline, and ammunition.

The Germans mounted their last big offensive against the town on Christmas Day 1944. When it was over and the defending Allied troops realized they had survived, they felt a new confidence. They had stopped the best the enemy could marshal against them. On December 26 a division from General Patton's Third Army plowed through an enemy roadblock and reached the town's perimeter. Paratroopers from the 101st Airborne climbed cautiously out of their foxholes to greet them. The stranglehold on Bastogne was broken.

"How we got here and what we saw on the way . . . doesn't enter into this story," Dot Avery wrote of the quartet of correspondents who reached the town the next day. Perhaps she was thinking of the sensibilities of her friends on the society page of the *Detroit Free Press*, friends for whom she had whipped up gastronomically perfect suppers in what now seemed like another life. Still, if these horrors had happened to American kids — and so many of them were only kids — how could she flinch from writing it, or they from reading what she wrote? "The town is still burning from German bombing," she reported. "There are the usual scenes of wreckage and desolation. Civilians are digging themselves out, picking up bits of junk and trying to salvage their homes. In a pile of rubble which had been an improvised hospital before bombs hit it, German prisoners and medical corpsmen are searching for bodies."

For all the havoc, the arrival of replacements had brought a crazy relief, a sense of holiday. Several soldiers invited Dot into their home in a small garage. They were boiling water for coffee, and she was grateful for a few sips against the bitter cold and constant mist that penetrated right through to the bone. She talked with a medical officer directing the search for bodies. He had a wild tale of having been trapped by enemy tanks and ringed with enemy artillery fire, of litter bearers attempting daring rescues of men in burning tanks while under murderous fire from snipers and machine guns. When at last they reached Bastogne, the Americans had expected a fully equipped hospital to be waiting, only to discover there was nothing. Men had gone around town begging for supplies from private homes to treat the wounded. Then on Christmas Eve six enemy planes had dive-bombed, hitting the makeshift hospital and setting it afire.

What the correspondents "saw on the way" to Bastogne was devastatingly multiplied by what faced them when they got there.

Arriving a day or so later, Martha Gellhorn felt very like a weary soldier herself. She had begun the month by driving over a sixteen-foot embankment, from which she suffered no more than bruises and a broken rib, but which served to remind her of her own mortality. She wrote to her editor at *Collier's* of her exhaustion. Sometimes the war seemed to have depleted her, wrung her dry. She felt unable to do justice in her writing to the terrible things she witnessed every day.

Gellhorn had had another unpleasant encounter with Hemingway in Luxembourg over Christmas, and she moved into Belgium with some relief. She and a colleague took the road, marginally safer than before, to Bastogne. They stopped at an ex-German gun position to consult with ten American soldiers there. A sergeant advised against continuing up the road, which was cut with small-arms fire, he said, and in any case a German counterattack was in the works — thirty tanks headed their way. "What are you going to do?" Gellhorn asked them. "Stay here," one of them said, and shrugged. War was lonely and individual work, Martha brooded in her piece for *Collier's*. "It is hard to realize how small it can get. Finally it can boil down to ten unshaven gaunt-looking young men, from anywhere in America, stationed on a vital road with German tanks coming in."

Gellhorn and her colleague compromised by taking a secondary road and stopping to consult at the farmhouse headquarters of the American general in command. A dead horse with spilling entrails blocked the front door. Only a few minutes before, a shell had landed in the farmyard, also killing a cow and wounding another, which was moaning softly in the passageway between house and barn. Martha's driver, heretofore silent, was bitter about the livestock, "all beat up this way. Goddammit, what they got to do with it?" he asked. "It's not their fault."

Bastogne, Gellhorn observed when they reached it, was "a German job of death and destruction . . . beautifully thorough." The wounded had been flown out, but the 101st Airborne was still there. Martha and her colleague could not understand the cheerfulness of the paratroopers. Not having experienced the previous couple of weeks up close, she had difficulty accepting that to have made it through against such odds, even when many of your buddies had not, left a heady sensation.

Back in Luxembourg on New Year's Eve, she ran into Bill Walton of *Time*. They contemplated visiting the front, but the front, as it turned out, was quiet. Fat snowflakes were falling softly. "We decided, like millions of other people, that we were most heartily sick of war," she wrote. "What we really wanted to do was borrow a sled and go coasting." They did borrow a sled — an unsteerable homemade variety — and were directed to a steep hill near an abandoned stone quarry where dozens of children were already descending on similar sleds. There were noisy planes nearby, and artillery directed at the planes, but the children paid no attention. "Screaming with joy, fear, and good spirits, they continued to slide down the hill," Martha noted, as she, Walton, and their driver stood watching them. "Children aren't so dumb," the driver said. "What I mean is, children got the right idea. What people ought to do is go coasting."

Indeed, it seemed the only sane occupation as bitter cold arrived in the Ardennes. At the First Army press camp, now inhabiting a convent in Tongres, it was so cold "that water brought us for washing froze almost before we could pour it into the basins," Iris Carpenter wrote. Blizzards dropped up to eighteen inches of snow, and the roads were sheets of ice. Driving became more hazardous than facing the enemy: it was then that Lee Carson smashed three jeeps in a single week, but that feat was not uncommon, and it was merely suggested that she try to be more careful.

The Luftwaffe celebrated the New Year with what would turn out to be their last great concentrated effort of the war. Among a group of reporters lying flattened against a roadside barn, Carpenter observed that until then she would not have believed it possible to lie in the snow and melt it to steaming point with perspiration. Two days later the Americans began to push the Germans back eastward. The going was slow over the ice, tanks skidding all over the place, Iris said, and the last thing you wanted to have skid into you was a tank.

First Army headquarters and press camp returned to Spa exactly a month after their near-panicky retreat. The proprietress at the Portugal welcomed them with open arms, and a party was held in Chambre Six. At headquarters General Courtney Hodges gave a press conference. "We shall continue bending the bulge backward right into Germany," he said, tracing his pointer along the map in the general direction of Bonn. The armies were already moving, pressing against the desperate resistance of Hitler's Panzer divisions.

The Battle of the Bulge exacted an enormous toll: some 19,000 American dead, 15,000 taken prisoner. On the other side, Hitler lost 100,000 killed, wounded, or captured in the Ardennes. Logistically speaking — which was of little comfort to families back home, of course — the Americans could afford the loss, while the Germans could not. Eisenhower had fresh troops on their way; Hitler had none.

26

Penetrating the Pacific Barriers

The Pacific theater presented an entirely different challenge for the woman war correspondent. Most offensives were of necessity island operations. American bombers took off from islands — Hawaii, Midway — or from aircraft carriers. Their targets were other islands — Guadalcanal, Guam, Saipan, Iwo Jima — on which, when taken, airstrips were built (or old ones repaired) for more bombers to reach other islands until the target was those islands that made up the Japanese nation itself. Ground troops reached their destination by ship, on which the men lived in close quarters for weeks. From those ships they were disgorged onto islands, and if they made it through the surf and onto the beach, and past the beach to the interior, there was not only the enemy to contend with — machine-gun fire, mines, snipers — but often a torrid climate, mosquitoes, dysentery, malaria. Small wonder that through 1944 only male reporters covered the offensives, and not always happily. But the successes of those troops meant that in time there were islands to which reporters of either sex could go with relative safety and minimal discomfort. It was then that General Douglas MacArthur's dictum that no women reporters be allowed in his Southwest Pacific theater of command, and similar restrictions on the part of Admiral Chester Nimitz, commander of the Pacific Ocean Area (POA), began to come under pressure from women and their advocates in the press.

No one exerted more pressure than the first woman to have been accredited as a war correspondent, Peggy Hull. She had reported the training of American troops in France in 1917, the mission to Vladivostok two years later, and the Japanese attack on Shanghai in 1932. Now Peggy Hull Deuell, widow of *New York Daily News* managing editor Harvey Deuell, renewed her old affiliation with the *Cleveland Plain Dealer*, which agreed to send her wherever she could get accreditation. But over fifty and overweight was not what the War Department judged appropriate for overseas. In time, however, her persistence wore them down, and for some months in 1944, from Hawaii, she reported the stories GIs told her when they returned there for hospitalization or on leave, or wrote her from more forward areas. Her informal style, alternately snappy and poignant, exactly suited her little stories. Still, she often felt shut out, belittled by the male correspondents around her. "Our presence in various fields is bitterly resented by the men we compete with," she noted. "Overwhelming obstacles are frequently set up to prevent us from working."

The overwhelming obstacles Annalee Whitmore Jacoby would face on her return to China that fall of 1944 did not originate with the U.S. military and had nothing to do with her sex. Three years had passed since she left Chungking and flew to Manila to marry Melville Jacoby, more than two since Mel's death on an Australian airfield. "Friendly fire" takes many forms; Mel's came by way of a propeller that detached from its plane, stormed across the field, and cut him to pieces in seconds. Annalee held that image before her eyes for a long time. She also retained memories of their perilous escape by boat to and then from Bataan, of night watches together on Cebu, of sitting close and whispering their hopes and plans — all for nothing. That great irrational called war cared nothing for hopes and plans.

After she returned to New York, Annalee Jacoby (she seldom used her maiden name now) went to the Time Inc. offices to discuss her future with the editors there. Work was what she wanted, all-engulfing work, and she asked for "an eighteen-hour-a-day job right in the middle of the war, if possible." But in 1942 that wasn't possible. It wasn't possible for her to go to the China-Burma-India theater as she requested, because women were not yet allowed there, and by the time they were, she was otherwise involved. Mostly, she was mourning — an activity postponed during the first rather crazy months of her widow-hood.

Back in China Theodore H. "Teddy" White, his emotions grafted to the image of his late best friend's wife, wrote to an editor at *Time* of his concern for Annalee and his hope that she might be persuaded to work in one of the Time Inc. offices. "I can't do a damn thing about her because she answers no letters she receives from China," he lamented. Still, he never stopped writing, and on his home leave early in 1944, White sought her out. He felt it was time to make his feelings known, to say aloud what Annalee must already have guessed. He asked her to spend the last two weeks of his leave in his company, and she agreed, but then turned around and took a job with *Time*, effectively aborting the experiment, if that was what it was. Perhaps for her it was still too soon; perhaps she could not so easily substitute Teddy's round, homely face for Mel's dark, handsome one, which still haunted her dreams.

White nevertheless clung to the prospect of Jacoby's return to Chungking, and together they sought government permission for her to join the Time Inc. staff as his assistant. Teddy returned to China, and that fall, exerting influence as only he could, Henry Luce managed to get Annalee back there. She was the only woman correspondent in res-idence.

Chungking no longer seemed to Jacoby the heroic little city it had once been. Air raids were rare now, the cavernous shelters hardly used, but there was more hunger. The city was full of refugees. The problem of inflation absorbed the Chinese to the detriment of all else. "All our old idealistic friends from 1941 had to do rather unsavory things in order to stay alive and feed their children," Annalee noted. "Chiang's troops were starving. Some didn't even have straw sandals to go into battle." The long-dormant war had become active as Japan launched an offensive aimed at capturing air bases the U.S. military had built across southeast China and from which they were bombing Japan. Ironically, by the time Japan took the bases, it hardly mattered. The air-fields in the Mariana Islands were operational, and Tokyo could be bombed from the south.

Jacoby found the city and her life there depressing. She and White gathered information and pounded out their stories, but they weren't stories that pleased Henry Luce. He did not want to know that China had lost its strategic importance in the conduct of the war, or that corruption under Chiang Kai-shek had reached such a state as to make normal commerce impossible, or that the army, also under Chiang, simply vanished into thin air when ordered to fight. He especially did not want to hear what Teddy and Annalee were reporting in dispatch after dispatch: that the only economy and the only army performing properly were Mao's economy and Mao's army operating out of Yenan.

White and Jacoby had rooms next to each other in the press hostel. Teddy hoped that proximity would help sway Annalee's affections, but that did not happen. In the middle of the compound lay the new Melville Jacoby Memorial Garden, assuring her late husband's subliminal presence in her life. Teddy was her colleague and her friend, but her heart was not in the relationship, and he knew it. For the time being, he put Annalee in charge of the Chungking bureau and went off to report the war.

It was during that period that Jacoby interviewed Chiang. When in 1941 she had worked for Madame Chiang's United China Relief, the Chiangs had liked and trusted her. Now her opinions were no longer in sync with those of her boss on the subject of Chiang. Luce, she noted, still saw him as "an honest Christian, beloved by his people," believed that "anyone who said otherwise was mistaken or Communist," and had recently appointed a like-minded man by the name of Whittaker Chambers to the post of foreign news editor. Annalee's interview produced little of note to report except Chiang's proposal to make Sian the postwar capital. "This seemed an unlikely place," she said, "lacking buildings, transportation, almost everything except charm, so I featured this in my dispatch and added some Chiang platitudes. Back came a long article, which went on for pages of questions I had not asked and answers Chiang had not given. Whittaker had made up the dialogue."

When Henry Luce positioned the Chambers version of her interview as a *Life* cover story, Jacoby realized it was time to resign and go home.

In the fall of 1944 women won the fight for accreditation to the navy, and Shelley Mydans applied. It was her chance to be back in action with Carl, but for the moment she was slated for Guam, which was under the command of Admiral Nimitz and now boasted a press office, while her husband was scheduled for the Philippines, under General MacArthur and still closed to women. *Life* had promised Carl Mydans he could cover the recapture of Manila, and he traveled all the way from France to be there.

The landings on Luzon occurred in January 1945. The action signaled the first kamikaze attacks of the war, one of which killed a friend and fellow *Life* reporter on another vessel, but MacArthur's flagship with Mydans aboard was spared. The immediate goal of the American forces was the prison camps, with the camp containing the survivors of the Bataan Death March as the first objective. When that sortie was successful, it was decided to risk a sixty-mile dash into the heart of Manila to liberate Santo Tomás, where Carl and Shelley had spent eight months of internment, and where after three long years some 3,700 Americans were still held.

Later Carl described to Shelley exactly what happened on that first day of February 1945. The jeep he shared with other reporters, including Frank Hewlett of UP whose wife was in Santo Tomás, was fourth in line after the tanks. There were rivers to ford and bullets to dodge. At one point an essential bridge had just been mined, but an officer dashed over and stamped out the burning fuses. A cheering populace greeted them in Manila, but again they did not pause, and night had fallen by the time they reached the entrance to the old university. The first tank turned in, and Carl was amazed to see, as he wrote later, "that gate and fence, which had stood so long between me and freedom, fall over like a painted illusion."

Mydans and Hewlett ran for the main building. Inside they could see by a few flickering candles that the lobby and great stairway were crowded with people who at first would not believe that the two men facing them were Americans. "If you are Americans," one said, "put that flashlight on yourself." Mydans turned the light on his own face. "I'm Carl Mydans," he said, and that was all he got out before he was mobbed.

This and much more was what Carl told Shelley when, a few weeks later, he flew to Guam. Shelley had been there for some weeks, and she was full of optimism about the progress of the war. Having just

297

witnessed how hard the Japanese were fighting in the Philippines, Carl was surprised by her confident assertions that a sense of futility was sweeping Japan and that defeat was now expected. He accompanied her to the briefing room in an oversized Quonset hut where the commanding officer had just informed rows of airmen sitting before him that their target that night would be — yes, again — Tokyo. The men, smoking, chewing gum, sipping coffee out of heavy mugs, faced a huge photo-mosaic that covered the entire wall, on which one could see every street and building still standing in the Tokyo-Kawasaki-Yokohama industrial area. As Shelley and Carl watched, a slender young intelligence officer aimed his pointer at one of the few sections not already burned to blackness on the photograph. "This is the area we're taking out tonight," he said, noting that it was light industrial, small aircraft engine plants, shops, some residential, mostly wooden structures. The population density ran at about 30,000 per square mile. He moved on to the weather pattern, and the men sat there immobile, inured to figures, lumping together information like "minimum ground wind" with "population 30,000 per square mile" as if they were equivalent.

Later Shelley showed Carl the file of Japanese home radio broadcasts. The city of Tokyo was a great wasteland, they read, "literally scorched to the ground," although Japanese civilians were still being told that to conform to an "unconditional surrender" would be foolish. That night they followed the B-29 crews out onto the airfield. As they stood watching the great planes lift one by one into the soft night air, they could only wonder how much longer the Japanese could hold out.

Later that winter, on assignment for *Life*, Shelley joined flight nurse Victoria Pavlowski on the middle leg of the 4,757-mile trip from Leyte in the Philippines to Hawaii. The nurses of the Army Air Transport Command had already brought tens of thousands of sick and wounded from their island battlefields back to home ground. The nurses were young and pretty, Shelley reported, and inordinately admired by their lonely charges, but their jobs were an endless succession of weariness and danger.

After they took off, Mydans took notes on Pavlowski's routine: taking temperatures, dispensing sleeping pills, codeine, or morphine for those needing it. Pavlowski brought out more blankets, as the heat on the ground had already been replaced by the cold of the sky. In the dim light the men who were not sleeping were watching her. "From the shadow of the litters I could see their eyes as they turned from staring above them to look at her neat head and slim shoulders in the baggy flight suit," Shelley wrote. When the two port-side engines suddenly cut out and the plane dropped, they looked to her for reassurance. Her face did not change. Grasping the nearest litter to steady herself, she leaned down and, smiling, spoke to a young soldier in a body cast. The engines cut in again and the plane steadied, but all Shelley could think of was the phrase "prepare to ditch," and the image of this kid swimming for his life in a body cast.

That called to mind stories she had heard other nurses tell. One, whose plane had crash-landed on a tiny island south of Guadalcanal, had managed to save all her patients, even the GI whose neck had been slit in the crash; she put a tube down his throat and syphoned out the blood with an ear syringe. When the rescue boat came, there wasn't enough room for them and her too, so she swam out to the ship anchored beyond the coral reefs. Another nurse, when the pilot told everyone to prepare to ditch, propped up and held close to her a young blind soldier until, two hours later, the plane limped in onto Hickam Field. Watching Victoria Pavlowski now, Shelley understood the combination of desperate tiredness and exhilaration on their faces when each trip was over.

At last MacArthur lifted the ban against women reporters, and Shelley was among the first invited to return to the Philippines. Nearly three years had passed since she left Manila, and she was anxious to see the city. Throngs of people filled the streets. She and Carl drove around to all the places they had known, such as the Bay View Hotel where they and the Jacobys were staying when the Japanese invaded, now only a shell. Navy landing craft had replaced the sailboats in the little harbor, but otherwise the city appeared to be returning to some kind of normalcy.

The gates were open at Santo Tomás when they reached it. Morning glories covered the bunker. All the prisoners had been sent home and the main building turned into an army hospital. Shelley and

Carl walked up to their old quarters. The wall between their two rooms had been torn down, and twenty-six GIs lay in rows of white beds where sixty-five prisoners once had lived. In the far corner a soldier, yellowed with jaundice, was reading. They went over to him. "This is where my husband slept when we were prisoners here," Shelley said, but he just stared at them, not comprehending.

27

Iwo Jima

The battle for Iwo Jima in February 1945 was the first in which women correspondents in the Pacific were allowed in a combat area. Accreditation to the navy (implying permission to travel on and report from navy vessels) had just come through, and only a few women — new to the Pacific, and to the war itself — were available to go. Patricia Lochridge was one.

Patricia Lochridge, *Woman's Home Companion*

Pat Lochridge grew up in Austin, Texas, where her father was editor and publisher of the *Austin Statesman*. After graduating from Wellesley and the Columbia School of Journalism, she followed the time-honored course of young journalists and joined the staff of a small daily paper — this one in Mexico, Missouri. It was valuable experience but lacking in glamour, and when in the late 1930s CBS, just forming a news staff, offered her a job at their Madison Avenue office, she grabbed it. It was not all news writing, she recalled; one reason it was offered to a woman was that, in the same time-honored way, she could double as secretary. It also fell to her to cover on weekends, and as Hitler's armies always invaded on weekends, it was Pat who would open the network and see that the latest news got on the air. She often worked seven days a week, and during vacations kept in the swing by writing magazine articles.

After Pearl Harbor, Lochridge went to Washington to work for

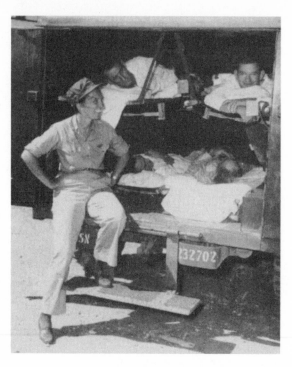

Patricia Lochridge with wounded ready for evacuation, Saipan, 1945.
STEVE BULL PERSONAL COLLECTION.

the Office of War Information (OWI), but left a year later for a job at Crowell Collier, publisher of *Collier's* and *Woman's Home Companion*. It was only natural that when an opening for a woman in the Pacific came up, the *Companion* asked Pat if she would like to go. There was a publicity angle to the position; she would be the magazine's emissary. Her uniform was made to order by Saks Fifth Avenue. She was photographed by Warner Brothers and promoted as the *Companion's* Fearless Girl Reporter, and she met regularly with advertisers. Uncomplaining, she was nevertheless grateful that this kind of hype was seldom seen by other reporters.

The voyage to Honolulu was an education in itself. The troopship was triple-loaded, which meant that each bunk was occupied by three persons alternately, eight hours each. Lochridge bunked with the nurses and played poker with air force officers.

Hawaii, under the command of Admiral Nimitz, was billed as a "forward area," although Pat later said, "Playing tennis with the

302

Dickey Chapelle.
PHOTO BY M/SGT. LEW LOWERY, USMC.
STATE HISTORICAL SOCIETY OF WISCONSIN.

Nimitzes was not my idea of activity for a forward area." Still, she managed to get one very good story, about the women who worked at Hickam Air Force Base doing repairs. "They lived in Quonset huts and worked the same kind of assembly line that women were doing in Nebraska or New York," Pat recalled later, but the newsworthy part was that they were available single women plunked down in a sea of men. On their off hours they went to Waikiki Beach, among other places, and inevitably formed relationships. Since this put them in the category of a hazard to "home and hearth," which the military did not want the home front to know about, Lochridge was convinced her story would not pass the censor if filed in a normal way. She solved that problem by prevailing upon a friendly air force colonel to pick her up at her hotel at 2 A.M. and take her to the night censor, who was believed to be more lenient. (Apparently she charmed the colonel that night — or perhaps she already had. He later became her second husband.)

In January 1945, Patricia Lochridge, Peggy Hull Deuell, and Barbara Finch, an American woman married to an Englishman and

303

working with him for the British wire service Reuters, received accreditation to the Pacific fleet. They were authorized to go to "Guam, Saipan, Tinian, Guadalcanal, New Hebrides, Angaur, Peleliu, Christmas, Funafuti, Samoa, Tongatabu [sic], Ulithi, Tarawa, Makin, Apamama [sic] and other . . . points in the POA (Pacific Ocean Area)." Within days Shelley Mydans and Bonnie Wiley of the AP had acquired the same. The dike was open.

Almost at once they began shipping out for Guam. There they were consigned to a single large tent near the commander's quarters, on the theory that the sentries there would protect them as well. Although Guam had been captured six months before, even on apparently secure islands a few desperate enemy holdouts remained. The unsecured island of the moment — the island toward which all focus had turned — was Iwo Jima.

Iwo Jima is small — some five miles long, and half that in breadth at its widest point. Because it afforded only one landing area, troops and press were thrown into close proximity. No one on Iwo was ever very far from anyone else, friend or foe, and there were a great many of the latter, well-armed and entrenched in strong fortifications. The importance of the island was its position. From bases on Saipan and Guam, B-29s could fly to Japan, unload their bombs, and return without refueling, but they needed the protection of fighter escorts, which had a shorter range. And there, directly in line between the Mariana Islands and central Japan, lay this volcanic bulge of sand and clay, dotted with stunted trees and devoid of animal life except for typhus-carrying mites.

The battle for Iwo Jima was mostly a Marine Corps operation. The navy supplied the transport, the shellfire that provided cover for the troops while landing, the planes that strafed Japanese positions from above, and the hospital ships that took on the wounded. But the assaults were made by marines, and the long lists of casualties were marine casualties.

Women correspondents covered the battle from the hospital ships. Pat Lochridge arrived on a cold gray morning, four days after the initial landing, aboard the hospital ship *Solace*. She stood on the windy upper deck with a group of doctors, dreading what she knew she must see in just a few more hours. Unsure how well she would handle it, she was grateful when a young surgeon handed her a small bottle of ammonia to use "if things get too rough and you feel faint."

Writing for a magazine and facing no immediate deadline, Lochridge could include considerably more detail than, say, the AP reporter Bonnie Wiley, whose Iwo trip two days before had of necessity been condensed into a few wire service dispatches. Pat described how the *Solace* maneuvered among battleships, cruisers, and carriers to anchor within several hundred yards of the battle-scarred, black sand beach. The gangplank was lowered, and almost immediately the ship was surrounded by small boats transporting the wounded from the beach, or from combat ships where they had found temporary refuge. The sea was rough, making the transfer difficult.

> The wounded came on and on. Some still had their rifles; others were naked except for their battle dressings. Most were in terrible pain. All were terribly brave. By late afternoon we had taken aboard almost four hundred patients, to be put into bunks, given transfusions and medicines; to be cleaned up and have their dressings changed; to be fed a hot dinner with perhaps a drink of medicinal whisky to warm them after their cold days on Iwo.
>
> By nightfall the neat shining white wards with their double-decked bunks were almost filled. On the once spotless white decks were little piles of dirty bloodstained clothing which had been cut off the men. The stain was everywhere — a splash on the toe of my shoe, little droplets on a railing where I rested my hand. You fortify yourself against it in the operating rooms, train yourself to ignore it on the doctors' white gowns. But there is no getting used to it everywhere.

Lochridge moved about the wards with the two chaplains, helping when and however they could, but only too aware that theirs was not the real work. That was done by the seventeen doctors, thirteen nurses, and 175 corpsmen who never rested. At dusk the *Solace* put out to sea so that its lighted decks and spotlighted red crosses would not indicate the position of the rest of the blacked-out fleet. There, as the ship rocked and pitched, the medical staff worked on. Abdominal wounds came first, then brain and chest operations, finally amputations. "Six men died," Lochridge reported. "But three hundred and ninety-six of the worst shot-up men in the war were still alive in the morning when we returned to our post beside Iwo's crowded bloody beach."

She had survived the first day. Amid all the suffering there had been one moment to raise the spirit. It had occurred quite early when a marine was carried on board swathed in bloody bandages, but volubly happy. "Take a look at that," he sang out, half rising from his stretcher to look back shoreward. Pat could just make out tiny figures struggling up the large extinct volcano known as Suribachi. "And then we saw it," she wrote later, "an American flag on the peak, snapping in the wind. The marine lay back and smiled. 'I helped put her there this morning,' he said."

In the press office on Guam, directly connected to the communications ship *Eldorado* anchored off Iwo Jima, a young woman was absorbing this news of the flag with increasing amazement. The teletype machine was monitored by a handful of rewrite experts whose job it was to relay dispatches from the battle zones. Watching it with them, Dickey Chapelle first learned that new marine units had arrived that morning. The rewrite men nodded; that had been expected. The staccato continued: AN UNCONFIRMED RUMOR . . . THE FLAG HAS BEEN SIGHTED ON THE TOP OF THE HIGHEST POINT OF THE SAVAGELY CONTESTED SOIL OF . . . The men thought that improbable. Still, the tension was palpable. Suddenly the teletype clicked on again: IT HAS BEEN OFFICIALLY CONFIRMED THAT THE FLAG OF THE UNITED STATES NOW FLIES FROM MOUNT SURIBACHI HIGHEST POINT OF THIS VOLCANIC ISLAND. The room erupted in a cheer.

Dickey Chapelle, *Life Story* magazine

Dickey Chapelle first heard the words "Iwo Jima" aboard the large transport plane *Martin Mars* bound for Honolulu. Born Georgette Louise Meyer, blond and blue-eyed, she grew up a chubby, nearsighted child in a Milwaukee suburb, always marching to a different drummer from her classmates. Her idol was Admiral Richard E. Byrd who first flew over the South Pole the year she was ten. Tired of being called Georgie, she took the name Dickey from him. Dickey was accepted at

M.I.T. on a full scholarship, highly unusual for a sixteen-year-old girl in 1935, but bored with her classes, she spent her days hanging around the Boston Navy Yard, or the airport, or watching the sophisticated tracking system at the Coast Guard station, and then describing the scene in stories for the *Boston Traveler.* It was a blow to her ego when she flunked out, but otherwise a relief. Migrating to New York, she contributed stories to the *New York Times* on air shows and daredevil flying exercises in which she signed on as a passenger in order to describe the sensations firsthand. At nineteen she took up photography with the same enthusiasm, and at twenty-two married her teacher, Tony Chapelle, a charming World War I navy photographer more than twice her age and, unknown to Dickey, still married to another woman.

After Pearl Harbor, Dickey received accreditation from the War Department and became a news photographer for *Look* magazine in the Caribbean where Tony's naval unit was combating German U-boats. U-boats were the big story, but one she was not allowed to tell. Although she worked for *Look*, she read *Life* avidly and wanted nothing more than to do cover stories or, better, *be* the cover story, as Margaret Bourke-White had once been. But Chapelle was not *Look*'s darling the way Bourke-White was *Life*'s; she was let go, and returned to New York to wait for a second chance.

That came in 1944 when she signed up with *Life Story*, a popular women's monthly, to do a series on "the ordinary doings and problems of women's lives," and turned it into something else. Although her husband was opposed, Dickey persuaded her editor to send her to the Pacific. Early in 1945 she became accredited to the U. S. Navy while doing a story on navy flight-nurse training, then made the trip out with a new contingent of flight nurses. All her life she remembered how privileged and special she felt on that flight — at twenty-five, the youngest woman correspondent there. When the copilot of the *Martin Mars* climbed back to where Dickey and the nurses were sitting among the mailbags to tell them the marines had landed on this little island, he had to spell I-w-o J-i-m-a for them.

By the time she hit the press room at navy headquarters in Hawaii, the news had turned bad. Whole units of assault troops were going in, only, it seemed, to be shot up or killed. Dickey decided this was the story for her. "I want you to be sure you'll be the first woman somewhere," her editor had whispered into her ear before she left. "Any of those islands will do." So when the public relations officer asked her where she would like to go, she did not pause: "As far forward as you'll let me." Her request, however, did not find a sympathetic ear in Admiral Harold Miller, head of navy PR in the Pacific. He had just the job for a woman photographer, he said: to document photographically the use of whole blood in the treatment of the wounded, thus advertising the need for more blood donations from the folks back home. It was a good cause, but not the kind of thing Chapelle knew her editor was hoping for. Still, she thought she should be able to achieve both goals together. Miller wrote her orders for the hospital ship *Samaritan*, and Dickey left for Iwo.

Pat Lochridge found her second day on the *Solace* more devastating than the first. For one thing, yesterday's men were better able today to talk of their experience, and she heard of nothing but impenetrable blockhouses, thousand-pound rockets, huge mortar shells, no way to take cover, and everyone shivering in the raw cold. Worse than his wildest nightmares, one marine told her. Whenever there was a new arrival, they were full of questions about their units, their friends. "Only once was it still," Lochridge recalled. "A red-haired corporal choked out the words: 'They got me when they killed John.' Each man knew that John was Gunnery Sergeant John Basilone, Congressional Medal of Honor veteran of Guadalcanal, whom all marines believed invulnerable. In the stillness I couldn't bear the expression on their faces."

That day the accumulated smells of blood, disinfectants, gangrene, and death became more pervasive. Lochridge went up on deck. She had arranged to be taken ashore to see how the doctors and corpsmen were operating. She found the beach littered with equipment and stores unloaded from the ships but not yet distributed. Mortar fire was still heavy. Medical personnel patched up the wounded temporarily in beach casualty stations, but sometimes they were wounded a second time, or even killed, while they waited for the small boats to take them to the hospital ship.

Lochridge returned to the *Solace* to find that the ship's crew had been evicted from their quarters to provide more beds. Death also made for more room. "Some live and you don't know why," one of the surgeons told her. "Others die and you don't know why either." That evening Pat and the surgeon, exhausted and drained, stood together on the quarterdeck as the *Solace* struck off for Saipan.

Peggy Hull Deuell was on Saipan. Japanese bombers no longer called there at night. "It is the time of the full moon," Deuell wrote, plainly infected by its lunar magic. "Under its soft light the camp becomes a landscape of surprising beauty. The tents look like small dark pyramids — dozens of them in orderly rows. The coconut palms, their tall gray trunks distinct in the moonlight, are great feather fans above the sleeping men."

But Peggy's quiet was sharply broken the night the *Solace* reached harbor. Over the public address system came the summons to stretcher bearers to report to the receiving stations. "They're coming in now," said the redheaded nurse in Peggy's tent, and they walked together up the hill to the brightly lighted platform in front of the Quonset hut lined with litters.

Gray blankets cover the quiet figures. Medical officers kneel beside the wounded and give their commands in a low voice. "Fracture — X-ray room," you hear, and a stretcher moves past. You look at the next litter, and the pallor, even in the deceiving night light, carries a significant warning. The pallor and the resignation, as if death had already been accepted. "Plasma now." The doctor speaks cryptly [*sic*] as if he does not want to waste further time even with words.

A young soldier smiles up at me from another litter. His blue eyes are bright. "Say, haven't I seen you before?" he asks. "Didn't I see you in Honolulu?" "Yes, I was there." . . . He talks with difficulty for his throat is encased in a vise-like cast. A bullet had gone through his mouth, taken out some of his teeth, and broken his neck — nonetheless he is cheerful. . . . Somehow his good humor, his banter, lifts the tragic pall from the scene. He, with the others, is just back from ash-covered, blood-saturated Iwo Jima, but from the wisecracks they toss at one another, from their bright remarks to the nurses and doctors, you would think they were just coming in from a football game.

Peggy Hull Deuell was proving her worth at last.

Dickey Chapelle's experience on the *Samaritan* was much like Lochridge's on the *Solace* except that Dickey saw it mostly through the lens of a camera. At the beginning she used that lens as insulation against shock. She stood by the gangway, trying to keep out of the way of the stretcher bearers, endlessly focusing and shooting. The wounded seemed to come in a stream that never slowed down, even when, more than once, she heard the doctor grunt to a boat crew that they had reached him too late. "Take him back," he said hoarsely. "We only have space for the living."

The second day was much like the first, except that Chapelle went through the wards to check on the men she had photographed the day before. Having no names as yet, she had carefully copied the numbers from each man's dog tags into her notebook. One marine sitting up on his bunk, an enormous bandage around his midsection, welcomed her enthusiastically, insisting she had taken his picture the previous day. Dickey didn't remember him, but there was his number in her notebook. The face across from her simply bore no resemblance to the one she had photographed; fourteen pints of blood fed into his veins had made that much difference. She photographed him again, and the two pictures, taken twenty-four hours apart, were used on posters for years afterward to attract blood donors.

Chapelle spent part of the day in one of the operating rooms, secured with a rope to the pipes overhead so that if she fainted, she would not fall on top of the patient. She found photographing amputations a grisly business. The surgeons averaged an amputation every thirty minutes, night and day, for three days running. Meanwhile, all the bunks were occupied, and men lay along the corridors on stretchers because there was nowhere to move them to. That evening the *Samaritan* threaded its way around the warships and, like the *Solace* before, left Iwo for Saipan.

Pat Lochridge did not return to Iwo Jima, but Dickey Chapelle felt there was something inconclusive about her time there. For one thing, she had not set foot on the island, and she probably heard that Lochridge had. For another, her few days with the wounded had only served to whet her appetite for combat experience. Back in the big tent on Guam, she mentioned this to Reuters correspondent Barbara Finch, sitting cross-legged on her canvas cot. It was Finch you went to when you needed specifics on the Pacific war. Among her most recent nuggets of information was the news that a field hospital had been set up by a captured airfield in the interior; Barbara had already flown there and back on an evac plane, and suggested that Dickey do the same. Dickey's orders, once obtained, specified that she would photograph procedures using whole blood at the field hospital at Motoyama Airfield One. The round-trip flight would leave at 3 A.M. and return the same day — the navy's way of insuring that no woman spent a night with the troops.

Chapelle's C-47 reached Iwo in good time, but had to circle a while over the airfield until sniper fire died down. When it landed, the pilot ordered her to hit the sand and keep running — no easy job carrying bulky camera equipment through ankle-deep volcanic ash. She set to work inside the three-tent hospital, where conditions were primitive in the extreme. Night operations took place by handheld flashlight. After photographing the whole-blood procedures, Dickey decided that she should have an exterior shot of the hospital as well. The trick to that was carrying twenty pounds of equipment up one of the fifteen-foot ridges — an accomplishment that left her more respectful of the marines with their seventy-pound packs.

On the ridge she found three young officers laughing at her struggle. They asked what she was doing, and she knew she should have explained that she was photographing the hospital, and then done just that. Instead, she blurted out what she wanted to be doing, which was looking for the front. No doubt envisioning the tale they would tell their fellows, the young men were happy to oblige. They tucked her into their weapons carrier and drove about forty minutes along a cratered lane toward Mount Suribachi, at which point they came to a halt. Gesturing toward the great sooty range of ridges, they informed her that this was "somewhere on the front."

Chapelle climbed laboriously up one of the ridges and looked around. She had no idea which direction to focus on; it looked the same everywhere. She solved the problem by setting up her tripod and photographing in a great circle. It was hot and windy up there, and she could hear what sounded like invisible winged insects all around. In the distance were a few tanks, and now and then a marine popped up from a hole in the honeycombed ridges, looked around, and ducked down again. Dickey found it pretty scary, and as soon as she had her photos, she stumbled back down. The waiting officers, no doubt thinking of the dressing-down they would have received had she been shot, gave her the same. Was she crazy? Didn't she know better than to stand up on a skyline and expose herself on all sides? Disgruntled, they returned her to the airfield.

Back in the big tent on Guam, Barbara Finch listened to her story and laughed at the part about the whizzing insects. There was no animal life on Iwo, she said; what Dickey had heard was sniper fire. It took Dickey a moment to digest that fact. Apparently, she'd been to the front, she'd been shot at, she'd survived. She had crossed the divide, and she felt wonderful. She floated down the hill to the Quonset known as the "zebra hut," after the stripes on the sleeves of the NCO (noncommissioned officer) reporters whose territory it was. Technically, it was off limits to civilians and officers, but it was handy, and as Finch had shown her, a woman could slip in quietly, type up her material, and slip out again. This evening, however — perhaps emboldened by her prowess in the field — Dickey typed up her story (the dateline read "March 5, 1945, Iwo Jima. Under Fire") and then didn't leave. Instead, as she recalled later, when she heard one of the men bitching about civilian reporters — how they didn't want to go forward and never wrote about the marines anyway — she forgot herself and tore into him at length, naming correspondents who had gone in with the troops from Guadalcanal on, and concluding with a summary of her own stories since arrival, all of them about marines. Her outburst was met by stunned silence. She should have left right then while she was ahead, but again, she didn't. "Now you just tell me," she remembered blaring forth, "is there anything else *this* civilian correspondent can do for the United States Marine Corps?"

The response was a resounding "Yes, ma'am!" accompanied by hoots of laughter. Chapelle flushed scarlet. The top NCO made his way across the room. "Come on, I'll take you home now," he said gently, and walked with her back up the hill, saluted, turned about, and retraced his steps. Dickey figured that from then on she'd be catching the jeep up to CINCPAC to do her typing. But the following morning when she started off to the civilian mess for breakfast, she was intercepted by three NCO correspondents. Why did she want to go eat "brass chow"? they asked. Theirs was much better. They took her to the big mess hall where she was amazed at the size of the portions and how good it tasted — and how comfortable she felt there. There was a lot of banter, much of it against officers, and as a correspondent holding captain's status, she might have felt defensive. But clearly it was not directed at her; rather, she felt that they were all *for* her. Suddenly her insecurities — at being the rookie reporter in the big tent, at having a husband back in the States who she knew was seeing other women — began to fade. Lew Lowery, photographer for *Leatherneck*, the Marine Corps magazine, even came over to speak to her, and referred to her in front of the others as "our girl."

This marked the beginning of Dickey Chapelle's love affair with the marines, which lasted the rest of her life.

28

Of Rain, Ruin, Relationships, and the Bridge at Remagen

The winter of 1945 was the worst of the war. Wearing their Wac long johns under thick wool fatigues, or dress uniforms topped by overcoats, the women correspondents were far better clothed than the civilians they moved among, friend or enemy. The weather was the Great Equalizer: it dealt the same heavy rains and bitter cold to both sides, and to all points along the front, from the northern reaches of the Rhine valley to the Vosges Mountains in Alsace and the Apennines in Italy. Nor were the cities spared; coal barges could not navigate on rivers swollen from constant rain. At the Scribe in Paris, there were two hours of heat each day. Women based there typed in their rooms with gloved hands. When Lee Miller went to the Palais Royal to see Colette, she photographed her in bed piled with fur coverings; they talked of the black market, the end of the war that for a while had seemed close and then wasn't, and the cold. "Parisians are colder than they have been any other winter of the war," Janet Flanner wrote in the *New Yorker*. "They are hungrier than they have been any other winter of the war. They are the hungriest they have been since the Prussian siege of Paris, when their grandparents ate mice."

Every week, it seemed, a new correspondent arrived. Some women brought years of valuable experience to their job, such as Virginia Lee Warren, veteran of the *Washington Post* and *Time* magazine, who replaced her husband, Milton Bracker, at the *New York Times* bureau in

Rome to free him for field reporting. The AP's Lyn Crost gave up a Washington staff job to cover the activities of those extraordinary Japanese-American soldiers in the 100th Infantry Battalion and the 442nd Regimental Combat Team in Italy and Alsace. But other new-comers were still in their twenties — less practiced, more concerned with proving themselves. Most prominent among these were Ann Stringer and Marguerite Higgins.

Ann Stringer, United Press

Ann Stringer arrived in Europe in the tender position of wife of a correspondent killed by enemy fire. She had grown up in Texas and gone to college there before marrying William Stringer, then UP bureau chief in Columbus, Ohio. After a stint on the *Columbus Citizen*, Ann too was hired by UP, and she and Bill were sent as a team to New York and Buenos Aires. But reporting the war in Europe was their goal, and when UP would not send them, Bill switched to Reuters and in the summer of 1944 left for France. Ann was to join him, but before that could happen, Bill, in a moment of bravado during the advance on Paris, drove his jeep into the town of Versailles and was hit by sniper fire.

News of her husband's death was the same news received by thousands of other young American women that summer, but it was less common among war correspondents. Only Annalee Jacoby had lost a husband, and that was not at the hands of the enemy. A sympathetic UP management offered to send Ann to Europe, only to find that SHAEF was reluctant to allow her on the Continent for fear she might prove as rash as her husband. In time, however, SHAEF reversed itself, and in the lobby of the Scribe in Paris the UP chief introduced her to Colonel Barney Oldfield, head of the Ninth Army press camp, and placed her in his care.

Everyone who knew Ann Stringer mentioned her beauty, but that she was both beautiful and bereaved lent her a special aura to which every healthy American male seemed susceptible. She was tall and slender, with shoulder-length light brown hair worn loose and what Oldfield referred to as "butter-melting" eyes. Wherever she went,

Ann Stringer interviewing GIs, Germany, 1945.
UPI/CORBIS-BETTMANN.

heads turned, which could be dangerous when the head belonged to the driver of your jeep. Unhappy at the proscription against women in the combat zone, she was eager to make good as a war correspondent and justify UP's faith in her. She also had in mind to complete what her husband had not been able to, although some officers feared she harbored a wish to complete it in the same way he had. Perhaps in her grief she saw no reason to be careful, causing every man around to conclude that he must be careful for her.

During February the Ninth Army moved steadily eastward, and Stringer with it. But her impatience was too evident and her timing too close for the officers at SHAEF when they saw her datelines in the *Herald Tribune* Paris edition. Oldfield received a teletype message reiterating the rule that a woman correspondent was to go "no further forward than women's services go," and that refusal to comply could cut short her stay with the Ninth or any other army. Personally, Oldfield believed that reporters of either sex should have the option of moving into a danger area as long as they were clear that was what they were doing. But his job was to enforce the rules, as he reminded the senior UP hand who com-

Marguerite Higgins.
UPI/CORBIS-BETTMANN.

plained when the message from SHAEF caused Ann to burst into tears.
The dateline "With the Ninth Army in Germany" was fine, Barney said,
but "With the First Troops in Jülich" would only cause trouble.

Early in March 1945 the First Army reached Cologne, and a few
days after its capture Janet Flanner, Marjorie "Dot" Avery, Catherine
Coyne, and Lee Miller arrived. They found lodging in an apartment
only slightly less shattered than most. Flanner was glad to be out of
Paris, which made her edgy. With the cold beginning to abate, nightlife
had returned, and for many GIs and journalists it had become the good-
time place. Life at the Scribe reflected that. Ravished Cologne better
suited her mood.

All four women recalled how horrible the destruction of Aachen
had seemed when they first saw it. Miller remembered climbing onto

some wreckage to photograph the cathedral and causing an avalanche of debris upon which she slid to the street. "Half-buried, putrefying flesh . . . clung to my hands, elbows and bottom," she had written. But now Cologne seemed worse. "Aachen died in a different way," Flanner noted; "its handsome melancholy skeleton is left upright; behind its elegant, carved facades, it was burned out. Cologne and its heavy, medieval pomp were blown up. By its river bank, Cologne lies recumbent, without beauty, shapeless in the rubble and loneliness of complete physical defeat."

Coyne agreed. One did not see a whole building anywhere, she wrote, only piles of rubble from which flew white flags, indicating that underneath homes were still operational. She could not imagine living for two years with no gas for cooking, no telephone, intermittent electricity, all while under frequent attack. On Sunday she watched with amazement as the citizens took their customary Sunday promenade along the rubble-lined streets; on Monday it was even more astonishing to see men setting off briskly from their bombed-out hovels with their briefcases as if going to the office. Where in fact they were going she could not guess. Avery was surprised by the plenitude of items not to be found anywhere else. An abundance of food was the most obvious, but little things, too, like paper clips (which were hardly available even in America), rubber items, even paper napkins. And how well dressed, if a little dusty, people seemed to be.

The four women were present in the cobbled prison yard the day more than fifty people were freed from the Klingelputz Gestapo prison. Avery described how the living had to be sorted from the dead, lying together as they were on the stone floors. First to walk out was a thin but lovely nineteen-year-old Belgian girl arrested for helping French prisoners elude the Germans, then starved and beaten in an attempt to make her talk. A young Frenchman with sunken cheeks but a disarming smile followed. After that, in no particular order, emerged a Dutchwoman caught with her husband and daughter listening to the BBC; a woman from Brussels who, unable to forget the five weeks she had spent naked in solitary confinement in the prison cellar, wept uncontrollably; an emaciated sixteen-year-old Dutch boy; and a little Russian girl who repeated the same phrases over and over, about the beatings and the hunger and the cold.

"They came out into the sunlight one by one," Avery reported, "and stood around the courtyard holding small suitcases or bundles. . . . To me it was a glimpse into an unknown and horrifying world." Flanner wrote of "a thin young Belgian, in what had once been good tweeds, praying over a mound of earth in the prison courtyard. His father and four other prisoners had been buried there the night before our soldiers came in." She was glad for the witness of her colleagues, so that their accounts, being the same, would be believed. Miller was as horrified by the implications as the facts. "This went on in a great German city," she pointed out, "where the inhabitants must have known and acquiesced or at the very least suspected and ignored the activities of their lovers and spouses and sons."

Before they left, the women visited the great cathedral, its twin spires the tallest in Europe. American bombers had made an effort to spare it, and indeed it was gauged to be only ten percent damaged, although you thought more when you walked ankle-deep through the debris and gazed at the leaden sky through two gaping holes in the roof, Coyne said. Flanner conjectured that "Cologne's panorama of ruin" would be what American soldiers could expect now in city after city. And however the Allies might eventually divide Germany, she wrote, "her cities, if they are like Cologne, are already divided into morsels of stone no bigger than your hand."

From the cathedral square the women looked out on what was left of the once great bridge spanning the Rhine, blown by the retreating Germans to a mass of twisted steel. The Allies would not cross the Rhine at Cologne.

March was also the month when that most controversial of women correspondents Marguerite Higgins moved out of Paris toward the front.

Marguerite Higgins, *New York Herald Tribune*

Born in Hong Kong, Marguerite Higgins was the only child of a steamship company agent, once an American World War I flier, and his French wife, whom he had met in a Paris bomb shelter. Maggie, as she was called, grew up fluent in French, and with an imagination steeped in her father's war stories. A graduate of the University of California at Berkeley, she apprenticed at several small California papers before entering the Columbia University School of Journalism on a scholarship. There she achieved two journalistic coups, genderwise: she was taken on by the *New York Herald Tribune* as their first female campus correspondent, and she was hired by them right after graduation in 1942. Despite an active social life revolving around the city room, Higgins got married that summer — to Stanley Moore, a young, upper-class leftist philosopher she had known in California, now an air force recruit. But neither job nor marriage met her expectations: she was soon openly unfaithful, as well as vocally desirous of quitting run-of-the-mill reporting to cover the war. That aspiration placed her at the bottom of a long list of hopefuls, and the *Herald Tribune* was not about to leapfrog her to the top — not at least until she persuaded publisher and feminist Helen Rogers Reid to do just that. By the fall of 1944 Higgins was accredited and off on the *Queen Mary*, if just barely.

The luxury-liner-now-troopship made the crossing from New York to Southampton twice a month, departing at midnight in an attempt to avoid any U-boats still about. On the night of the sailing, seven of the eight expected correspondents were assembled on deck. The *Queen Mary* approached Ambrose Light, and the pilot was lowered over the side. But when the ladder was raised, reporters, crew, and an entire army regiment were amazed to see a young woman in full army uniform clinging to it, blond hair blowing out from under her helmet. Marguerite Higgins was off to war, and the style of her leave-taking was only one of many unorthodox acts etched into the minds of her fellow correspondents.

Marguerite's husband Stanley, posted in London, had a room at the Savoy reserved for her. While she awaited her orders to the Continent, they had several months together, dining and dancing as well as working. But the honeymoon idyll soon turned to frustration. If their goals had ever been the same, they were no longer; for Maggie, life as a wife quickly paled before that of a war correspondent. In January 1945 they parted ways. At the Scribe in Paris, Higgins worked hard. Her French stood her in good stead: she read all the Paris dailies before writing her own copy, often on politics or the economic situation. She had also taken on the position of "foreign correspondent" for *Mademoiselle* magazine, to which she posted stories on wartime fashion and lifestyle, along with dramatic tales told her by refugees from the newly liberated countries. But she wanted nothing so much as to go to the front, and was delighted when, in mid-March, she was sent to the Ninth Air Force base in Germany. Others were not so pleased.

Maggie Higgins was well remembered by her female colleagues. Their lack of enthusiasm owed something to her youth (twenty-four), her half-innocent, half-sexy kind of prettiness, and her wealth of energy at a time when many of them were very tired. It owed much also to her doing, as a matter of course, what most of them scorned to do, which was to use her femininity to get something she could not acquire otherwise — not that she was the only one ever to do *that*. Then there was her driven personality, the ambition that fueled her often frenetic activity, her solipsism — attributes that were not always pleasant to be around. Helen Kirkpatrick recalled that she, Lee Miller, Higgins, and a fourth correspondent went to the outskirts of Cologne and took over a house for a day or two. There was no running water, and the beds were all in the same room. Everyone except Maggie wanted the window open at night, but each time it was opened, she would get up and close it. The unwritten rule of correspondents — that new arrivals defer to the old hands — she blatantly ignored. The old hands in this case had never met anyone so determined, and so adept at tramping on toes.

From Higgins's point of view, she did not have time for social amenities. She had come to the war very late; probably only a few weeks remained, and she had to make the most of them, she just *had* to. Nothing else mattered. But to the women whose paths she crossed — none of whose papers were competitors of hers — certain things did matter, like courtesy, an attempt at cleanliness, a sense of humor, and what they saw as a reasonable view of one's place in the universe. In that spring of 1945 these were not Maggie's strong points, and she was not easily forgiven.

Marguerite Higgins's radical views on sex constituted another point of contention with many of the women correspondents. The subject of sex was a touchy one. There were few discernible signs of a sexual revolution in the 1940s; even during the war, with their boyfriends and fiancés going off to possible death, "nice girls" were expected to say no and remain virgins, although, of course, many did not. The practices of women correspondents were similarly varied. After Lee Carson went to Europe, Pat Lochridge moved into her Washington apartment for a time, and was startled to find a stack of condoms in her medicine cabinet. The profession of journalism was hardly immune to the double standard of the time, as Carson had discovered, or rediscovered, when she joined the First Army press camp and was accused of getting human interest stories by dancing with the troops. Women were attacked for trading sex for information and thereby advancing their careers, which in fact happened rarely, but no one suggested that the men involved might have borne part of the blame.

Whatever happened in private, most women were discreet on the job. They were more apt to form liaisons with other reporters with whom they had regular contact than with the military, although both occurred. Some women — Catherine Coyne was one — were outspoken in their opposition to women engaging in relationships with male colleagues who they knew had wives back home, but others, probably the majority, had no blanket rules. War had a way of breaking down absolutes.

With the ratio between men and women in the press so skewed, most women had more opportunities for sex, or relationships leading to sex, than they cared to think about. A woman working out of a particular press camp spent much of her time in a jeep, so it was well to be choosy about who her companions were. Iris Carpenter traveled with two British correspondents, and it became awkward for her when one of them became emotionally attached and wanted more than just jeep time. Lee Carson began sharing a jeep with her AP competitor, Don Whitehead, in a close, steady relationship that drove the ever-suspicious AP head, Wes Gallagher, crazy. Calm and dependable in a crisis, Whitehead was also married, but few people condemned the strong mutual attachment between two people who were so happy in it themselves. "Lee was quite frank about it," Carpenter said later. "She felt she needed sex, that it made her forget the daily horror of the war. Other people didn't feel it comforted them in any way. For me there was too much else to think about — there was so much horror that sex didn't belong somehow. People are all different."

Intent though she was on establishing her credentials, Ann Stringer found it hard to ignore the men who flocked around her. She had difficulty resolving her feelings about her husband's death, and was often depressed because she could not reconcile the dualities of her nature. She had moved to the First Army where Lee Carson and Iris Carpenter might have helped her, but there is no indication she sought help from them. Perhaps she saw Lee (INS) as the competition, and Iris was not without her English reserve. Stringer was still under SHAEF prohibition from combat situations, which meant she had to move about judiciously and be careful how she worded her datelines. It also meant she had to seek out her own transportation, although INS photographer Allan Jackson was happy to oblige with a seat in his "liberated" Ford V8 convertible coupé.

One day Stringer and Jackson drove up to the market town of Eschweiler to visit the Fourth Division. They happened to catch a tank battle in the street; the Americans won, but there were dead and wounded. It was always distressing to correspondents, particularly women, to see young Americans die, and to Ann, with her husband always in mind, this was especially true. After the battle it was too late to reach First Army headquarters before dark, so Ann wrote her story and Allan his captions, and the press officer sent these back by courier and found them quarters for the night in a German farmhouse. They were lodged over the barn where they could hear the cows and feel the warmth and smell the odors coming up through cracks in the floor. Their hosts provided fresh eggs, bread, and milk for breakfast, and they made coffee from their own supply. It was blissful to linger there over the barn, to absorb the simple country sounds and smells — for Ann, a few hours of healing after the stress of the previous day and the recurrent images she carried with her.

But not all relationships were fresh and exciting. To the relief of both parties involved, an old one was reaching dissolution. Early that March Martha Gellhorn was in London, in bed with flu at the Dorchester when Hemingway came to see her. Assured of Allied success in the war, he was on his way home, i.e., to the Finca Vigía, the farmhouse outside Havana that Martha had discovered and renovated, and where they had lived, sometimes together, seldom in harmony. He would divorce her in Cuba, Ernest said; that was the simplest solution, since both were residents there. She acquiesced, grateful that she need not leave the war for a spell in Reno. Her first thought was to change the name on her passport back to Gellhorn. "I wanted above all to be free of him and his name," she said. At the time Hemingway thought he wanted to be free of her as well, but in fact this remained throughout his life the most traumatic of all his separations.

Nowhere that winter were the women very far from the Rhine. That great waterway was a major logistical obstacle, and one that carried mystical importance as well. Now that the Siegfried Line had proved vulnerable, the river was the only significant barrier between Allied forces and the heart of Germany. Hitler's armies retreated steadily eastward, blowing up bridges behind them.

British Field Marshal Sir Bernard Montgomery and General George S. Patton, commander of the Third Army, both assumed the goal of crossing the Rhine as a personal mission. Women were among the correspondents who had linked up with Patton's forces. Catherine Coyne recalled a briefing he held at this time at which she and Dot Avery were present. "He came in with his raincoat and his gun belt with the two ivory-handled pistols, his fluffy white hair and his foxy grandpa voice. He stood up there, and his aide said, as a kind of preemptive strike, 'There are women here,' and he replied, 'So I see.' He said to us, 'You'll have to excuse my language.' Every time he spoke of the enemy, he called them the 'son-of-a-bitch' Germans or Krauts or whatever. And every time he did that, he'd turn to Dot and me and apologize. It made her furious, that he would single us out that way, but I thought it was very funny."

Virginia Irwin was with Patton's Fourth Armored Division when they made their dash to the Rhine. On the morning of March 5, 1945, what Irwin referred to (in print) as "the hard-bitten, horny-handed tankers of the Fourth Armored" set out from the little village of Erdorf. By the night of the seventh they had cut through six German divisions to the Rhine valley. In their wake the smoke of burning German vehicles and oil dumps lay like a dense fog. Those Germans still alive were "scared witless, begging to be taken prisoners," Virginia wrote. There were about four thousand of them; other booty included an estimated thousand vehicles, not including tanks, an ordnance depot intact, and piles of artillery and other equipment.

The Fourth Armored was moving so fast, Irwin reported, and the nearest infantry support was so far behind, that they might at any time have been cut off by the Germans. "It was not a comfortable feeling sitting up with these tankers at the fingertip of the attenuated spearhead only as wide as the road we had traveled," she said. The prisoners were so numerous that there was no way to accommodate them but to send them westward, on foot, unarmed, often unaccompanied. "Everywhere, as I traveled today up to the most favored forward tank position, the krauts are getting in the way of military traffic. In their stumbling long overcoats they march in straggling columns with their 'leader' waving a white flag like a way-station depot master trying to flag a fast freight."

On the morning of the ninth, Irwin drifted down for a closer look at the Rhine, then stopped in at headquarters for a cup of coffee, where she learned that the route she had just taken was in range of six 105 howitzers. Anything might have happened, and why Virginia was so far to the front is not clear. As the *Saint Louis Post-Dispatch*'s primary correspondent, she may have acquired special status, or perhaps she and Patton had spent a rainy evening sitting around cussing the enemy together. Certainly, in the six months since she "shook like an aspen leaf" on encountering the enemy on the road to Paris, the cowardly lioness had found her courage.

While Irwin waited with Patton's Fourth Armored, patrols of the First Army's Ninth Armored Division to the north were battling down the west bank of the Rhine to link up with them. One patrol, the Fourteenth Tank Battalion, had orders to take the town of Remagen, site of the old Ludendorff railway bridge, which the Allied command assumed the Germans would by now have destroyed. But as Iris Carpenter told the story, the patrol came out of the woods above the town to see the bridge still there, "strung from the face of a five-hundred-foot black cliff to the cream-colored huddle of houses which was Remagen village, across one of the most breathtakingly beautiful stretches of waterway in the world." Not only was it beautifully intact, it was crowded with German tanks and troops streaming eastward.

What happened next, Carpenter reported, was this: A platoon of tanks twisted down the hairpin road to Remagen, where the crew learned that the bridge was wired to be blown up at four that afternoon. It was then three-fifteen. Company A Infantry of the First Army Armored Division reached the bridge at ten minutes to four to find the Germans desperately trying to blow the charges early; they had succeeded in knocking out a support pier and blasting a large hole in the bridge surface about two-thirds of the way across. But three Company A engineers, working feverishly, managed to cut the wires of the forty-pound explosives below deck, and then sped across the bridge to cut the main cable. When that proved too thick for their instruments, they shot it through, and the infantry started across in the face of German machine-gun fire. While two sharpshooter sergeants picked off the enemy gunners, the rest of Company A raced over and up against the face of the cliff. The Germans above tried everything to dislodge them, including hurling rocks, but the Americans held. After dark the tanks and tank destroyers started across the narrow bridge, its surface mere planks laid across the railroad tracks. One vehicle slipped off the roadway and hung precariously near the edge, holding up traffic when every moment was precious, but somehow it was towed off and the procession resumed.

General Courtney Hodges, First Army commander, when notified, ordered troops in the area to "get everything you've got over." "Pour everything you've got across!" General Omar Bradley, Ike's second in command, shouted into the telephone. Everyone began to see the Remagen bridge as the conduit for a quick Allied victory — that is, until word came from SHAEF that three divisions across would be quite enough, and everyone else was to continue with the execution of Montgomery's northern offensive as planned. The British field marshal had been promised the prize of first across the Rhine, and he was not happy with this impulsive, unplanned pounce of the American First Army.

Back in Spa, Iris Carpenter, Lee Carson, and Ann Stringer had been complaining that the First Army press camp was too far behind the lines, and never more so than when word came of the events at Remagen. When Carpenter, her jeep buddies, and driver left Spa at four the next morning, it was cold with a dismal rain. Before long they were wet through and covered with yellow ooze from passing vehicles. As bad as the weather, the terrain was narrow and twisted, and marked by craters which, to the surprise of the Allies, German civilians were filling in. Nobody had asked them to, Iris said; they saw that it needed doing, grabbed shovels, and set to work. But if this was a bright spot in the trip, it was the only one. She and her jeep buddies were united in their opinion that for anything but crossing the Rhine, they would not be there.

After seven hours they came within sight of the bridge. "The narrow road looped steeply through woods and vineyards to bring us opposite twin gray stone towers, and a long ribbon of boardwalk that disappeared into the black cliff face on the far bank," Iris reported. An MP told them to park their jeep under the bridge and foot it over with the infantry, "but keep ten paces between you and the next guy — it's hot around here!"

Writing of it later, Carpenter did not mention the gunfire on the way across. What she remembered, while traversing the narrow footpath above the steely gray and fast-flowing river, was the view in front of her: "the incredible loveliness of the Rhineland — schloss-drowned hills, terraced vineyards, and cream-and-yellow villages looking like bunches of primroses tucked into the country's corsage." She also remembered the fair-haired German soldier they had to step over. "Don't look at his face, Iris," her colleague turned to warn her, but she did, and thought there could be nothing so blue as those eyes. Then, having reached the tunnel at the far end, they solemnly shook hands before beginning accelerated interviews of everyone in sight, especially the proud troops of the Ninth Armored.

Later they recrossed the bridge to an accompaniment of shells, but the river road home proved even more hazardous. It was seven o'clock when they pulled into Spa. Aching from the long hard ride and the tension, Iris plunked herself down next to Lee Carson who was already pounding away at her typewriter. Both were mud-caked and disheveled, but they had crossed the Rhine and made it back to tell the tale. "German armed forces on both the east and western banks of the Rhine deteriorated into a state of complete chaos today in the sector where the U.S. 1st Army made a spectacular surprise crossing of the Rhine," Lee wrote. "The Germans frantically scoured their front for reserves to throw against the rapidly-expanding Remagen front. But in the meantime, American tanks, heavy guns, men and materials poured across the bridge in an endless stream."

Both women went back to the bridge the next day — Lee without her helmet, having left it "at home on the piano." "Home" is an existential in wartime. Lee and Iris walked across the bridge together; enemy artillery fire had been pounding it since dawn, and ack-ack batteries were going strong. At one point they were down at the river bank with other reporters inspecting some engineering when five ME-109s approached. "We gazed confidently at the planes zooming down until the ack-ack let loose and then everyone wished he had paid a little more attention to aircraft identification instruction," Lee reported. "By the time I swan-dived into a foxhole some yards from the road the planes were so close I could see the pilots in the cockpits. The combination of falling flak, enemy strafing and bombing made the foxhole seem entirely inadequate. For the first time I felt like a high priority target, hand-picked by Berlin." But the "hand-picked" target proved instead to be the London *Daily Telegraph* correspondent, one of their "family" (another wartime existential) at Spa, who had not dodged an incoming shell quite fast enough. "One minute he was there, alive, talking to us, and the next he was gone," Iris recalled later. "I realized then it could happen to any of us."

Ann Stringer and Dot Avery also crossed the bridge at Remagen. Refused jeep transport to the combat zone, Stringer resorted to begging a ride from a general in a tank. It is hard to imagine that SHAEF was happy to read her account of crossing the bridge at five miles an hour in an open jeep with enemy artillery shells "swooshing overhead, landing much too close for comfort," not to mention "the spiraling swish" of American shells, "almost as terrifying." Nor were they likely to have appreciated word that a "burning jeep and truck sending off hot flames and black smoke" had greeted her on the other side, or that a German fighter, hit by American fire, had dived so low over them that they "could see the frantic pilot trying to extricate himself." Clearly, Ann had determined to cover the war on her own terms.

Dot Avery drove down from Cologne a few days later. The road remained exposed to German shell fire, but by the time she reached Remagen, engineers had constructed a new pontoon bridge parallel to the old steel railroad one. For all its efforts, the enemy had not been able to slow the American passage across the Rhine, Dot wrote, and the morale of the American soldiers had risen immeasurably: "Nothing has cheered the men like this since the fall of Paris." Crossing on the old bridge, still under constant shelling, she wrote her story from a cellar in what was left of the village of Erpel on the far side. "Crossing takes some doing," she reported. "You wait your turn in a long line of tanks, guns, trucks and ambulances. . . . You just sit there in line, feeling like an oyster — open and helpless."

For a while longer the old Ludendorff railroad bridge hung suspended next to the new pontoon bridge over the Rhine. Then one day, damaged by shelling, its structure weakened under the weight of heavy equipment, it gave way and sank into the river forever.

29

The Month of April: The Advance

For women correspondents, April 1945 was both a dream come true and a nightmare. The Rhine crossings were already legend, but once east of the Rhine, there was little organized resistance. The front was everywhere and nowhere: no one knew where from day to day, sometimes hour to hour. It was at the same time both wide open and so hazardous that the women had to weigh their movements carefully. Lone jeeps with a party of four, reporters' usual mode of travel, were at serious disadvantage in an area where an enemy soldier or civilian, not yet disarmed, could pick off his victims and then grab the jeep for his own purposes. No longer were women denied access to the press camps; rather, they were encouraged to use them as bases, and they did, glad for a "safe house" come evening. With the end of the war in sight, no one wanted to become a statistic — the only woman correspondent killed in World War II.

Margaret Bourke-White had spent much of the winter of 1944–45 on the interminable Italian front, during which yet another set of irreplaceable negatives on their way to *Life* had been lost by the army. In an attempt at compensation, *Life* sent her to Germany. She linked up with General Patton's Third Army and settled briefly into a house requisitioned as the Air Power Press Camp in Frankfurt. But her reputation for risk-taking preceded her. The commanding officer assigned a tall, handsome corporal, the division's best rifleman, to protect her. "Never let that woman out of your sight," the CO warned.

Bourke-White found just-captured Frankfurt a mangled ruin. Twisted figures of newly fallen dead were scattered about, but it was the living that caught her eye. Women climbed out of the darkness of their cellars into the light and wandered about dazed. She photographed an old man who came along leading a horse; he had been ordered to bring it to town for the German army, and it was hard for him to comprehend that there was no longer a German army in Frankfurt to receive it.

Helen Kirkpatrick, Virginia Irwin, and Marguerite Higgins reached Frankfurt by Easter Sunday, the first of April. Helen reported that fierce fires were still burning. The German population of half a million had diminished by two-thirds; 106 Jews out of an original 30,000 remained in this, the Rothschilds' hometown, but that there were any at all was surprising. Also in Frankfurt were some 20,000 "emancipated slaves," people who had spent the war years at hard labor in Nazi munitions factories or on farms, more commonly referred to as displaced persons or DPs. In Germany Allied forces conquered and liberated simultaneously. Irwin too wrote of this "great army of Hitler slaves," who celebrated Easter by raiding Frankfurt cellars. "You could tell that the taste of freedom was sweet," she reported. "Emaciated men grown gaunt on the potato-peeling soup and black-bread diet of the German labor camps staggered grinning under the weight of gunnysacks full of provisions for the feast."

Marguerite Higgins wrote of a Frankfurt where roofs were a rarity, where twisted steel girders were all that remained of a vast airplane propeller factory. In Hoechst she interviewed a young leader of Hitler Youth now in the city jail. Later that month she moved south to the Sixth Army Group press camp in Rosenheim, south of Munich, from where she drove out daily to newly captured Bavarian towns. Further afield, she reported a jet fighter factory buried deep in a mountain in Kahla, Thuringia, and in a cellar five stories below the Franconian castle of Lichtenfels, the discovery of the library and secret documents of top Nazi Alfred Rosenberg. The subject she as yet avoided was the general havoc and desolation, the crumpled bodies in American uniform, young like herself, lying dead in a foreign town with a name few of them could have pronounced. What she saw bore little relation to her father's stories of gallantry and glory in World War I.

Eleanor Packard and Patricia Lochridge also worked out of the Sixth Army Group press camp south of Munich. UP had sent Packard up from Italy, and Lochridge had moved on to Europe from the Pacific; she was the only woman to cover both theaters. She roomed with Packard, whose no-nonsense attitude and professionalism she admired. In Bavaria the information each jeep crew brought back was shared with other correspondents over dinner at the local gasthaus — "group journalism," Pat called it. It rankled her and Eleanor that Higgins went out on her own and refused to share her material. That was not playing fair, Lochridge said, and harmful to the development of women in journalism, too. Higgins didn't care what they thought. She wanted to be known as a reporter who got stories no one else did, and she succeeded. "Maybe it didn't matter," Pat admitted later. "Maybe there's room in a war for a person like her."

Bourke-White and Kirkpatrick moved on to Kassel with the Eightieth Infantry. The sun filtered through yellow bomb dust, which lay thick on the crushed contours of the buildings. It seemed to Margaret "that people had always lived in the crevasses and ridges of a country like the surface of the moon." Helen recorded her impressions of the next town, Schweinfurt:

> Death rained down yesterday and the day before yesterday — from our planes and from our guns, and from German guns. German shells fell with curious impartiality on their own men. . . .
>
> While this organized death was being dealt out, unofficial death came to a good many citizens of Schweinfurt. Hans Friedlich, only one month in the army, reached his home town in time to die, slowly, from a bullet in the lungs. They laid him out on the floor of the hospital chapel, uncovered and still bleeding. Two hours later they laid his wife beside him, covered by a sheet. . . .
>
> The town's streets are littered with dead — soldiers and

civilians. Nobody has had time to bury them, or even to glance at these odd, twisted, ragdoll remnants of human beings.

The press camp on the outskirts of Schweinfurt was a dark but commodious house, a welcome distance from the town center and the unburied dead. The woman who owned the house was very dignified, the press officer said, and no one was to loot anything, including the little gold coffee cups with swastikas on them in the china cabinet. One evening Helen was organizing dinner, trying to make something palatable out of K-rations while the others were relaxing, when a jeepful of medics brought the news: President Roosevelt was dead. GIs began to flock in, seeking their own kind. "They'd heard it from the Stars and Stripes network," Helen said, "and they were all in tears."

Catherine Coyne and Dot Avery were at the press camp in Frankfurt when word came. Avery talked to a trainload of Third Army frontline soldiers waiting to depart for Paris on a long-anticipated furlough. Their spirits were noticeably dampened by what they felt as a personal loss. Many times she had heard soldiers say, with varying degrees of seriousness, that they were going to write the president to complain about this or that aspect of the war. They thought of him as a sympathetic friend. Passing a homeless French boy who had attached himself to the outfit as a chef's assistant, Avery saw tears running down his cheeks. "Le président est mort," he wept. "Poor world!"

Coyne talked with black soldiers from a mortar section, mostly from South Carolina. They had slept several nights in bombed houses, and their clothes smelled of spent explosives. "He was the one guy who knew what the score was," one of them lamented, meaning that he would have known what to do when the war was over. "President Roosevelt had *plans*," another declared. "Right now when we're going like a cyclone, to have this happen!" "It's funny," said a third, "you see death every day, you walk over corpses and do not notice, then something like this happens and you tighten all up inside." Almost as an afterthought they asked who the new president was. "Harry Truman," Coyne told them. "Never heard of him," they said.

At the Scribe in Paris Ruth Cowan reported that correspondents hung about the desk, stunned. Her own story for AP was on the president's wife, who had been instrumental in sending her overseas. Before the war Cowan had accompanied Eleanor Roosevelt across the country, covering her visits to farm picnics, coal mines, health clinics, and schools. Now she was no longer first lady, but she would not disappear — Ruth was sure of that. Pat Lochridge agreed; she had known the Roosevelts in Washington (the fact that she had come down with polio when young had cemented their relationship). She recalled how once at dinner she had dared to chide the president for breaking crackers into his soup, and often over tea had reported to Mrs. Roosevelt on what people "in the real world" were saying.

Janet Flanner wrote that "the sorrow the French felt at losing Roosevelt seemed like someone's private unhappiness multiplied by millions." If they remembered his opposition to de Gaulle, they were not mentioning it. "On the Rue Scribe, a sergeant in a jeep held up traffic while he received the condolences of two elderly French spinsters," she reported. At the Place de la Madeleine a patriarchal flower vendor passed out pink tulips to startled paratroopers, and on Sunday great crowds gathered at Notre Dame where, from behind the high altar, came the trumpet call of taps. "'The Star-Spangled Banner' was played slowly as a dead march," Flanner wrote, after which followed "a prayer of intercession to the Virgin Queen of Heaven for the soul of a Democratic, Episcopalian President."

"We all wondered when the war would end," Margaret Bourke-White recalled later. "Logically, it should have been over; there was no real reason for the Germans to go on fighting. Prisoners were being taken by the tens of thousands. During each day's advance we caught up with whole cattle cars of German wounded, without mattresses, straw, or food. Victory for the Reich could be only the dream of a madman."

But some Germans, the fanatic SS troops and Hitler Youth in particular, did go on fighting, and the erratic front lines remained dangerous. Across central Germany there were long fingerlike extensions of Allied-conquered territory, while in between might be large undefined German-held pockets. Once when Bourke-White's jeep companions flagged down an American oil truck for gas, the driver warned them not

"Helen Kirkpatrick drove the lead jeep."
HELEN KIRKPATRICK PERSONAL COLLECTION.

to slow down for anybody over the next thirty miles, especially in wooded areas; forty SS men had attacked their convoy there the previous night.

In the safest of circumstances, jeep navigation was an acquired skill that not everyone possessed. In their little press convoy "it was Helen Kirkpatrick who read the maps, charted our course, and drove the lead jeep," Bourke-White said. "She loved to sail along so fast, however, that the Colonel was always in a dither, knowing that before the day was over her exuberant little jeep would disappear into the distance and leave the rest of our convoy far behind." Margaret admired Helen's expertise with "the extra gears which could be called on for almost perpendicular hills." Catherine Coyne also drove her press jeep for a while, "after our driver had steeplechased a ditch and landed us in a field," she

Suicide scene in the Leipzig City Hall, April 1945.
MARGARET BOURKE-WHITE/*LIFE* MAGAZINE. © TIME INC.

said, and added that when she dreamed about being killed, it was always by jeep accident.

Never again in their lives would the women see death take so many forms as in that single month of April 1945. Leipzig was a case in point. Bourke-White, Kirkpatrick, and Dot Avery went in on the heels of the American troops; Lee Miller, Iris Carpenter, and Lee Carson followed. A resident of the town took Carson to view what remained of the house of a bazooka factory director who, just as the Americans crashed the city gates, committed suicide and took a hundred or so friends with him. He had invited them to a banquet, at the conclusion of which he touched a button under the table and blasted them all to bits.

Even that was less bizarre than the contents of the eighteenth-century Gothic city hall that a GI brought to the attention of Bill Walton of *Time*. Walton immediately sent for Bourke-White, who loaded up her equipment, rushed over, and followed Bill up three flights of stone steps and through a pair of padded soundproof doors. "Reclining on the ponderous leather furniture was a family group, so intimate, so life-like, that it was hard to realize these people were no longer living," Margaret wrote later. The Leipzig city treasurer sat at his desk, head in hands. His wife reclined serenely in an overstuffed armchair, while their daughter rested on a stiff leather couch, a pillow under her pretty head, her little Red Cross cap slightly askew. Family documents were set out in an orderly manner on the desk, along with an empty bottle of Pyrimal. A similar tableau of silent and apparently painless death was repeated in every room.

The story spread, and Lee Miller brought her own camera onto the scene. Iris Carpenter described the family of the burgomaster, including his daughter, a contemporary of the little Red Cross worker, with an Easter note from her soldier-sweetheart in her hand. The men had taken their poison in cognac, the women in lemonade. One imagines them watching, from windows high enough to afford an unimpeded view, the thundering approach of American tanks and troops, and acting accordingly.

But for American women correspondents, it was contact with their own soldiers, newly released from POW camps, that left them most moved. Virginia Irwin found it difficult to write dispassionately of the "haggard and half-starved Allied prisoners of war, ghost-like remnants of an 'army' of 30,000 men condemned by the Germans to a two-month, 500-mile starvation march across Germany." One group she came upon in a POW hospital had been "starved, beaten and herded across Germany like animals." An American chaplain taken prisoner in Holland told her he had buried many who died after reaching the hospital. But others had not made it that far. Everyone had an incident to relate — Americans stoned as they walked through German towns, a GI shot for picking potato peelings out of a garbage pail, another who begged a German woman for a cup of water only to have a guard strike it down and beat him to insensibility.

"We ate snow when the Germans weren't looking," a sergeant told Virginia. "Sometimes we managed to steal a little wheat or dry mash that they fed to the cows, and in the night we would soak this in water and eat it." On "lucky" days they were issued a piece of black bread and a bit of cheese, plus a pound of meat to share fifty ways. The men stole anything vaguely edible, he said; he himself had just missed detection when he liberated a rabbit from a coop, skinned it, and devoured it raw. But a friend had been caught and beaten to death for digging a turnip out of a field.

Virginia reported that when they set out on the return march from the prison camp, the men carried a blanket and some personal belongings, which, in their increasing exhaustion, were one by one discarded. Some died just before the Americans arrived, some just after. Those alive but too weak to care for themselves were lying two or three to a bed, resting until they were strong enough to evacuate to a proper hospital. Having lost a great deal of weight, they could no longer digest solid food, but were living on powdered milk mixed with water, a glassful every two hours. Virginia spent as many hours as she could spare at their bedsides.

Helen Kirkpatrick too talked to Allied prisoners of war, most captured during the Battle of the Bulge. They were obsessed with food, having lived for months on "grass soup" — a watery substance made from greens and potatoes — and a little bread they said tasted like black sawdust. More than a hundred had been sent to work at the oil plants in Leuna or Zeitz, but were so weak by the time they arrived that the personnel director considered them useless. Lee Miller reported that some of the newly freed British had been imprisoned for five years; they had a better survival rate than the Americans, she said, because "they knew all the secrets — when to be arrogant, stupid, argumentatively clever, or plain deaf." And in devastated Trier, Catherine Coyne watched liberated French and British soldiers struggling against hysterical laughter and tears as they crowded into boxcars for the journey across the German border to freedom.

Women, too, were crossing that border. One Sunday Janet Flanner went to a Paris train station to report the arrival of three hundred Frenchwomen from the camp at Ravensbrück, in the marshes near Berlin. Their faces gray-green in color, eyes that "seemed to see but not to take in," they were met by a nearly silent crowd carrying lilac branches, including General de Gaulle, who wept, Flanner said. Some women could not be recognized even by their husbands who had come to meet them. "There was a general, anguished babble of search, of finding or not finding. There was almost no joy . . . too much suffering lay behind this homecoming." Although the select three hundred had been the healthiest in the camp, eleven had died en route. "One matron, six years ago renowned in Paris for her elegance, had become a bent, dazed, shabby old woman," Janet wrote. "When her smartly attired brother, who met her, said, like an automaton, 'Where is your luggage?,' she silently handed him what looked like a dirty black sweater fastened with safety pins around whatever small belongings were rolled inside."

There was no longer any doubt that Flanner had found a new voice, and an enormously effective one. This was true in a literal sense as well — she had been broadcasting that winter and spring for the Blue Network. Her broadcasts were more personal than her "Letters"; she allowed herself to speak her feelings on what she observed. Several had dealt with the inefficiency and lack of feeling accorded returned prisoners of war by the French minister of deportees. Janet thought the incompetence of the French in this matter only slightly less appalling than American lack of concern for, and aid to, the French people, who were still doing without basic items like pots and pans, bed linens, and knives for peeling onions, the only vegetable yet available in the Parisian markets.

Flanner's contemporary Sigrid Schultz, beleaguered Berlin bureau chief for the *Chicago Tribune* before America's entry into the war, returned to Europe that spring. She had spent three years in New York and its bucolic Connecticut environs, writing for the *Tribune, Collier's,* and *McCall's.* Early in 1944 she published *Germany Will Try It Again* — a general denunciation of that country and a warning against false sentimentalism toward its people. Back in Germany now and reporting for the *Tribune* and *McCall's,* she saw nothing that caused her to change her mind. She had left a Germany of prideful Nazis; she returned to find people denying their affiliation, soft-pedaling their allegiance. Even in Nuremberg, once home to the Nazi Party congresses, this was so — although admittedly there was not much left of that lovely medieval city. But there as in all the once important Nazi towns she visited, Schultz heard the same refrain: "We are the little people. We had nothing to say in Germany."

Virtually all the correspondents following the victorious Allied troops encountered the same national denial. "No one is a Nazi. No one ever was," Martha Gellhorn, traveling with a regiment of the Eighty-second Airborne, wrote in prose laced with sarcasm. "To see a whole nation passing the buck is not an enlightening spectacle. It is clear that all you have to do in Germany, in order to lead the country, is to be successful; if you stop being successful, no one will admit they ever heard of you."

The big story that last week of April 1945, and for many the climactic moment of the war, belonged to the First Army — more specifically to a platoon of the First Battalion and another of the Third Battalion of the 273d Infantry Regiment, Sixty-ninth Division, who within a few hours of each other on the afternoon of April 25 would link up with the Russians near the town of Torgau.

That the Red Army was not far away had become apparent to Lee Carson, Iris Carpenter, and others in the First Army press camp by the change in makeup of the moving humanity clogging the roads. Displaced persons liberated from the work camps were now joined by German civilians trekking westward. Rumor spread that Germany was to be divided into zones occupied by the victorious powers, and the Soviet Union, naturally, would have the eastern zone. The Russians were not expected to show much sympathy toward their old foe at Stalingrad.

The Americans were not prepared for this latest exodus. They had halted west of the Mulde River, to await formal contact with the approaching Russians, when the order went out that all German civilians east of the Mulde must stay there. Only freed Allied prisoners of war, DPs trying to get home, and surrendering German soldiers were allowed across. The wrecks of bridges that remained were carefully policed, and the identification of each person was carefully checked. "Men, women and children wept and pleaded as they attempted to alibi or beg admittance into 'protective' American arms," Carson reported.

Among the Nazis turned back was a German princess distantly related to Queen Victoria and her husband, professor of American history at the University of Leipzig. "Well, lady, you're not crossing the river," Lee quoted a lieutenant from Nebraska barking at the princess. "You're staying right here. Even if you did get across, which you won't, it wouldn't do you any good because the Russians are coming right in here. We're going to give them a bang-up welcome, too." Rejected Germans settled on the river bank, hoping for a change of policy. They sat there for days, Iris wrote, in absolute despair.

Meanwhile, the area between the Mulde and Elbe Rivers was being patrolled by eager GIs, ostensibly looking for American POWs, but actually hoping to be the first to make contact with the Russians. On April 25 this at last occurred. As Carson and Carpenter both reported, a six-jeep, twenty-man patrol under Lieutenant Albert Kotzebue sighted a single Russian cavalryman east of the Elbe about three o'clock. The Americans promptly crossed the river and were taken to Krunitz where Lieutenant Kotzebue was presented to the Russian commanding general. News of the encounter was flashed by radio to the Sixty-ninth Division command post: "Mission accomplished. Contact made. Arrangements being made for a formal meeting."

That same afternoon, however, Lieutenant William D. Robertson in a single jeep with a corporal and two enlisted men, out hunting for POWs, they said, became aware of soldiers on the other side of the Elbe who they decided were Russians. As Robertson later told the story to Carson, Carpenter, and others, he hurriedly painted a rough approximation of an American flag, missing a few stripes and many stars, on a large sheet of paper, and waved it madly. Then he inched his way on his hands and knees along the girders of what was left of the bridge. A Russian private crawled toward him from the other side. In the middle, clinging to a girder and with the river swirling below them, they shook hands.

That solemn ceremony having been satisfactorily completed, the four Americans located a boat and crossed to the east bank to meet "the rest of the gang. The Russians offered sardines, biscuits, and chocolate," Carson reported, and there was "an all-around swapping of rank and insignia, toasts with German schnapps out of Russian canteens

341

Iris Carpenter interviewing the first GIs
to make contact with the Russians, Torgau, 1945.
UPI/CORBIS-BETTMANN.

shouted noisily in two languages, neither of which was understood by
the other side." "We just said 'Hi-yah, here's to you' and shook hands,"
Robertson told her.

Although no reporter was present at either event, they heard about
it soon enough, and by the next day Carson and Carpenter were joined
by Dot Avery, Catherine Coyne, Virginia Irwin, Lee Miller, and dozens
of male correspondents who headed their jeeps for Torgau. Ann
Stringer's arrival was much more dramatic. Stringer had once again run
afoul of army regulations and had been ordered to retreat to Paris.
Instead, she was touring about with her INS photographer friend Allan
Jackson in his old Ford. Coming upon two Piper Cubs, they persuaded
the pilots to take them up for a view of the Elbe River front. They had
not flown far before Ann heard voices speaking a recognizable Russian
on her plane's radio. She asked to land at Torgau to investigate. They
came down in a clover field, climbed over two roadblocks, and suddenly

Virginia Irwin (facing camera) during dance
celebrating the U.S.-Russian linkup, Torgau, April 1945.
U. S. ARMY PHOTOGRAPH.

saw a young man running toward them. "Down the street of Torgau
came a Russian youth wearing blue shorts and a gray cap with a red
hammer and sickle on it," Stringer began her story. "'Bravo,
Americanski!' he yelled. 'Bravo comrades!' He was dripping wet
because he had swum the Elbe River to greet us."

Stringer went on to describe "the small fleet of shaky boats and
canoes," one of which she, the two pilots, and Jackson took across, and
how the Russians on the far side "rushed down to the river bank
through the tall, wet grass" and helped them beach the canoe. They
were taken to meet the regimental commander. "We gave the Russians
our autographs. They gave us theirs. The commander invited us to
lunch. He said I was the first American woman he and his troops had
ever seen, and he seated me in the place of honor on his right." After
which followed an expansive lunch, including a series of toasts with a
variety of intoxicants.

At last they returned to the river where a racing shell awaited them,
but while the Russians were helping her into it, Stringer accidentally

pitched headlong into the Elbe, blurring the notes she had taken down so carefully. And how to file her story anyway once she wrote it? she worried aloud as they approached the far bank, landed, climbed back into the Piper Cubs, and headed west. She could not return to the press camp. Just then her pilot spotted a C-47 and came down beside it. Yes, it was leaving for Paris shortly, and the pilot would (with pleasure!) take her along. Ann sat on one wing and typed her story. Eventually she reached a military field outside Paris, hitchhiked to the Scribe, filed her story, and collapsed.

There were a lot of glum faces, mostly male, at the First Army press camp when reporters there found out they'd been scooped.

Still, all the women's stories received front-page — some banner-headline — placement. Lee Carson described "carnival scenes" on the east bank of the Elbe. "Conversation is sincere if short-circuited by lack of a mutual tongue," she reported. "The Russians are handing over captured German lugers to the Doughboys, who in return are giving away everything from radios to shaving soap." At a regimental command post Carson recorded the toast given by a Russian major with a working knowledge of English: "Today we have the most happy day in our lives. At Moscow and Stalingrad in 1941 and 1942 we have the most difficult days of our lives. Now our great friends the Americans we have met one another. It end up the enemy. Long live our great leader. Long live America's great leader."

The Russians, Carson said, are "like overgrown, bearish children, good-natured, abrupt, and direct. Their handshakes are guaranteed bone-crushers. Their bearhugs are rib-crackers." But she survived intact.

Everyone (except Ann Stringer) was present a day or two later for the ceremony in a sunny meadow when General E. F. Reinhardt of the Sixty-ninth Infantry Division crossed the Elbe in a rowboat to meet his counterpart, the youthful General Vladimir Roussakov of the Fifty-eighth Guards Division of the Red Army. They shook hands, posed for innumerable pictures by both news and amateur photographers, and then retired to a barracks to feast on captured German eggs, black bread, cheese, and twice-captured champagne.

Catherine Coyne reported that the Yanks were at the river bank first thing that morning with a big sign reading "East Meets West, Courtesy 69th Division," and Russian soldiers came swarming across in racing skiffs to stroll along the towpath with the Americans and try out each other's firearms. Dot Avery compared the day to a cross between a circus and the armistice celebration after the First World War. She and Coyne crossed over to the Russian side with a lieutenant from the Ukraine, three Siberian captains, and an obliging American officer for protection. One of the Siberians pinned the brass star from his cap onto Catherine's jacket, and she and Dot were offered "a strange assortment of impossible drinks," she said. After that the Russians sang, and when they asked for an American song in return, Catherine and Dot sang "Birmingham Jail," which the Seventh Airborne had sung as they flew to jump east of the Rhine.

Iris Carpenter reported that the mile or so of road between the river and the village was lined with flag-waving Russian soldiers, every third or fourth one a Red Army woman wearing the "guard's star" awarded to four-year veterans. Lunch for officers was served in the garden of a small villa. "On a plum tree on one side hung a crepe-framed picture of Roosevelt. On an apple tree on the other was a picture of Stalin." The American generals were presented with the red silk flag of the Thirty-fourth Corps, said to have flown over Stalingrad throughout the battle. "There was more food than any of the Americans present had ever seen on any table at any one time — and more liquor," Iris recalled. "Women soldiers brought the steaming dishes first to the officers' table and then took them to the enlisted men's party across the street. Enlisted men, however, were served with a kiss and embrace."

After lunch came the dancing. All around them were sounds of the harmonica, accordion, or mandolin, Avery reported. A Russian major grabbed her and whirled her into the circle. "At first I thought etiquette would compel me to try the leaping and boot-slapping step that seemed customary," she said, "but my partner compromised on a rather elaborate form of ballroom dancing." In a moment Coyne and Virginia Irwin were dancing too, while Russian women soldiers and nurses cheered. Lee Miller ran up to photograph the event, and someone had a newsreel camera going (the footage was included in the movie "The Last

Days of Hitler," with Alec Guinness, providing a rare immortality for that day in their lives.)

"It was a day of laughter," Coyne said in concluding her story:

American soldiers laughed when they danced Russian and hill-billy dances. They laughed when they crossed the river in the frail craft, they laughed as they skirted mines on our side of the Elbe . . . and they laughed almost tearfully when they met half-starved Americans escaped from prisoner of war camps like Pfc. Frank Bartz, machine gunner with the Seventh Armored Division captured in the December breakthrough, as he crawled into my jeep. Bartz struggled to keep back his tears when he asked between laughter and sobs: 'Say, is this war over or has everybody just gone crazy?' "

30

The Month of April:
The Camps

The day was fast approaching, all the women were aware, when the Allies would liberate one or another of the concentration camps known to be scattered about Germany, and going in to report what they found would be that day's job. Buchenwald, on a wooded hill outside Weimar, was the first. It was freed by the Eightieth Division of the U.S. Third Army on April 10, 1945. Reporters at the Air Power Press Camp in Frankfurt were flown there at once.

Who among the women had not dreaded what she would see, worried how she would bear up under it, wondered from what inner resource she would find the strength to write her story? In the end, as they discovered, it was their professionalism that carried them through — that and the realization that it was up to them to record for posterity what had happened, against any denial in times to come. They had no choice but to take in the smell — stench was a more accurate term — and the sight of living men and boys who were all eyes and bones and gaping mouths, who looked and talked, walked or crawled or lay in the barracks, four or five to a bunk, too weak to raise their heads in greeting. Perhaps a little wave of the hand, a tiny smile. These were men multiplied by thousands: 20,000 at Buchenwald, not including the 6,000 who had died the previous month alone. Battlefield dead had become a familiar sight to women reporters, but to move about among 20,000 living dead, *that* was new to their experience.

Sigrid Schultz, Helen Kirkpatrick, and Marguerite Higgins went in that first day. From her post as Berlin bureau chief for the *Chicago Tribune*, Schultz had been among the first to warn the world of the existence of the camps; nothing at Buchenwald was likely to surprise her. In fact, she had a private mission: Paris academicians of her acquaintance had begged her to try to locate certain promising young students who had been arrested and taken right out of school to slave labor camps. She had a long list of names. Ascertaining who in the camp were French, she selected a young man and showed him her list. He was amazed at being spoken to in French. "I think I knew two of them," he said. "They will not be coming home." When Schultz asked what had been his work in the camp, he replied, "Madame, j'ai été un cheval." He described nearby stone quarries where inmates had daily loaded huge stones onto a special contraption which they were then ordered to pull to one work site or another. "When a man fell because his back was broken by the weight and effort, he was shot. . . . When we suffered internal injuries, we tried to hide them. Somehow I survived, but so far I have not been able to find any of my French fellow-horses."

This same young man suggested that it might do a lot of good for those in the "so-called hospital" to hear in their own language that they were free, and perhaps if she had the courage, she could do that. Sigrid followed him to "where men were dying on three-tiered bunks, with blood and everything else dripping from tier to tier." Walking down the line of bunks, she delivered her message in French, assuring the men again and again that they were free, and that help was on its way. "One of the pitiful bearded creatures raised himself a little and stuck out a groping hand, which I took," she recalled. "'C'est vrai, qu'on est libre?' he whispered. I talked about the chestnuts that were in bloom in Paris, and of the planes that were being readied to take prisoners home with all the semblance of optimism I could muster. I was rewarded by a wonderfully peaceful smile as he let go of my hand and sank back on his bunk."

Maggie Higgins, with her fluent French, might have performed a similar function, but she did not. Her celebrated lack of sensitivity was never more obvious than in the skepticism with which she entered Buchenwald. Like many in the U.S. military, she seems to have doubted, not the existence of the camps, but that they were as bad as rumored. Determined not to be handed, or to hand on, an "atrocity line" she could not verify, she put her emotions on hold and set out to interrogate those prisoners in condition to reply. She was after the facts: names of victims, names of guards, dates, details of mass executions. Perhaps she saw this as an angle that no one else would think of, that would set her story apart from the others. When it became abundantly clear that the deprivation, torture, and deaths were not exaggerated, she was, to her credit, deeply ashamed.

Photographers Margaret Bourke-White and Lee Miller were present to chronicle the reactions of the citizens of Weimar to a special tour of their "neighborhood camp." General Patton was so angry at what he had seen there, Bourke-White recalled, that he ordered a thousand civilians to attend, and the MPs, equally enraged, doubled that number. They ushered the townspeople past the heaps of dead, more than twelve hundred still unburied; Margaret said that the women fainted or wept and the men covered their faces, but Sigrid Schultz, who scolded a group of women who persisted in looking at the sky, said *she* didn't see anyone faint. Maggie Higgins wrote that a few put their hands over their eyes when confronted by the sight of half-burned human bodies still in the ovens, but an officer had ordered them to look because, he said, it was they who were responsible. Lee Miller noted that, in any case, much of it had been cleared away by then. She and Margaret had photographed the horror in all its starkness.

Perhaps to atone for her initial callousness, Marguerite Higgins gave an exhaustive accounting of what had occurred at Buchenwald. She noted that four French generals and a number of European diplomats had died there, as well as Allied fliers who had bailed out over Germany, thirty of them American. They had been hanged, she reported: the Gestapo forced the prisoners to hang their own comrades. There were also children at Buchenwald. Maggie asked a boy of eight, in charge of his three-year-old brother, why he was there. "I am Jewish," he replied. When she enquired about his parents, he said with no sign of emotion, "All the older people were burned up." She found Jewish boys, now sixteen, who had been there since they were eight or nine.

Higgins also reported the memorial service held one evening for the dead. The prison band, in grim remembrance, played the same tune they had played twice each day under the Nazis. Each man stood by the flag of his homeland, fifteen flags in all, including the prewar German flag for the anti-Nazi inmates of that country. A large American flag was draped on the platform, and behind it a wreath to commemorate the dead with the inscription: "Buchenwald Concentration Camp — Fifty-One Thousand." After brief tributes and the playing of taps, the once prisoners, led by the children, filed silently away.

Twelve days after the camp's liberation, Helen Kirkpatrick was able to report that the thousands of skeletons there were returning slowly to life under the care of the 120th Evacuation Hospital, assisted by inmate doctors. The death rate was down from a hundred per day to thirty. Most men were suffering from starvation and dehydration, she said, but there were also cases of tuberculosis and typhus. Helen ran across a German Jew who had been a professor in Geneva when she was there; he recognized her, but had to tell her who he was. "It was pretty awful," she recalled.

Janet Flanner waited almost three weeks before going to Buchenwald. It was quieter by then, and she knew from reports what to expect. Her guide, a gentle young Jewish inmate from Prague, took her from building to building, pointing out the crematorium and gallows as well as the primroses growing in abundance. She had not expected still to see corpses, but a dozen had been discovered in some forgotten nook only that morning, and were lying in a heap, stiff and naked, their mouths open as if they were hungry. She and her guide sat down on the steps. Neither of them spoke.

Correspondents visited the newly liberated camps wherever they could reach them. At Lager Dora outside Nordhausen in central Germany, Iris Carpenter, accompanying the Seventh Corps of the First Army, found starving men and women lying two and three to a bunk, living and dead together. V-1 rockets had been made there, and hundreds of corpses were piled against the factory walls which, if bombed, might have buried them. But that had not happened, Carpenter wrote, so General Collins selected a peaceful green hillside for the burial site. When the burgomaster objected that the field was private property, he was informed that there was no more private property as such in that part of Germany. The general ordered the leading citizens of Nordhausen, appropriately attired, to bury the dead with their own hands. Iris described how American soldiers stood guard while black-coated men dug twenty-four long graves in regulation army pattern, wrapped the bodies in makeshift shrouds and, having been refused the use of army trucks, bore them on planks of wood or old doors or whatever could be found to the open graves. There were 2,017 dead. When all were interred, prayers were said, the graves were filled in, and the surface raked fine and sowed with grass seed. Not until then were the townspeople released.

Ann Stringer also went to Nordhausen. It was a raw experience to go in just after the troops, she said; there was little to distinguish the living from the dead. You really had to grit your teeth to put what you'd seen into words, to set it down on the page.

"The spring wind ruffled a white flag of surrender, nothing else moved." That was Lee Carson's first impression of the Erla work camp near Leipzig when she and Don Whitehead, Margaret Bourke-White, and Bill Walton arrived there on the afternoon of April 23. The work camp was not their planned destination, Bourke-White said; they had been looking for an aircraft small-parts factory in the suburb of Erla. Driving along a narrow country road with plowed fields on either side, they began to smell a strange odor unlike any they had smelled before. Across a small meadow they saw a high barbed-wire fence, which at first seemed to surround nothing but a flagpole with a white flag at the top. A soldier with them opened the locked gates with a hand grenade, and they found themselves standing at the edge of a carpet of bones. Along the barbed wire barrier were charred human figures in postures indicating they had been trying to escape. Scattered among the bones were nails from the building, dozens of little graniteware bowls, and a scattering of spoons. The ground was still warm, and the smell was overpowering.

"We stood frozen with horror," Carson reported. Walton recalled walking about with Bourke-White, both of them sobbing. Then he quietly threw up. Margaret got out her camera, but Walton could not bring himself to take notes. After a while, from across the field, they saw a skeletal figure in prison uniform coming toward them, and within a

351

Charred human remains at the Erla work camp, Germany, April 1945.
MARGARET BOURKE-WHITE/*LIFE* MAGAZINE. © TIME INC.

short time, perhaps seeing the American jeeps, others emerged. "They fell into each other's arms," Margaret said, "while standing up to their ankles in bones."

Their story was simple. There had been about three hundred fifty prisoners, workers in the aircraft factory. Advised that American troops would arrive soon, the SS guards worked out a plan. They carried a large vat of soup into a wooden barracks to entice the prisoners inside, locked the doors, secured the windows, poured on some inflammable substance, and set the barracks alight. A few men, human torches, fought their way out somehow; it was they who were caught, charred but still recognizable as human, on the barbed wire. About eighteen — those now returning — were outside the enclosure, and escaped the grim fate of their fellows.

Sigrid Schultz also went to Erla and reported additional details to the *Chicago Tribune*. The irony was that no one had known the camp was there. Had those correspondents not been out looking for the small-parts factory that afternoon, perhaps no one would ever have seen, or reported, or exposed that particular footnote of inhumanity.

In fact, no one had been aware there were so many camps. At Landsberg, near the Austrian border, Eleanor Packard watched as inhabitants of nearby villages were brought to view the bodies of about five hundred males, most of them Jewish, all used as slave labor until they got sick and were declared not worth wasting food on. "Most were naked," she wrote. "Their gaunt skeleton frameworks looked more like gruesome waxworks from a horror museum than human beings." Another six hundred were still alive, if barely, while a detachment of four thousand had been moved back behind German lines. But with the Russians closing in, there wasn't much space behind German lines anymore.

Virginia Irwin, traveling with Third Army troops, stole a visit up a winding wagon trail to Hitler's great "abortion camp" high in the Neideraula Staatsforst. To this clump of flimsy wooden structures enclosed in barbed wire were sent pregnant Russian and Polish women who, as slaves, were not permitted to have children. They came and went, Irwin discovered, to undergo "operations" that were less often abortions than induced deliveries in which the baby always died. Each woman had already signed a paper giving permission for her baby to be killed. The death rate for the mothers was estimated at sixty percent.

Irwin visited the delivery room. Pine planks set on two-by-fours and covered with filthy oilcloth served as the delivery table; recovery took place on a metal cot covered with coarse straw-filled ticking. Instruments "of dark ages crudity" were arranged in rows on open shelves. Hands were washed and utensils "sterilized" in a couple of dishpans into which was poured water and a little disinfectant — "when disinfectant is available," she was told. The induced delivery of women in the later months of pregnancy had been described to her, Virginia said, but was "too barbaric for print."

In the "recuperation wards," the odor of infection lay heavy, and the pall of death was almost perceptible. Downhill from the camp, surrounded by pines, was the graveyard, "probably the most unpretentious in all of Europe," Irwin wrote. The mothers that died were buried with a number. The babies were tossed into any open grave.

Janet Flanner did not go to Ravensbrück; lying as it did in the marshes north of Berlin, it was liberated late, and fell into the Russian zone. But a young member of the French bourgeois resistance movement was in a group of three hundred Frenchwomen exchanged for four hundred German women early that April, and agreed to talk with her about it. Colette (not her real name) shrank from revealing too much, for fear of reprisals against the thirty thousand women still there, but she said quite a lot, which appeared in Genêt's "Letter from Paris" for April 25.

Colette had been arrested in May 1943 at age twenty-five. Friends described her as a "big-boned, attractive, still adolescent looking brunette, individualistic, healthy, strong-willed." When Flanner met her nearly two years later, her torso seemed all shoulder bones. Her mind was clear, but starvation had resulted in loss of memory, which embarrassed her. She talked mostly about the other women, and answered only some of Janet's questions about the camp itself. Colette told her that Ravensbrück was made up of twenty-five buildings, each supposed to house up to five hundred women, but housing twelve hundred while she was there. There was one bunk for every four women, so they slept on their side, head to foot to head to foot. Between thirty and fifty died every day, but the same number of replacements always seemed to arrive. A corpse would be carried by her bunkmates to the washroom and piled on the cold tile floor; some women had the job of disposing of them further, but Colette worked elsewhere.

Wake-up call was between two and two-thirty, after which came morning count, lasting two hours. You had to stand without moving or talking, even should the person beside you faint or fall dead. When Colette first arrived, there was a breakfast of ersatz coffee and a bit of black bread, but later this was omitted. The workday began: some women dug drainage ditches in the sandy marshes; others sorted uniforms taken off dead or captured Russians, which were always full of lice and probably typhus and cholera as well. Colette worked in the Siemens electric factory two miles away. At first the women working at Siemens marched there each morning, back to camp for the midday meal, once more to the factory, and back again in the evening. There was no supper. When the women trained for the factory began to die too fast, a unit was set up nearer the camp to conserve their energy.

Since she could not eat at night, Colette told Janet, she washed herself, which helped to keep her going. Her will, and later her hate, worked in her favor as well. Punishment for possessing a piece of jewelry, or a prayer book, came in the form of a beating on the bare buttocks with a heavy stick. The top number was twenty-five strokes. Some women died outright; others developed septicemia from unhealed flesh wounds. As at all the camps, Ravensbrück was run by SS men; there were German women under the SS, and Polish women under the German. Colette's mother mailed her a parcel every day, but in a year only ten reached her. They were usually consumed by various persons in charge.

Because women were constantly dying, others always arriving, beatings regularly handed out and new illnesses acquired, Ravensbrück seemed like a busy place, whereas in fact there was hardly anything to talk about, and no one had the strength to talk anyway. At night the prisoners lay in agonized exhaustion instead of sleep. That spring the barracks were freshly painted on the outside. It appeared the SS wanted the camp to look its best for whatever might happen, but Colette left before anything did. One day three hundred inmates were given civilian clothes, including stockings and scarves for their heads, and put on trucks driven by Canadian POWs. On a bad stretch in a small Bavarian town they ran out of gasoline and no more could be found, but when three days later some was found, they moved on. At last they crossed the border into Switzerland. Several of the older women, having tasted freedom, died, but the rest made it to Paris.

Janet Flanner's simple recitation of this young Frenchwoman's ordeal as prisoner of the Nazis caused quite a stir when it appeared in the *New Yorker* that spring. To her American sisters — healthy, well fed, above all *safe* — that Colette survived at all was almost incomprehensible.

Marguerite Higgins's dream of journalistic triumph came true with the liberation of the camp at Dachau in southern Germany by the Forty-second and Forty-fifth divisions of the U.S. Seventh Army. She had joined forces with *Stars and Stripes* reporter Peter Furst, an American of German birth and Jewish parentage, who understood the geography and people of his native land and possessed a strong survival instinct. Furst admired Maggie's sharp mind and instinctive courage, and she in turn was not put off by his recklessness. Hurtling along in their jeep, aspiring to be the first reporters to reach the camp that afternoon of April 29, they discovered that eleven kilometers of unsecured road separated them from their destination, and that the battle for a nearby town was perhaps not yet over. But then perhaps it was. They continued on.

A town draped in white sheets was an encouraging sign, followed in short order by straggling detachments of German troops, lugging their arms but happy to surrender them. Higgins and Furst loaded them into their jeep until it was full; by then Maggie was less afraid of being shot by a German than she was that one of the grenades rattling around in the back of the jeep would go off. In the town of Dachau they were informed that American troops were still fighting the SS on the northern perimeter of the camp, but that buildings on the south side had been observed flying white flags. That was all they needed to hear: a little detour around the fighting and they would be there. As they neared the entrance, the heavy smell of decay became increasingly strong. Some fifty boxcars were sidetracked outside the gate; the men in the cars had been alive when shoved in there; they were now corpses, dead and rotting. A few who had crawled or been pulled out were lying on the ground, shot or beaten to death. Maggie turned aside, convulsed with nausea.

But there was no time to pause. Joined by two jeeps from the Forty-second Infantry, they approached the SS general at the main gate. Higgins explained that the American officers would accept his surrender, but she and her companion wanted an SS officer to escort them to where the prisoners were confined. They positioned this officer on the hood of their jeep and took off, but even with this recognizable deterrent, Maggie found machine guns trained on them from one of the watchtowers. Running, she realized, was no longer an option. Instead, she turned to face them and called out, "Kommen Sie hier, bitte. Wir sind Amerikaner." They complied, with their hands raised.

Higgins continued her story in the *Herald Tribune*:

There was not a soul in the yard when the gate was opened. As we learned later, the prisoners themselves had taken over control of their inclosure the night before, refusing to obey any further orders from the German guards, who had retreated to the outside. The prisoners maintained strict discipline among themselves, remaining close to their barracks so as not to give the S.S. men an excuse for mass murder.

But the minute the two of us entered a jangled barrage of "Are you Americans?" in about sixteen languages came from the barracks 200 yards from the gate. An affirmative nod caused pandemonium.

Tattered, emaciated men, weeping, yelling and shouting "Long live America!" swept toward the gate in a mob. Those who could not walk limped or crawled. In the confusion they were so hysterically happy that they took the S.S. man for an American. During a wild five minutes he was patted on the back, paraded on shoulders and embraced enthusiastically by prisoners. The arrival of the American soldiers soon straightened out the situation.

I happened to be the first through the gate, and the first person to rush up to me turned out to be a Polish Catholic priest, a deputy of August Cardinal Hlond, Primate of Poland, who was not a little startled to discover that the helmeted, uniformed, begoggled individual he had so heartily embraced was not a man.

Meanwhile, troops from the Forty-second and Forty-fifth made their way into the encampment where they, too, were cheered and hugged. A just-released American flier showed them about the camp: the crowded barracks, the torture room, the crematorium with its piles of corpses, the place where men knelt to be shot in the back of the head. It was a day of conflicting emotions. It was also a front-page story, the unchallenged scoop Maggie had sought. To crown her triumph, for her participation in the liberation of Dachau she was awarded an army campaign ribbon, to her immense pride.

Patricia Lochridge and Lee Miller reached Dachau the next day. A half century later Pat recalled the boxcars — "dead men spilling out of the boxcars all over the ground." The memory that still shocked her was "the little kids, four and five years old, running around these prisoners to see if there was anything to take. I've often tried to think why

Prisoners scavenging a rubbish dump, Dachau, April 1945.
PHOTO BY LEE MILLER. © LEE MILLER ARCHIVES.

they did that," she mused, "and all I could say was that these prisoners really didn't look human anymore. They were so very dead."

Lochridge was present for the compulsory visit to the camp of twenty-five of the town's leading citizens, men and women. She described them walking solemnly along, looking straight ahead, feigning to be unaffected by the condition of the camp and its inhabitants. It was the crematorium that got through to them. So many hundreds of bodies were not easily ignored.

Afterward she went about the town talking to people, pressing them to respond. How was it possible, she asked the town's master baker, that he would not have talked with his customers of what went on at the camp? He protested innocence. "The business at the camp was none of our affair," the town's leading physician told her. "We were shamefully deceived, there was nothing we could do." He insisted he was not a Nazi and therefore not culpable, but the following day she met a "proud Hitlerite," the official barber for the SS troops at the camp. "You Americans are such sentimentalists," he sneered. The town matriarch, when approached, was surprised at Pat's interest. "The state put them there," she said, dismissing any culpability. "They weren't good Germans. Most of them weren't Aryan." Lochridge questioned another woman whom she had seen crying over the bodies stacked like wood at the crematorium. "Nothing more terrible could have been done than was done at Dachau," the hausfrau admitted. "But most Germans weren't involved. The Fuehrer couldn't have known about it. He would never have permitted such suffering." Only one woman voiced reactions that Pat could relate to. Her husband had been sentenced to a year's internment in Dachau for disobeying a military order, and she had moved from Hamburg with her children to be near him. But she had never been allowed to see him, she said, until the day the Americans liberated him.

Lee Miller hooted at the idea that the townspeople of Dachau could have been unaware of what went on in the camp. She pointed out that it was only just outside the town, and that the railway siding into it ran right past a number of fine villas. She photographed it all. In a small canal running beside the camp a number of dead SS personnel floated, "slithered along in the current, along with a dead dog or two and smashed rifles," she wrote. She also visited the angora rabbit farm, an industry of the prison; the rabbits and the workhorses in the stable were much better cared for than the humans, she noted, although that would not have taken much doing. "Dachau had everything you'll ever hear or close your ears to about a concentration camp," Miller concluded.

Martha Gellhorn reached Dachau a few days later. She did not rush to the fray anymore; she had not done that since she was the first woman to set foot in France after D Day and then was penalized for it. By the time she got to Torgau, the Russians were no longer permitting Americans to cross onto their side of the Elbe. But in the end that hardly mattered, because while she waited, what seemed like half the Russian army poured across to the American side, which made for perhaps an even better story.

This was true at Dachau, too: five or six days after the camp's liberation the story was a different one, but just as good. The 116th and 127th Evacuation Hospitals were well into operation. Buildings had been scrubbed clean and smelled of antiseptic, office buildings had been made into wards, and the houses in which the SS officers had lived were now luxurious quarters for the nurses. These houses were just across a stretch of grass from the crematorium, Martha noted; the SS wives and children had lived, apparently contentedly, in the midst of that smell and activity.

The boxcars at the camp's entrance had been emptied and the bodies buried, but in one of the hospitals Gellhorn saw a tall Polish man, the only survivor of the boxcar dead. "Now he stood on the bones that were his legs and talked," she said, "and then suddenly he wept. 'Everyone is dead,' he said. A Polish doctor, five years a prisoner, tried to encourage him. 'In four weeks you will be a young man again,' he said. 'You will be fine.' " But Martha did not believe his eyes would ever again be like other people's eyes.

In her article for *Collier's*, Gellhorn reported certain experiments the doctors had witnessed: to see how long an aviator could go without oxygen, for example, or how long pilots could survive in salt water at low temperatures, as might happen if they were shot down over the English Channel. Great vats of seawater were used for that one; prisoners stood in the seawater up to their necks. The limit was two and a half hours at minus eight degrees centigrade. Martha also visited the "jail" where so-called *Nacht und Nebel* (night and mist) men lived in small white cells, without contact with anyone or ever going outside. How they had borne this treatment was not known, as they were among the eight thousand men who, two days before the Americans arrived, had been taken out on the final transport.

Gellhorn was still at Dachau when the German army surrendered. She found that suitable. "For surely the war was made to abolish Dachau and all the other places like Dachau and everything that Dachau stands for," she wrote. "We are not entirely guiltless, we the Allies, because it took us twelve years to open the gates of Dachau. We were blind and unbelieving and slow, and that we can never be again."

31

The Longed-for Day

By May Day rumors were flying that the war would end that day, tomorrow at the latest, that it had already ended but nobody was being told, that this or that crisis was holding up the inevitable. Each rumor provided the little thrust of flame that fueled the next. All were premature. May 1 was also the day that units of the Forty-fifth Division, U.S. Seventh Army, reached Munich. This was Hitler's favorite city; since the 1920s he had occupied an apartment at 16 Prinzregentenplatz. In the mid-thirties he had bought the building, converting the ground floor to quarters for his SS guards and installing bombproof shelters in the basement.

With the sanction of the Forty-fifth, Lee Miller promptly moved in. The place lacked charm, she said, but connected to Hitler's bedroom (decorated in chintz) was a very pleasant bathroom, and Lee always liked a good bath. Her *Life* photographer friend Dave Scherman took a picture of her bathing in Hitler's tub, which became a classic of the noncombative side of the war. Miller was less appreciative of Hitler's sculpture and paintings, but it gave one pause to sit at the conference table where Franco and Mussolini had conferred with the Fuehrer and where Chamberlain had given away Czechoslovakia.

With a guide, Miller went about Munich photographing what had and had not survived Allied bombing. Among the former was a little stucco house, a gift from Hitler to his mistress, Eva Braun. The concrete sentry box inside the gate was unoccupied, and the front door lock shot through. Inside, Lee was fascinated. She labeled the living room "newly bought suburban"; on one table was a brass globe of the world

Lee Miller enjoys a bath in Hitler's bathtub, Munich, May 1945.
PHOTO BY DAVID E. SCHERMAN. © LEE MILLER ARCHIVES.

that opened to reveal liqueur glasses. The kitchen did not appear much used. Upstairs, Eva's ice blue satin coverlet lay pristine, and although her closet was mostly empty, her desk was fitted out with blotters, rulers, pen points, pencils, clips, and stacks of stationery. The medicine chest in the bathroom was stuffed.

Before she left, Lee took a nap on Eva's bed and tried the telephones marked "Berlin" and "Berchtesgaden." There was no connection.

It was also on the first of May that news of Hitler's death in his bunker in Berlin came over Hamburg radio. No woman correspondent reported having heard the actual broadcast — the "Achtung! Achtung!" and three rolls of the drum, followed by the statement that "our Fuehrer, Adolf Hitler . . . fell for Germany this afternoon in his operational headquarters in the Reich Chancellery." Grand Admiral Karl Dönitz, announced as his successor, then took up the microphone to talk of Hitler's "hero's death" and his life of service for Germany,

Virginia Irwin and jeep driver Sgt. Johnny Wilson in Berlin, May 1945.
SAINT LOUIS POST-DISPATCH.

followed by a call to every German to "maintain order and discipline" and "do his duty at his own post."

The word "fallen" was no doubt purposely chosen to imply that Russian soldiers had charged the chancellery and shot the Fuehrer as he sent final orders to his generals. In fact, Hitler had not left his bunker, a thirty-two-room structure below the chancellery, since emerging on his birthday, April 20, to "review the troops" — in this case, a nearby SS division and a little group of Hitler Youth. Joseph and Magda Goebbels were there with their six children. Eva Braun had come up from Munich with a wardrobe of clothes (which might explain why Lee Miller found so little in her closet), prepared to die with "poor, poor Adolf" whom she saw as betrayed by all.

The truth was that he was betrayed by those who most mattered — marshal of the Reich Goering, Sigrid Schultz's old adversary, who tried a last-minute grab for power, and even more treacherously by Heinrich Himmler, head of the SS, who made an offer of surrender to the western Allies. It was after Hitler heard that, and learned of Mussolini's capture and public execution — a fate he himself feared — that he determined on a quick suicide. On April 29 he married Eva, and on the thirtieth, with Russian tanks a half mile away, they lunched, said their goodbyes, and retired. Hitler put a gun to his head; his bride took cyanide. As planned, their bodies were wrapped in gray army blankets, soaked with gasoline, and burned in the little garden just outside the bunker entrance. Only a few people knew of these events until later, but what could immediately be observed by anyone near the Platz der Republik that afternoon was the red Soviet flag flying from the Reichstag.

The capture of Berlin was an event like none other in the entire war, as Virginia Irwin was about to tell the world. She was one of the first three Americans there — although the capital had been decreed absolutely out of bounds to the Allied press. Lee Carson tried, but failed to make it.

Irwin's grand adventure began on the day of the Russian-American celebration by the Elbe. She and Andrew Tully of the *Boston Traveler* had conned a jeep from the Twenty-sixth Infantry, along with driver Sergeant Johnny Wilson. They found a way to ferry the jeep across, as presumably Carson and her buddy, Don Whitehead of AP, did with his "liberated" Mercedes. After the feast and a dance or two with Russian officers, the women joined their fellow conspirators and sneaked off, headed for Berlin.

Carson and Whitehead had a little bad luck. First, they lost their map, or rather it was blown away when Lee was using it for a napkin on her lap while she ate a K-ration. Then a gasket blew. A Soviet truck towed them straight through what she referred to later as "the whole Russian army." "We ran right across their line of march," she said. "The Russians were simply furious. Big Mongols they were, with wide faces and narrow eyes, waving their arms at us and cursing, 'Goddam Amerikanski!' " By the time a mechanic had been found and the car fixed, the fighting was too heavy for them to continue. "The Russians were walking on a carpet of dead Germans," she recalled. "We tried to angle through and finally got caught between the Russian and German lines." Opting to stick with the Russians, they were taken to a command post for questioning and held for three days before their credentials were pronounced satisfactory.

Irwin's better luck was indicated by the banner headline above her story, POST-DISPATCH REPORTER GETS INTO BERLIN:

> From Torgau we started north, behind the Russian lines, traveling sometimes over deserted roads through dark forests. At other times we hit highways clogged with the great body of the Russian Army, beating along in its motley array of horse-drawn vehicles of all sorts.
>
> There were Russian troops riding in American 2½-ton trucks. There were Russian troops riding in two wheeled carts, phaetons, in old-fashioned pony carts, in gypsy wagons, and surreys with fringed tops. They rode in everything that could be pulled.
>
> The wagons were filled with hay and the soldiers lay on top of the hay like an army taking a holiday and going on a mass hayride.... The fierce fighting men of the Red Army in their tunics and great boots, shabby and ragged after their long war, riding toward Berlin in their strange assortment of vehicles, singing their fighting songs, drinking vodka, were like so many holiday-makers going on a picnic.

Traveling with the forward units, a crude handmade American flag flying from their jeep, the trio were well into Berlin by evening. The dead lay all about, on sidewalks, in front yards. Russian vehicles clogged the streets, while horses, freed from their supply carts, ran about loose. "But the Russians were happy — with an almost indescribably wild joy," Virginia wrote with feeling. "They were in Berlin. In this German capital lies their true revenge for Leningrad and Stalingrad, for Sevastopol and Moscow."

Irwin was not even much worried when they were labeled possible spies and taken to a regimental command post in what was left of a German home. The guards-major quickly cleared them of suspicion and invited them to stay. There was no electricity or running water, but he had his Cossack orderly — "a fierce Mongolian with a great scar on his left cheek" — take Virginia a dishpan of water, along with German face powder, perfume, and a cracked mirror. Thus tidied up, she descended to a dinner that defied description. A candelabra of upturned milk bottles and a pickle-jar vase full of spring flowers adorned the table. Servers passed huge platefuls of food, not all of which Irwin could identify, although the liquor was always vodka. "After each course there were toasts to 'the late and great President Roosevelt,' to Stalin, to President Truman, to Churchill, to 'Capt. André Tooley,' to 'Capt. Veergeenee Erween,' to the Red Army, to the American Army, to 'Sarjaunt Wilson,' and 'to the American jeep.' "

"Sarjaunt" Johnny Wilson was so excited at being the first GI to get to Berlin that he could hardly eat. The Russians had discovered a beat-up old Victrola, so after dinner there was dancing. A young captain, adept at the jitterbug, danced with Virginia, and when she could twirl no longer, he grabbed Johnny. The three exhausted Americans soon caved in and were shown to their rooms. "Captain Veergeenee" sat down to write her story, the flame of her candle fluttering from the artillery only a few blocks away. It was the most exciting experience that could happen to a reporter, she said. "It is all unreal. Russian officers in their worn tunics bedecked with the medals of Leningrad, Stalingrad, and all the other great Russian battles, are unreal. The whole battle is somehow unreal."

Unreality continued all the next day. After a breakfast of charred veal and potatoes washed down with hot milk and vodka, the three Americans moved in a circuitous route about the city, trying to get to the center but often blocked by artillery and sniper fire. The little flag on their jeep was a sign for Russian soldiers to gather round; Virginia said she shook hands until her right wrist was paralyzed and smiled until her ears ached. Accustomed to streamlined American supply, she could not get over the hodgepodge of the Russian army. "Great herds of sheep and cows are mixed in with armored cars and half-tracks with household belongings lashed to their sides. Super tanks tangle with a fantastic mess of horse-drawn vehicles, many driven by soldiers with their heads swathed in bandages, and all loaded down with ammunition, food, women, wounded soldiers, and animals." Through it all the

Russian artillery was letting go with barrage after barrage. "The earth shakes," Virginia reported. "The air stinks of cordite and the dead. All Berlin seems confusion."

Later, trying to make sense of the past few days, she likened the experience to having been caught in a giant whirlpool of destruction; at times she thought she must have imagined much of what she had seen.

The women, for example — not the Red Army women, but the secretaries, laundresses, traffic cops, all riding in hay wagons with the infantry — that had been unexpected. The transport was positively medieval. And what should she make of the time she got out of the jeep to shake hands with a milling mob of Russian soldiers, one of whom was serenading her on an accordion, to find she was standing in the middle of a yard of German dead? And the noise — whenever a column came to a halt, there would be (besides the artillery) "an unearthly din of truck horns mixed with the neighing of horses, the bleating of sheep, the cackling of chickens," while some Russian folk tune was being wildly rendered on an accordion and men were shouting at each other in their unintelligible tongue.

It was mad, she said, but wonderful.

On the evening of the second day, mindful of their need to file their stories, Irwin and Tully said goodbye to the guards-major and, with "Sarjaunt Johnny" at the wheel, headed west out of Berlin. They reached the Elbe that night and hid out with a couple of British POWs. At dawn, after the Russians refused to take them across, Virginia stood on the bank and yelled, "I'm an American woman, come and get me away from these Russians." Two assault boats put out from the opposite shore. At the Weimar press camp they learned that stories written from Berlin could not get clearance. Friends in the Ninth Air Force saw them to Paris; there they discovered that SHAEF had suspended them, meaning they could neither send stories out nor communicate with their home offices. In a scribbled note to Joseph Pulitzer that passed the censors only because it did not mention Berlin, Irwin informed him that she was suspended and could not file, asked him to call her mother and tell her she was safe, and noted that she would need a thousand dollars "if I am to stay any length of time." Pulitzer, figuring she was on to something, complied.

During the following week five more reporters returned from Berlin with their own stories; they, too, were suspended. Irwin remained the only woman among them. By the time their combined dispatches were allowed through, the impact of the scoop was decidedly lessened. Nevertheless, the first of her three-part front-page series ran under a lovely photograph of her at her typewriter — not the Virginia of three parts perspiration to one part bomb rubble dust, not the dancing, whirling Virginia or the bottoms-up on the vodka Virginia, but the serious correspondent Virginia, the unquestionably brave Virginia, who had done her newspaper proud.

When Hitler's death became known, there was a dash for his mountain retreat at Berchtesgaden. Lee Miller and Dave Scherman drove like mad over rugged terrain; at one point their little Chevrolet slid right off the road and had to be pulled back on course by a handy army bulldozer. Further along they crossed paths with an abandoned 1939 Mercedes under the dubious care of a group of GIs, who were persuaded to relinquish it in exchange for posing with Lee for their hometown papers. "Ludmilla" proved better equipped for the difficult roads, and they arrived just after the Third Division, Seventh Army, ousted the resident SS troops who, before their retreat into the forest, set fire to the chalet. Miller and Scherman scrambled up the back of the mountain and held their flashguns for each other as they photographed Hitler's beloved Eagle's Nest going up in flames. Later Lee described the moment:

> The mountainside was a mess of craters, Hitler's own house was still standing with the roof slightly askew and the fire which the SS troopers set as a final salute was lashing out the windows. I crawled up and down . . . and looked at the empty flagpole which had carried the last Nazi banner to fly over the redoubt. The departing SS had ripped the swastika center from it, but left the red cloth.
>
> There was a sunset to color the snowy mountain tops, and it was warm enough by the fires. Two more fires started on the peak opposite like beacons and the soldiers on the jeep kept their machine guns ready, because if there were any unsurrendered vengeful Nazis around we were a beautiful target in the firelight.

The next day saw a free-for-all of souvenir hunting. Marguerite Higgins was there: "Stores of china, glassware, linen and silver lay in vast quantities in the cupboards and storerooms lining the passageways," she wrote. Soldiers and correspondents alike seized whatever they could stuff into their knapsacks. By the time Helen Kirkpatrick and Bill Walton arrived a few days later, little remained. "The GIs had stripped the place," Walton said. The only thing he could find to take was an ice cube container. Helen discovered a frying pan. They hadn't had lunch yet, and they had some A-rations, so there near the rubble that had been Hitler's beloved retreat, they built a little fire and cooked powdered eggs and bacon.

The war in Italy ended at noon on May 2. On the fourth, Field Marshal Montgomery accepted the surrender of all German forces in Holland, Denmark, and northwestern Germany, and Admiral Dönitz, Hitler's appointed successor, ordered German U-boats still at sea to return to port and surrender. German Army Group G in Bavaria capitulated, and on May 5 much of Prague was seized by resistance fighters. But the surrender that counted was the one at General Eisenhower's headquarters at the schoolhouse in Rheims, France.

Controversy about that — as far as the press was concerned — continues to this day. General Alfred Jodl represented Germany, General Walter Bedell Smith (Eisenhower's chief of staff) the Allies, and General Ivan Suslaparov the Soviet Union. All plans were highly secret. The signing was planned for May 7, and active hostilities were to end at one minute past midnight on that day. But no one — or almost no one — in the press knew these details.

Lael Wertenbaker of *Time-Life* knew because, Lael said, Ike told Wert and Wert told her. (Lael had remained in Paris when everybody else fanned out over the Continent because, you might know, she was pregnant again. She was the only pregnant woman in the U.S. Army allowed to stay at her job — or so she believed.) Apparently Wert had been out at SHAEF and caught sight of one of the German generals and guessed something was up, so Eisenhower had felt obliged to call him in and tell him about the surrender plans. "But Ike said," Lael continued, "'If you breathe one word you'll be court-martialed. This is a serious secret.' So Wert whispered it to me in the middle of the night in the middle of our double bed, but I didn't tell, and he said nothing more. And then he was left out of the surrender. The army guy in charge just made his own list of people who could attend. And Wert wasn't on it."

Helen Kirkpatrick rushed back to Paris from Berchtesgaden to find she wasn't on it either. "A general who had been assigned as the Poohbah for the press corps in Paris, by himself and without consulting any correspondents, set up a pool of correspondents to go witness the surrender. On what basis he made his choices, none of us ever knew. Obviously they had to make choices, but they could have consulted the press corps — we had a sort of loose organization — to see that the major newspapers and magazines and wire services were involved. But he didn't do that."

Realizing what was about to happen in Rheims without them, Kirkpatrick, Wertenbaker, and two other male reporters drove there to join other excluded colleagues pacing about outside the schoolhouse. Helen at least wiggled to where she could see over some heads, but she did not find that satisfactory, and they returned to Paris. There events soon became even more bizarre. The story could not be released. It had been impressed upon those who attended the surrender that nothing must be said until it had formally been announced by SHAEF. Military officers understood that all had agreed. Those who had been there unofficially, such as Kirkpatrick, also felt bound by the rules, as did others who heard about it later that day. The censors had their instructions, and the phone lines were monitored. Correspondents back at the Scribe stayed up all night expecting news, but none came. Later the press was told that permission for release could not be given until the documents had been "signed," or "ratified," in Berlin.

Years later it was reliably reported that owing to an oversight, the surrender agreement signed at Rheims had not been the one previously approved by the Russians — a fact that was not noticed until the Russian signatory returned to his headquarters in Berlin. The correct documents had to be located and flown there for a second signing by representatives of all parties on May 8. The delay in SHAEF's announcement of the surrender was thus longer than expected. But Edward Kennedy, an AP reporter throughout the war, decided that circumstances had changed and he was no longer bound by what he may or may not previously have agreed to. He found a line to London open and phoned in his story. The London AP office, which also knew of the ban, released the story anyway.

The brouhaha that followed was of the first order. Eisenhower was furious. The AP was briefly suspended and Kennedy disaccredited. Most correspondents felt they had been cut out twice, first by the military and then by one of their own. Seeing what all had agreed would be a shared story appear everywhere under Kennedy's byline was doubly galling. Fifty-four correspondents, including Kirkpatrick, signed a strongly worded statement in condemnation of Kennedy and the AP. They also criticized SHAEF for security so lax that such a thing could happen. In time, some reporters defended Kennedy, but the bitterness remained.

Meanwhile, just as they had done throughout the war, Marjorie "Dot" Avery and Catherine Coyne turned up for the story but stayed out of the fray. They were practical women, and when they couldn't get into the schoolhouse, they looked about for a related story to do instead. They talked to the GIs assigned to guard the German officers and to the Wac who managed the guest house and to the three Wac secretaries to the general staff. Avery was able to report that during the ceremony Eisenhower sat "in his office with his feet comfortably perched on his desk, his spectacles half down on his nose, engrossed in a Western-story magazine." Coyne expanded: "Those who saw him said he was completely relaxed as he waited for signatures to make his triumph official. Nobody is supposed to know about these signatures until three o'clock tomorrow afternoon but news of desperately fought for and long prayed for peace petered out to the world. Residents of this champagne center of France, glimpsing enemy officers in speeding staff cars, guessed the news."

Those "enemy officers" turned out to be the chief of the German army staff, the commander in chief of the German navy, and a colonel with the war office. Avery wrote that all three men were courteous, had ramrod bearing, and wore exquisite clothes. Each night they placed their shining boots outside their doors to be polished yet further; although the MPs refused, a GI orderly took on the task. They spent their time working in their rooms or telephoning or eating or walking in the garden "with their hands behind their backs in a manner of classic moments of history."

Coyne reported that chief of staff General Jodl, the only one who held membership in the Nazi Party, admired the "Sad Sack" cartoons and *Yank* magazine. Otherwise he was found by the American MPs to be arrogant, impatient, and cold as steel. But the Germans did look like soldiers, the MPs admitted, while the American generals, including Eisenhower, looked like competent businessmen in uniform.

The majority of correspondents were not in Paris and thus not affected by events there or in Rheims. Margaret Bourke-White, photographing the harbor at Bremerhaven from a Piper Cub, passed a C-47 "trailing a curtain of fluttering white flakes behind it . . . leaflets to inform the German people below that World War II had come to an end."

Lee Miller and Dave Scherman were at the press camp in Rosenheim, south of Munich, working on their stories when a soldier walked in. "I thought you guys might want to know Germany has just surrendered," he said. Lee kept right on typing. "Thanks," she said. Then she stopped. "Shit! That's blown my first paragraph!"

In Salzburg the Third Division, Seventh Army, had taken as headquarters the camouflaged palace that once belonged to the prince-archbishops of the city. Marguerite Higgins was sitting in the spacious tree-shaded grounds talking with the soldiers when they heard the news. That night there was a party. "At exactly one minute after midnight — the official hour of the war's end — we all went out on the balcony to see the artillery guns of the division flash in celebration into the sky," Higgins reported. "Red and blue flares, tracer bullets, ack-ack guns, tank guns, fired into the midnight sky for the last time on this front." Below them the valley reverberated with the noise. Maggie found it a tremendous and moving experience.

"We sat in the press camp now in a small hotel back at Weimar and wrote our last dispatches," Iris Carpenter recalled. At the command posts bottles of schnapps and wine and cognac were being cracked open. The battle maps on the walls were still marked with the little squares and crosses and numbers that meant this corps, that division, that regiment. The scrawls that indicated heavy fire from a strongly entrenched enemy didn't have to be feared anymore, she thought, and the brown and green and blue markings could be thought of simply as hills and forests and rivers instead of how many men might be wounded or die in taking them.

The First Army press camp decided to have a party. "We swept typewriters off the tables in the copy-room," Carpenter wrote. "We rolled up the maps. We filled great jugs full of lilac boughs." Everybody put on his or her best uniform. Lee Carson was going to wear a skirt until she remembered she had nothing but combat boots to wear it with, so settled for "pinks" and her best jacket. General Courtney Hodges, First Army commander, came with his staff, as did the division commanders with their staffs and the public relations and intelligence officers. "We were even friendly to the censors," Iris said.

"In Paris the war ended the way it began — with marching," Janet

Catherine Coyne, Marjorie Avery, and other colleagues
celebrating V-E Day and Coyne's birthday, Germany, 1945.
SCHLESINGER LIBRARY, RADCLIFFE COLLEGE.

Virginia Cowles and Martha Gellhorn, during the West End run of
their play about two women war correspondents in Italy, with actors
Ralph Michael and Irene Worth, London, 1946.
UPI/CORBIS-BETTMANN.

Flanner reported in her "Letter from Paris" of May 11, 1945. It began
with the French soldiers marching off to the war and it ended with the
French civilians marching around into the peace." They had started
marching just after de Gaulle's announcement came over the loud-
speaker system at 3 P.M., and thousands were still marching at dawn.

"V-E Day was like an occupation of Paris by Parisians," Flanner
continued. "They streamed out onto their city's avenues and boulevards
and took possession of them from curb to curb. They paved the
Champs-Elysées with their moving, serried bodies. . . . The babble and
the shuffle of feet drowned out the sound of the stentorian churchbells
that clanged for peace and even the cannon firing from the
Invalides. . . . All anyone cared about was to keep moving, to keep
shouting, to keep singing snatches of the 'Marseillaise' — 'Le jour de
gloire est arrivé . . . marchons, marchons.' "

It was mostly a young crowd, Janet noticed. By midnight crowds
had thinned sufficiently for the long lines of young men and women
holding hands to stretch out like cut-out paper dolls. It was they who
screamed joyfully at the huge American planes roaring over the tips of

the chestnut trees on the Champs-Elysées, and they who shouted at the skyrockets that shot through the night sky. "It was the new postwar generation," she said, "running free and mixed on the streets, celebrating peace with a fine freedom which their parents, young in 1918, had certainly not known."

Ann Stringer too was in Paris that day. It was a hard time for her; she could not help thinking of her husband, who had died nearby the previous August, just before the liberation of the city. Her friend Allan Jackson drove into Paris to spend the day with her, and then, since neither of them had anything else immediately to do, they drove to Normandy where Bill Stringer was buried. Jackson had traded in his old Ford coupé for a liberated BMW, so the ride was made in comfort. Ann had only a vague idea where the U.S. military cemetery was, but at last it was found outside the town of Staint-André. It was large and still very bare; there had not yet been time for anyone to plant a lawn. Allan stayed by the car, and Ann entered the gate to a sea of white crosses. Later she described how, as she walked along the first row, she felt as if she were being pulled toward the center, and then suddenly there she was in front of the cross with the marking that read "William J. Stringer, Jr." She sat there a little while, Allan said, and then returned to the car and they drove back to Paris.

32

"It Is Not Over, Over Here"

In the Pacific, Peggy Hull Deuell heard the news of V-E Day while at "A Little Army Camp in the South Seas." Peggy's datelines were never very explicit. Sometimes she was "On the Road to Tokyo" or at "A Remote Army Post." Most often she was just "Somewhere in the Pacific." She and her boys had been hanging around the radios in the orderly room for days, she said, trying to filter out the news through the static. When at last V-E Day was announced during mess, no one could work up much excitement. Some of the men had been at that station for thirty-eight months, which was longer than any regular American forces had been in the European theater, Hull pointed out. "It is over on that side of the world, but it is not over, over here."

This particular war was over, however, for photographer Dickey Chapelle. Her appetite for combat whetted by the experience of being under fire on Iwo Jima, she managed to go ashore on still-unsecured Okinawa against the precise order of her commanding officer, and to spend six nights there — or was it eight? The admiral was so mad that the actual number was unclear.

Except for its strategic location, fertile Okinawa had little in common with the volcanic ash of Iwo Jima. It was a large island, with farms and a sizable civilian population. Two marine and four army divisions had landed there on April 1, 1945, without a shot being fired. The USS *Relief*, with Chapelle aboard, joined 1,500 other American ships anchored in the harbor. But unlike Iwo Jima, there was little at the beginning for the medical staff to do, as yet no wounded marines in need of whole blood for Dickey to photograph.

On her third day of inactivity, Chapelle organized a photo opportunity for herself: she followed fifty cases of blood from the *Relief*, via LCI, LST, and "duck," shoreward, except that she herself could not land. The next day, toting camera and life preserver (a storm was in progress), she caught a ride to the *Eldorado*, the communications ship, where she complained to Commander Smith about lack of subject material and asked to be allowed to go ashore in search of casualties. Smith, who did not know of Admiral Miller's ban, agreed that she might go to Brown Beach to photograph the delivery of blood to the army field hospital, returning by nightfall. But the coxswain who delivered her to an amphtrac (amphibious tractor) informed her that it would be impossible to pick her up that day, as an order had gone out to secure all small craft. Dickey was exultant. Her own initiative had brought about one of the "firsts" her editor wanted — first woman reporter on Okinawa. Now luck had handed her another — first woman to spend the night on an island during combat. That these "firsts" might have their day of reckoning, she pushed to the back of her mind.

No one onshore knew where Brown Beach was, but a couple of MPs happened by and took her on a harrowing ride to the marine command post. There men were digging in for an anticipated counterattack, and their commander's reaction at the sight of Chapelle was an instantaneous "Get that broad the hell out of here!" At Marine Corps press headquarters, where she spent that night, she was no more welcome. That night the kamikaze attacks began. They came in waves, some 350 planes in all, suicide pilots hurtling toward the new American strongholds on the island or at selected ships offshore. Six American ships were sunk.

John Lardner, a celebrated Pacific correspondent and one of Dickey's inhospitable tentmates, set down his impressions of her visit in a dispatch to NANA: "The nerves of the boys in our tent section were somewhat demoralized by the presence of the first American woman to go ashore on Okinawa, Miss Dickie Chapelle." She was there, he continued, because her boat had landed her too late for the return trip to her ship that day. She was "small, bespectacled, and almost invisible under her standard steel helmet," and "came drifting drowsily out of the tent with the rest of us from time to time during the night to huddle in ditches or foxholes."

Back on Guam a livid Admiral Miller read Lardner's dispatch, and an angry missive from the commander of the Joint Expeditionary Forces. By then the forces on Okinawa were engaged in full combat. Chapelle moved on to the Sixth Marine Division where the general, although nonplussed at her arrival, was too courteous to chew her out. Conditions did not allow for her return that day either, and she spent the night in his tent. On the following day there was too much traffic on the road, and the day after that she found a jeep traveling to a field hospital and hitched a ride to do a story there. She spent that night holding a heavy navy flashlight while the resident doctor operated on an ambush victim.

Late on the sixth day after her landing, some eight hundred yards in advance of the front, her jeep was pulled over by a weary MP who could no longer continue the charade that he had not seen her. "Don't you know there's an order to arrest you on sight, ma'am?" he asked, and directed her to the PR office nearby.

Chapelle, a pro at marine lingo by this time, let off a few colorful re-joinders, but she went. She was arrested, was evacuated with the casualties, and reached a hospital ship just before two days of even heavier kamikaze attacks in which twenty American ships were lost. In due time she was returned to Guam. Admiral Miller had transferred on to Washington, but had left instructions to relieve Dickey of her credentials. The navy wanted to send her home by slow boat, but the army flew her in style — to annoy the navy, some said. Her husband Tony was waiting.

Chapelle did her best to get her credentials restored. Her editor at *Life Story* himself wrote to the navy: "It is our considered opinion that the decision to discipline Mrs. Chapelle was made largely because of her sex." But the navy was not interested in editors' opinions. In fact, her editor lost interest himself after he saw her photographs — too "dirty" for his publication, he said. They appeared instead in the December issue of *Cosmopolitan*.

No one ever pretended that it was an equal opportunity war.

Other women went to Okinawa later, after the guns had been silent for a while. On all the islands, a reporter who moved into the interior was likely to encounter clusters of Japanese, soldiers and civilians alike, who did not know what they should do next, if indeed they even knew that their army had lost. Shelley Mydans met up with some on Guam. The American military had ceased thinking of them as dangerous, Mydans said in her piece for *Life*, but wanted them out of there anyway. Japanese POW volunteers newly indoctrinated with a smattering of psychological warfare went back into the jungle to make contact with the holdouts. They stressed the difficulty of jungle life and the need Japan would have for men like them. "Your family and friends are worrying about you," they said. "Give up now and live to rebuild Japan for them."

One officer, after nearly a year in hiding, had become a Guam legend, Shelley said, and she described his emergence from the jungle with his little troop of faithful:

Now he stood in the clearing, ready to surrender to the Americans. With him was his lieutenant, his orderly — who from time to time wiped the sweat from the officer's forehead — and thirty-three ragged soldiers. When Colonel Howard Stent, USMC, arrived in his jeep, the Japanese officer snapped his men to attention. "You are now prisoners of war," he said. "This is no disgrace. It is a mistake to think of it as such." The thirty-five men turned toward their emperor in Tokyo and bowed, eyes closed. Then they went off to the prisoners' stockade.

All spring Shelley had watched as the B-29s flew out of the Marianas to bomb the large industrial centers of Japan — Tokyo, Yokohama, Nagoya, Kawasaki, Kobe, Osaka. She knew that the bombs they dropped were incendiary bombs filled with jellified petrol. Everything they touched went up in flames. One raid left the heart of Tokyo so hot that the water in the canals boiled. The casualties were in the hundreds of thousands; exact numbers were only guesswork as so little could be identified afterwards. By summer the steel and chemical industries had collapsed. There was not enough fuel for boats to travel between the islands, and the railroads would soon cease to function. There was not enough food anywhere.

In May the Allies had sent out peace feelers through the Japanese legation in Switzerland, but they were met with silence. In June, after the steep cost of American lives on Okinawa had been assessed, the Southwest Pacific Command foresaw that the price of invading Japan, planned for the fall, could be very high. By July it seemed clear that saturation bombing was not pushing the surrender process forward as hoped. It was in the middle of that month that an atomic device was detonated in the desert of New Mexico. President Truman saw the device as a military weapon, and neither Churchill nor Stalin voiced objections to its use. There were those in Truman's cabinet who pushed for a more explicit warning to Japan, and a feeler to the effect that the emperor's abdication might not be required for surrender, but others disagreed. On July 26, the Potsdam Declaration was issued with an ultimatum: accept unconditional surrender or face absolute destruction. The Japanese announced they would ignore the ultimatum.

None of the women correspondents in the Pacific or anywhere else (and probably none of the men) knew of the inner workings of this period of the war. Shelley Mydans had no idea that two bombs — one uranium, one plutonium — were being assembled right there on Tinian, on the other side of Saipan from Guam, nor did she know until afterward, when everybody else learned too, of their explosion on August 6 and 9 on Hiroshima and Nagasaki respectively, and the resulting horror and devastation. On August 10, the Japanese government sued for peace, asking only that Hirohito remain as emperor. The request was granted.

Hirohito, a small and gentle man, a marine biologist who kept a portrait of Abraham Lincoln in his study, was present at the final meeting of the Japanese Supreme War Council. Although there were officers on the council still holding out, the emperor said they would accept the terms offered. Then he broadcast over the radio to all the people of Japan, wherever they might be, that the war was over.

33

Women Winding Up a War

Then they were war correspondents without a war. When they woke at dawn, there was quiet; they had been released from the boom and crash and ack-ack of the bombs, the mortars, the artillery, even the little ping of sniper fire. These were sounds that most of them would now put behind them, along with sights like torn-up young bodies, along with smells they hoped never again to know. But their jobs had not ended; they were still reporters, still under contract to go, to see, to write. The terrible tension, which had vitalized them and at the same time drained them, had already begun to dwindle. They would have to be careful not to lose all momentum.

Now there were few rules as to where a reporter of either sex could or could not go, except for the vast area to the east that the Soviets were claiming as theirs, and where even before the surrender they were posting guards and denying entry. Iris Carpenter went to Prague the day after V-E Day with colleagues from the First Army press corps. On the return trip, retracing their way through twenty kilometers of what, between afternoon and night, had become the Russian lines, they found themselves among hordes of Germans trying desperately to get across to the American side. Wounded soldiers crowded into wagons of every sort, men hobbled on crutches or were pushed by nurses in handtrucks, civilians trudged along. At the sign "Limit of Advance for American Troops" Carpenter watched a weary GI shoo them all into custody as he would sheep or cattle. Many were the same Germans Hitler had uprooted and sent to populate the Sudetenland a decade before. Another little irony of the war.

None of the women relaxed for more than maybe a day. Eleanor

Packard was on hand to report the surrender of Hermann Goering to the Seventh Army, although her story lacked the drama of Patricia Lochridge's version in which the Reichsmarshall surrendered to members of the press, his car full of fried chicken and wine that was promptly devoured by that same press. In Berchtesgaden Lochridge moved into a house with officers of the 101st Airborne and, dubbed by them Fraülein Kommandante, governed the town for a week, reopening the banks so that elderly citizens would have money for food. Also in Berchtesgaden, Marguerite Higgins wrote of the fabulous art treasures uncovered in the tunnels below Goering's villa. Valued at more than two billion dollars, they included four Rembrandts, several Rubenses, and van Gogh's *Sunflowers* and *Bridge at Arles*.

Life sent Margaret Bourke-White to Essen in the Ruhr valley to interview and photograph Alfred Krupp, who headed the once massive armament works that had supplied Hitler's troops. Before that, the Krupp family had armed the Kaiser's troops in 1914, the Prussians in the Franco-Prussian War of 1870, and both sides in the 1866 Austro-Prussian War. Although the current Krupp, about Margaret's age, had been forced to relinquish his 117-room mansion to the Allied Control Commission and move into his servants' quarters, he remained, she noted drily, one of the wealthiest men in Europe.

In the last of their many cooperative ventures, Marjorie "Dot" Avery and Catherine Coyne flew to liberated Norway. They were shocked to find arrogant Germans still strolling about with Lugers on their hips and speeding through towns in their accustomed staff cars, except for the uncustomary white flags flying from their windshields. Even so, Catherine reported, witnessing the peace was a joyful alternative to covering the war. In Oslo, the long-planned celebration began at dawn with hundreds of Red Cross women thronging the streets, singing. Later marching bands, resistance fighters, and children paraded through the town. On the balcony of the royal palace, Crown Prince Olaf stood in worn British battle dress; he had returned from England only a few days before, Dot said, and "the people almost tore themselves apart welcoming him."

Vienna had been divided into five zones of occupation: American, British, French, Russian, and "international." Ann Stringer went in with the first convoy of Western correspondents. From there she and her buddy, INS photographer Allan Jackson, took off for Budapest on one of her typical unauthorized jaunts. They crossed back and forth over a Danube littered with corpses of undeterminable age and origin. Later they drove across Yugoslavia to Bulgaria, and on to Bucharest. Stringer, like Higgins a lady-come-lately to the war, was determined to stretch her odyssey to its limit.

In Vienna both Stringer and Lee Miller sought out and interviewed the Russian dancer and choreographer Vaslav Nijinsky and his wife Romola. Miller found the Nijinskys in the "international zone." Madame Nijinsky had hidden her deranged husband throughout the war, afraid that the Nazis would remove him to one of their infamous camps. "He's like a nice speechless backward child," Lee cabled back to *Vogue*. She wrote of his excitement at hearing Russian spoken again, and how Russian soldiers, shocked that "the great Nijinskaya had no shoes," cut pieces of red leather from a sofa and made her some sandals.

But the peace brought little of its elusive quality into Lee Miller's own life. She had thrown herself heart and soul into the war, thriving on the vagrant life, and now she could not easily relinquish it. In England, where British *Vogue* hailed her with parties and accolades, she felt displaced and depressed. She returned to Paris, but there her bouts of depression deepened. Sometimes she lay in bed weeping all day. Her buddy, photographer Dave Scherman, was there; he could make her laugh, and, in time, laugh at herself.

Marguerite Higgins's adjustment problems were of a different kind. Much of her reporting that summer she did in the company of George Milar of the London *Daily Express*, who also figured personally in pieces she did for *Mademoiselle*. Milar was a journalist who had joined the Rifle Brigade early in the war, had been captured in North Africa, escaped from a POW camp and returned to England, and then had parachuted back into France to work with the resistance. He was as handsome as he was brave, and Maggie was soon in love as never before. They passed idyllic days by the Wolfgangsee and swam nude in mountain lakes before setting out for Paris in a smart sports car she had liberated from a fleet that once belonged to Ribbentrop. In Paris problems emerged. Milar planned to settle down in a small English village to write fiction — not the postwar life Higgins saw for herself. Nor could

Milar see her there. He returned to England and abruptly married. Maggie was crushed. To be denied something she wanted badly was not in her experience. As with Dorothy Thompson nearly twenty years before, salvation lay in work. In that first year after the war, Higgins was credited with the most front-page stories of any foreign correspondent.

On the Fourth of July, the Russians formally handed over to the Americans their designated area of Berlin. An emotional Sigrid Schultz was part of the first contingent of correspondents who drove in convoy from Weimar to Halle and then on through a steady rain across the Russian sector to the capital. Press officer Barney Oldfield, in charge of lodging, recalled her eagerness to see what was left of the Wilhelmstrasse.

Ray Daniell and Tania Long arrived to open the postwar *New York Times* Berlin bureau. Berliners had been hard at work, and much of the rubble had by then been removed. Always practical, Tania discovered a house with electricity and plumbing still intact; she ascertained from the startled maid that the owners were away and informed the maid that she and her husband would be moving in. The Long family furniture and books and paintings had been stored in a large warehouse when she and her mother left Berlin in 1939; most of the warehouse was a shambles, but the corner holding her family goods stood firm, its contents in excellent condition. Berlin neighbors still harbored Tania's mother's silver, and even the family parrot, left with the maid, was noisily alive and well.

Shattered Berlin was slowly returning to life. In the evenings Tania and Ray could drop by the open-air cafés, go to the theater, a concert, or the movies. There was horseracing at Karlshorst again on Sundays, boating on the Wannsee, and of course the zoo. The beloved zoo had not fared well despite dedicated keepers who had done their best to keep the animals alive. Only one elephant and a few monkeys had survived.

Berliners complained a lot, Tania said, but exhibited none of the sullenness she had encountered in Bavaria. She located the *Times*'s prewar secretary and opened the bureau for business.

Helen Kirkpatrick and Janet Flanner spent much of July and August in a small, shoddy, crowded chamber of the high court of France

385

covering the trial for treason of eighty-nine-year-old Marshal Philippe Pétain, head of the Vichy government. Kirkpatrick sat within a few feet of the white-moustached leader in his immaculate uniform, his sole decoration the Médaille Militaire, France's highest award. He listened to the testimony, she said, "with the air of injured innocence of a male Joan of Arc." Léon Blum, the Socialist former premier who had been imprisoned at Dachau, was the first to declare that Pétain was indeed a traitor.

Flanner wrote that the trial, held in "an atmosphere in which all the men seem faintly fallible and all the methods slightly illegal," tarnished everyone it touched. At one point each politician testifying was asked by the judge how treason should be defined. Blum's response impressed her most: "An absence of moral confidence was the basis of the Vichy government, and that is treason," he said. "Treason is the act of selling out." In the end it was Pétain's own words that condemned him, Janet noted. In one radio broadcast he had said: "The responsibility for our defeat lies with the democratic political regime of France." His buckling under Nazi pressure for more conformance with the anti-Jewish laws didn't help either: of the 120,000 French Jews deported, only 1,500 returned.

A few women simply went home. Lael Wertenbaker, now noticeably pregnant and having trouble adjusting her uniform, was one. She and Wert flew home, anxious to see their son, delighted at the subsequent birth of their little daughter. Mary Welsh had already gone, having requested a year's sabbatical from *Time*. In Cuba Hemingway was waiting.

Sonia Tomara, confined to the U.S. General Hospital in Neuilly with pneumonia during much of the spring, flew back to the States late in April; an exhausted Ruth Cowan, sent over as a war correspondent in that long-ago winter of 1942–43, did the same. Although her stories had been much appreciated back home, Wes Gallagher — commonly known as "the AP's field marshal on the western front" — had never ceased to give her a hard time. Nor was it to the AP's credit that its only long-term female reporter in the European theater was never made to feel part of the staff.

Virginia Irwin, disaccredited, went home to find herself a bona fide hometown hero. She was named "woman of the year" for "distinguished war coverage" by the Organization of Business and Professional Women. The War Department saw it differently, however; it was two years before they forgave her Berlin escapade and reaccredited her.

Lee Carson managed to hitch an early plane back to New York. She scooted right over to the INS office in her battle dress — GI pants, Eisenhower blouse, paratrooper's boots — excited to be home, tired, but bubbling over with talk. The next day she gave a press conference in her hotel room, wearing a blouse and a short gray-green skirt, those lovely long legs no longer hidden.

Gradually, the others followed. One could not hang on forever, although some who stayed to cover the Nuremberg trials stretched it out for a year or longer. A few women — Carpenter was one — planned to go to the Pacific theater, and sailed to America with that intent, but the war against Japan ended before that could happen.

Waiting for a place on a returning troopship could be a slow process. Martha Gellhorn flew from Scotland in a C-54 transport carrying wounded; she qualified because she was doing a story on them. The trip to the airfield, the on-loading, had been a strain, and at first all the men did was sleep, or lie there thinking because everyone else seemed to be asleep. "There are many things you think about when you are coming home after a war," Gellhorn wrote with her characteristic perceptiveness.

> You think in small amazed snatches, saying to yourself, how in God's name did they get all those ships there on D Day; and how did they ever straighten out that freezing rat race when the Germans broke through the Ardennes; and how did anybody survive Italy? . . . You wonder how it all worked; it was too big to work, big and crazy. But it had worked and here we were, rocking in a large calm plane, with the Air Transport Command looking after us like a mother and bringing us home.

These wounded were all young, Gellhorn continued, between nineteen and twenty-one mostly, plus one old man of twenty-five. After that first sleep, they began to talk. No one complained. If they hurt somewhere, they turned their faces to the side of the plane to hide it. "It was a nice plane full of nice people," Martha noted, "even though it smelled pretty awful the way wounds and bodies and drainage bottles will smell; and it was a happy plane. I couldn't even imagine what home would be like because home was written on everyone's face so lovingly, so hopefully; home must be the end of the rainbow. Then we landed late at night at Mitchel Field and everyone was silent when the doors opened and the hot air of American summer came in."

In the Pacific, going home was still mostly on the schedule books. Shelley Mydans was in Manila for the preliminary surrender conference held in the crack-walled city hall that she remembered from better days. On August 28, 1945, General MacArthur arrived in Yokohama to head the American occupation and reconstitution of Japan. The battleship USS *Missouri*, flagship of the Pacific fleet, sailed into Tokyo Bay, and on the morning of September 2, one-legged Japanese foreign minister Mamoru Shigemitsu, in striped pants and top hat and carrying a cane, limped aboard with General Yoshijiro Umezu of the general staff. The surrender documents, in Japanese and English, lay on a long table; Shigemitsu, with great dignity, signed them both, followed by Umezu. Then MacArthur came forward, flanked by Lieutenant General Jonathan M. Wainwright, in whose charge he had left Corregidor, and Lieutenant General Sir Arthur Percival, who had commanded Singapore for Britain — both not long released from Japanese POW camps. MacArthur signed, followed by Admiral Nimitz and delegates from the Allied powers. The general gave a brief and conciliatory little speech, and then the war was really over.

And the men in the Pacific, too, were on their way home. First, again, the wounded, then the men who had been out there so long — on the tiny atolls and in the remote ack-ack batteries and up in the hills outside Manila. Like their fellows in Europe, they went home to moms and dads, kid brothers and sisters, sweethearts and wives, and to babies they had never seen, now no longer babies. In both theaters, women reporters described their return. It was scary, this going home — and the women found it scary for themselves, too. Like the GIs on the atolls, some of them had been out there so long. But they had gained their own kind of victory; they had truly proved themselves. The recognition they had earned was not only for themselves, because most of them thought their achievements were just what any woman lucky enough to have been in their place would have accomplished, but for their sisters coming after them. If they had not exactly made rough paths smooth — smooth was too much to hope for — they had made them passable. Passable would do.

The women went home, not so much to a particular person as to old friends, and to a life that would have to be painstakingly re-assembled. Martha Gellhorn — whose last home was now occupied by another — said it gave one a kind of desperate feeling. "For the war, the hated and perilous and mad, had been home for a long time too; every-one had learned how to live in it, everyone had something to do, some-thing that looked necessary, and now we were back in this beautiful big safe place called home and what would become of us?"

Epilogue

What the women in these pages did after the war, and how women journalists to follow seized the advantage and succeeded — or failed, or were prevented by new circumstances from carrying that advantage through — is the story of the last half century. It is as varied as the number of women involved, and has many of the same highs and lows that have appeared in these pages. Feminism was a boon, but not a decisive one. From what they accomplished in a male world, these correspondents would appear to have been on the cusp of the feminist movement, but in fact no woman I interviewed claimed affiliation or even affinity with it. Most saw its value for women a generation or two down the line. Times change.

A number of correspondents of both sexes joined the great postwar fraternity of the psychically displaced. The wide field of operation that the war had provided was no more. Only a favored few were assigned to cover areas that had required dozens a short time before, and in most cases men received priority. Women who returned to their local papers often found themselves in positions that seemed, after all they had been through, inconsequential, bordering on trivial. Adjustment was not easy.

Dorothy Thompson and Sigrid Schultz, heads of opposition news bureaus in prewar Berlin, confronted each other again as contributors to the two major postwar women's magazines, *Ladies' Home Journal* and *McCall's* respectively. An out-of-character ending for pioneering women, one might think, but politically the world had passed them by. Both were out of sync with the postwar era, Schultz in her disapproval of rapprochement with Germany, Thompson in her pro-Arab, anti-Zionist stance. At least for Dorothy, those years, marked by her marriage to a Viennese-born Czech émigré artist, were happy ones.

Janet Flanner's "Letter from Paris" continued to appear in the *New Yorker* for another thirty years. For so long a period of passionate writing, "Genêt" was awarded the Légion d'Honneur. She had more devoted friends than anyone could count: from the past, Solita Solano, with whom she had first escaped to Paris, and Noel Murphy, who remained on the farm at Orgeval; Natalia Murray, with whom she later lived in New York; and many, too, from the next generation. Her writing was always paramount. "I've never wanted to do anything else," she affirmed late in her life. "I'd rather write than eat, than eat with good wine, even."

Josephine Herbst worked for the OSS (Office of Strategic Services) in Washington during the war. Most of her later years she spent at her simple country house in Erwinna, Pennsylvania. She divided her time between her writing (mostly poetry) and a host of friends, but she never got over her divorce and loved her husband until she died.

Frances Davis married a Harvard professor. She wrote for the rest of her life, but never returned to journalism.

At the end of the war Sonia Tomara left the staff of the *New York Herald Tribune* to marry Colonel William Clark, a legal officer on Eisenhower's staff, later a judge. Clark was drafted by General Lucius Clay to reform the German courts, and they lived for six years in Berlin. Back in America they settled in Princeton. Tomara had never wanted to be on the world's stage; her goal had been to report it from second row center, but she relinquished that position, too, without regret. She had at last found the solid love, "the security and personal peace," that had eluded her in her long years of uprooted existence.

Eleanor and Reynolds Packard remained in Rome. They switched their allegiance from UP to the *New York Daily News*, but still frequented the same cafés on the Via Veneto and played bridge with old friends.

Betty Wason wrote *Miracle in Hellas* about her time in Greece, followed by twenty-three other books. She continued her work in broadcasting, hosting a talk show in Washington, serving as women's editor for Voice of America, and for six years moderating "Author Rap Sessions" on NBC.

Life continued to send Margaret Bourke-White to war-torn areas of the globe. She covered India's struggle for freedom from Great Britain and the bloody civil strife between Muslims and Hindus, photographing Gandhi often and visiting him only hours before his assassination. Her camera took her a perilous two miles deep into the gold mines of South Africa, and high into the mountains of Korea to shoot the guerrilla warfare occurring there. Several men passed in and out of her life. On the plane trip home from Korea she became aware of a dull ache in her left arm and leg, first signs of the Parkinson's disease that she would fight for nearly twenty years until her death.

After the war the *Chicago Daily News* was taken over by the *New York Post*, and Helen Kirkpatrick accepted the job of roving European correspondent. She traveled to Moscow, then to India to cover the last days of the British raj, and on to Pakistan, Afghanistan, and Turkey. But she never felt at home at the *Post*, and resigned. From government-related jobs in Paris and Washington, she assumed charge of the USIA in Europe, accompanying Secretary of State Dean Acheson as his press officer. Not long thereafter, she met Robbins Milbank of a prominent New England family, married him, gave up her far-flung career, and settled into new roles as wife, stepmother, occasional teacher, civic leader. In recognition of her wartime and postwar activities, she was awarded the Légion d'Honneur, the Médaille de la Reconnaissance, and the U.S. Medal of Freedom.

Mary Welsh gave in to Ernest Hemingway's need for a wife who was only a wife and, with their marriage in 1946, gave up all regular reporting. Hemingway gave up nothing, certainly not his drinking or bullying. They lived mostly at Finca Vigía in Cuba, with seasons in Key West, and in Ketchum, Idaho. Their efforts to have a child were nearly fatal to Mary, and Ernest suffered yet another head wound when, on safari in Africa, their plane crashed in the jungle. In 1961 he died of a self-inflicted gunshot wound, and Mary assumed the laborious job of custodian of his work.

After their postwar stint in Berlin, Tania Long and her husband Ray Daniell moved on to London and finally New York. Too much time had passed for Tania to make a real family with her son; their relationship became another of the casualties of war. In time she and Ray were sent to the Canadian capital, Ottawa, where they worked contentedly

together for eleven years. After Ray's death Tania became the PR director for music at the National Arts Centre of Canada.

Lee Miller married Roland Penrose shortly before their son,
Antony, was born. Picasso and Henry Moore were only two of the many
luminaries of the art world who visited them on their farm in East
Sussex, but neither the pastoral life nor motherhood held Lee's attention for long, and during the 1950s her chronic depression, fueled by
alcoholism, returned. It did not help that Roland, not she, was com-
missioned to write a biography of Picasso, or that Roland fell in love
with a slim and beautiful young woman, neither of which Lee was anymore. She was saved by two new interests, cooking and music, both of
which competed with photography for her time. After her death, the
Lee Miller Archives were established in Chiddingly, East Sussex,
England.

Ruth Cowan returned to Washington and to her old desk at the
AP office. She was assigned to the Congressional press gallery and later
to the House Armed Services Committee and the Pentagon, and was
elected president of the Women's National Press Club. The AP
frowned on employing married women or anyone over the age of fifty-
five. On nearing that age, she resigned and surprised everyone by marrying Bradley Nash, a kind and supportive man who had held various
government posts. They retired to his farm in Harper's Ferry, West
Virginia.

A few years after the war Lael Tucker Laird Wertenbaker and her
little family went down to live in the Basque country of France. Wert
quit his job at Time Inc. and they freelanced and began to write fiction.
It was there Wert learned he had cancer, and it was the long experience
of his dying — in full knowledge, and in the heart of his family — that
prompted Lael to write *Death of a Man*, a seminal work on the right of
a patient to know the truth about his condition and to choose how he
wished to die. She wrote six other nonfiction works, six novels, and
three children's books.

Virginia Cowles continued as a roving correspondent for the
Sunday Times of London and received the Order of the British Empire
for her war reporting. She and Martha Gellhorn collaborated on a play
about two women reporters on the Italian front (it opened in London

Janet Flanner at the Pétain trial, Paris, July–August 1945.
LIBRARY OF CONGRESS.

to enthusiastic reviews, but lasted only four days on Broadway, where its humor was not understood). As soon as could be arranged after his return from a German POW camp, Virginia married Aidan Crawley. He was elected to Parliament, and they raised three children. Over the years she wrote biographies of Winston Churchill, the Marlborough and Rothschild families, Kaiser Wilhelm, and Edward VII. She died in an automobile accident on the Continent in 1983.

Martha Gellhorn settled in London, where she continued to write both fiction and nonfiction. She made a stab at family life — adopted an Italian orphan and married retired *Time* editor T. S. Matthews — but neither endeavor was successful. As the war heated up in Vietnam, she traveled there to report its effect on civilians, sending back eyewitness accounts of human suffering that were devastating in their indictment of U.S. policy. She was barred from returning. Subsequently she covered the Arab-Israeli conflict, wars in El Salvador and Nicaragua, and the United States invasion of Panama; all her life she was both fascinated and repelled by war. She lived in London, Mexico, Italy, Kenya, and an isolated cottage in South Wales. Besides collections of her journalism, she published five novels, fourteen novellas, and two collections of short stories.

Having put off childbearing during the war years, Shelley Mydans had a son and daughter in quick succession and worked as a commentator for Time Inc. radio network news. She and the children joined Carl in Tokyo where he was serving as *Time-Life* bureau chief. Shelley reported on a half-time basis, held down the bureau when Carl traveled, and worried about neglecting her children. Back in New York she returned to fiction; besides *The Open City*, her novel about Americans interned by the Japanese, she published a fictional treatment of Thomas à Becket and other books. Carl became one of the foremost news photographers in the country.

Annalee Jacoby joined Teddy White in the passionate enterprise of writing the true story of China at war, and simultaneously advocating that America get out of China. *Thunder out of China* was a success, the collaboration less so. Both were strong-willed, their views were not identical, and White's emotional ties to Jacoby affected his professionalism. They parted. In 1950 Annalee married writer Clifton Fadiman, emcee of the radio and TV show *Information Please* and later head of the Book of the Month Club.

Iris Carpenter married redheaded Colonel Russell F. Akers Jr., operations officer for the First Army whom she first met at the press camp just before the Battle of the Bulge. She became a U.S. citizen, and her two children joined her in America, but the marriage was not the success she had hoped for. She wrote *No Woman's World*, about the war as she had experienced it, and continued to report from Washington for the *Boston Globe* and several English papers.

Carpenter's press camp colleague Lee Carson was hardly back in New York before the wife of her AP buddy Don Whitehead paid her a visit, pistol in hand. Carson, who had had enough of firearms, relinquished any claims. Over the next two decades she worked for a variety of magazines, married twice, then died, still young, of cancer.

Marjorie "Dot" Avery and Catherine Coyne, dubbed by Coyne "the Rover Girls Abroad," parted ways, although they kept in touch for the rest of their lives. Avery married the former editor of the *Detroit Free Press*, Andrew Bernhard, and taught English and journalism at the

University of Pittsburgh. At age ninety-one, knowing she had not long to live, she asked her housekeeper to take all her war stories and notebooks and burn them; no one, she said, would care about *that* anymore. Catherine Coyne returned to the *Boston Herald*, but resigned a few years later to marry Judge Eugene A. Hudson. She lived the rest of her life beside a tidal river on Cape Cod.

Predictably, Virginia Irwin had problems adjusting to civilian life, although the *Saint Louis Post-Dispatch* was proud of her wartime success and assigned her important stories such as the postwar status of the Oak Ridge atomic bomb project. A series on reentry problems experienced by men and women of the military was closer to her heart. She moved to New York and for fourteen years wrote feature articles from there, but never achieved her lifelong goal to make it into the *Post-Dispatch* newsroom.

Patricia Lochridge continued her career in journalism for most of her active life. She was a natural muckraker: she was hassled by lawyers for the trucking industry for exposing how trucks tear up highways, and was sued in the New Orleans courts for reporting the black market there. She married several times and had four sons. For a while she worked in PR for UNICEF, and she was instrumental in building the Scottsdale Art Center in Arizona before moving to Hawaii, where she lectured for many years at the university.

Ann Stringer and Marguerite Higgins, both of whom came late to the war, remained for the postwar scene in Europe. Stringer was still turning heads, and hearts: Dan DeLuce of the AP divorced his wife of many years to marry her, a union that lasted only a few weeks. Stringer continued to report for UP, mostly from Berlin, covering the blockade and the American airlift there. In 1949 she married the German-born American photographer Hank Ries and moved with him to New York. That union continued for three decades but brought Ann little happiness.

Soon after the war's end Marguerite Higgins was appointed head of the *Herald Tribune* Berlin bureau. When the Korean conflict began, she flew to Seoul, hoping to find in Korea the complete war she had missed in Europe. She risked her life more than once, was ordered out of the country and then ordered back in, and won a Pulitzer Prize for her front-line dispatches. She married General William Hall, director of army intelligence, whom she had known in Berlin. They settled in Washington and had three children (Maggie accompanied Vice President Richard Nixon to the Soviet Union when eight months pregnant with the last). Beginning in 1953, she traveled frequently to Vietnam, but she could not remain objective, and used her column to voice her strong dissent with U.S. policy there. Eventually she broke with her editors on the subject and, after twenty-two years with the *Herald Tribune*, resigned and became a columnist for *Newsday*. Following her tenth and most taxing tour in 1965, Higgins came down with a rare tropical disease, but continued to write her column from her hospital bed during the two months before her death at age forty-five.

Dickey Chapelle and her husband Tony spent two postwar years traveling about Germany and eastern Europe, photographing and documenting the feeding and medical stations set up by the American Friends Service Committee. Dickey assembled some ten thousand negatives on the work of relief organizations. After she and Tony parted in the mid-1950s, *Life* sent her to Austria to record the stories of Hungarian refugees crossing the border after the Soviet-crushed revolt. Dickey seized the opportunity to slip into Hungary with a small camera and penicillin for the wounded, but was caught and imprisoned for months. Undaunted, she later covered revolutions in Algeria and Cuba, marine operations in Lebanon and the Dominican Republic, and the war in Vietnam. She always arranged to be in the field with her beloved marines, parachuted with them several times into the thick of the fighting, and was killed by shrapnel from a land mine near Da Nang in November 1965. She was forty-six, and remains the only American woman war correspondent killed in action.

World War II has been labeled "the good war"; it may have been a just war, but no war is ever good. Still, good things emerge from bad situations, and a lot of positive changes for women came out of World War II. For one thing, they found they could do things they had never imagined doing. In the Stateside job market women were courted; they took jobs and learned skills and gained a self-confidence they might never have acquired otherwise. They worked in munitions factories and on farms; they went up into the skies as pilots, and deep underground as miners. Women who served in the military, particularly those sent to the combat zones, expanded their world as they never could have done on their own; an ex-Wac and dear friend of mine, now over ninety, speaks of her tour of duty in the Pacific theater as the happiest time of her life. Even mothers (like my own) who found themselves a single parent for the duration met the challenge with creativity and pride.

Although women war correspondents were continuing in a field in which they were already established, the seriousness of the war lent a gravitas to their work that it might not have achieved otherwise. Their daring and their sheer endurance was extraordinary. That there were too many of them to brush off as anomalies served to raise the level of possibility for women journalists across the country. The women I spoke with were interested in the feminist movement of the next generation, and tended to support their younger sisters in this endeavor, but none saw herself in that light. Their loyalty was directed to their vocation, their colleagues, the boss at home who had sent them into the field, and the reporters of both sexes among whom they lived and worked. Had it been otherwise, they may never have attained so much, and come home heroes, as they did indeed.

Notes

1. The Groundbreakers

1   Biographical material on Dorothy Thompson comes from Marion K. Sanders, *Dorothy Thompson*; Peter Kurth, *American Cassandra*; Vincent Sheean, *Dorothy & Red* (Boston: Houghton Mifflin, 1963); and Jack Alexander, "The Girl from Syracuse," *Saturday Evening Post*, May 18 and 25, 1940.

2   **"I am so scared of marriage"** — Thompson to Rose Wilder Lane, September 3, 1921, quoted by William Holtz, *Dorothy Thompson and Rose Wilder Lane: Forty Years of Friendship* (Columbia: University of Missouri Press, 1991).

3   Biographical material on Sigrid Schultz is taken primarily from the Sigrid Schultz Papers, State Historical Society of Wisconsin, Madison.

4   **warmly welcomed by the "news gang" . . . "sketchy" grasp of languages** — Schultz, notes in the Sigrid Schultz Papers.

5   **"Good old work!"** — Kurth, *American Cassandra*, p. 103.

5   **She selected . . . ace pilot Captain Hermann Goering** — *Overseas Press Club Cookbook*, ed. Sigrid Schultz (Garden City: Doubleday, 1962), p. 147.

6   **Schultz later recalled that Hitler** — Schultz, interviews by Alan Green, February 1971, Sigrid Shultz Papers.

6   **"I was a little nervous"** — Thompson, *"I Saw Hitler!"* as quoted in Sanders, *Dorothy Thompson*, p. 167.

7   **"six thousand boys"** — Thompson, "Goodbye to Germany," *Harper's*, December 1934.

7   **"Dorothy Thompson, American writer"** — Schultz, *Chicago Tribune*, August 26, 1934.

8   **"My offense was to think"** — Thompson, *New York Times*, August 27, 1934.

8   General biographical material on Janet Flanner comes from Brenda Wineapple, *Genêt*.

10   **"As a ruler of a great European power"** — "Führer" ran in the *New Yorker* on
      February 29 and March 7 and 14, 1936; reprinted in *Janet Flanner's World*, pp.
      7–28.

2. Cassandras of the Coming Storm

13   Biographical material on Helen Kirkpatrick comes from a Washington Press
      Club Foundation interview by Anne S. Kasper, April 1990, and an interview with
      the author, June 1991.

15   **"The French and British consulted"** — Kirkpatrick, Kasper interview, p. 41.

15   Biographical material on Josephine Herbst comes from Elinor Langer, *Josephine
      Herbst*.

16   **In the first of six installments** — Josephine Herbst, "Behind the Swastika,"
      New York Post, 1935, reprinted in pamphlet form by the Anti-Nazi Foundation,
      January 1936.

16   **"The newspaper, the radio"** — Ibid., p. 3.

17   **"For anyone who knew Germany"** — Ibid., pp. 10–11.

17   **Herbst wrote despairingly of walking through Berlin** — Ibid., pp. 19–20.

19   **So a backup ploy . . . was inaugurated** — Sigrid Schultz, "Hermann Goering's
      'Dragon from Chicago,'" *How I Got That Story*, David Brown and W. Richard
      Bruner, eds. (New York: E. P. Dutton, 1967), pp. 76–78.

19   **Schultz decided the time had come** — Ibid., pp. 78–81.

20   **The *Chicago Tribune* had begun a series of articles** — Frederick S. Voss,
      Reporting the War, p. 5.

22   Biographical material on Martha Gellhorn comes from Carl Rollyson's biogra-
      phy *Nothing Ever Happens to the Brave*, from introductory pieces in her collec-
      tion *The Face of War*, and from various biographies of Ernest Hemingway.

3. Apprentices in Spain

25   Biographical material on Eleanor Packard comes from *Current Biography 1941*,
      pp. 647–648.

27   **Reynolds became enamored of a Mongolian woman** — Harrison Salisbury,
      interview by author, August 8, 1992.

27   **In the fall of 1935 they were on their way** — Reynolds and Eleanor Packard, *Balcony Empire*, pp. 17–36.

28   Material on Frances Davis in Spain comes from *My Shadow in the Sun*; biographical material is taken from her *A Fearful Innocence* (Kent, Ohio: Kent State University Press, 1981).

30   **"Reinforcements have been sent"** — Davis, *My Shadow*, pp. 108–110.

31   **"a grim journalistic picnic"** — *Current Biography 1941*, p. 648.

32   **FROM ONE NEWSPAPER WOMAN** — Davis, *My Shadow*, p. 220.

33   Biographical material on Virginia Cowles comes from *Current Biography 1942* and her own account in *Looking for Trouble*.

33   **She expected a solemn, black-uniformed dictator** — *Looking for Trouble*, pp. 245–249.

34   **Josephine Herbst, dragging a knapsack** — Herbst, "The Starched Blue Sky of Spain," reprinted in the *Noble Savage*, I, 1960, pp. 80–81.

35   **He knew she would get there, he said** — Kenneth S. Lynn, *Hemingway*, p. 468.

35   **"The shellholes, the camouflaged trucks"** — Cowles, *Looking for Trouble*, p. 14.

35   **Martha wrote that "the sun was too warm"** — Gellhorn, "Only the Shells Whine," *Collier's*, July 17, 1937.

35   **"The heavy shelling usually came"** — Herbst, "Starched Blue Sky," p. 84.

35   **Herbst and Cowles waited out** — Ibid., pp. 108–110; Cowles, *Looking for Trouble*, p. 30.

36   **"Looking out the door"** — Gellhorn, "Only the Shells Whine."

37   **she had tagged along behind** — Gellhorn, introduction to "The War in Spain," *The Face of War*, p. 16.

37   **Their cohabitation became clear** — Carlos Baker, *Ernest Hemingway: A Life Story*, p. 308.

37   **Josephine Herbst remembered how the correspondents** — Herbst, "Starched Blue Sky," pp. 94–95.

37   **"beautiful Saks Fifth Avenue pants"** — Ibid., p. 83.

38   **This front provided the baptism** — Cowles, *Looking for Trouble*, pp. 21–25.

38   **Her chance came one morning** — Herbst, "Starched Blue Sky," pp. 84–92.

39   **Gellhorn described a visit** — Gellhorn, "Only the Shells Whine."

40   **Josephine Herbst noted that** — Herbst, "Starched Blue Sky," *Noble Savage*, I, p. 115.

40   **Virginia Cowles became embroiled in a situation** — Cowles, *Looking for Trouble*, pp. 40–52.

41   **Josephine Herbst, too, thought** — Herbst, "Starched Blue Sky," *Noble Savage*, I, pp. 115–116.

42   **Virginia Cowles managed to cross the border once more** — Cowles, *Looking for Trouble*, pp. 62–93.

42   **Eleanor and Reynolds Packard reported the Nationalist victory** — Packard, *Balcony Empire*, p. 57.

4. The Lessons of Czechoslovakia

43   Biographical material on Margaret Bourke-White comes primarily from Vicki Goldberg's fine eponymous biography, augmented by Bourke-White's *Portrait of Myself*.

46   **"I was learning that to understand"** — Bourke-White, *Portrait*, p. 134.

47   **"These are German islands"** — Erskine Caldwell and Margaret Bourke-White, *North of the Danube* (New York: Viking Press, 1939).

49   **Virginia Cowles . . . arrived in the Sudetenland** — Cowles, *Looking for Trouble*, pp. 116–120.

49   **"We're on an island now"** — Gellhorn, "The Lord Will Provide for England," *Collier's*, September 17, 1938.

49   **"Martha was infuriated"** — Cowles, *Looking for Trouble*, p. 127.

49   **"Fancy going round to the pubs"** — Ibid.

50   **Nuremberg to cover the annual Nazi Party congress** — Cowles, *Looking for Trouble*, pp. 141–151.

52   **correspondents who flocked to Berchtesgaden** — Schultz, *Chicago Tribune*, September 15, 1938.

53   *Sunday Times* **articles on Spain** — Cowles, *Looking for Trouble*, p. 107.

53   **Kirkpatrick had a clear view of the prime minister's return** — Kirkpatrick, *Under the British Umbrella*, pp. vii–viii.

53   **"The Czechs had one of the best armies"** — Kirkpatrick, Kasper interview, p. 30.

53   **along the Hungarian-Czechoslovakian border** — Flanner, "Letter from Budapest," *New Yorker*, September 17, 1938, in *Janet Flanner's World*, p. 46; Wineapple, *Genêt*, pp. 153–154.

54   **Back in France, she sat huddled by the radio** — Wineapple, *Genêt*, p. 154.

54   **In her Paris letter of October 2** — Flanner, *Paris Was Yesterday*, pp. 219–220.

55   **"Our state will not be the smallest"** — Cowles, *Looking for Trouble*, p. 171.

55   **Knickerbocker, Whitaker, and Cowles ... cover the crossing ... into Czechoslovakia** — Ibid., pp. 171–177; John T. Whitaker, *We Cannot Escape History* (New York: Macmillan, 1943), pp. 144–147.

55   **"Tell me, did you find ... any bitter feeling"** — Cowles, *Looking for Trouble*, p. 181.

56   **"On all the roads in Czechoslovakia"** — Gellhorn, "Obituary of a Democracy, *Collier's*, December 1938; reprinted in her *The View from the Ground*, p. 49.

56   **"They stood along the curb and waited"** — Ibid., p. 63.

56   **"It's like war, Mary thought"** — Gellhorn, *A Stricken Field*, p. 56.

57   **"with wild eyes and stunned, exhausted faces"** — Ibid., p. 94.

57   **"didn't see a single refugee"** — Ibid., Afterword, p. 308.

5. One Thought, One Holy Mission: Poland

59   **"a sudden, swift and agonized death"** — Kirkpatrick, *Under the British Umbrella*, p. 282.

59   Biographical material on Sonia Tomara comes primarily from her unpublished memoir made available by family members.

59   **"a dark, rather mysterious young woman"** — Robert St. John, *Foreign Correspondent* (Garden City: Doubleday, 1957), p. 97.

60   **"blood was still running"** — Tomara, unpublished memoir, p. 67.

60   **"to plunge again into the thick of things"** — Ibid., p. 84.

61   **"passed from ... one party to the other"** — Ibid., p. 90.

62   **On landing in France, she felt . . . impending catastrophe** — Tomara, *New York Herald Tribune*, August 1, 1940.

63   **In Prague for Czech army maneuvers** — William Shirer, *Berlin Diary*, p. 122.

63   **Eleanor decided to fly to Tirana** — Packard, *Balcony Empire*, pp. 79–86.

64   **Sigrid Schultz was unearthing a . . . Nazi maneuver** — Voss, *Reporting the War*, p. 5.

65   **invited . . . to join Ciano for lunch on the beach** — Cowles, *Looking for Trouble*, pp. 251–53.

65   **Helen Kirkpatrick began to sleuth out the German scenario for war** — Kirkpatrick, *Umbrella*, p. 290.

66   **"I spent it in the country"** — Ibid., pp. 304–305.

66   **Cowles flew into Berlin's Tempelhof** — Cowles, *Looking for Trouble*, pp. 258–261.

67   **Sonia Tomara was . . . in Warsaw** — Tomara, "Democracies' Envoys at Warsaw Ask Beck If He'll Compromise," *New York Herald Tribune*, August 28–31, 1939.

67   **On Friday she was awakened** — Tomara, "Poland Says It Is Making a Hard Fight," *New York Herald Tribune*, September 3, 1939; unpublished memoir, pp. 165–167.

68   **boys and girls assembled** — Kirkpatrick, *Umbrella*, p. 334.

68   **Chamberlain . . . spoke first of Hitler's "senseless ambitions"** — Ibid., p. 335.

68   **Sonia Tomara was not heard from again** — Tomara, unpublished memoir, p. 173.

69   **"I saw high members of the Foreign Office confer"** — Tomara, "Polish Cabinet Hides in Secret Isolated Town," *New York Herald Tribune*, September 12, 1939; unpublished memoir, pp. 173–182.

69   **In her next dispatch** — Tomara, "Smigly-Rydz Ignored Advice of Allied Staffs" and "Germans Push on Lemberg to Cut Supply Line," *New York Herald Tribune*, September 11 and 14, 1939.

69   **On September 15 Tomara crossed back** — Tomara, "Polish Morale Cracking Under Swift Invasion," "Planes Wreak Havoc as Poles Flee Invaders," and "Poland's Task Too Formidable," *New York Herald Tribune*, September 15, 16, and 18, 1939.

70   **"This morning the Polish government learned"** — Tomara, *New York Herald Times*, September 22, 1939.

6. Waiting for Hitler: The Phony War

71   **Flanner decided to return home** — Wineapple, *Genêt*, pp. 159–165.

72   **American Friends of France** — Anne Morgan had performed significant relief work after World War I with her American Friends for Devastated France, later called the Comité Américain pour le Secours Civil. By fall 1939 an operation to evacuate handicapped people from Paris was already underway.

72   **what would be her last *New Yorker* piece** — Flanner, "Letter from Bordeaux," *New Yorker,* September 24, 1939; reprinted in *Janet Flanner's World*, pp. 47–50.

72   **"Both much too used to looking out"** — Goldberg, *Margaret Bourke-White*, pp. 216–217.

73   **She wrote her husband** — Ibid., p. 227.

74   Biographical material on Betty Wason comes from *Current Biography 1943*, pp. 806–808; David H. Hosley and Gayle K. Yamada, *Hard News*, pp. 17–21; and Wason's correspondence with the author.

75   **"Down the road ran King Haakon"** — *Current Biography 1943*, p. 807.

75   **Her next challenge** — Ibid.; Leland Stowe, *No Other Road to Freedom* (New York: Alfred A. Knopf, 1941); Wason, "Her Own Stories," *Purdue Alumnus*, November/December 1995, pp. 21–25.

76   **the Commons jeered him wildly** — Kirkpatrick, "His Cabinet Job in Grave Peril, Writer Asserts," *Chicago Daily News*, May 7, 1940.

76   **"I like your stuff"** — Kirkpatrick, Kasper interview, p. 33.

76   **When . . . Kirkpatrick sailed** — Ibid., pp. 20–21.

77   **"a swing around the hot-spot circle"** — Kurth, *American Cassandra*, p. 315.

77   **The Simplon Express . . . met the Orient Express** — Tomara, "Germany's Path to the East — Belgrade," *New York Herald Tribune*, January 9, 1940.

77   **In Belgrade correspondents stayed** — Sonia Tomara's Balkan period is detailed in her unpublished memoir, pp. 178–182.

78   **when the Germans invaded Norway** — Edward W. Beattie, Jr., *"Freely to Pass"* (New York: Thomas Y. Crowell, 1942), p. 235.

78   **Tomara ... drove to the Rumanian-Soviet border** — Derek Patmore, *Balkan Correspondent* (New York: Harper & Brothers, 1941), p. 78–79.

79   **"Who knows? Maybe some time"** — Kurth, *American Cassandra*, p. 307.

79   **"The soldier stands face to face"** — Thompson, "On the Record," May 13, 1940.

7. Fleeing France

81   **Meanwhile, refugees . . . "two thirds of them women and children"** — Tomara, "Refugee Plight in France Dims Polish Disaster," *New York Herald Tribune*, May 23, 1940.

81   **a photograph in the *New York Mirror*** — Wineapple, *Genêt*, p. 161.

82   **"all fainting and vomiting, poor women"** — Ibid., p. 162.

82   **"Hundreds of them filed through"** — Cowles, *Looking for Trouble*, pp. 359–360.

83   Biographical material on Mary Welsh comes primarily from her autobiography, *How It Was*.

83   **Welsh procured an assignment with the Royal Air Force** — Ibid., p. 47.

83   **"clothes, coiffure and savoir-faire"** — Ibid., p. 33.

85   **"Parisians look at the sky with one thought"** — Tomara, "Parisians Face Danger Calmly, Trust Weygand," *New York Herald Tribune*, June 7, 1940.

85   **"river of gold flowing"** — Tomara, "Paris Hears Rumble of Gunfire But Keeps Confidence in Army," *New York Herald Tribune*, June 10, 1940.

85   **Mary Welsh felt the days winding down** — Mary Welsh Hemingway, *How It Was*, pp. 49–51.

87   **Virginia grabbed the first available plane** — Cowles, *Looking for Trouble*, pp. 363–371.

88   **Sonia and Irina and a . . . friend started out** — Tomara, "Reporter With Paris Refugees Describes Nightmare Flight," *New York Herald Tribune*, June 15, 1940.

89   **"All her life she had been troubled"** — Cowles, *Looking for Trouble*, p. 386.

89   **"It is with a heavy heart"** — Tomara, "French Conceal Despair, Move As Automatons," *New York Herald Tribune*, June 19, 1940.

90   **Sonia Tomara remained . . . to help the *Herald Tribune* Paris correspondent** — Tomara, unpublished memoir, pp. 200–205.

90   **Virginia Cowles described the white sand** — Cowles, *Looking for Trouble*, pp. 390–394.

8. Braving the Blitz

92   Biographical material on Tania Long comes primarily from an interview by the author, September 1991.

94   **"Hitler's storm troopers stood about on street corners"** — Ibid.

95   **"Don't let them palm off any second-raters"** — Raymond Daniell, *Civilians Must Fight*, pp. 69–71.

95   **Long and Daniell spent more and more time together** — Ibid., pp. 223–225.

96   **"In front of you stretched"** — Cowles, *Looking for Trouble*, pp. 404–405.

97   **"You have no feeling of carnage"** — Kirkpatrick, "Air War Like a Prize Fight, Observer Finds," *Chicago Daily News*, August 17, 1940.

97   **Virginia Cowles . . . drove down to Dover . . . Invasion Weekend** — Cowles, *Looking for Trouble*, pp. 430–431.

98   **"handsome and brave" pilots** — Ibid., p. 405.

98   **Cowles had a particular connection with the 601 Squadron** — Ibid., pp. 277–278.

98   **"We made out a batch of tiny white specks"** — Ibid., pp. 414–416.

99   **Mary Welsh and . . . Noel Monks were at the movies** — Welsh, *How It Was*, p. 59.

99   **"For nearly ten miles in the East End"** — Long, "Poor Suffer Worst in London As Bombs Cut a Ten-Mile Swath," *New York Herald Tribune*, September 9, 1940.

99   **Kirkpatrick . . . had gone downriver with the fire brigade** — Kirkpatrick, author interview, June 1991.

100   **"London still stood this morning"** — Kirkpatrick, *Chicago Daily News*, September 9, 1940.

100 **went down to Cliveden at the invitation of Lord and Lady Astor** — Kirkpatrick, Kasper interview, p. 51.

100 **The windows of Tania Long's house** — Long, "Herald Tribune's London Staff Joins 'Bombs Up Our Street' Club," *New York Herald Tribune*, September 11, 1940.

100 **Virginia Cowles was dining with a friend at Claridge's** — Cowles, *Looking for Trouble*, p. 422.

100 **"Husbands and wives . . . born and raised"** — Welsh, *How It Was*, p. 63.

101 **"hung around the edges of an incident"** — Ibid., p. 66.

101 **"These were some of London's dead"** — Ibid., p. 63.

102 **"It is still the Abraham Lincoln Room, madam"** — Kirkpatrick, *Chicago Daily News*, September 13, 1940.

102 **the management at the Savoy understood** — Long, author interview.

102 **Ray snored and woke up one night** — Daniell, *Civilians Must Fight*, pp. 278–279.

103 **"When one hears bombs coming"** — Long, "The Savoy and Carlton Damaged During Nazi Raids on London," *New York Herald Tribune*, November 29, 1940.

103 **Long and Daniell, driving through the blacked-out night"** — Long, "Midlands City a Scene of Horror, Homes Leveled, Noted Cathedral Gone," *New York Herald Tribune*, November 16, 1940.

103 **"Thin wisps of smoke still rose"** — Long, "Coventry Lays Dead to Rest in Common Grave," *New York Herald Tribune*, November 21, 1940.

104 **"American women reporters now active"** — *New York Herald Tribune*, February 15, 1941.

9. Working Under the Swastika

106 Biographical material on Lael Tucker Wertenbaker comes from an interview by the author, August 1991.

109 **"A full moon lit up the sprawling city"** — Long, *New York Herald Tribune*, October 16, 1940.

110 **Schultz and Shirer would broadcast sequentially** — "Recollections of Air Raids," Sigrid Schultz Papers.

110 **Her instructions from . . . McCormick were clear** — Schultz, interview, p. 48.

110 **"because of her independence"** — William Shirer, *Berlin Diary*, p. 462.

111 **Officials had warned her** — Schultz to Colonel Robert R. McCormick, February 24, 1941; Sigrid Schultz Papers.

111 **she carried several stories out in her head** — Schultz interview, p. 48.

112 **Burdette would later prove** — *Nation*, July 16, 1955, p. 3; David Caute, *The Great Fear* (New York: Simon & Schuster, 1978), p. 451; obituary, *New York Times*, May 21, 1993.

112 **The Italian campaign took place** — Wason, *Miracle in Hellas*, pp. 16–21.

113 **"tough Australians with wide-brimmed hats"** — Ibid., p. 24.

114 **She had become romantically involved** — Wason to the author, June 10, 1943.

114 **"worrying about seconds while the world crashed"** — Wason, *Miracle*, p. 29.

115 **"The Germans are boasting"** — Ibid., p. 26.

115 **"You had better not depend on me"** — Ibid., p. 46.

116 **Only when German correspondents . . . received orders to depart** — *Current Biography 1943*, p. 808.

10. Margaret Bourke-White Shoots the Russian War

117 **Bourke-White and Caldwell flew with six-hundred-plus pounds of luggage** — Bourke-White, *Shooting the Russian War*, p. 5.

117 **They could travel about . . . almost at will** — Bourke-White, "A *Life* Photographer Looks at Moscow a Week Before the Nazi Invasion Began," *Life*, August 11, 1941.

117 **Even when she happened into a church** — Bourke-White, "Religion in Russia," *Life*, October 13, 1941.

118 **an "opium dream" of an opportunity** — Bourke-White, "A Photographer in Moscow," *Harper's*, March 1942.

118 **driving . . . from one collective farm to another** — Bourke-White, *Shooting*, p. 5.

118 **Bourke-White . . . and Caldwell got a "raid pass"** — Erskine Caldwell, *All-Out on the Road to Smolensk* (New York: Duell, Sloan & Pearce, 1942), p. 87.

118 **set up her camera on the embassy roof** — Bourke-White, *Shooting*, pp. 89–90; Bourke-White, *Portrait*, pp. 176–177; Henry C. Cassidy, *Moscow Dateline* (Boston: Houghton Mifflin, 1943), pp. 95–96.

119 **"I would creep out on the balcony"** — Bourke-White, *Portrait*, pp. 178–179.

120 Bourke-White's visit to the Kremlin to photograph Stalin is variously described in *Shooting*, pp. 211–215; *Portrait*, pp. 174–186; and "A Photographer in Moscow," pp. 417–419.

121 **Erskine thought Lozovsky bore a distinct resemblance** — Caldwell, *Smolensk*, pp. 91–97.

122 **In mid-September the press bureau notified** — Bourke-White, *Shooting*, pp. 221–222.

122 **the party set out in M1 sedans** — Ibid., pp 227–231; Whitman Bassow, *The Moscow Correspondents* (New York: William Morrow, 1988), pp. 100–101.

123 **More enemy planes followed them** — The trip to the front is chronicled by Bourke-White in *Shooting*, pp. 244–270, and "A Photographer in Moscow," pp. 419–420.

11. Treading Water, Marking Time

126 **She regularly took her message in person** — Kurth, *American Cassandra*, p. 332.

126 **"The Abbey stands"** — Thompson, "On the Record," May 14, 1941, quoted in Kurth, *American Cassandra*, pp. 335–337.

127 **"sang for their supper"** — Lael Wertenbaker, interview.

128 **Mary Welsh did a piece for *Life*** — Welsh, "No Time For Tears," *Life*, August 4, 1941.

130 **Favorite restaurants and neighborhood shops** — Packard, *Balcony Empire*, p. 316.

130 **Japanese nationals in Rome were . . . overfriendly** — Ibid., pp. 327–328.

12. China Hands

131 **A small number of American women** — Material on Edna Lee Booker is taken from her *News Is My Job* (New York: Macmillan, 1941); on Agnes Smedley from her *Battle Hymn of China* (New York: Alfred A. Knopf, 1943), and from Janice R. MacKinnon and Stephen R. MacKinnon, *Agnes Smedley: The Life and Times of an American Radical* (Berkeley: University of California Press, 1988); Material on Helen Foster (Snow) comes from her *My China Years* (New York: William Morrow, 1984); on Peggy Hull from Wilda M. Smith and Eleanor A. Bogart, *The Wars of Peggy Hull*; and on Emily Hahn from her book *China to Me*.

133 Biographical material on Shelley Smith Mydans is based on Carl Mydans, *More Than Meets the Eye*, and an interview by the author, December 1991.

135 **Most of the occupants of the press hostel** — Stephen R. MacKinnon and Oris Friesen, *China Reporting*; Peter Rand, *China Hands*; Hahn, *China to Me*; S. Mydans, interview.

136 **"hardy Chungking perennial"** — Hahn, *China to Me*, p. 162.

136 **a soldier climbed onto a box** — C. Mydans, *More Than Meets the Eye*, pp. 45–46.

136 **"But Carl and I were young"** — S. Mydans, interview.

137 **"report on the Chinese army in action"** — Gellhorn, *Travels with Myself and Another*, pp. 19–24.

137 **a story on the CNAC passenger-mail flight** — Gellhorn, "Flight Into Peril," *Collier's*, May 31, 1941.

137 **"Beautiful hopeless country"** — Gellhorn, *Travels*, pp. 27–29.

138 **a rusty Chris-Craft towing a sampan** — Gellhorn, "These, Our Mountains," *Collier's*, June 28, 1941; reprinted as "The Canton Front" in *The Face of War*, pp. 74–76.

138 **Gellhorn's introduction to "the Chinese army in action"** — *Travels*, pp. 40–47

141 Biographical material on Annalee Whitmore Jacoby comes from Rand, *China Hands*, pp. 212–217.

143 **"Being a radical young person"** — S. Mydans, interview.

143 **"these two stony rulers cared nothing for ... their people"** — Gellhorn, *Travels*, p. 58.

143 **Smith and Mydans went to the tiny room** — S. Mydans, interview.

144   recalled his "brilliant amused eyes" — Gellhorn, *Travels*, pp. 59–60.

144   Mydans, Smith, and Mel Jacoby visited the Yellow River front — C. Mydans, *More Than Meets the Eye*, pp. 50–55; S. Mydans, interview.

145   Martha . . . had developed "China rot" — Gellhorn, *Travels*, p. 60.

145   Her U.C. "saw the Chinese as people" — Ibid., p. 56.

145   Ernest was like a "beached whale" — Ibid., pp. 62–63.

145   "the legendary silent-footed Oriental" — Gellhorn, "Singapore Scenario," *Collier's*, August 9, 1941.

146   Mel Jacoby sent a message to Annalee — Rand, *China Hands*, p. 218.

146   On the last day of November — C. Mydans, *More Than Meets the Eye*, pp. 60–61.

13. Facing the War That Is Our War Now

148   "A naval base somewhere in the Pacific" — Welsh, *How It Was*, p. 74.

148   "I hadn't the faintest idea where Pearl Harbor was" — Lael Wertenbaker, interview.

149   the company gathered there was "flabbergasted" — Kirkpatrick, personal diary, entry for December 8, 1941.

149   Eleanor Packard was in the UP office in Rome — Packard, *Balcony Empire*, p. 329.

149   Ezra Pound dropped by — Ibid., pp. 250–251.

149   By Wednesday, December 10, it was clear — Ibid., pp. 5–16; 330–333.

151   Mel and Annalee . . . lay asleep in their room — Annalee Whitmore Jacoby, "I Saw It Happen in Manila," *Liberty*, January 24, 1942; C. Mydans, *More Than Meets the Eye*, p. 62.

152   "We just got in position" — S. Mydans, *Life*, December 22, 1941.

152   "searchlights cutting the sky into parallelograms" — A. W. Jacoby, "I Saw It Happen."

152   "Friday, December 12. Manila's tenth air-raid alarm on" — Ibid.

154   "Bitterly regret your request not available here" — S. Mydans, interview.

154 **But Annalee was present at USAFFE . . . headquarters** — Clark Lee, *They Call It Pacific*, p. 80.

154 **Christmas morning was quiet** — S. Mydans, interview.

154 **"Especially you . . . on their blacklist"** — Lee, *Pacific*, p. 118.

155 **On the last afternoon of the year** — Ibid., pp. 151–155.

155 **At dawn on January 2** — C. Mydans, *More Than Meets the Eye*, p. 68.

155 **The city "lay ringed by fire"** — C. and S. Mydans, "Tomorrow We Will Be Free," *Life*, December 6, 1943.

155 **Orders were issued** — S. Mydans, *The Open City*, pp. 26–39; C. Mydans, *More Than Meets the Eye*, pp. 71–73; Frances Long, "Yankee Girl," *Life*, September 7, 1942; S. Mydans, interview.

156 **There could be no Dunkirk here** — A. W. Jacoby, "With MacArthur," *Liberty*, April 18, 1942.

157 **She selected several nurse's reports and edited them** — A. W. Jacoby, "Bataan Nurses," *Life*, June 15, 1942.

157 **it occurred to them that if they . . . could just get their story out** — Lee, *Pacific*, p. 246.

157 **Again it was Mel who found a boat** — Melville Jacoby, "Farewell to Bataan," reprinted in *They Were There*, Curt Riess, ed. (Freeport, NY: Books for Libraries Press, 1944), pp. 424–426.

158 **They took turns standing watch** — Lee, *Pacific*, p. 257.

158 **"There was always a tight feeling in our stomachs"** — "A Letter from the Publisher," *Time*, November 27, 1944.

14. Women Behind Walls: Manila, Siena, Shanghai

159 **Had she seriously considered capture** — Gwen Dew, "Hong Kong 1942," reprinted in *They Were There*, Curt Riess, ed., pp. 442–445.

159 **Their internment was billed as a "military necessity"** — Doris Kearns Goodwin, *No Ordinary Time*, pp. 321–322.

160 **The internees were left to organize their own lives** — Life in Santo Tomás is variously taken from S. Mydans, *The Open City*, pp. 56–60; C. Mydans, *More*

Than Meets the Eye, pp. 71–77; Frances Long, "Yankee Girl," *Life*, September 7, 1942; C. and S. Mydans, "Tomorrow We Will Be Free"; S. Mydans, interview.

163 **"Had he heard the news?"** — C. Mydans, *More Than Meets the Eye*, pp. 78–80.

163 **Eleanor and Reynolds Packard had never worried much** — E. and R. Packard, *Balcony Empire*, pp. 334–342.

164 **This was truly "polite confinement"** — Ibid., pp. 343–346.

164 **the exchange was on** — Ibid., pp. 350–352.

165 **The last diplomatic train left . . . for Lisbon** — Ibid., pp. 352–358.

166 **Shelley Smith and Carl Mydans were also on the move** — The trip on the Japanese freighter *Maya Maru*, the months in Shanghai, internment in Chapei, and journey on the *Teia Maru* to freedom comes from C. Mydans, *More Than Meets the Eye*, pp. 82–116; C. and S. Mydans, "Tomorrow We Will Be Free"; S. Mydans, interview.

15. Learning the Rules, Dressing the Part

172 **Kirkpatrick described how . . . workers . . . gathered** — Kirkpatrick, "Gen. Chaney, Air Expert, Heads Yanks in Britain," *Chicago Daily News*, January 27, 1942.

172 **Mary concentrated on the nuts and bolts** — Welsh, "A.E.F. in Ireland," *Life*, February 23, 1942.

174 **a visit from King George and Queen Elizabeth** — Kirkpatrick, "King, Queen Find A.E.F. is 'Colossal,'" *Chicago Daily News*, June 27, 1942.

174 **Tania's son felt displaced by this stranger** — Long, interview.

175 **Long went down to Dover to report** — Long, "The White Caves of Dover," *New York Times Magazine*, May 10, 1942.

176 **Americans polled in an OWI . . . survey** — David Reynolds, *Rich Relations*, p. 34.

176 **Erskine Caldwell . . . was not happy about his wife's choice** — Goldberg, *Margaret Bourke-White*, p. 253.

176 **there to photograph their first mission** — Bourke-White, "U.S. High-Altitude Bombers Hit Nazis," *Life*, October 19, 1942.

177 **"May the *Flying Flitgun* bring to the enemy"** — Goldberg, *Margaret Bourke-White*, p. 253.

177 **Charles Wertenbaker . . . arrived at the London office** — Lael Tucker Wertenbaker, *Death of a Man* (Boston: Beacon Press, 1957), pp. 159–160; Tucker, interview.

177 **"to see the things we wanted to see"** — Wertenbaker, *Death of a Man*, p. 160.

178 **"It was hard leaving Steve"** — Wertenbaker, interview.

178 **women correspondents . . . found their customary easy movement . . . obstructed** — Kirkpatrick, Kasper interview, p. 32.

178 **So she went to Helen Rogers Reid** — Julia Edwards, *Women of the World*, p. 123.

179 **Reid had . . . "the persistence of gravity"** — Barbara Sicherman and Carol Hurd Green, *Notable American Women: The Modern Period*, pp. 574–575.

179 **"Somewhere on the coast of Africa"** — Tomara, "Air Transports Use Africa Base on Jungle Edge," *New York Herald Tribune*, August 24, 1942.

16. Women on Trial: North Africa

180 Biographical material on Ruth Cowan comes from a Washington Press Club Foundation interview by Margot Knight, September 26, 1987, and an unpublished memoir.

182 **Then in December a story came over the teletype** — Cowan, memoir, p. 56.

182 **"So you want to go to war?"** — Ibid., pp. 60–61.

183 **Cowan began the process** — Ibid., pp. 62–82.

184 *Life* **reporter Lincoln Barnett . . . had no idea** — Goldberg, *Margaret Bourke-White*, p. 256.

184 **she set about persuading the U.S. Army Air Force** — Ibid., p. 257.

184 **She was assigned to the flagship** — Bourke-White, *Portrait*, pp. 204–205.

185 **the torpedo awakened her** — Bourke-White, "Women in Lifeboats," *Life*, February 22, 1943.

185 **"This must be fear"** — Bourke-White, *Portrait*, pp. 208–209.

185 **water up to her hips** — Bourke-White, "Women in Lifeboats."

187   **Everyone was determinedly roughing it** — Cowan, "First Waacs in Africa Sang Way Through Hardships, Perils at Sea," AP dispatch, January 31, 1943.

188   **Wes Gallagher . . . suggested that when Cowan's ship returned** — Cowan to Robert Bunnelle, AP London office, February 13, 1943; Knight interview, pp. 23–25.

188   **"Don't encourage more women to come to Africa"** — Edwards, *Women of the World*, p. 151.

189   **"I never thought women could live a life so hard"** — Cowan (AP), "Nurses Working 12-Hour Shifts in Front Lines Hospital in Tunisia," *Saint Louis Post-Dispatch*, February 21, 1943.

189   **General Jimmy Doolittle . . . had her flown to the Ninety-seventh Bomb Group** — Bourke-White, *Portrait*, p. 117.

189   **"In the evening . . . she left with the general"** — Goldberg, *Margaret Bourke-White*, p. 263.

191   **"You can do one of two things"** — Ibid.

191   **she did not recall having given a thought** — Bourke-White, *Portrait*, p. 226.

191   **The Flying Fortresses set off at dawn** — "*Life*'s Bourke-White Goes Bombing," *Life*, March 1, 1943.

192   **"Oh, that's just what I want, that's a beautiful angle!"** — Goldberg, *Margaret Bourke-White*, p. 267.

192   **"the first woman ever to fly with a U.S. combat crew over enemy soil"** — "*Life*'s Bourke-White."

192   **In the company of four officers, they headed for the rear** — Cowan (AP), "Girls in Hitch-Hike Flight As Nazis Approach," *The Evening Sun*, Baltimore, March 9, 1943.

17. Touching Base on Five Continents

193   Biographical material on Lee Miller comes from two studies by her son, Antony Penrose: *The Lives of Lee Miller* and *Lee Miller's War*.

196   **Her earlier nonchalance vanished** — Welsh, *How It Was*, p. 83.

196   **the long separation had left both of them changed** — Ibid., p. 84.

196   **A new Japanese offensive was pressing westward** — Tomara, "Crucial Battle for 'Rice Bowl' Worries China, *New York Herald Tribune*, May 21, 1943.

196   **she sat with other correspondents in the courtyard** — Tomara, "Chinese Doubt Foe Can Drive to Chungking," *New York Herald Tribune*, May 29, 1943.

196   **Leaving felt a bit like treason** — Tomara, "Farewell to Chungking," *New York Herald Tribune*, August 9, 1943.

197   **she hitched a ride in a bomber** — Tomara, "Sonia Tomara Flies in a Raid over Hankow," *New York Herald Tribune*, August 24, 1943.

198   **"You do feel the war here"** — Tomara, "U.S. Flyers in China Find Zeros Keep Coming," *New York Herald Tribune*, September 12, 1943.

198   **she forwarded dispatches on the invasion of Sicily** — Kirkpatrick, "Island Attacked by Land, Sea, Air," *Chicago Daily News*, July 10, 1943.

198   **Italy's withdrawal from the war** — Kirkpatrick, "Disunity in Italy Heralds Its Crackup, Neutrals Say," *Chicago Daily News*, July 13, 1943.

198   **Carl and Shelley Mydans were on the final lap** — S. Mydans, "Letter from Mormugao," *Life*, November 29, 1943; "Americans' Return," *Life*, December 20, 1943; C. Mydans, *More Than Meets the Eye*, chapters 22 and 23.

18. Slogging Through Italy

200   **General Eisenhower charged that she had maneuvered herself** — Goldberg, *Margaret Bourke-White*, p. 274.

201   **She described how a thorough job of mine clearance** — Bourke-White, *They Called It "Purple Heart Valley,"* pp. 28–30.

201   **he was full of praises for her work** — Goldberg, *Margaret Bourke-White*, p. 276.

202   **He had, he said, written to ask his wife for a divorce** — Ibid., p. 277.

202   **She was quartered in a monastery** — Bourke-White, *Purple Heart Valley*, pp. 49–51.

202   **Their route . . . encompassed a newly completed Bailey bridge** — Ibid., pp. 42–48.

203   **Bourke-White returned exhausted to her cell** — Ibid., pp. 66–67.

204 **[Helen] lived with the nurses in a tent** — Kirkpatrick, Kasper interview, pp. 68–69.

204 **Still in her combat boots, Helen flew back** — Kirkpatrick, author interview.

205 **two days after the Anzio landings** — Tomara, "Nazis Counter-Attack on Cassino Front," *New York Herald Tribune*, January 25, 1944; "5th Army Fights Nazis Trying to Escape Noose," *New York Herald Tribune*, January 26, 1944.

205 **It was hard to photograph such suffering** — Bourke-White, *Purple Heart Valley*, pp. 111–113; "Evacuation Hospital," *Life*, February 21, 1944.

205 **More dramatic were the photos taken at the Eleventh Field Hospital** — Bourke-White, *Purple Heart Valley*, pp. 123–132.

206 **"Everything was so still, so pure"** — Ibid., p. 134.

206 **Her negatives and notes routinely traveled to the Pentagon** — Goldberg, *Bourke-White*, pp. 283–284.

207 **"I would give anything to be part of the invasion"** — Lynn, *Hemingway*, p. 505.

207 **"The French held these mountains"** — Gellhorn, "Visit Italy," *Collier's*, May 6, 1944.

208 **"It smelled of many things, of men and dampness"** — Gellhorn, "Postcards from Italy," *Collier's*, July 1, 1944.

208 **She celebrated Easter with two hundred soldiers** — Tomara, "Easter in Italy: Americans Pray Within Earshot of German Lines," *New York Herald Tribune*, April 10, 1944.

209 **Later that spring she reached Cassino** — Tomara, "Italian Front at a Standstill," *New York Herald Tribune*, April 13, 1944.

210 **A risky jaunt into Cassino** — William H. Stoneman, "Martha Gellhorn Sets Out to See Cassino; Shot At, Dives Into Ditch," *Saint Louis Post-Dispatch*, February 29, 1944.

19. New Women Come Over for Overlord

212 Biographical material on Virginia Irwin comes primarily from Anne R. Kenney, " 'She Got to Berlin': Virginia Irwin, *St. Louis Post-Dispatch* War Correspondent."

213   Biographical material on Lee Carson is taken from assorted news articles and Julia Edwards, *Women of the World*, pp. 156–160.

213   **"best-looking woman correspondent,"** *Newsweek*, March 19, 1945, p. 88.

214   Biographical material on Iris Carpenter comes from assorted profile pieces in the *Boston Globe*; Edwards, *Women of the World*, pp. 153–156; and an interview by the author, October 1994.

214   **"My husband had found another woman"** — Carpenter, interview.

215   **"She could get interviews from anybody"** — Colonel Barney Oldfield, to the author, May 1994.

215   Biographical material on Marjorie "Dot" Avery is taken from assorted articles in the *Detroit Free Press* and reminiscences of friends.

216   Biographical material on Catherine Coyne comes from an interview by the author, February 1992, and reminiscences of friends.

217   **"There was nothing glorious about going off to war"** — Coyne, "Embarkation Grim Business for Troops," *Boston Herald*, May 30, 1944.

219   **her appointed place on the correspondents' committee** — Kirkpatrick, Kasper interview, pp. 69–70; author interview.

219   **a key man in the Polish underground** — Kirkpatrick, "Poles Writing Air Legends in Europe's Skies," *Chicago Daily News*, January 30, 1944.

219   **interviewed three Poles for her story** — Gellhorn, "Three Poles," *Collier's*, March 18, 1944.

220   **Martha . . . "had devoted her entire attention to . . . Polish pilots"** — Welsh, *How It Was*, p. 93.

221   **she was very gay that . . . spring** — William Walton, author interview, May 1994.

221   **Martha Gellhorn had returned to Cuba** — Carlos Baker, *Ernest Hemingway*, p. 387.

221   **Welsh was lunching with Irwin Shaw** — Ibid., p. 389.

221   **"I don't know you, Mary. . . . But I want to marry you."** — Welsh, *How It Was*, p. 95.

222   **the car in which Hemingway was a passenger** — Baker, *Ernest Hemingway*, p. 391; Lynn, *Hemingway*, pp. 508–509; James R. Mellow, *Hemingway*, p. 531.

222   **"Woods and hedgerows were spiky with guns"** — Carpenter, *No Woman's World*, pp. 15–16.

20. D Day

224 **"At about 4 a.m. on June 6"** — Welsh, *How It Was*, p. 99.

225 **"The correspondents who were going with the troops"** — Kirkpatrick, Kasper interview, p. 71.

225 **"The first landings today"** — Kirkpatrick, "Superb Plans Give Edge to Allied Forces," *Chicago Daily News*, June 6, 1944.

225 **"I was fast asleep"** — Avery, "Londoners Sober But Happy All D-Day," *Detroit Free Press*, June 7, 1944.

226 **Catherine Coyne had received a similar call** — Coyne, interview.

226 **also there in that "great guarded room"** — Gellhorn, "Over and Back," *Collier's*, July 22, 1944.

227 **"Wherever troops hit France on those Omaha beaches"** — Carpenter, *No Woman's World*, pp. 29–30.

227 **On D Day plus one Catherine Coyne hitchhiked** — Coyne, "Catherine Coyne in England," *Boston Herald*, June 17, 1944.

228 **"Great formations of gliders rose in the air"** — Avery, "Invasion Gliders Blanket Sky Over England," *Detroit Free Press*, June 8, 1944.

228 **stood on the dock of a military port marshaling area** — Cowan, AP dispatch, June 6, 1944.

229 **Lee Carson . . . found . . . a seat on a plane** — Oldfield, *Never a Shot in Anger*, p. 104; Edwards, *Women of the World*, p. 156.

229 **Martha Gellhorn crossed the Channel in a hospital ship** — Gellhorn, "The Wounded Come Home," *Collier's*, August 5, 1944.

230 **The army press office took a dim view** — Rollyson, *Nothing Ever Happens to the Brave*, p. 199.

231 **The next woman correspondent to step onto French soil** — Carpenter, *No Woman's World*, pp. 29–31.

231 **"Some of the men who made the first assault"** — Avery, "Normandy's Casualties Come Back," *Detroit Free Press*, June 11, 1944.

232 **"There was something macabre"** — Welsh, *How It Was*, p. 101.

233 **people had gone back to sleeping in the shelters** — Long, "Worse Than the Blitz," *New York Times Magazine*, July 30, 1944.

233 **"The infernal machine seemed to be buzzing down upon us"** — Coyne,

"Londoners Calm, Even Scornful Despite 2752 Dead by Robots," *Boston Herald*, July 6, 1944.

233 **"There were streets where, for several miles"** — Kirkpatrick, "Still Digging Yank Dead From Robot Bomb Debris," *Chicago Daily News*, July 7, 1944.

234 **expected to be gone no more than thirty-six hours** — Cowan, AP dispatch, July 14, 1944.

234 **Carpenter interpreted the term "beachhead" to include Cherbourg** — Edwards, *Women of the World*, p. 157.

21. Trekking North from Rome

236 **she was already breaking protocol** — Reynolds Packard (UP), "Press, Including Woman in Slacks, Calls on Pope," *New York World-Telegram*, June 8, 1944.

236 **Packard underwent the unsettling experience** — R. Packard, "Eleanor Packard Shows Italians She's No Spy," *New York World-Telegram*, July 10, 1944.

237 **All they talked about . . . was the Russian army** — Gellhorn, "The Carpathian Lancers," *The Face of the War*, p. 121. *Collier's* did not publish this article, perhaps because it appeared critical of America's Russian allies.

237 **"We moved the next day and every day after that"** — Ibid.

238 **"The U.S. 7th Army"** — E. Packard (UP), "Sea and Sky Troops Rip Defenses, Swarm Ashore Between Nice, Marseille," *New York World-Telegram*, August 15, 1944.

239 **the [FFI] took it upon themselves to seize Bordeaux** — E. Packard (UP), "Biggest Port Is Liberated," *New York World-Telegram*, August 23, 1944.

239 **Martha Gellhorn attached herself to the First Canadian Corps** — Gellhorn, "Cracking the Gothic Line," *Collier's*, October 28, 1944.

239 **"Suddenly you see antlike figures of infantry"** — Ibid.

240 **her request to cover the Normandy invasion** — Goldberg, *Margaret Bourke-White*, p. 284.

240 **Bourke-White was anxious to renew her connection** — Ibid., p. 285.

240 **"I love you. I will marry you. Maggie."** — Ibid.

241 **"During the month she's been in Italy"** — Ibid., p. 286.

22. That Summer in France

242   **(an exasperated Iris Carpenter pointed out)** — Carpenter, *No Woman's World*, p. 48.

243   **"It was terribly humiliating, the way I went to war"** — Coyne, interview.

243   **The Wacs were allowed to mingle with nearby troops** — Coyne, "Miss Coyne Joins WACs in Invasion," *Boston Herald*, July 12, 1944.

243   **Irwin thought it incongruous** — Irwin, "Three Missouri Girls Land With Wacs in France," *Saint Louis Post-Dispatch*, July 17, 1944.

243   **the Wacs went ashore . . . singing the "Marseillaise"** — Coyne, "Mass. Girls Share Hardships of GI," *Boston Herald*, July 14, 1944.

243   **"like the sand-houses prairie dogs make"** — Avery, "Marjorie Avery Camps with the WACs in Orchard," *Detroit Free Press*, July 21, 1944.

245   **"whose voice even at two o'clock in the morning"** — Coyne, "Catherine Coyne on the War Front," column, *Boston Herald*, August 5, 1944.

245   **It had rained all day** — Avery, "Rain Invades Dinner Party for WAC Officers," *Detroit Free Press*, July 27, 1944.

245   **"such a mechanical, well-organized operation"** — Long, interview.

246   **The sisters were at first suspicious** — Tomara, "Shopkeepers in Cherbourg Breathe Freely," Tomara, *New York Herald Tribune*, August 2, 1944.

246   **Lee Miller . . . boarded a plane for Normandy** — Miller, "U.S.A. Tent Hospital," *Vogue*, September 15, 1944.

248   **"the most exciting journalistic experience of my war"** — Penrose, *The Lives of Lee Miller*, p. 118.

248   **Iris Carpenter and Ruth Cowan started out** — Carpenter, *No Woman's World*, pp. 47–65.

249   **"Ruth was a straightforward person"** — Carpenter, interview.

250   **"It's not safe in England"** — Kirkpatrick's account of her Normandy experience July-August 1944 is taken from her "Rennes Wild with Joy at Yank Victory," *Chicago Daily News*, August 5, 1944; Kasper interview, pp. 72–73; and author interview.

251   **Lee Miller grabbed at a chance** — Miller, "France Free Again," *Vogue*, October 15, 1944.

254 **"Drawn up in front of the city hall"** — Coyne, "DeGaulle at Rennes Lights Battle Spark," Coyne, *Boston Herald*, August 22, 1944.

254 **felt he was much moved** — Carpenter, *No Woman's World*, pp. 98–99.

254 **"She was rubbing eau de cologne all over herself"** — Coyne, interview.

255 **Helen in her khaki Wac underwear** — Walton, interview, May 1994.

255 **"These Frenchmen were going out of their minds"** — Kirkpatrick, Kasper interview, pp. 73–74.

23. Liberating Paris

256 **when word came "everybody fell into line"** — Kirkpatrick, Kasper interview, p. 74.

257 **Charles Wertenbaker and Robert Capa told their driver** — Oldfield, *Never a Shot in Anger*, p. 110.

257 **"I will never forget the next morning"** — Kirkpatrick, Kasper interview, p. 74.

257 **"My heart was so tense"** — Tomara, *New York Herald Tribune*, August 29, 1944.

258 **One of her first stories . . . was on the mechanics of that uprising** —Tomara, *New York Herald Tribune*, August 31, 1944.

258 **An order had been out on [Carson]** — Oldfield, *Never a Shot in Anger*, p. 111.

258 **she took sole charge of six German soldiers** — J. C. Oestreicher, *The World Is Their Beat*, p. 225.

258 **"Madame want to buy a beautiful rug very cheap?"** — Ibid.

258 **she was apprehensive as to what kind of welcome** — Oldfield, *Never a Shot in Anger*, pp. 111–112.

258–59 **"deliciously, deliriously back in real France,"** — Welsh, *How It Was*, p. 108.

259 **"Daughter . . . sit still and drink this good brandy"** — Baker, *Ernest Hemingway*, p. 417.

259 **she and Reinhart . . . turned back to Notre Dame** — Kirkpatrick, "On-Spot Story by Kirkpatrick," *Chicago Daily News*, August 26, 1944.

260 **"The generals' car arrived on the dot of 4:15"** — Ibid.

261   **went over to the *Chicago Daily News* office** — Kirkpatrick, Kasper interview, p. 75.

261   **"sprawled in hideously awkward death"** — Coyne, "Petals, Wine, Kisses Power Paris Drive," *Boston Herald*, August 25, 1944.

261   **Marjorie Avery reported shelled houses** — Avery, "Writer Sees Few Outward Signs of War," *Detroit Free Press*, September 2, 1944.

261   **"I arrived exhausted by my share of . . . handshakes"** — Penrose, *Lee Miller's War*, p. 67.

261   **Virginia Irwin and British reporter Judy Barden took a roundabout route** — Barden, "Girl Reporters Got Lost in Front Lines," *New York Sun*, August 31, 1944.

262   **Tania Long drove down from Cherbourg** — Long, "It's Still the Same Glowing Paris," *New York Times Magazine*, September 10, 1944.

263   **Ruth Cowan's was to recover her blondness** — Overseas Press Club of America, *Deadline Delayed* (New York: E. P. Dutton, 1947).

264   **Picasso, whom she found at his studio** — Miller, "In Paris . . . Picasso, Eluard, Bérard," *Vogue*, October 15, 1944.

264   **"Even I, conservative Boston spinster that I am"** — Coyne, "'Spinster' Coyne Turns Cheek to Kisses of a Grateful Paris," *Boston Herald*, August 28, 1944.

264   **thought the painter looked like a Prudential Insurance collector** — Coyne, interview.

264   **Another day Miller invited Coyne up to her room** — Ibid.

266   **Lael Wertenbaker wanted desperately to come to newly liberated Paris** — Wertenbaker, interview.

266   **Jesus Christ Himself Lee** — Reynolds, *Rich Relations*, p. 105.

267   **Marjorie Avery interviewed Lucien LeLong** — Avery, "Paris Dressmakers Hail Liberation of Fashions," *Detroit Free Press*, September 11, 1944.

267   **The horror of it was almost too much to take in** — Tomara, "Germans Shot 75,000 During Reign in Paris," *New York Herald Tribune*, September 2, 1944.

268   **"When you first go into the chamber you disbelieve everything"** — Coyne, "Gestapo Hot Air Jets Tortured Parisians Before Execution," *Boston Herald*, September 3, 1944.

268   **visited . . . a member of the underground** — Kirkpatrick, "Victim's Story Bares Gestapo Bestialities," *Chicago Daily News*, October 13, 1944.

269 **"They simply locked men and women there in the wet unending dark"** — Gellhorn, "The Wounds of Paris," *Collier's*, November 4, 1944.

269 **"It is impossible to write properly of such monstrous . . . cruelty"** — Ibid.

270 **A sympathetic Robert Capa found her in tears** — Richard Whelan, *Robert Capa* (New York: Alfred A. Knopf, 1985), p. 228.

270 **"Mary and I live at the Ritz"** — Mellow, *Hemingway*, p. 536.

271 **One night Marlene Dietrich met them for dinner** — Ibid., p. 540.

271 **"jerking, jumping, hair-in-eyes GIs"** — Carson (INS), "Paris Jitterbugs Stomp in Open After 4 Years in Secret Groove," *New York Journal-American*, September 21, 1944.

24. Crossing the Siegfried Line

273 **Her visit, scheduled for three days** — Kenney, "She Got to Berlin," p. 467.

273 **how the Eighty-second . . . dropped . . . onto the Dutch countryside** — Gellhorn, "Rough and Tumble," *Collier's*, December 2, 1944.

274 **Nijmegen . . . was the subject** — Gellhorn, "Death of a Dutch Town," *Collier's*, December 23, 1944; reprinted as "A Little Dutch Town" in *The Face of War*.

274 **"The battles had been recent ones"** — Avery, "Marjorie Avery Stands on German Soil," *Detroit Free Press*, October 3, 1944.

275 **"There was about it constant beauty"** — Coyne, "Miss Coyne Finds Luftwaffe No Myth, in Rhine Bridge Blow," *Boston Herald*, October 4, 1944.

276 **Iris had begun to fear the war would be over** — Carpenter, *No Woman's World*, p. 130.

277 **"the wolf in correspondent's clothing"** — Carson, "I Love My Fellow Correspondents — but," *Cosmopolitan*, January 1945.

277 **Janet Flanner returned to Paris** — Wineapple, *Genêt*, pp. 183–186.

278 **"Paris is still a mass of uncoordinated individuals"** — Flanner, "Letter from Paris," *New Yorker*, December 15, 1944; reprinted in *Paris Journal 1944–1965*, p. 3.

279 **arrived . . . to cover its surrender** — Carpenter, *No Woman's World*, pp. 170–174.

279 **"The American 100th Division is cleaning the Germans out"** — Tomara, "Strasbourg Hit By Artillery on Banks of Rhine," *New York Herald Tribune*, November 27, 1944.

280 **That afternoon Sonia . . . went forty miles by jeep to Struthof** — Tomara, "Nazis Cremated 1,665 Women at Camp in Alsace," *New York Herald Tribune*, December 10, 1944.

281 **Avery and Coyne were visiting an area of "static warfare"** — Avery, "Reporter Dines in German Pillbox," *Detroit Free Press*, November 26, 1944.

281 **Back on the Luxembourg side** — Coyne, "Miss Coyne Dines on Venison at Brilliant Front Line Party," *Boston Herald*, November 25, 1944.

25. The Battle of the Bulge

283 **SHAEF . . . granted Lee Carson and Iris Carpenter full accreditation** — Carpenter, *No Woman's World*, p. 189.

283 **"They can go wherever their reporter's conscience drives them"** — Ibid., p. 190.

283 **they began by disliking each other intensely** — Carpenter, interview.

284 **About ten o'clock one night** — Carpenter, *No Woman's World*, pp. 196–197.

285 **"The Germans have broken through"** — Ibid., pp. 207–208.

285 **"Retreat in the face of Germany's . . . counteroffensive"** — Carson, "Yanks Vow They'll Avenge Retreat," *New York Journal-American*, December 18, 1944.

286 **Iris . . . set out for Fifth Corps headquarters** — Carpenter, *No Woman's World*, pp. 210–212.

287 **"A field artillery battery"** — Carson (INS), "GI-Clad Nazis Led Drive in Jeeps," *New York Journal-American*, December 20, 1944.

287 **"We were very much a family"** — Carpenter, interview.

287 **"I've got a wife and a couple of kids"** — Carpenter, *No Woman's World*, pp. 218–219.

288 **"I spent Christmas Eve on the line"** — J. C. Oestreicher, *The World Is Their Beat*, pp. 221–222.

288 **"The convoys were huge, fantastic"** — Coyne, "Holly in Helmets, GIs Rumble to Battle Cheering Belgians," *Boston Herald*, December 24, 1944.

289 **"How we got here and what we saw"** — Avery, "Bastogne Desolate After Liberation," *Detroit Free Press*, December 30, 1944.

290 **She wrote to her editor at *Collier's* of her exhaustion** — Amy Porter, "This Week's Work," *Collier's*, February 3, 1945.

290 **She and a colleague took the road . . . to Bastogne** — Gellhorn, "The Battle of the Bulge," in *The Face of War*, pp. 145–152.

291 **it was so cold "that water brought us for washing froze"** — Carpenter, *No Woman's World*, pp. 224–226.

292 **First Army headquarters and press camp returned to Spa** — Ibid., p. 233.

26. Penetrating the Pacific Barriers

294 **"Our presence in various fields is bitterly resented"** — Deuell, *Cleveland Plain Dealer*, October 3, 1944.

294 **"an eighteen-hour-a-day job"** — "A Letter From the Publisher," *Time*, November 27, 1944.

295 **"I can't do a damn thing about her"** — Rand, *China Hands*, pp. 231–232.

295 **"All our old idealistic friends from 1941"** — MacKinnon and Friesen, *China Reporting*, p. 51.

296 **"an honest Christian, beloved by his people"** — Annalee Jacoby Fadiman to the author, October 27, 1992.

297 **on that first day of February 1945** — C. Mydans, *More Than Meets the Eye*, pp. 182–191.

297 **Shelley . . . was full of optimism about the progress of the war** — Ibid., pp. 206–207.

299 **"From the shadow of the litters I could see their eyes"** — S. Mydans, "Flight Nurse," *Life*, February 12, 1945.

299 **At last MacArthur lifted the ban** — C. Mydans, *More Than Meets the Eye*, p. 208.

27. Iwo Jima

301 Biographical material on Patricia Lochridge is taken from an interview by her son Steve Bull, May 1995.

302 **"Playing tennis with the Nimitzes was not my idea of activity for a forward area"** — Lochridge, interview.

304 **They were authorized to go to "Guam, Saipan ..."** — Smith and Bogart, *The Wars of Peggy Hull*, p. 245.

304 **Pat Lochridge arrived on a cold gray morning** — Lochridge, "Solace at Iwo," *Woman's Home Companion*, May 1945.

305 **"The wounded came on and on"** — Ibid.

306 **In the press office on Guam** — Dickey Chapelle, *What's A Woman Doing Here?*, pp. 67–68.

306 Biographical material on Dickey Chapelle comes from her autobiography, *What's A Woman Doing Here?*; Roberta Ostroff, *Fire in the Wind*; and assorted material in the Dickey Chapelle Collection, State Historical Society of Wisconsin.

307 **"I want you to be sure you'll be the first"** — Ostroff, *Fire in the Wind*, p. 88.

308 **"Only once was it still"** — Lochridge, "Solace at Iwo."

308 **"Some live and you don't know why"** — Ibid.

309 **"It is the time of the full moon"** — Deuell, "The Wounded Return," *Cleveland Plain Dealer*, April 4, 1945.

309 **"Gray blankets cover the quiet figures"** — Ibid.

310 **Dickey Chapelle's experience on the *Samaritan*** — Chapelle, *What's a Woman Doing Here?*, chapters 4 and 5.

311 **Back in the big tent on Guam** — Ibid., chapter 6; Ostroff, *Fire in the Wind*, pp. 104–105.

311 **Chapelle's C-47 reached Iwo** — Dickey's escapade on Iwo is taken from *What's a Woman Doing Here?*, chapter 6.

312 **"Now you just tell me"** — Ostroff, *Fire in the Wind*, pp. 105–107.

28. Of Rain, Ruin, Relationships, and the Bridge at Remagen

314 **When Lee Miller went ... to see Colette** — Miller, "Colette," *Vogue*, March 1, 1945.

314 **"Parisians are colder than they have been"** — Flanner, "Letter from Paris," *New Yorker*, January 17, 1945.

315   Biographical material on Ann Stringer is taken from Julia Edwards, *Women of the World*, pp. 165–167.

315   **"butter-melting eyes"** — Oldfield, *Never a Shot in Anger*, p. 189.

316   **her timing too close for the officers at SHAEF** — Ibid., pp. 189–191.

317   **Flanner was glad to be out of Paris** — Wineapple, *Genêt*, pp. 188–189.

317   **Miller remembered climbing onto some wreckage** — Penrose, *Lee Miller's War*, p. 169.

318   **"Aachen died in a different way"** — Flanner, "Letter from Cologne," *New Yorker*, March 19, 1945; reprinted in *Janet Flanner's World*, p. 92.

318   **One did not see a whole building anywhere** — Coyne, "Old Glory Defies Hun Shells High Above Cologne Rubble," *Boston Herald*, March 11, 1945.

318   **On Sunday she watched with amazement** — Coyne, "Cologne's Hymn of 'Nazi Hate' Has No Fear of Yank Rulers," *Boston Herald*, March 14, 1945.

318   **Avery was surprised by the plenitude of items** — Avery, "Cologne Germans Eat Plenty and Dress Well," *Detroit Free Press*, March 18, 1945.

318   **the living had to be sorted from the dead** — Avery, "Murderers Roam City of Cologne," *Detroit Free Press*, March 19, 1945.

319   **"They came out into the sunlight"** — Avery, "Freed Prisoners Still Have Hope," *Detroit Free Press*, March 20, 1945.

319   **"a thin young Belgian . . . praying over a mound"** — Flanner, "Letter from Cologne."

319   **"This went on in a great German city"** — Penrose, *Lee Miller's War*, p. 166.

319   **it was gauged to be only ten percent damaged** — Coyne, "Three-Fourths of Fine Arts of Ancient Cologne in Rubble," *Boston Herald*, March 18, 1945.

319   **"Cologne's panorama of ruin"** — Flanner, "Letter from Cologne."

319   Biographical material on Marguerite Higgins is taken from Antoinette May, *Witness to War*.

321   **Helen Kirkpatrick recalled** — Kirkpatrick, interview.

322   **After Lee Carson went to Europe** — Lochridge, interview.

322   **Iris Carpenter traveled with two British correspondents** — Carpenter, interview.

322   **Lee Carson began sharing a jeep** — Walton, interview.

322   **"Lee was quite frank about it"** — Carpenter, interview.

323 **One day Stringer and Jackson drove** — Allan Jackson, "Ann Stringer, Memories of a Lady War Correspondent" (unpublished).

324 **"I wanted above all to be free"** — Bernice Kert, *The Hemingway Women*, p. 417.

324 **"He came in with his raincoat and his gun belt"** — Coyne, interview.

324 **"the hard-bitten, horny-handed tankers"** — Irwin, "4th Armored Yanks Bluffed Way Through 6 Nazi Divisions," *Saint Louis Post-Dispatch*, March 12, 1945.

325 **But as Iris Carpenter told the story** — her account of the Remagen episode is found in *No Woman's World*, pp. 271–277.

328 **"German armed forces on both . . . banks of the Rhine"** — Carson (INS), "Crossing Threw Nazis into Chaos," *New York Journal-American*, March 9, 1945.

328 **"We gazed confidently at the planes"** — Carson (INS), "Bridgehead Becomes Hot Shooting Gallery," *New York Journal-American*, March 11, 1945.

328 **"One minute he was there, alive"** — Carpenter, interview.

328 **her account of crossing the bridge** — Stringer (UP), "Nazis Hurling 'Everything' But Yanks Are Unstoppable," *Detroit Free Press*, March 11, 1945.

329 **"Nothing has cheered the men like this"** — Avery, "Bridgehead Yanks Are Confident," *Detroit Free Press*, March 15, 1945.

29. The Month of April: The Advance

331 **"Never let that woman out of your sight"** — Bourke-White, *"Dear Fatherland, Rest Quietly,"* p. 38.

331 **Helen reported that fierce fires were still burning** — Kirkpatrick, "Frankfurt in Chaos," *Chicago Daily News*, April 2, 1945.

331 **Also in Frankfurt were some 20,000 "emancipated slaves"** — Kirkpatrick, "Slave Hordes Streaming to Rhine," *Chicago Daily News*, April 4, 1945.

331 **a Frankfurt where roofs were a rarity** — Higgins, "Key Frankfurt Arms Factories Found Wrecked," *New York Herald Tribune*, April 1, 1945.

331 **In Hoechst she interviewed** — Higgins, "Youth Leader Is Indignant at Arrest by U.S.," *New York Herald Tribune*, April 17, 1945.

331 **she reported a jet fighter factory** — Higgins, "Jet-Plane Plant Cut by Nazis in Mountainside," *New York Herald Tribune*, April 19, 1945.

331 **below the Franconian castle of Lichtenfels** — Higgins, "Americans Find Nazi Archives in Castle Vault," *New York Herald Tribune*, April 24, 1945.

332 **It rankled her and Eleanor** — Lochridge, interview.

332 **It seemed to Margaret "that people had always lived in the crevasses"** — Bourke-White, *"Dear Fatherland,"* p. 44.

332 **"Death rained down yesterday"** — Kirkpatrick, "'Ragdoll' Dead Litter Streets of Nazi City," *Chicago Daily News*, April 13, 1945.

333 **"They'd heard it from the Stars and Stripes network"** — Kirkpatrick, interview.

333 **Avery talked to a trainload of . . . soldiers** — Avery, *Detroit Free Press*, April 14, 1945.

333 **Coyne talked with black soldiers from a mortar section** — Coyne, *Boston Herald*, April 15, 1945.

333 **At the Scribe in Paris** — Cowan, AP dispatch, April 13, 1945.

334 **Pat Lochridge . . . had known the Roosevelts in Washington** — Lochridge, interview.

334 **"the sorrow the French felt at losing Roosevelt"** — Flanner, "Letter from Paris," *New Yorker*, April 19, 1945; reprinted in *Paris Journal 1944–1965*, pp. 23–24.

334 **"We all wondered when the war would end"** — Bourke-White, *"Dear Fatherland,"* pp. 47–48.

335 **"it was Helen Kirkpatrick who read the maps"** — Ibid., pp. 48–49.

335 **"after our driver had steeplechased a ditch"** — Coyne, interview.

336 **what remained of the house of a bazooka factory director** — Carson, "Leipzig Tycoon Dines 100, Blows Them to Pieces," *New York Journal-American*, April 19, 1945.

336 **"Reclining on the ponderous leather furniture"** — Bourke-White, *"Dear Fatherland,"* pp. 49–51.

337 **the family of the burgomaster** — Carpenter, *No Woman's World*, p. 311.

337 **Virginia Irwin found it difficult to write** — Irwin, "Nazis Starved, Beat, Killed Prisoners on Long March," *Saint Louis Post-Dispatch*, April 6, 1945.

337 **"We ate snow when the Germans weren't looking"** — Ibid.

338 **Helen Kirkpatrick too talked to Allied prisoners of war** — Kirkpatrick, "Yanks Made to Build Nazi Ambush," *Chicago Daily News*, April 11, 1945.

338 **Lee Miller reported** — Penrose, *Lee Miller's War*, p. 178.

338 **Catherine Coyne watched liberated French and British soldiers** — Coyne, "War Slaves Start on Long Road Back," *Boston Herald*, April 12, 1945.

338 **One Sunday Janet Flanner went to a Paris train station** — Flanner, "Letter from Paris," *New Yorker*, April 19, 1945; reprinted in *Paris Journal 1944–1965*, pp. 25–26.

339 **Her broadcasts were more personal** — Wineapple, *Genêt*, pp. 190–191.

339 **She had left a Germany of prideful Nazis** — Schultz, "The 'Little People' of Germany," *McCall's*, June 1945.

339 **"No one is a Nazi"** — Gellhorn, "We Were Never Nazis," *Collier's*, May 26, 1945.

340 **"Men, women and children wept"** — Carson, "Nazis Frantically Seek Yank Lines," *New York Journal-American*, April 26, 1945.

341 **They sat there for days, Iris wrote** — Carpenter, *No Woman's World*, p. 319.

341 **"Mission accomplished"** — Carson, "Yank Met Russ on Elbe River," *New York Journal-American*, April 27, 1945.

341 **Robertson later told the story** — Carpenter, *No Woman's World*, pp. 322–323.

341 **the four Americans located a boat** — Carson, "Yank Met Russ on Elbe River."

342 **"Down the street of Torgau came a Russian youth"** — Stringer (UP), "Reds Swim Elbe, Hail 'Americanskis'," *New York World Telegram*, April 27, 1945.

344 **Lee Carson described "carnival scenes"** — Carson, "Yank Met Russ on Elbe River."

344 **the Yanks were at the river bank** — Coyne, "Russians 'Dance Feet Off' Miss Coyne in Link-up Fete," *Boston Herald*, April 27, 1945.

344 **Dot Avery compared the day** — Avery, "Yanks, Reds Dance," *Detroit Free Press*, April 28, 1945.

345 **the mile or so of road** — Carpenter, *No Woman's World*, p. 325.

345 **"At first I thought etiquette would compel me"** — Avery, "Marjorie Avery Makes History with a Dance," *Detroit Free Press*, May 20, 1945.

345 **"It was a day of laughter"** — Coyne, "Russians 'Dance Feet Off' Miss Coyne."

30. The Month of April: The Camps

347   **not including the 6,000** — This figure varies: Helen Kirkpatrick's report put it at 15,000.

348   **In fact, she had a private mission** — Schultz, Green interviews.

348   **Determined not to be handed . . . an "atrocity line"** — May, *Witness to War*, pp. 82–83.

349   **General Patton was so angry** — Bourke-White, *"Dear Fatherland,"* p. 74.

349   *she* **didn't see anyone faint** — Schultz, notes in the Sigrid Schultz Papers.

349   **a few put their hands over their eyes** — Higgins, "Army Forces Weimar Citizens to View Buchenwald's Horrors," *New York Herald Tribune*, April 18, 1945.

349   **Marguerite Higgins gave an exhaustive accounting** — Ibid.

349   **also reported the memorial service** — Higgins, "The 51,000 Dead of Buchenwald Honored by the 20,000 Living," *New York Herald Tribune*, April 21, 1945.

350   **Twelve days after the camp's liberation** — Kirkpatrick, "3,000 Skeletons Come Slowly Back to Life," *Chicago Daily News*, April 24, 1945.

350   **Helen ran across a German Jew** — Kirkpatrick, interview.

350   **Janet Flanner waited almost three weeks** — Flanner, letter to Solita Solano, April 16, 1945, in Wineapple, *Genêt*, p. 192.

350   **At Lager Dora . . . starving men and women** — Carpenter, *No Woman's World*, pp. 293–295.

351   **Ann Stringer also went to Nordhausen** — Stringer (UP), "10,000 Dead and Dying in Nazi Horror Plant," *New York World Telegram*, April 14, 1945.

351   **"The spring wind ruffled a white flag"** — Carson (INS), "Nazi Massacre of War Slaves," *New York Journal-American*, April 23, 1945.

351   **The work camp was not their planned destination** — Bourke-White, *"Dear Fatherland,"* p. 76.

351   **Walton recalled walking about . . . sobbing** — Walton, interview.

353   **At Landsberg** — E. Packard (UP), "Germans View Victims' Bodies, Voice Sorrow," *New York World Telegram*, April 30, 1945.

353   **a visit . . . to Hitler's great "abortion camp"** — Irwin, "Nazis Killed Slave

Women, Babies in 'Murder-Before-Birth' Camp," *Saint Louis Post-Dispatch*, April 15, 1945.

354 **Janet Flanner did not go to Ravensbrück** — Flanner, "Letter from Paris," *New Yorker*, April 25, 1945.

356 **Marguerite Higgins's dream of journalistic triumph** — May, *Witness to War*, pp. 87–91; Higgins, "Finale in the West," *Mademoiselle*, July 1945.

357 **"There was not a soul in the yard"** — Higgins, "33,000 Dachau Captives Freed by 7th Army," *New York Herald Tribune*, May 1, 1945.

358 **recalled the boxcars** — Lochridge, "Are Germans Human?" *Woman's Home Companion*, July 1945.

359 **Lee Miller hooted at the idea** — Penrose, *Lee Miller's War*, p. 182.

360 **By the time she got to Torgau** — Gellhorn, "The Russians' Invisible Wall," *Collier's*, June 30, 1945.

360 **This was true at Dachau, too** — Gellhorn, "Dachau: Experimental Murder," *Collier's*, June 23, 1945.

31. The Longed-for Day

362 **Lee Miller promptly moved in** — Penrose, *Lee Miller's War*, pp. 191–199.

365 **Carson and Whitehead had a little bad luck** — Carson interview by Dwight Bentel of *Editor & Publisher*, spring 1945; Oestreicher, *The World Is Their Beat*, pp. 225–227.

366 **Irwin's better luck** — Stories of her Berlin coup were delayed by censors, but appeared under banner headlines in the *Saint Louis Post-Dispatch* for May 8, 9, and 10, 1945.

368 **On the evening of the second day** — Kenney, "She Got to Berlin," pp. 473–474.

369 **Lee Miller and Dave Scherman drove like mad** — Penrose, *The Lives of Lee Miller*, p. 143.

369 **"The mountainside was a mess of craters"** — Penrose, *Lee Miller's War*, p. 200.

370 **"Stores of china, glassware, linen and silver"** — Higgins, "U.S. Flag Flies Over Ruins of Berchtesgaden," *New York Herald Tribune*, May 7, 1945.

370   **By the time Helen Kirkpatrick and Bill Walton arrived** — Walton, interview.

370   **Lael Wertenbaker of *Time-Life* knew** — Wertenbaker, interview.

371   **"A general who had been assigned as the Poohbah"** — Kirkpatrick, interview.

371   **Years later it was reliably reported** — Robert Murphy, *Diplomat Among Warriors* (Garden City: Doubleday, 1964), pp. 240–241.

372   **during the ceremony Eisenhower sat** — Avery, " 'Ike' Reads a Cowboy Story as Enemy Capitulates," *Detroit Free Press*, May 9, 1945.

372   **"Those who saw him said"** — Coyne, "His Feet on Desk, 'Ike' Reads 'Westerns' as Germans Sign," *Boston Herald*, May 9, 1945.

373   **photographing . . . Bremerhaven from a Piper Cub** — Bourke-White, *"Dear Fatherland,"* pp. 55–60.

373   **Lee Miller and Dave Scherman were at the press camp** — Penrose, *The Lives of Lee Miller*, p. 144.

373   **"At exactly one minute after midnight"** — Higgins, "Finale in the West," *Mademoiselle*, July 1945.

373   **"We sat in the press camp"** — Carpenter, *No Woman's World*, pp. 330–332.

374   **"In Paris the war ended the way it began"** — Flanner, "Letter from Paris," *New Yorker*, May 11, 1945; reprinted in *Paris Journal 1944–1965*, pp. 26–27.

376   **Ann Stringer too was in Paris** — telephone interview of Allan Jackson by author, July 15, 1994.

32. "It Is Not Over, Over Here"

377   **Peggy Hull Deuell heard the news** — Deuell, "V-E Day No Fiesta," *Cleveland Plain Dealer*, May 21, 1945.

377   **Dickey . . . managed to go ashore on still-unsecured Okinawa** — Notes labeled "4–5 April 1945, Okinawa Harbor," Dickey Chapelle Collection; Chapelle, *What's A Woman Doing Here?*, pp. 97–127; Ostroff, *Fire in the Wind*, pp. 108–125.

378   **John Lardner . . . set down his impressions** — Lardner, radio dispatch to NANA, April 6, 1945.

380 **Shelley Mydans met up with some [Japanese] on Guam** — S. Mydans, "Guam Holdouts Give Up," July 2, 1945.

380 **"Now he stood in the clearing"** — Ibid.

33. Women Winding Up a War

382 **to Prague the day after V-E Day** — Carpenter, *No Woman's World*, pp. 333–338.

383 **on hand to report the surrender** — E. Packard (UP), "Goering Held by 7th Army," *New York World-Telegram*, May 9, 1945.

383 **Patricia Lochridge's version** — Lochridge, interview.

383 **fabulous art treasures** — Higgins, "2,000,000,000 Art Loot Seized in Nazi Caches," and "$500,000,000 in Art Captured at Goering Villa," *New York Herald Tribune*, May 14 and 21, 1945.

383 *Life* **sent Margaret Bourke-White to Essen** — Bourke-White, "The Krupps," *Life*, August 27, 1945.

383 **Marjorie "Dot" Avery and Catherine Coyne flew to liberated Norway** — Avery, "Nazi Army in Norway Still Carrying Arms," *Detroit Free Press*, May 22, 1945; Coyne, "Norse 'Forgive' Nazi Soldiers Who Still Keep Guns, Live Well," *Boston Herald*, May 19, 1945.

383 **"the people almost tore themselves apart"** — Avery, "Norse Hail Freedom in Big Parade," *Detroit Free Press*, May 21, 1945.

383 **Ann Stringer went in with the first convoy** — Jackson, "Ann Stringer, Memories"; Edwards, *Women of the World*, pp. 172–173.

384 **Lee Miller sought out and interviewed . . . Nijinsky** — Penrose, *The Lives of Lee Miller*, p. 154.

384 **In England, where British *Vogue* hailed her return** — Ibid., pp. 146–147.

384 **Much of her reporting that summer** — Higgins, "Voices of the Defeated," *Mademoiselle*, August 1945; May, *Witness to War*, pp. 93–101.

385 **Ray Daniell and Tania Long arrived** — Long, "This Is Berlin — Without Hitler," *New York Times Magazine*, July 22, 1945; interview.

385 **Helen . . . spent much of July and August** — Kirkpatrick, "Petain's Supporters Decry Reynaud Attack," *Chicago Daily News*, July 25, 1945.

386   **the trial . . . tarnished everyone** — Flanner, "Letter from Paris," *New Yorker,* July 26, 1945; reprinted in *Paris Journal 1944–1965,* pp. 31–35.

386   **Lael Wertenbaker, now noticeably pregnant** — Wertenbaker, interview.

386   **Sonia Tomara, confined to the U.S. General Hospital** — Tomara, unpublished memoir.

386   **an exhausted Ruth Cowan** — Cowan to "Ed" (probably Edward Kennedy of the AP), April 25, 1945, Schlesinger Library, Radcliffe College.

387   **Virginia Irwin, disaccredited** — Kenney, "She Got to Berlin," p. 476.

387   **Lee Carson managed to hitch an early plane** — Oestreicher, *The World Is Their Beat,* p. 225.

387   **Carpenter . . . planned to go to the Pacific theater** — Carpenter, interview.

387   **Martha Gellhorn flew from Scotland** — Gellhorn, "You're on Your Way Home," *Collier's,* September 22, 1945.

387   **"You think in small amazed snatches"** — Ibid.

389   **"For the war, the hated and perilous and mad"** — Ibid.

Epilogue

390   **What the women in these pages did** — except where indicated, biographical material included here comes from sources previously noted.

391   **"I've never wanted to do anything else"** — Mimi Mead, "Janet Flanner recalls joys of Paris lifetime," Women's News Service, December 26, 1971.

Selected Bibliography

Baker, Carlos. *Ernest Hemingway: A Life Story*. New York: Charles Scribner's Sons, 1969.

Belford, Barbara. *Brilliant Bylines: A Biographical Anthology of Notable Newspaperwomen in America*. New York: Columbia University Press, 1986.

Bourke-White, Margaret. *"Dear Fatherland, Rest Quietly."* New York: Simon & Schuster, 1946.

———. *Portrait of Myself*. New York: Simon & Schuster, 1963.

———. *Shooting the Russian War*. New York: Simon & Schuster, 1942.

———. *They Called It "Purple Heart Valley."* New York: Simon & Schuster, 1944.

Calvocoressi, Peter, Guy Wint, and John Pritchard. *Total War*. Revised edition. New York: Pantheon, 1989.

Carpenter, Iris. *No Woman's World*. Boston: Houghton Mifflin, 1946.

Chapelle, Dickey. *What's a Woman Doing Here?* New York: William Morrow, 1961.

———. Unpublished papers, State Historical Society of Wisconsin, Madison.

Cowles, Virginia. *Looking for Trouble*. New York: Harper & Brothers, 1941.

Daniell, Raymond. *Civilians Must Fight*. New York: Doubleday, Doran, 1941.

Davis, Frances. *My Shadow in the Sun*. New York: Carrick & Evans, 1940.

Edwards, Julia. *Women of the World: The Great Foreign Correspondents*. Boston: Houghton Mifflin, 1988.

Flanner, Janet. *Janet Flanner's World: Uncollected Writings 1932–1975*, edited by Irving Drutman. New York: Harcourt Brace Jovanovich, 1979.

———. *Paris Journal 1944–1965*, edited by William Shawn. New York: Atheneum, 1965.

———. *Paris Was Yesterday 1925–1939*, edited by Irving Drutman. New York: Viking Press, 1972.

Gellhorn, Martha. *The Face of War*. New York: Atlantic Monthly Press, 1988.

———. *A Stricken Field*. New York: Charles Scribner's Sons, 1940.

———. *Travels with Myself and Another*. New York: Dodd, Mead, 1978.

———. *The View from the Ground*. New York: Atlantic Monthly Press, 1988.

Goldberg, Vicki. *Margaret Bourke-White*. New York: Harper & Row, 1986.

Goodwin, Doris Kearns. *No Ordinary Time*. New York: Simon & Schuster, 1994.

Hahn, Emily. *China to Me: A Partial Autobiography*. Philadelphia: Blakiston, 1944.

Hemingway, Mary Welsh. *How It Was*. New York: Alfred A. Knopf, 1976.

Higgins, Marguerite. *News Is a Singular Thing*. Garden City: Doubleday, 1955.

Hohenberg, John. *Foreign Correspondence: The Great Reporters and Their Times*. New York: Columbia University Press, 1964.

Hosley, David H. and Gayle K. Yamada. *Hard News: Women in Broadcast Journalism*. New York: Greenwood Press, 1982.

Keegan, John. *The Second World War*. New York: Viking Penguin, 1989.

Kenney, Anne R. "'She Got to Berlin': Virginia Irwin, *St. Louis Post Dispatch* War Correspondent." *Missouri Historical Review*, Vol. LXXIX, No. 4, July 1985.

Kert, Bernice. *The Hemingway Women*. New York, W. W. Norton, 1983.

Kirkpatrick, Helen. *Under the British Umbrella*. New York: Charles Scribner's Sons, 1939.

———. *See* Milbank, Helen Kirkpatrick.

Kurth, Peter. *American Cassandra: The Life of Dorothy Thompson*. Boston: Little, Brown, 1990.

Langer, Elinor. *Josephine Herbst*. Boston: Little, Brown, 1983.

Lee, Clark. *They Call It Pacific*. New York: Viking Press, 1943.

Lynn, Kenneth S. *Hemingway*. New York: Simon & Schuster, 1987.

MacKinnon, Stephen R. and Oris Friesen. *China Reporting*. Berkeley: University of California Press, 1987.

Marzolf, Marion. *Up From the Footnote: A History of Women Journalists*. New York: Hastings House, 1977.

May, Antoinette. *Witness to War: A Biography of Marguerite Higgins*. New York: Beaufort Books, 1983.

Mellow, James R. *Hemingway: A Life Without Consequences*. New York: Addison Wesley, 1992.

Messenger, Charles. *The Chronological Atlas of World War Two*. New York: Macmillan, 1989.

Milbank, Helen Kirkpatrick. Interview by Anne S. Kasper, April 1990. Women in Journalism Oral History Project of the Washington Press Club Foundation.

Moats, Alice-Leone. *Blind Date With Mars*. Garden City: Doubleday, Doran, 1943.

Mydans, Carl. *More Than Meets the Eye*. New York: Harper & Brothers, 1959.

Mydans, Shelley Smith. *The Open City*. Garden City: Doubleday, Doran, 1945.

Oestreicher, J. C. *The World Is Their Beat*. New York: Duell, Sloan & Pearce, 1945.

Oldfield, Colonel Barney. *Never a Shot in Anger*. Santa Barbara: Capra Press, 1956.

Ostroff, Roberta. *Fire in the Wind: The Life of Dickey Chapelle*. New York: Ballantine Books, 1992.

Packard, Reynolds and Eleanor. *Balcony Empire*. New York: Oxford, 1942.

Penrose, Antony. *The Lives of Lee Miller*. New York: Holt, Rinehart & Winston, 1985.

Penrose, Antony, editor. *Lee Miller's War*. Boston: Little, Brown, 1992.

Rand, Peter. *China Hands*. New York: Simon & Schuster, 1995.

Reynolds, David. *Rich Relations: The American Occupation of Britain, 1942–1945*. New York: Random House, 1995.

Rollyson, Carl. *Nothing Ever Happens to the Brave: The Story of Martha Gellhorn*. New York: St. Martin's Press, 1990.

Sanders, Marion K. *Dorothy Thompson: A Legend in Her Time*. Boston: Houghton Mifflin, 1973.

Schultz, Sigrid. Interview by Harold Hutchings for *Chicago Tribune*, April 5–6, 1977. Sigrid Schultz Papers, State Historical Society of Wisconsin, Madison.

———. Interview by Alan Green, February 12, 1971. Sigrid Schultz Papers, State Historical Society of Wisconsin, Madison.

Shirer, William. *Berlin Diary*. New York: Alfred A. Knopf, 1941.

———. *The Rise and Fall of the Third Reich*. New York: Simon & Schuster, 1960.

———. *Twentieth Century Journey: The Nightmare Years, 1930–1940*. Boston: Little, Brown, 1984.

Sicherman, Barbara and Carol Hurd Green, *Notable American Women: The Modern Period*. Cambridge: Belknap Press (Harvard), 1980.

Smith, Wilda M. and Eleanor A. Bogart. *The Wars of Peggy Hull: The Life and Times of a War Correspondent*. El Paso: Texas Western Press, 1991.

Voss, Frederick S. *Reporting the War: The Journalistic Coverage of World War II*. Washington: Smithsonian Institution Press, 1994.

Wason, Elizabeth. *Miracle in Hellas*. New York: Macmillan, 1943.

Welsh, Mary. *See* Hemingway, Mary Welsh.

White, Theodore H. and Annalee Jacoby. *Thunder out of China*. New York: William Sloane, 1946.

Wineapple, Brenda. *Genêt: A Biography of Janet Flanner*. New York, Ticknor & Fields, 1989.

Index

Aachen, 276–77, 317–18
Abraham Lincoln Brigade, 38, 39
accreditation, 176, 178, 212–13,
    283–84, 296–97, 301, 303–4
Acheson, Dean, 392
Air Power Press Camp, 330, 347
Akers, Russell F., Jr., 284, 395
Albania, 63–64, 113
Albany Times Union, 22
Alfiero, Dino, 65
Algiers, 180, 182–84, 187–88,
    192–93, 208
Alsace, 279–80
American Expeditionary Force,
    171–73
American Friends of France, 72, 81
American Friends Service
    Committee, 397
American Red Cross, 1, 96, 212
Anderson, Margaret, 71–72
Anderson, Maxwell, 15, 37
Angly, Ed, 95
anti-Semitism, 17, 23, 47–48, 195,
    220
Ardennes, 284, 285
Army Air Transport Command, 298
arrests of reporters, 150–51, 163–65.
    See also internment

Associated Press (AP), 77, 181, 188,
    192, 386
Athenée Palace (Bucharest),
    78
Atkinson, J. Hampton, 177, 189,
    201
atomic bombs, on Japan, 381
Auden, W. H., 25
Aulock, Colonel von, 251,
    253
Auxiliary Territorial Service (ATS),
    128, 195
Avery, Marjorie "Dot": Bastogne,
    288–90; Cologne, 317–19; death
    of FDR, 333–34; Holland para-
    chute mission, 273–76; Leipzig,
    336–37; in liberated Paris, 261,
    267, 271; "London Diary," 216;
    Nijmegen, 274; Normandy inva-
    sion, 225–26, 228, 231–32;
    Norway after surrender, 383; and
    Patton, 324; post–D Day France,
    242–44; postwar adjustment,
    395–96; Remagen bridge, 328–29;
    Rheims surrender, 372–73;
    Russian-U.S. meeting in Torgau,
    342, 345; Siegfried Line, 281–
    82

Badoglio, Pietro, 28, 198
Bailey bridge incident, 202–3
Balkans, 112
Bard, Josef, 2, 4, 5, 127
Barden, Judy, 244, 261–62
Barnes, Ralph, 94, 95
Barnett, Lincoln, 184
Basilone, John, 308
Bastogne (Belgium), 288–91
Bataan, 155–58, 162, 297
Battle of Britain, 96, 98–105
Battle of the Bulge, 284–92
BBC, 78, 164, 214
Beaton, Cecil, 195
Beattie, Ed, 78
Beaverbrook, Lord, 83
Belden, Jack, 135, 136
Belgium, 79, 81
Beneš, Eduard, 55, 56
Benjamin, Anna, xv, 43, 59
Berchtesgaden, 369–70, 383
Berlin, 4–5, 127–28; Allied capture
    of, 365–69; post-surrender, 385;
    prewar, 16–18; at start of war,
    94–95; wartime, 109–12
Bernhard, Andrew, 395
Binder, Carroll, 76
biological warfare, Japanese, 108–9
Birmingham (England), 103
Blitz on London, 99–105
Blue Network, 339
Blum, Léon, 386
Bockhorst, John Arthur, 279
Bolshevism, 5, 59–60
Boni, Bill, 285, 287–88
Booker, Edna Lee, 131, 132
Boston Globe, 215, 283
Boston Herald, 216, 217
Boston Traveler, 307
Bourke-White, Margaret, 43–48,
    334; accreditation, 176, 178; B-17
    bombing mission, 176, 184,
    189–91; Bailey bridge, 202–3;

Bavaria, 332–33; Buchenwald,
    349; Czechoslovakia, 47–48;
    "Dear Fatherland, Rest Quietly,"
    241; Erla work camp, 351–53; and
    Erskine Caldwell, 46, 47, 72–73,
    176; *Fortune* magazine, 45;
    Frankfurt, 330–31; German attack
    on USSR, 117–24; German sur-
    render, 373; Italy, 200–203,
    205–7, 240; and J. Hampton
    Atkinson, 189; Krupp interview,
    383; Leipzig, 336–37; *Life* assign-
    ments, 47, 73–74, 176, 184–87,
    391–92; and Luce, 45–46; North
    Africa, 183–87, 189–91; *North of
    the Danube*, 48; and Papurt,
    201–2, 206, 240–41; *Purple Heart
    Valley*, 201, 206; *Shooting the
    Russian War*, 122; Stalin pho-
    tographs, 120–21; violations of
    army regulations, 200–201;
    "Women in Lifeboats" *(Life)*,
    184–87; *You Have Seen Their Faces*,
    46
Boussard, Henri, 257
Bracker, Milton, 314
Bradley, Omar, 219, 326
Braun, Eva, 362–63, 364, 365
Brewer, Sam, 77, 78
Brines, Russell, 154, 155
British Expeditionary Force, 83
Brooklyn Daily Eagle, 113
Bruce, David, 96
Buchenwald concentration camp,
    347–50
Burdette, Winston, 76, 112–13
buzz bombs (V-1s), 232–33, 250,
    350

Caen (France), 234
Caldwell, Erskine, 48, 184; and
    Bourke-White, 46, 47, 72–73,
    176; *North of the Danube*, 48;

Russia, 117–19, 121–24; *You Have Seen Their Faces*, 46
Camp Kilmer (New Jersey), 183
Capa, Robert, 255, 257, 270
Cardozo, Major, 29, 31
Carpathian Lancers, 237
Carpenter, Iris, 214, 215, 216, 242, 323; Aachen, 276–77; accreditation, 283–84; Battle of the Bulge, 285–88, 291–92; court-martial of, 234; de Gaulle speech, 253–54; German surrender, 373–74; hospitals, post–D Day, 248; Huertgen Forest, 284; Lager Dora camp, 350–51; Leipzig, 336–37; in liberated Paris, 261; Metz surrender, 278–79; Mulde River press camp, 340–41; Normandy invasion, 222–23, 227, 231, 234; *No Woman's World*, 395; post–D Day France, 248; post-surrender, 382, 387; postwar adjustment, 395; Remagen, 325–28; Russian-U.S. meeting in Torgau, 342, 345; views on wartime sex, 322–23
Carson, Lee, 213–14, 242, 323, 326, 365–66, 374; Aachen, 276–77; accreditation, 283–84; Battle of the Bulge, 285–88, 291–92; Erla work camp, 351–53; Leipzig, 336–37; in liberated Paris, 258, 271; Mulde River press camp, 340–41; Normandy invasion, 229; post-surrender, 387; postwar adjustment, 395; Rhine crossing, 327–28; Russian-U.S. meeting in Torgau, 342, 345; views on wartime sex, 322–23
Carter, Ernestine, *Grim Glory: Pictures of Britain Under Fire*, 195
Cassidy, Henry, 119
Cassino (Italy), 209–10
Catholic Church, 77

CBS, 74–76, 110, 112, 113, 114, 116, 301
censorship, 16, 31–32, 42, 53, 101, 112, 114, 115, 146, 154, 156, 206–7, 219, 242, 253, 283, 284, 296, 303, 368–69
Chamberlain, Neville, 52, 53, 54, 55–56, 59, 68, 76, 104
Chambers, Whittaker, 296
Channel crossing, 243–44
Chapelle, Dickey (Georgette Louise Meyer), 306–8; Iwo Jima, 310–13; Okinawa, 377–80; postwar adjustment, 397
Chapelle, Tony, 307
Cherbourg (France), 234
Chiang Kai-shek, 132, 134, 135, 143, 296
Chiang Kai-shek (Madame), 142–43, 296
Chicago Daily News, 28, 32, 58, 65, 76, 83, 129, 172–73, 204, 211, 219, 225, 261, 271, 392
Chicago Daily Times, 214
Chicago Tribune, 4, 7–8, 20–21, 29, 52, 58, 64–65, 77, 78, 110, 339, 348
China, 27, 131–46, 159–69, 196–98, 294–96
China-Burma-India theater (CBI), 179, 196, 294–95
China National Aviation Company, 133
China Press, 131
Choltitz, Dietrich von, 256
Chou En-lai, 131, 135, 143–44
Chungking (China), 134–36, 146, 196, 295–96
Churchill, Winston, 76, 89, 97, 104, 118, 127, 149, 381
Ciano, Count, 65, 77
Clark, William, 391
Clark Field (Manila), 151, 154

Cleveland Plain Dealer, 294

Cocteau, Jean, 271; *Blood of a Poet* (film), 194

Codreanu, Corneliu, 74

Colette (camp survivor), 354–56

Colette (writer), 314

Collier, Crowell, 302

Collier's, 24, 36, 39–40, 49, 56, 137–40, 207, 219, 229–31, 273–74, 290, 302, 339, 360–61

Collins, General, 350–51

Cologne, 317–19

Communism, 40, 117

Company A Infantry, First Army Armored Division, 326

concentration camps, 17, 20, 280–81, 347–61

Corregidor, 157, 162

Cosmopolitan, 131, 379

Coventry (England), 103–4

Cowan, Ruth, 180–84; North Africa, 180, 182–83, 187–88, 192; death of FDR, 333–34; hospitals, post–D Day, 248; in liberated Paris, 263–64; Normandy invasion, 228–29, 234; post–D Day France, 248–49; post-surrender, 386; postwar adjustment, 393

Cowles, Virginia, 33–36, 58, 66–67, 82, 92, 239; Battle of Britain, 96–99; Czechoslovakia, 49; England, prewar, 49–50; France, 89, 90; Hitler's Nuremberg speech, 51–52; Italy, prewar, 65; Italy, wartime, 207–8; London Blitz, 100; Madrid, 34–38; Spain, 42; Mussolini interview, 33; Nationalist Nazi Party congress, 50–52; and Neville Chamberlain, 55–56; Order of the British Empire, 393; Paris, 86–87; postwar adjustment, 393–94; Prague,

54–56; Soviet indoctrination incident, 40–41; *Sunday Times* articles on Spain, 53

Coyne, Catherine, 28, 216–19, 267, 335; Bastogne, 288–90; Cologne, 317–19; death of FDR, 333–34; de Gaulle speech, 253–54; Gestapo activities, 268; Holland parachute mission, 273; in liberated Paris, 261, 264–66; London, V-1 rockets, 233; Nijmegen, 274–76; Normandy invasion, 226, 227–28; Norway after surrender, 383; and Patton, 324; post–D Day France, 242–44; postwar adjustment, 395, 396; prisoners of war, 338; Rheims surrender, 372–73; Russian-U.S. meeting in Torgau, 342, 345–46; Siegfried Line, 281–82; views on wartime sex, 322

Crawley, Aidan, 98, 394

Cronin, Ray, 155

Crost, Lyn, 315

Curtis syndicate, 2

Czechoslovakia, 47–57, 59, 72

Dachau, 356–61

Daily Express (London), 37, 62, 83, 214, 384

Daily Herald (London), 132, 215

Daily Mail (London), 29, 30–32, 69, 78, 83

Daily Mirror (London), 87

Daily News, 68

Daily Telegraph (London), 14, 52

Daniell, Raymond, 95–96, 112, 174–75, 262; in liberated Paris, 271; London Blitz, 102–3; postwar adjustment, 392–93; postwar Berlin, 385

Davis, Frances, 28–33, 40, 391

D Day, 224–34. *See also* Normandy invasion; Overlord

de Gaulle, Charles, 91, 254, 259–60, 338
del Drago, Prince and Princess, 65
DeLuce, Dan, 396
Denmark, 74–76, 370
Denny, Harold, 164
Detroit Free Press, 216, 225, 232
Detroit News, 159
Deuell, Harvey, 294
Deuell, Peggy Hull, xv–xvi, 132, 294, 303–4, 309–10, 377
Dew, Gwen, 159
"Dickson, John." *See* Schultz, Sigrid
Dietrich, Marlene, 271
displaced persons, 331, 340. *See also* refugees
Dixon, Jeanne, 187
Dlugoszowski, General, 65
Dönitz, Karl, 363–64, 370
Doolittle, Jimmy, 189
Dos Passos, John, 15, 25, 34, 39, 41
Dover (England), 96–97, 175
Duncan, Elspeth, 184, 186
Dunkirk, 82
Duranty, Walter, 78
Durdin, Tillman and Peggy, 135

Economist, 52
Egypt, 27
Eighth Army, British, 239
Eightieth Division, Third Army, 347
Eightieth Infantry, 332
Eighty-second Airborne, 273–74, 340
Eisenhower, Dwight D., 170, 180, 200, 219, 224, 250, 256, 285, 370–72
Eleventh Field Hospital, 205–6
Elliott, John, 29, 90
Emergency Relief Administration, 23
England: declaration of war, 68; German attack, 92–105; German

civilian sympathy for, 109–10; prewar, 49–50; support of Soviet Union, 118; U.S. mood toward, 1941, 175
Erla work camp, 351–53
espionage, alleged, 40–41, 236–37
Ethiopia, 27
European Theater of Operations, U.S. Army (ETOUSA), 170
Excelsior Hotel (Siena), 163–64
Express (London), 14

Fadiman, Clifton, 395
Fascism, 12, 42, 149. *See also* Nazi Party
feminist movement, 390, 398
Feversham, Lord, 49
Fifth Army, 200, 208, 235, 239
Fifth Corps, 286
Fifth General Hospital, 247
Fifty-eighth Guards Division of the Red Army, 344
Fifty-fifth Division, 362
Finch, Barbara, 303–4, 311, 312
First Army, 272, 276–77, 283, 284, 285–87, 291–92, 317, 323, 340, 374–75
First Battalion, First Army, 340–46
First British Airborne, 273–74
First Canadian Corps, 239
First Division, 225
Flanner, Janet (Genêt), 8–11, 71–72, 81–82, 314; Blue Network, 339; Buchenwald, 350; Cologne, 317–19; death of FDR, 334; female prisoners of war, 338–39; "Fuehrer," 10–11; Légion d'honneur, 391; "Letter(s) from Paris" (*New Yorker*), 8, 10, 53–54, 72, 277–78, 354–56, 374–76, 391; "Peace in Our Time" (*New Yorker*), 54; Pétain trial, 385–86
Flannery, Harry, 116

Fleeson, Doris, 245
Flying Flitgun (B-17), 177, 184, 189
Flying Fortresses (B-17s), 191
Foreign Policy Association, 14
Fortune, 45, 106
Forty-fifth Division, 356–58, 362
Forty-fourth Evacuation Hospital, 246–47
Forty-second Division, 356–58
Foster, Helen, 132
442nd Regimental Combat Team, 315
Fourteenth Tank Battalion, 325
Fourteenth U.S. Air Force Forward Echelon, 197–98
Fourth Armored Division, 323–26
Fourth Infantry Division, 258
France; capitulation to Hitler, 89–91; and death of FDR, 334; declaration of war, 68; post–D Day, 242–55; refugees in, 81–91; southern, Allies in, 238–39. *See also* Paris
Franco, General, 25–26, 31, 32, 41
Frankfurt, 330–32
Frankfurter Zeitung, 131
Frankish, Jack, 285, 287, 288
French Forces of the Interior (FFI), 239, 250, 254, 258, 259, 269, 280
Fuller, Margaret, 59
Furst, Peter, 356–58

Gallagher, Wes, 116, 188, 192, 322, 386
Gandhi, 392
Gavin, James, 273
Gellhorn, Edna, 21–23
Gellhorn, Martha, 21–24, 34, 35–36, 39–40, 211, 267, 272, 340; Bastogne, 290–91; Chiang Kai-shek, 143; China, 136–40, 145; Chou En-lai, 144; Dachau, 360–61; "Death of a Dutch Town"

(Collier's), 274; England, prewar, 49–50; flouting of restrictions, 229–31, 235; Gestapo activities, 269–70; Gothic Line, 239–40; and Hemingway, 24, 37, 39, 41, 56, 136–40, 207, 221–22, 230–31, 270–71, 323–24; Holland parachute mission, 273–74; Hotel Florida, 36; Italy, 207–8, 235; Madrid, 34–40; Normandy invasion, 226, 229–31; "Obituary of a Democracy" *(Collier's)*, 56; Palace Hotel, 39–40; Polish refugees, 219–20, 237–38; post-surrender, 387–88, 389; postwar adjustment, 393–95; Prague, 56–57; "Rough and Tumble" *(Collier's)*, 273–74; Singapore, 145–46; *A Stricken Field*, 56–57; *Travels with Myself and Another*, 137; *The Trouble I've Seen*, 23; "The Wounded Come Home" *(Collier's)*, 229–31
George, Lloyd, 53
George VI, King, and Queen Elizabeth, 172–73
German people, postwar reactions, 339–40, 349, 359–60
Germany; advance on Belgium and Holland, 79; advance on Czechoslovakia, 47–48, 59; advance on Denmark and Norway, 74–76; advance on England, 92–105; advance on France, 81–91; advance on Greece, 112–16; advance on North Africa, 191–92; advance on Paris, 89; advance on Poland, 62, 67; advance on Soviet Union, 117–24; attitude toward U.S., 129; division of, 1945, 340–41; Italian alliance with, 149–51; Italian campaign, 202–3; Italian retreat, 200–210; Malmédy Massacre,

286–87; mobilization of, pre–World War II, 65–68; and Normandy invasion, 232–34; pockets held, in face of defeat, 251, 334–35; prewar tension, 16–21; surrender in Europe, 370–71, 374–76; torture tactics, 267–70. *See also* Nazi Party
Gestapo, 17, 267–70, 318–19
Goebbels, Joseph, 111, 364
Goering, Hermann, 5, 19–20, 66, 97, 98, 364–65, 383
Gothic Line (Italy), 239–40
Graham, Betty, 135, 143
Grand Hotel (Dover), 96
Gran Vía Hotel (Madrid), 34–35, 36–37
Grave (Holland), 276
Great Britain. *See* England
Greece, German attack on, 112–16
Guam, 297–98, 304, 380
Guernica, 42

Hahn, Emily, 132–33, 168
Haldane, Charlotte Burghes, 122
Haldane, J. B. S, 38, 122
Halifax, Lord Charles, 76
Hall, Flem, 274
Hall, William, 396–97
Hanfstaengl, Ernst Sedgwick, 6, 11
Harbin (Manchuria), 107–9
Hargrove, Rosette, 246
Harper's, 7
Harriman, Kathleen, 170
Hawaii, 129, 148–52, 302–3
Healy, Tom, 87
Hearst, William Randolph, Jr., 258
Hemingway, Ernest, 15, 24, 34, 35–36, 143, 145, 255, 259, 278, 290, 386; *For Whom the Bell Tolls*, 137; and Gellhorn, 24, 37, 39, 41, 56, 136–40, 207, 221–22, 230–31, 270–71, 323–24; Paris liberation,

256–57; and Welsh, 221–22, 270–71, 392
Hemingway, Hadley, 37, 270
Hemingway, Pauline, 37
Hendaye (France), 28, 29, 31
Herald (London), 14
Herald Tribune, 52, 62, 68, 81, 87, 90, 101–2, 174, 178, 316, 357–58, 396, 397
Herbst, Josephine, 15–19, 33, 34, 35–36, 37, 39, 40, 41; "Behind the Swastika" (*New York Post*), 16–19; and John Herrmann, 16; postwar adjustment, 391
Herrmann, John, 15
Hersey, John, 141–42
Hewlett, Frank, 297
Hickam Air Force Base, 303
Higgins, Marguerite, 319–21; Berchtesgaden, 370, 383; Buchenwald, 347–50; Dachau, 356–58; Frankfurt, 331–32; and George Milar, 384–85; German surrender, 373; Paris, 320–21; postwar adjustment, 396; Pulitzer Prize, 396–97; views on wartime sex, 321
Himmler, Heinrich, 365
Hirohito, Emperor, 381
Hiroshima, atomic bomb on, 381
Hitler, Adolf, 4, 5–6, 7, 8, 12, 15, 47, 50–52, 54, 59, 82, 279–80; buzz bombs, 232–33; and Count Ciano, 65; death of, 363–65; Flanner portrait of, 10–11; German underground resistance to, prewar, 16–19; Munich residence, 362; and Neville Chamberlain, 52, 68; Nuremberg speech, 51–52; orders to destroy Paris, 256; Schultz interview, 5–6; and Soviet Union, prewar, 64–65; Thompson interview, 6

Hitler Youth, 21, 331, 364
Hobby, Oveta Culp, 179
Hodges, Courtney, 292, 326, 374
Holland, 79, 81, 160, 273–76, 370
home leave, during wartime, 195–96
Hong Kong, 159
Hopkins, Harry, 120
Horst (photographer), 277–78
Hotel Adlon (Berlin), 4, 5, 7, 109
Hotel Deutscher Hof (Nuremberg), 50
Hotel Florida (Madrid), 34, 35, 36
Hôtel Saint-Germain-des-Prés (Paris), 10, 53
Hôtel Scribe (Paris), 258, 262, 272, 278
House Un-American Activities Committee, 122
Houston Chronicle, 181
Hudson, Eugene A., 396
Huertgen Forest, 284
Hull, Peggy. *See* Deuell, Peggy Hull
Hutton, Graham, 52

Imatz Hotel (Hendaye), 29
India, 196, 392
Indochina, 159–69
infiltrators, 285
insignia, for reporters, 171
International Brigades, 38
International News Service (INS), 31, 131, 187, 213, 214
Internews, 161
internment, 155–56, 159–69, 297, 299–300. *See also* arrests of reporters
Invasion Weekend (Britain), 97–98
Irwin, Virginia, 212–13; "abortion camp," 353–54; capture of Berlin, 365–69; de Gaulle speech, 253–54; flouting of SHAEF regulations, 273; Frankfurt, 331; in liberated Paris, 261–62; with

Patton's Fourth Armored Division, 324–25; post–D Day France, 242–44; post-surrender, 387; postwar adjustment, 396; POW releases, 337–38; Russian-U.S. meeting in Torgau, 342, 345
Italy, 25, 62–64, 77, 163; advance on Albania, 63–64; attitude toward U.S., 129–30; end of war, 370; Fascist state, 12; German-Japanese alliance, 149–51; during German retreat, 200–210, 235–41; Gothic Line, 239–40; and Greece, 113; incarceration of U.S. reporters, 163–65; and Pearl Harbor, 149; surrender to Allies, 198
Iwo Jima, 304–13

Jackson, Allan, 323, 342, 376, 384
Jacoby, Annalee Whitmore, 154; *Babes in Arms* (film), 141; Bataan, 156–58; Chiang Kai-shek interview, 296; Chungking, 140–43, 294–96; Japanese bombing of Manila, 152–53; Philippines, 154–58, 160, 162; postwar adjustment, 395; *Thunder out of China*, 395; and Theodore H. White, 295–96, 395
Jacoby, Melville, 135, 136, 141–43, 152, 294; death of, 163; memorial garden to, 296; Philippines, 146, 154–58, 160, 162; Yellow River front, 144–45
Japan, 146, 298; advances on China, 132–33, 295; atomic bombs, 380; attitude toward U.S., 129; biological warfare, 108–9; bombing of Clark Field, 151–58; bombing of Pearl Harbor, 129, 148–52; courting of U.S. favor, 130; final months of war, 377–81; Italian

alliance with, 149–51; prisoners of war, 380; surrender documents, 388

Japanese Americans, internment of, in U.S. West, 159–60

Japanese Supreme War Council, 381

Jews, 220, 274. *See also* anti-Semitism

Jodl, Alfred, 370, 373

Joint Expeditionary Force, 379

Jouvenel, Bertrand de, 23, 29

Juin, Alphonse, 259

kamikaze attacks, 297, 378

Kennedy, Edward, 77, 371–72

Kennedy, Joseph P., 149

Kerr, Walter, 87

Kirkpatrick, Helen, 13–15, 58–59, 65–66, 68, 76–77, 92, 102, 128–29, 170, 242, 267, 272, 278, 321; AEF in Great Britain, 171–74; awards of, 392; Britain, 96–97; Battle of Bavaria, 332–33; Berchtesgaden, 370; Battle of Britain, 96–97; Buchenwald, 347–50; Frankfurt, 331; Gestapo activities, 268–69; Italy, 203–4; jeep-driving habits, 335; Leipzig, 336–37; in liberated Paris, 256–57, 271; London, V-1 rockets, 233; London Blitz, 99–100; Normandy invasion, 225; North Africa, 198; Overlord, 219; Paris liberation and de Gaulle, 259–61; Pearl Harbor, 148–49; Pétain trial, 385–86; post–D Day France, 250–51, 255; postwar adjustment, 392; prewar reporting, 52–53; prisoners of war, 338; Rheims surrender, 371; *This Terrible Peace*, 58

Klingelputz Gestapo prison, 318–19

Knickerbocker, "Knick," 54–55, 97

Knox, Frank, 58, 76, 83, 204, 219

Koenig, Marie-Pierre, 250, 259

Kotzebue, Albert, 341

Krupp, Alfred, 15, 383

Kuhn, Irene Corbally, 132

Ladies' Home Journal, 390

Lager Dora (Nordhausen) camp, 350–51

Laird, Stephen, 106–9, 112, 127–28, 148, 177–78

Landsberg camp, 353

Langen, Baron Wolfgang von, 150

Lardner, John, 378–79

The Last Days of Hitler (film), 345

League of Nations, 12, 22, 57

Leatherneck magazine, 313

Leclerc, Philippe, 256–57, 259

Lee, Clark, 154, 155, 157, 158

Lee, John Clifford Hodges, 266

Leipzig, 336–37

LeLong, Lucien, 267

Lend-Lease program, 125

Lennox, Victor Gordon, 52

Lewis, Dorothy Thompson. *See* Thompson, Dorothy

Lewis, Ervin, 274

Lewis, Sinclair, 5, 79, 127

Liberty, 152–53, 157

Life, 47, 73–74, 120, 122, 133–34, 135, 143, 146, 279, 391–92, 397; Bataan hospitals (A. Jacoby), 157; Bourke-White assignments, 47, 73–74, 175–76, 184–87, 189–91, 205–7, 383, 391–92; Chiang Kai-shek interview (A. Jacoby), 296; conscription of women (Welsh), 128; Japanese bombing of Manila (Mydans), 151–54; nurses in Pacific theater (Mydans), 298–99

Life Story, 307

Literary Digest, 133

Little Review, 71

Lochridge, Patricia, 301–6, 310; Dachau, 358–60; death of FDR, 334; Goering surrender, 383; Iwo Jima hospital ship, 304–6, 308–9; Munich, 332; postwar adjustment, 396; views on wartime sex, 322

London: Blitz, 99–105; D Day, 233; eve of World War II, 68; V-1 rockets, 233; wartime, 126–128, 196

Long, Tania, 92–96, 110, 170, 178; award, 104–5; England, 174–75; in liberated Paris, 262, 271; London V-1 rockets, 233; London Blitz, 99, 100, 102–5; marital decisions, 174–75; post–D Day, in France, 245; postwar adjustment, 392–93; postwar Berlin, 385; return to U.S., 112

Look magazine, 307

Lowery, Lew, 313

Lozovsky, Solomon A., 121

LSTs, 230, 231, 232

Luce, Clare Boothe, 142, 271

Luce, Henry, 45, 46, 134, 141, 142, 295, 296

Luftwaffe, 96, 98–105, 114, 291

MacArthur, Douglas, 152, 156, 162, 293, 297, 299, 388

Mademoiselle, 321, 384

Madrid, 35–36

Madura, SS, 90

Maginot Line, 15, 79, 86

Majorca, 32–33

Malmédy Massacre, 286–87

Malraux, André, 25

Manchester (England), 103

Manchester Guardian, 14, 132

Mao Tse-tung, 131, 296

Marin, Jean, 251

Marine Corps, 304–13, 377, 378

Marshall, George C., 170

Martin, Robert P. "Pepper," 135

Marxism, 40

Massock, Dick, 164

Le Matin, 61

Matthews, Herbert, 41, 164

Matthews, T. S., 394

Maya Maru (boat), 166–67

Mayborn, Frank, 258

McCall's, 339, 390

McClure, Robert, 187, 192, 198

McCormick, Robert, 52, 111

McLaughlin, Kathleen, 104

Metz (France), surrender of, 278–79

Milar, George, 384–85

Milbank, Robbins, 392

Miller, Harold, 308, 379

Miller, Lee, 193–95, 314, 321; archives of (England), 393; Berchtesgaden, 369; Buchenwald, 349; Cologne, 317–19; Dachau, 358–60; de Gaulle speech, 254–55; German surrender, 373; hospital, post–D Day France, 246–47; Leipzig, 336–37; in liberated Paris, 261, 264–66; Munich, 362–63; Nijinsky interview, 384; and Picasso, 194, 264; postwar adjustment, 384, 393; Russian-U.S. meeting in Torgau, 341; Saint Malo, 251–53

Missouri, USS, 388

Mitford, Unity Valkyrie, 50–51

Molotov, Vyacheslav, 120

Monks, Noel, 83, 86, 90, 99, 148, 196, 221, 270

Montgomery, Bernard, 234, 250, 324, 370

Moore, Henry, 195, 393

Moore, Stanley, 320

Morgan, Anne, 72, 81

Morris, Johnny, 279

Moscow, 118–20, 124

Motoyama Airfield One (Iwo Jima), 311
Mowrer, Edgar Ansel, 4, 28, 32
Mowrer, Paul Scott, 76
Munich, 332, 362–63
Munich conference, 53, 54, 55
Murata (Spain), 38–39
Murphy, Noel Haskins, 10, 53–54, 71, 72, 81–82, 278, 391
Murray, Natalia Danesi, 278, 391
Murrow, Edward R., 104; *Grim Glory: Pictures of Britain Under Fire*, 195
Mussolini, Benito, 12, 33, 62–64, 129–30, 149–50, 198, 365
Mutual Radio Network, 110
Mydans, Carl, 133–36, 143–45, 146, 151, 154–56, 160–63, 166–69, 198–99, 216, 297–98, 299–300
Mydans, Shelley Smith, 133, 198–99, 304; accreditation, 296–97; Chiang Kai-shek, 143; China, 133–36; Chou En-lai, 143–44; Guam, 297–98; Japan, 380; Japanese bombing of Manila, 151–52, 153–54; *Life* report on Pacific nurses, 298–99; *The Open City*, 395; Pearl Harbor, 151; Philippines, 146, 154–56, 160, 299–300; postwar adjustment, 395; Santo Tomás, 160–63, 166–67; Shanghai, 167–69; Yellow River front, 144–45
Myrdal, Gunnar, 13

Nagasaki, atomic bomb on, 381
Narkomindel, 121
Nash, Bradley, 393
Nation, 16, 132
Nazi Party, 5, 15–16, 20–21, 23, 50–52, 110–11, 340. *See also* Fascism
NBC, 146

Neideraula Staatsforst "abortion camp," 353–54
Netherlands. *See* Holland
Newark Ledger, 94
New Masses, 16
New Republic, 22
News of the Day (newsreels), 279
Newspaper Enterprise Association, 246
Newsweek, 113
New Yorker, 10, 71, 81, 277; "Letter(s) from Paris" (Flanner), 8, 10, 53–54, 72, 278, 354–56, 374–76, 391; "Peace in Our Time" (Flanner), 54; "Reporter at Large" (Hahn), 132
New York Evening Post, 2
New York Herald Tribune, 14, 15, 29, 59, 62, 77, 94, 95, 100, 110, 178, 196, 211, 216, 279, 320
New York Mirror, 81
New York Newspaper Women's Club, 104–5
New York Post, 16–19, 46, 392
New York Sun, 132
New York Times, 41, 77, 78, 101–2, 104, 112, 135, 164, 174, 175, 178, 271, 307, 314–15, 385
New York Times Sunday Magazine, 175, 246
Nijinsky, Romola and Vaslav, 384
Nijmegen (Holland), 273–76
Nimitz, Chester, 293, 297, 302–3, 388
Nineteenth Corps, 249
Nineteenth Tactical Air Command of the Ninth Air Force, 273
Ninety-seventh Bomber Group, 189, 200
Ninth Air Force, 368
Ninth Armored Division, First Army, 323–27
Ninth Army, 272, 285, 315–17

Nixon, Richard, 397
Noailles, Vicomtesse de, 278
nonaggression treaty, 64–65, 117, 118
Normandy invasion, 224–34. *See also* D Day; Overlord
"Norman Smith" (pseudonym), 114
North Africa, 180, 182–92, 198
North American Newspaper Alliance, 24
North-China Daily News, 132
Norway, 74–76, 383
Nuremberg trials, 387
nurses, 189, 206, 247, 298–99, 305–6

Office of War Information (OWI), 176
Okinawa, 377–80
Olaf, Crown Prince, 383
Oldfield, Barney, 215, 315, 385
Olympus Line defense (Greece), 114, 115
101st Airborne, 273–74, 288, 289, 291, 383
116th Evacuation Hospital, 360
120th Evacuation Hospital, 350
127th Evacuation Hospital, 360
100th Division, 279
100th Infantry Battalion, 315
Organization of Business and Professional Women, 387
Orwell, George, 25
Oumansky, Ambassador, 122
Overlord (code name), 211, 219, 225. *See also* D Day; Normandy invasion

Pacific Ocean Area (POA), 293, 304
Pacific theater, 293, 298–99, 301, 303–4, 307–8, 377–81, 388
Packard, Eleanor, 25–28, 58, 129–30, 198; Ethiopia, 27–28;

Goering surrender, 382–83; internment in Italy, 163–65; Italian advance on Albania, 63–64; Italy, 235–37; Landsberg camp, 353; mistaken for a spy, 236–37; Munich, 332; Pearl Harbor bombing, 149–51; postwar adjustment, 391; southern France, 238–39; Spain, 28, 32, 42
Packard, Reynolds, 25–28, 42, 58, 129–30, 149–51, 163–65, 198, 235, 238, 391
Palace Hotel (Shanghai), 167
Papurt, Maxine Cohen, 240–41
Papurt, Maxwell Jerome, 201–2, 206, 240–41
Paris, 83–91, 256–71, 277–78, 320–21, 374–76
Paris-Soir, 29, 51, 67
Patmore, Derek, 78–79
Patton, George S., 198, 250, 251, 278, 289, 324–25, 349
Pavlowski, Victoria, 298–99
Pearl Harbor, 129, 148–52
Penrose, Roland, 194–95, 266, 393
Percival, Arthur, 388
Pétain, Marshal Henri Philippe, 89, 91, 386
Philadelphia Public Ledger, 1, 2
"Phil Brown" (pseudonym), 113–15
Philippines, 146–47, 151–58, 159–63, 297
Photo-Secession group, 43
Picasso, Pablo, 194, 264, 393
Pius XII, Pope, 77, 235–36
PM (New York daily), 74, 117, 129
Poland, 62, 65, 67–70, 72; refugees, 219–20, 237–38
Porter, Katherine Anne, 15
Portugal, 165
Potsdam Declaration, 381
Pound, Ezra, 149

Prague, 54–56, 370
prisoners of war (POWs), 286–87, 337–39, 340–41, 380
Pulitzer, Joseph, 368

Quintanilla, Pepe, 36

Ravensbrück camp, 338, 354–56
Ray, Man, 194
Reader's Digest, 141
refugees, 81–91, 219–20, 237–38. *See also* displaced persons
Reid, Helen Rogers, 178–79, 320
Reid, Robert, 259
Reinhardt, E. F., 344
Reinhart, John, 256, 259
Relief, USS, 377
Remagen, 325–29
reporters. *See* women reporters
Reuben James, 129
Reynaud, Paul, 89
Rheims (France), 370–72
Rhine, 324–29
Rhineland, 14
Ribbentrop, Joachim von, 50, 65
Ries, Hank, 396
Robb, Inez Callaway, 187, 188, 192
Robertson, Ben, 100
Robertson, William D., 341
Roosevelt, Eleanor, 23, 105, 182, 188, 274, 334
Roosevelt, Franklin D., 125, 149, 156, 218, 333–34, 345
Rosenberg, Alfred, 331
Roussakov, Vladimir, 344
Royal Air Force, 82, 83, 96, 98, 109, 110, 114–15, 219, 228
Russia. *See* Soviet Union
Ryan, Cornelius, 231; *The Longest Day*, 231

S., Heinrich von (friend of Tomara), 77–78
Saint-Exupéry, Antoine de, 25
Saint Louis Post-Dispatch, 22, 212, 273
Saint Malo (France), 251–53
Saipan, 309–10
Salter, Cedric, 69, 78
Samaritan (hospital ship), 308, 310
San Antonio Evening News, 181
Santo Tomás camp, 155–56, 160–63, 166, 297, 299–300
Sauerwein, Jules, 61–62
Savoy Hotel (London), 101–2, 126
Scherman, David, 195, 252–53, 266, 362, 369, 373, 384
Schmidt, Johannes, 64
Schultz, Sigrid, 3–8, 18–21, 58, 94, 385; Berchtesgaden, 52; Buchenwald, 347–50; Erla work camp, 353; *Germany Will Try It Again*, 339; Hitler interview, 5–6; "John Dickson" alias, 20, 64; leaving Germany, 11; Mutual Radio Network, 110–111; Nazi politics, 20–21; postwar adjustment, 390; return to Germany (1945), 339; Soviet-German nonaggression pact, 64–65
Schweinfurt, 332–33
Scottsboro case, 16
Scripps-Canfield syndicate, 132
Second Armored Division, French, 255–57, 280
Seventh Airborne, 345
Seventh Army, 272, 279, 280, 283, 362, 369, 373, 383
sex, wartime views on, 321–24
sexism, 26, 53, 58–59, 76–77, 83, 95, 113, 177–78, 181, 183, 188, 192, 198, 211, 216, 242, 250, 253, 272, 277, 283, 293–94, 299, 316, 323–24, 379

SHAEF (Supreme Headquarters Allied Expeditionary Force), 226, 242, 258, 272, 279, 315, 323, 328, 368, 371, 372
Shanghai, 132, 136, 166, 167–68
Shapiro, Henry, 119
Shaw, Irwin, 221, 255, 259
Sheean, Vincent, 96
Shigemitsu, Mamoru, 388
Shipley, Mrs., 178
Shirer, William, 63, 74–75, 110; *Berlin Diary*, 111
Siegfried Line, 274, 281, 324
Singapore, 145–46
Sino-Japanese War, 132–33
601st Squadron, 98
Sixth Army Group press camp, 332
Sixth Marine Division, 379
Sixty-ninth Division, 340, 341–46
Smart Set magazine, 16
Smedley, Agnes, 131–32
Smith, Walter Bedell, 370, 378
Snow, Edgar, 132
Solace (hospital ship), 304–6, 308–9
Solano, Solita, 10, 71, 72, 391
Southwest Pacific theater, 293
Soviet Union, 25, 59–61, 117–24; advance on Poland, 237; alliance with Germany against Poland, 70; Bourke-White in, 45, 117–24; German attack on, 117–24; and Hitler, prewar, 64–65; postwar, 382; Spanish Civil War, 40–41; switch to Allied cause, 125; takes Berlin, 365–69; Torgau meeting with U.S. forces, 340, 341–46; U.S. attitudes toward, 122, 175
Spain, 24, 165
Spanish Civil War, 25–26, 28–33, 34–42
Spender, Stephen, 25
Stalin, 118, 120–21, 345, 381
Stars and Stripes, 356

Steichen, Edward, 194
Stein, Gertrude, 72
Steinhardt, Ambassador, 120
Stoneman, Bill, 58
Stowe, Leland, 62, 75–76
Stringer, Ann, 315–17, 326, 376; First Army, 323; Lager Dora camp, 351; Nijinsky interview, 384; Ninth Army in Germany, 315–17; postwar adjustment, 383–84, 396; Remagen bridge, 328–29; Russian-U.S. meeting in Torgau, 342–44; views on wartime sex, 323
Stringer, William, 315
Strong, Anna Louise, 132
Struthof camp, 280–81
Sudetenland, 47, 49, 57, 62
Sulzberger, Cy, 77
Summersby, Kay, 184, 187
Sunday Chronicle, 126
Sunday Times (London), 49, 53, 58, 65
Sun Yat-sen, Madame, 131
Suslaparov, Ivan, 370
Sweden, 74, 75

Taylor, Edmond, 29
Teheran Conference, 204
Tenth Armored, 289
Third Army, 250–51, 272, 278–79, 284, 285, 289, 324, 330, 333, 347
Third Battalion of the 273rd Infantry Regiment, Sixty-ninth Division, 340, 341–46
Third Division, 369, 373, 383
Thirty-eighth Evacuation Hospital, 205–7
Thirty-sixth (Texas) Division, 205–6
Thompson, Dorothy, 1–2, 4–5, 6–7, 28, 32, 58, 178, 193; banished from Germany, 7–8; Europe 1940 trip, 76–77, 79–80; Hitler inter-

view, 6, 8; as mother, 6–7; "On the Record," 125–26; postwar adjustment, 390; and Sinclair Lewis, 5, 79, 127; in wartime England, 126–27

T'ien Hsia magazine, 132

Tiger tanks, 285–86

Tigne, Dixie, 170

Time, 106–7, 135, 142, 177, 314

Time Inc. (*Time-Life*), 101, 134, 135, 221, 294–95

Tomara, Irina, 87–88, 90

Tomara, Sonia, 59–62, 77–79, 81, 178, 239, 272; accreditation, 283; Algiers, 1944, 208; Alsace, 279–80; CBI theater, 196–98; de Gaulle speech, 254–55; France, 85, 87–90; France, post–D Day, 245; Gestapo activities, 267–68; Italy, 204–5, 208–10; in liberated Paris, 257–58, 271; post-surrender, 386; postwar adjustment, 391; Slavic roots of, 77–79; Struthof concentration camp, 280–81; Teheran Conference, 204; war in Poland, 67–70

Tong, Hollington, 135–36

Torgau, 340, 341–46

Transradio News, 74

Truman, Harry S., 333, 381

Tucker, Lael. *See* Wertenbaker, Lael Tucker Laird

Tully, Andrew, 365

Twelfth Air Force, 189

Twelfth Army Group, 272

Twenty-sixth Infantry, 365–68

203rd General Hospital, 263

Umezu, Yoshijiro, 388

uniforms, for reporters, 170–71

United China Relief, 141–42, 143, 296

United Kingdom. *See* England

United Press (UP), 22, 26, 78

United States: attitude toward Great Britain, 175; attitude toward Soviet Union, 122, 175; attitude toward war, 104–5, 125–26, 129–30; and bombing of Manila, 153–54; and bombing of Pearl Harbor, 148–52; Torgau meeting with Russian forces, 340, 341–46

U.S. Army Forces Far East (USAFFE), 154

V-E Day, 362–76

Versailles Treaty, 14

Victor Emmanuel, King, 198

Vienna, 383–84

Vogue, 22, 193, 194, 195, 246–47, 271, 384

Voice of America, 391

V-1s. *See* buzz bombs

Waafs (Air Force), 128, 228

Wacs (Army). *See* Women's Auxiliary Army Corps

Wainwright, Jonathan M., 388

Walton, William, 221, 255, 291, 336, 351, 370

Warren, Virginia Lee, 314–15

Warsaw, 67–69

Washington Post, 314

Wason, Betty, 105; Hitler's advance on Greece, 112–16; *Miracle in Hellas*, 116, 391; postwar adjustment, 391; Scandinavia, 74–76

Weil, Simone, 25

Weller, George, 116

Wells, H. G., 127

Welsh, Mary, 82–85, 92, 170, 171–72, 239; conscription of women, 128; France, 85–86, 90; and Hemingway, 221–22, 270–71, 392; in liberated Paris, 258–59; London Blitz, 99–101; London on D Day,

Welsh, Mary (*continued*)
224; London, V-1 rockets,
232–33; Pearl Harbor bombing,
148; post-surrender, 386; return
to England after home leave,
195–96
Wertenbaker, Charles, 177–78, 255,
257, 259, 370–71
Wertenbaker, Lael Tucker Laird,
106–10, 112, 170, 177; *Death of a
Man*, 393; in liberated Paris, 266;
London, 127–28; Pearl Harbor
bombing, 148; post-surrender,
386; postwar adjustment, 393;
Rheims surrender, 370–71; trip to
Berlin via Japan and Russia, 107–9
West, Rebecca, 25
West Wall, 276
Weyland, Otto P., 273
Whitaker, John, 32, 54–55
White, Theodore H., 135, 295, 395
Whitehall Letter, 52
Whitehead, Don, 322, 351, 365–66
Whitmore, Annalee. *See* Jacoby,
Annalee Whitmore
Wiley, Bonnie, 304, 305
Wilhelmina, Queen of the
Netherlands, 100
Willis, Jerome, 40
Wilson, Johnny, 365, 366–69
Winant, John Gilbert, 149, 207

winter of 1945, 314
Withers, Audrey, 247
Wolf, Margaret, 241
Woman's Home Companion, 302
Woman's Land Army, 128
women: conscription of, 128; suffrage movement, 1, 21; World
War II, and changes in status of,
397–98
women reporters, 272–73, 276–77;
arrests of, 150–51, 163–65; opening of Pacific theater to, 301,
303–4; opening of post–D Day
France to, 242–55; uniforms,
170–71; as untapped resource for
female at-home war readership,
211–12; wartime restrictions on,
170–71, 176–78, 234, 293,
294–95. *See also* sexism
Women's Auxiliary Army Corps
(WAAC; Wacs), 170, 180, 182–83,
185, 188, 242–43
Women's National Press Club,
393
Woolf, Padre, 164–65
Woollcott, Alexander, 129
Wrens (Navy), 128, 195

Yugoslavia, 63

Zog, King, 63–64